# THE PROFESSOR

# THE PROFESSOR

## Arsène Wenger at Arsenal

## Myles Palmer

## Dedication

*For Johnny Brooks, Keith McCormack, Vic Brooks, Chick Gilks, Steve Shaw, Dave 'Fido' Findlay, Mal Chadwick, John Turner, Dick Labrom, Kevin Taylor, Keith Bell, Dave Murby, Sean Hobson, Joe Matthews, Bob Crow and John Storey – the Manchester University footballers who gave me so many of my happiest Wednesdays and Saturdays.*

This edition published in Great Britain in 2004 by
Virgin Books Ltd
Thames Wharf Studios
Rainville Road
London W6 9HA

Published in paperback in 2002 by Virgin Books Ltd

First published in hardback in 2001 by Virgin Books Ltd

A catalogue record for the book is available from the British Library.

ISBN 0 7535 0980 6

Typeset by TW Typesetting, Plymouth, Devon
Printed and bound in Great Britain by
Mackays of Chatham PLC

# CONTENTS

# ACKNOWLEDGEMENTS

I would like to thank my journalist friends, especially Nigel Bidmead, Philippe Auclair, Gary Jacob, Kaz Mochlinksi and, in particular, the prolific and inspirational Rob Hughes, the man UEFA chief Lennart Johannson and I regard as the conscience of football. Sincere thanks are also due to Ian Grant, who created *www.anr.uk.com*, our website, where I kick ideas around, mostly about Arsenal and England. We have been heartened by most of the e-mails we receive. Conversations with Mitch Lawrence, Alexis Grower, Doug D'Arcy, Stewart Joseph, Kelvin Lewis and Mark Jacob have been entertaining and illuminating. Thanks also to Virgin, for the title of the book, which I did not like at first. The Professor is a good title and now, several years down the line, with the book in its third paperback version, the title seems more than just a title. It is becoming a brand.

# PREFACE

Arsène Wenger said that 23 February, 2004, was one of the most important days in Arsenal's history.

After years of negotiations, the loans to build Ashburton Grove, their new stadium, were finally in place. In a statement to the Stock Exchange, the club announced that Ashburton Properties had obtained a £260 million loan from six banks. The money would be repaid over fourteen years. Director Danny Fiszman said that the 60,000-seat stadium, which will open in August 2006, would help to make Arsenal one of the biggest clubs in Europe.

Fiszman, Arsenal's chief shareholder, said, 'After four and a half years our dream becomes reality. All is in place to enable us to build the new stadium. We have only been able to get to this stage thanks to the dedication, tenacity, commitment and hard work of our whole project team – it has taken substantial sacrifices to get as far as we have.'

The success of Arsène Wenger had hugely increased the demand for tickets at Highbury, the club's home for 91 years, so the ground was far too small to hold all the people who wanted to see England's finest team. He had signed gifted players from all over world, won six major trophies with a stylish brand of power football, thrilled millions of fans, and slain the monster of Manchester Megastore PLC.

After regaining the Premiership title in 2004, Wenger said, 'The key for us was quality play and our attitude. In any job consistency is a sign of quality. I don't believe in miracles. I believe in good quality of work.'

The general public only see Arsène Wenger on television before or after games, when he is usually being diplomatic and plausible. His steely determination is not too obvious, and his droll sense of humour only comes over intermittently. Away from the cameras, the Professor is deeply competitive, but he is also good fun, good company, as well.

Two of my favourite Arsène moments came on the green, green grass of Hertfordshire, far from the terraced streets around Highbury. The first was at Sopwell House, the hotel outside St Albans that Arsenal used before their training complex was built. The players used to change at the hotel, get on their bus to London Colney, come back after training to use the showers and jacuzzi, and then eat lunch in the restaurant.

It was early August and Arsène was due to give a pre-season press conference and because it was a warm summer day we sat round a table on the lawn outside. It was intimate, informal, just the manager and seven journalists. He was very relaxed and he seemed to be, already, one of us, an adopted Englishman, a gentleman-adventurer chatting in the garden of his mansion, a sporting explorer ready to face any challenge that the new season could bring, even though he knew that every season is an open-ended expedition, an adventure that has a starting date, but you never know where it will take you. He loves the action, the competition, but he knew there was no action yet. It would come soon enough and he was ready. You could feel he was ready.

Three years later, I was at the new training ground for one of UEFA's mandatory press conferences and the reporters were indoors while the photographers were snapping a practice session. All the players were there, except Bergkamp, and they were rehearsing how to defend a high ball and create a fast break. It was just before the FA Cup Final against Liverpool and I reckoned Matthew Upson had been told to imitate Emile Heskey

Wenger's assistant Bora Primorac was launching the ball high down the middle and Upson was jumping with the defender, and they were trying to pick the loose ball up instantly and pass it forward very quickly up the left side to Henry or Pires, then feed Kanu, or play Ljungberg in, for a shot at Stuart Taylor, who was shouting at his defenders. As the high ball went forward again, Upson jumped high and collided with Keown, who fell heavily. Some of the players hesitated to see if Keown was hurt, but the manager made an under-arm motion with both hands that said: play on!

For me, that was it. That signal revealed one obsession of this football *auteur*, an element of his originality. Arsène Wenger is the most audacious and inventive choreographer of counter-attacks that football has ever known and many of his team's best moves start with that first pass from the back third, which has to be early and forward. He does not like to see the ball passed sideways, if it can be passed forward. But it can only be passed forward if the shape is right, if every player is in the right position at the moment the ball is won, which can be any time, anywhere on the pitch. As Auxerre coach Guy Roux ruefully noted, 'They're capable of scoring within five seconds of getting the ball back.'

But the $64,000 question is: Can that style ever win the Champions League? Can quick-passing, narrow football open up teams as sophisticated as Deportivo La Coruna, Valencia and Ajax? Putting it another way, do Arsenal have enough ways of scoring a goal in Europe?

# PROLOGUE: MISSION STATEMENT

The twenty-second of September 1996. A Sunday morning in a hospitality suite in the Clock End at Highbury. Arsenal chairman Peter Hill-Wood stands on a small stage covered in red cloth, welcoming the assembled television crews, journalists, radio reporters and photographers. He is about to introduce the new Arsenal manager, who has flown in overnight from Japan. This press conference is a big moment, one the fans and the media have been wondering about for weeks. Everyone wants to know: who is this Arsène Wenger?

Is he a hard case like George Graham?

A blarney merchant like Terry Neill?

A tactician like Don Howe?

A chequebook cowboy like Ron Atkinson?

A brilliant bully like Brian Clough?

An inarticulate genius judge of horseflesh like Bob Paisley?

A combative workaholic like Alex Ferguson?

The main problem at Arsenal is an ageing team. The team will have to change and at the same time continue to be successful. We do not know how long the period of transition will prove to last, nor how expensive or painful it will be. The challenge is a fundamental one which all modern businesses have to face: the management of change.

A tall, slim Frenchman walks in and steps up on to the dais. Arsène Wenger is, we quickly realise, a completely different animal. He is not like George Graham, not like Bruce Rioch, not like anybody we have seen before. He has an ambassadorial presence. He is firm, calm, diplomatic and very articulate, handling a variety of testing questions with great fluency. He is authoritative, but in a friendly, accessible way. He seems to be a man of great analytical intelligence. Everything he says makes sense and he does not waste many words. It is a flawless performance, and while it is a valuable press conference in the sense that he answers each

question honestly and clearly, without the usual evasions, it is
something else too, something like a political or military briefing,
almost a lecture. A mission statement.

Clearly, Arsène Wenger is a gentleman rather than a well-
groomed bully on his best behaviour. A gentleman is someone who
can be trusted. A gentleman's word is his bond. A gentleman has
good manners and is public-spirited. A gentleman has firm
principles and unimpeachable integrity. A gentleman has an aura
of charm and intelligence. A gentleman, above all, is someone who
can demonstrate grace under pressure, and Arsène Wenger will
need that quality above all in his new job.

Today's football managers are powerful figures, household
names, superstars of the biggest sport in the world, ringmasters
who try to control forty players and fifty reporters, but they are also
lion-tamers who put their heads in the lion's mouth twice a week.
That is pressure. They live and die by decisions made in front of
40,000 people and twelve television cameras. It is a highly
nerve-racking job, but it is well paid. And somebody has to do it.

They have also become, in this Sky-hyped age of the Premiership, vital news providers. The managers want to be liked by the
viewers and listeners and readers and they need the approval of the
reporters who transmit their predictions, reactions and excuses.
Arsène Wenger knows he has to walk a fine line, knows he has to
be very careful about what he says while appearing to be friendly,
reasonable and candid. If reporters like him they will tend to
ignore his mistakes and forget to highlight the occasions when he
contradicts himself. However, his words must have substance,
especially topical substance, because he is feeding a machine which
services a huge appetite for news about football clubs and star
players. And if that tightrope is not tricky enough to walk, he has
to talk informatively about his players knowing that they will see
and hear and read what he has said. Every manager uses the media
to wind up a player at times, to challenge him, to punish him, to
remind him of his responsibilities.

So what did Wenger say at that inaugural press conference that
so impressed everyone? First of all he said that he had been
frustrated by the delay in securing his release from Nagoya

Grampus Eight, who had now hired Portuguese coach Carlos Queiroz. 'I had the feeling that I put Arsenal in an awkward situation. It was a very difficult situation for the board, which was severely attacked. Fortunately, the team has done very well and is in a good position. That makes me quite confident for the future.'

He had been offered the job over a month before, in the second week of August, and had not taken long to make up his mind. 'I love English football because the roots of football are here. I like the spirit of the games, and at Arsenal I like the appearance of the club and the potential of the club. It's another step in my personal development. I've worked and been successful in France for ten years, and I've been successful in Japan for two years, where I had to create something from nothing and had to adapt personally. To go to another country with a football club at a high level and be successful is a very big challenge for me.'

He admitted that he had also been approached by the FA. 'Before I had contact with Arsenal Glenn Hoddle had contacted me. When he took over the international team he asked me if I would take over as technical director of the FA. I asked him for time to think it over, and we agreed that I would call him back in August. But then I had contact from Arsenal. I told Glenn I would take over at Arsenal because I love to work on the field. I am not at an age where I would like to work in administration. So I chose Arsenal because I think it's better for me. I think I know all the best players in England. I know all the international players, I know all the clubs, I know how the teams play, the organisation. Some of the grounds I don't know, but generally I think I know what's going on here. I was always interested when I started my career. I went every year to other countries to see how they were working and I think I have a good knowledge of international football.'

Press reports had already been linking him with South American stars like Leonardo and Ortega, and with German midfielder Matthias Sammer, but he denied an interest in any of them. 'The people who write those stories have good imagination – and expensive imagination. There's no truth in them at all. I have some ideas about players I might sign, but nothing concrete. When you speak about players you want you always end up paying double what they're worth, and many times you don't make the agreement.' When asked about new acquisition Patrick Vieira, he said, 'I think he's a great midfielder because he's a fighter. He's able to win the ball. And he's a very good passer.' He emphasised that Vieira, at the time an under-21 international, would be a great asset to the French national team in the future.

He was asked if he had a message for the Arsenal fans. 'My aspiration is that when Arsenal fans come here they are happy. It's up to the players and me to present the game that they love. Also, I want the fans to help us in difficult periods of the season when they are inside the gates. Because no team can be attractive and fantastic for the whole season.' He added that the absence of a manager in recent weeks had not caused a crisis in morale at the club – quite the opposite. 'I was very surprised. I read all the press but every time I had contact with the board they were very strong and very determined.

'I have the feeling today that the team also reacted very well. So the crisis was around the club but never inside the club. I feel only one pressure, my inside pressure to win and to do well. When you are in a job as long as I've been now, you get used to the outside pressure. The only important pressure is what you feel from yourself, to be strong, to work hard, to make an attractive game, and to go on and win the game. All the rest, I'm used to it now. Of course at the beginning of my career it was not easy, but these kind of pressures are much easier now.'

He said he hoped to marry continental sophistication with the red-blooded fighting spirit of English football, giving Arsenal the best of both worlds. 'That's my challenge. But I think English football has changed in the last four or five years. Everything is internationalised today. Could you imagine four years ago that Ravanelli and Juninho would play in Middlesbrough? The way of playing has changed very quickly, and I don't see a big difference now between English football and the game in other countries. In Euro 96, England played more technically than some other countries, more of a passing game. I think the difference is very small now.'

The new boss continued to preach evolution rather than revolution. 'I want the team to develop what they are doing now.

Football made of movement, a collective game of quick passing and quick movement. I think we will have to improve, and that will be the main target of every player, individually and collectively. I would like to bring in my collective touch, the way I see things. You can never say in advance how long it will take, but for the players to get used to my way of working will take two months. I like real, modern football. That means compact lines, of zones, of quick, coordinated movements with a good technique. I play 4–4–2 if I can. It is very adaptable because you can change easily to 4–3–3 or 4–5–1. It is really strange because in Europe people are going to the English system of 4–4–2 and England is going the other way. But with three at the back you have to come a little deeper, and I like offensive football and winning the ball early. It is much more difficult to pressurise up the field with three at the back.

'There are two challenges. The first is for me to adapt to the team and the qualities of English players. The second is for them to adapt to my ideas. I want to improve the squad with my ideas, and if we really need somebody, I'll try to bring somebody in. I don't want to destroy the strengths of the team, the spirit, the mental strength they showed in a difficult period before I arrived. There are many talented players here. But after I assess them maybe we'll bring one or two young players in.'

Football is much bigger in England than in France, a point he acknowledged. 'The game is important here. You have the feeling that you're working with something that is part of the life of the people. That's very exciting. People carry on supporting, from father to son, and you really live with your club, and that gives you the feeling that you always have somebody behind you. Arsenal did well in the recent past, and also in the distant past. I think I can help this club be successful and take a further step forward. And after me somebody else will come in and help the club even more. The life of a club never stops. Also, the spirit of the players. They are always able to fight to reverse games. You can see a game where one team is leading 2–0, but anything can happen here because the players have a generosity that you don't find in Latin countries.'

Wenger is a personal friend of the vice-chairman, David Dein, so he was asked whether he thought, if things did not work out,

Dein would get rid of him. 'If you are a friend or not, when things don't work well you will always have problems. I don't think that will affect our friendship. The work is one thing and the friendship is another. What is important on one side has nothing to do with the friendship. The work is the work, and it has to be effective. If I'm here it's not because I'm a friend of the vice-chairman of Arsenal. It's because the board of Arsenal think I have the right qualities to work here, and it's up to me to prove they made the right choice.' He denied, however, that he was under pressure to be an instant success. 'I want to win every game. That's the only important pressure for me. Instant success is demanded everywhere, it's the same all over the world. I believe you have to work with your ideas, do quality work, and after that hope for the best.'

For Arsenal to introduce a new manager in this way on such a day was unprecedented. Peter Hill-Wood, a gracious old-Etonian banker, apologised for interrupting our Sunday, thanked us for coming, and invited us to stay for lunch. I chatted briefly with David Dein and his friend Danny Fiszman, and then joined assistant manager Pat Rice for lunch. We talked about Spurs and Gerry Francis.

Overall, Arsène Wenger came over as a serious technocrat who knew he was accepting a serious responsibility. He was everything we wanted him to be and more than we expected. His opening address was memorable because he somehow hit on exactly the right mixture of realism, optimism and humility. When it was all over we could safely point to a number of qualities in the new manager. We could say that Wenger was straightforward ('I love English football'), very ambitious ('I want to win every game'), a traditionalist ('the life of a club never stops'), idealistic ('my aspiration is that when Arsenal fans come here they are happy') and wholly comfortable when it came to accepting full responsibility ('it's up to the players and me to present the game that they love'). He was also pragmatic ('I don't want to destroy the strengths of the team, the spirit, the mental strength they showed in a difficult period before I arrived'), an experienced manager confident about his qualifications for the job ('I want to improve the squad with my ideas').

Luckily for Wenger, midfielder Patrick Vieira, whom Arsenal had signed on his recommendation, had already played twice by mid-September and shown his class. The twenty-year-old, who was signed from AC Milan for £3.5 million, had come on as a substitute for Ray Parlour in a 4–1 demolition of Sheffield Wednesday, then made a superb first start in a 2–0 victory at Middlesbrough which hoisted Arsenal up to third place in the table. Arsenal fans had long craved somebody who could pass the ball in midfield, so they welcomed Vieira. The powerful, skilful, exciting number four was exactly what Arsenal needed. Had any of those fans been able to ask the new manager one question that day, it would probably have been, 'Please sir, can you sign six more like Vieira?' David Dein had sent videos of each game by courier to Japan and Wenger had addressed the team's biggest and most long-standing problem even before he had arrived.

Although his arrival seemed to have been messy, there was a feeling that it might turn out to be remarkably well timed. He did not have to follow George Graham directly, and since Chelsea now had Ruud Gullit at the helm, it seemed less risky, less radical, for Arsenal to hire an overseas coach. In terms of British football, and in terms of Arsenal's history, that September gathering proved to be a milestone, a signpost pointing to a promising future.

Listening to Arsène Wenger that day, you could not help thinking: this guy is different class. If this guy is half as good at talking to footballers as he is at talking to us then Alex Ferguson will have a serious rival again. George Graham built a winning team, but this guy might go one step beyond that. This guy might build a great team, a magnificent team, a thrilling team that can win everything in sight: the Premier League, the FA Cup, the European Champions Cup, the Grand National, the Olympic Games, everything!

In the days following that Sunday press conference I called friends with global connections in football to ask about Wenger. One said, 'He's a runner-up, not a winner. He finishes second too often.' Another said, 'A cautious man who likes weak people round him. He's aristocratic, rich, doesn't need football. Why did he spend seven years in a tax haven in Monaco? And why go to Japan?

A backwater, a graveyard. The stadiums are full because it is hyped
so much, but the Japs don't know what they're watching.'

All of which made the next few years an interesting prospect.

# 1. FRANCE

*I think you'll find that managers do go in phases. There are certain facets of the game that they concentrate on, and then they move on. They're always changing, they're always learning, they're always maturing, aren't they?*

Mark Hateley, ex-Monaco striker

Arsène Wenger was born in Strasbourg on 22 October 1949 and grew up in Duttlenheim, a village of 2,500 people ten miles south-west of the city. His father, Alphonse, was a businessman and restaurateur, but also a football enthusiast who managed the village team in which his sons played. The Alsace region, of which Strasbourg is the capital, had been the subject of a territorial struggle between France and Germany for hundreds of years, but the area had been very much under French control since the end of the Second World War. Still, in the footballing world Racing Club de Strasbourg were always beaten by German teams, so the teenage Wenger, football already his passion, became fascinated by German clubs.

His father took him to see games in Germany, where Borussia Mönchengladbach became his favourite team. This was where his love of exciting, penetrating football first took hold. 'I was attracted by a game of movement, of counter-attack, based on speed and dynamism. That was what mattered to me,' he later recalled. The bright schoolboy knew that a goal was the most exciting moment in a football match, but he could also see that the moment when one team lost the ball and the other team gained possession was a moment alive with many thrilling possibilities.

Despite this passion already coursing through his veins, Gilbert Guntzburger, an older team-mate of the teenage Wenger in the 1968/69 FC Duttlenheim amateur side, remembered Arsène as a boy who had a more solemn disposition than his brother. 'He was so very serious. He was exactly the opposite of his older brother Guy. Guy liked a drink and a laugh. Not Arsène.' Serious, but in love with football. Alsace at that time was an area steeped in religion and the boys had to receive permission from their priest to go and play football because that meant missing vespers, the evening prayers. The young footballers, cycling past the church on their way to the pitch, used to cross themselves.

The community was so small that it was hard to find eleven boys of similar age, so Arsène did not play team football until he was twelve. But he was a regular from then on, and a decent player. A picture of Alphonse and a fourteen-year-old Arsène with the 1963/64 Duttlenheim team is still kept in the club office. Claude Wenger (no relation), now in charge of publicity at FC Duttlenheim, remembered his former team-mate as a good dribbler, a two-footed midfielder who could score goals. 'He was the club's top scorer with thirteen in 1968/69. But he had such intelligence, such vision. Those were his greatest assets.'

At that time Raymond 'Max' Hild, the coach at Mutzig, an amateur team in the Third Division, discovered the eighteen-year-old Wenger playing for Duttlenheim, signed him and made him his captain. Together they won the Alsace Cup. When Hild moved to Vauban, another amateur club, he took Wenger with him, and in 1978, when Hild became coach of Strasbourg, he once again persuaded Wenger to go with him, to join his first professional club. So the lanky amateur followed his coaching guru from club to club, but he continued his studies in economics, sociology, German and English and graduated from Strasbourg University.

Hild recalled, 'As a player he was an attacking midfielder who would score around eight goals a season from distance. He was not so good with his head around the opposing goal, but he could certainly use it to read the game. Mental speed was his great strength. He played eleven championship games and a UEFA Cup tie, but building clubs from the foundation is where his future always belonged.' Strasbourg reporter Michael Kapfer, who used to watch Wenger play from the press box, said, 'He had two or three games for the first team when they won the French Championship in 1979. But the match I'll always remember is the away leg of a UEFA Cup tie in the German town of Duisburg. It was the only European tie he ever played – he wasn't in the home leg when we drew 0–0. He played as a central defender in the away leg. It was an absolute disaster as Strasbourg lost 4–0. Arsène stayed an amateur because he chose to remain at university.'

Educated people are usually more aware of what they do not know, and Wenger realised that speaking English would be useful to him, as well as helping him with his studies, so he came to England during the close season. He later said, 'When you are a professional footballer, you spend your holidays at Club Med. Me, I bought an air ticket to London. A friend advised me to go to Cambridge where I hired a bike and enrolled on a three-week English course. My team-mates thought I was mad.'

Not only mad – too high-brow as well. Robert Felix, a back-room man at Strasbourg, remembered how Wenger never quite fitted in with the other players, who liked him but found him too sophisticated, and added that the Frenchman 'could play anywhere and he could be relied upon. But the truth is he was not really good enough to be a professional. I think that was the reason he did not turn pro, more than wanting to stay at university. He knew he was not good enough.'

Max Hild says that Wenger was about thirty when he finally asked him if he could help to coach the kids at Strasbourg, even though coaching 'wasn't a career he had ever thought about. His goal was to succeed his father at the Comptoir de l'Est, the family car-parts business.' Nevertheless, Wenger earned his manager's diploma in Paris in 1981 and he became Strasbourg's youth coach the same year. Robert Felix recalled him being 'brilliant with the youngsters. A perfect example for all young players. Even then he was a big man with an aura. You knew he was going to become a great coach.'

In 1983 Wenger moved to the French Riviera to take charge of the Cannes youth scheme, and a year later he was offered, and accepted, his first job as a manager. Aldo Platini, father of Michel, said, 'Arsène stood out at coaching meetings. I recommended him for his first job as a senior coach with my club Nancy.' In Wenger's first season in charge there, 1984/85, Nancy finished twelfth in the league and at the end of his second season they were eighteenth and had to win a play-off match to avoid relegation. The tiny club stayed up but continued to struggle, unable to afford the kind of players Wenger wanted, and the following year they were relegated. Aldo Platini said, 'It wasn't Arsène's fault. He had no money to spend. Monaco wanted him halfway through his spell with us. He wasn't sacked. He simply left us to join them.'

Mark Hateley joined Monaco from Milan in 1987 just as Wenger was arriving from Nancy. A tall, ebullient striker, the son of Tony Hateley, a big centre-forward who scored 200 goals for Notts County, Aston Villa, Chelsea, Liverpool, Coventry and Birmingham, Mark Hateley was greatly encouraged to learn that another English player, Glenn Hoddle, would be playing with him. 'At that particular time Glenn was supposed to be signing for Paris Saint Germain but hadn't signed on the dotted line,' he said. 'His agent was my agent. He had a chat with Wenger and we got him down to Monaco with us. We had an Ivory Coast player, Fofana, a very, very quick winger, but apart from myself and Glenn it was mostly French players.'

Hateley had left Portsmouth when he was 21, when English football training was still archaic. He immediately began to profit from the more professional training routines used in Italy, where even the smaller clubs prepared in a more technical, intelligent and detailed manner. He was pleased to see that Monaco under Arsène Wenger was no different. 'The training abroad was way in front of the British scene and it's only recently that we've got on to the same wavelength. Training camps, *retiros*, had been in existence for twenty years when I arrived. Milanello had been there long before that. At Milan you did your running, you did your weights, your diet was monitored. You were educated, and when you're a young lad you're easily educated anyway. We had a lot of doctors – the medical side was very, very good. It was the same at Monaco.'

But he found it hard, after playing in front of 80,000 people in Milan, to play in front of much smaller crowds in the principality. 'That was the most difficult thing about it. Summer season was good in Monaco because you had a lot of tourists there who would come and watch the games, so you could be getting between nine and thirteen thousand. But the winter periods you were as low as three thousand. That was the hardest thing we had to battle with. That's where self-motivation comes in.'

Hateley won most of his England caps when he was at Milan, partly because he suffered a serious injury at Monaco which stopped him playing for nineteen months. Most French fans, he reckoned, judged strikers purely by their goal tallies, 'but I don't think Wenger saw it like that. It was very much a team game and I was a team player. I worked very, very hard for the team and I used to create more goals than I would score. The first year we won the league and the cup and I finished second top goalscorer behind Papin. All in all it was a great experience and a great year for myself and Glenn. That first season was fantastic for me, for all the players, for the club, everybody. Monaco hadn't won anything for a long, long time, so to win the league and get into the European Cup was a feat beyond anybody's imagination.'

George Weah, a naive teenager from Liberia, was also brought in to Monaco during Wenger's first season. Wenger later recalled having to be very patient when he worked one-on-one with Weah. 'He came and he was nobody and he was on his own. He worked a lot because he had the desire. When you are a manager and you feel the appetite of somebody you'd be guilty if you didn't try to help. What makes you sad is when you meet talent and he hasn't the desire to achieve something. It's a bit like being a father, where you help a child achieve something. If you give them a good education and if they make their way, you're happy.' Hateley was impressed by Wenger's new signing, despite the fact that Weah came into the team in his position. 'It wasn't till I got the injury in the October of the second season that George came into the team. That's where he came through. He had unbelievable ability. He would do some unbelievable things with the ball. And, as you would expect from a nineteen-year-old, some unbelievably poor things, like tripping over the ball, or something silly.'

In Mark Hateley, George Weah and, later, Jurgen Klinsmann, Wenger had three genuine centre-forwards, all of whom could head the ball, yet when he went to Arsenal he never signed that type of player. 'Perhaps he went through a phase,' said Hateley. 'I think you'll find that managers do go in phases. There are certain facets of the game that they concentrate on, and then they move on. They're always changing, they're always learning, they're always maturing, aren't they? I liked to head the ball, and Klinsmann could head the ball, but we had more to our games than just heading the ball. George Weah was the same.'

Jean-Pierre Hopp, a friend of Wenger's from Nancy, went to visit him a year after he had taken over at Monaco and was amazed by his selfless commitment to the cause. 'The car park at the training ground was full of Mercedes, BMWs and Porsches – and parked alongside was Arsène's Renault 17. I've never seen a coach as determined and committed as him. He had a girlfriend back in Strasbourg but hardly ever had the time to see her.' Mark Hateley had a similar impression of the young workaholic coach. 'When I was at Monaco, Arsène was very, very intense. Every spare minute was football. It was football, football, football.' It was something of a shock for the England striker because his previous coach had been much older and more philosophical. 'Nils Liedholm, when I was at Milan, was sixty years old and had played in World Cup Finals and was well respected. He'd got all the knowledge of a footballing man. When I was 21 he was ideal for me because he had bags of time for me. I went from that to Arsène, who taught me something else, a lot about discipline and self-belief. He added that to my game.'

It was Wenger who first saw that Glenn Hoddle had coaching potential, although that development seemed improbable when Hoddle and Hateley were playing together, as the latter recalled. 'We sat down and talked about the game, I think all players do that. But when players are playing the one thing they've got on their mind is playing the game and nothing else. You don't think about not playing, and then going into coaching. You always think you're gonna keep playing. But that time does come. It was unfortunate for Glenn that he didn't come abroad at an earlier age. Michel Platini once said that had Glenn been born a Frenchman he'd have played over a hundred games for France.'

Hateley laughed when asked what system Monaco used to play under Wenger. 'We played the system where you have to win! With good players you can play any formation. Whether it's 4–4–2, you're interchanging all the time, 3–5–2, whatever you wanna play. We played with wide men sometimes and we played with three at the back at other times. We had Patrick Battiston playing at the back for us, and Amoros at full-back. We had a lot of good players who could play in different positions at different times in the game.

'Another young lad coming through was Emmanuel Petit. He was just coming into the set-up. He was a centre-half originally, then a left-back, and midfield on and off. Honestly, when he was a young sixteen-year-old he was ever so strong. Physically very strong, running very strong. Absolutely non-stop. Very few of us can do that. He had all the attributes and he was always gonna be a good player.'

Hateley later played for Glasgow Rangers, does radio work in Scotland now, and also has a Champions League show on Thursday nights on Scottish television, but he recalled that phase of his career, working with Wenger in a warm climate on the Riviera, with great affection and gratitude. 'Living down on the south coast, you have the heat and the Mediterranean diet: fish, salads, pasta – it's all conducive to a healthy lifestyle and weight loss.'

In 1989 Monaco got to the French Cup Final but lost 4–3 to Marseilles. They also reached the quarter-final of the European Cup, losing 1–0 to Galatasaray at home and drawing the second leg in Cologne, where UEFA had decreed they must play after crowd trouble in Istanbul. Two years later they took their revenge on Marseilles by beating them 1–0 to win the French Cup. The following year they won through to the final again but the match was cancelled after a major stadium accident during the other semi-final in Bastia, as a result of which 3,000 people were injured and twenty killed. That tragedy happened the night before Monaco were due to meet Werder Bremen in Lisbon in the Cup Winners Cup Final. The team, traumatised by the accident which involved friends of the players, lost the final 2–0.

In 1994, Wenger's Monaco were European Cup semi-finalists, and their line-up included Klinsmann, Youri Djorkaeff and the brilliant Belgian Enzo Scifo. They beat AEK Athens and Steaua Bucharest to reach the last eight, which was in two mini-leagues of four clubs. There they defeated Spartak Moscow and Galatasaray but lost twice to the mighty Barcelona, then managed by Johan Cruyff. But they qualified for a semi-final place, only to come up against an awesome AC Milan team which included the likes of Paolo Maldini, Marcel Desailly and Dejan Savicevic. They were soundly beaten 3–0, and Milan went on to thrash Barcelona 4–0 in the final.

After seven seasons of consistently good results, and having proved that he could discover talent as well as work with stars, Wenger had become much more successful as a coach than he ever was as a player, and his reputation grew apace. Bayern Munich wanted him, but Monaco refused to let him leave. A man of integrity, Wenger did not walk out on them. Ironically, a few months into the following season, 1994/95, after some indifferent results, he was sacked. It was time for Wenger to move on, to move away.

Years later, in January 2001, Wenger stated that bribery and corruption had influenced his decision to leave his native country. 'One of the reasons I moved away from France was that I suffered from that when I was manager of Monaco.' He was referring to the match-fixing scandal involving Marseilles president Bernard Tapie, who was eventually jailed for a year for bribing three Valenciennes players in a 1–0 win in 1993, en route to the club's fifth consecutive French title. Marseilles were stripped of their 1993 European Cup and relegated. 'Everybody knew they did it many times, bribing three players on one team. We were runners-up to them every year. I don't think it is a problem in English football. Our credibility depends on honest football. We knew it was happening in France although I was never approached to throw a game. It is down to officials and regulations in football to protect the game. I'm in football because I love football. I am happy that the players are earning a lot of money because I have always fought for that. But it has brought a lot of people to the game who don't care about football, only money.'

Having turned away from French football, Wenger decided to take his expertise to the other side of the world.

# 2. JAPAN

*He's a god there. He did a good job at Grampus Eight, took over a struggling team, lifted it all up. Stojkovic, the big star there, was under-performing and he got him playing again, to everyone's delight.*

Steve Perryman

Tokyo had staged the Olympic Games in 1964 and Japan had continued to boom right through the sixties, seventies and eighties, enjoying unprecedented economic growth. During that time the Japanese built up powerful, world-famous corporations which did business on every continent, companies like Sony, Toyota and Nissan. Japanese society is corporate in flavour, with hierarchies that everyone understands and a general assumption that people work towards shared objectives under highly qualified leaders. In mainstream Japanese life company workers live together, work together, achieve together and even play together.

The most popular sports in Japan in 1995 were sumo wrestling, baseball and golf, but Japan wanted to bid for the 2002 World Cup so they had launched their first professional football league in May 1993. The J-League comprised ten clubs – Kashima Antlers, Jef United, (Mitsubishi) Urawa Red Diamonds, Yomiuri Verdy, Yokohama Marinos, AS Flugels, Shimizu S-Pulse, Nagoya Grampus Eight, Gamba Osaka and Sanfrecce Hiroshima – each backed by a major company and each allowed three foreign players. It was agreed that no game should finish in a draw, so golden-goal extra time was played followed by penalties if necessary.

A few of these J-League clubs were formed from already existing amateur teams such as Nissan, but since the football clubs themselves had only just been created there was no history of rivalry or acrimony between them. The Japanese saw sport as entertainment rather than as tribal warfare, so the atmosphere at games was fresher, more innocent; there was a lot of female support and no need for heavy policing or strict segregation. Visiting team buses were never bombarded with abuse or rude gestures, fans were not hypercritical when a player made a mistake and it was safe for the teams to travel to other cities by *shinkansen* (bullet trains) without fear of being harassed.

Nagoya is the Detroit of Japan, an industrial city of two million people situated 150 miles west of Tokyo. The city had spent £12 million on a new stadium with a 30,000 capacity and in 1993 imported Gary Lineker and two Brazilians as their three overseas players. The following year they signed the former Yugoslavia captain Dragan Stojkovic. Other teams followed suit. Zico, the Brazilian star of the 1982 World Cup, came out of retirement to play for Kashima Antlers, although he had already reached the age of forty.

The trade was not just in players, although French coaches were not exactly fashionable in 1995. But Wenger had done well at Monaco and earned a reputation as a cultured technician of the game. He was respected as a team-mechanic, someone who could create a harmonious squad, refine individual players and combine them to create a balanced, efficient unit. He was also known for his diplomacy, for his knack of tailoring what he had to say to fit the person or group he was addressing, so his personality was as important as his knowledge. When people talked to him they found a multilingual man with an impressive command of detail, but one who could also see the bigger picture, the landscape beyond his next match. He also had the patience to work with young, inexperienced players, which some top coaches lack.

So the question was not: why did the Japanese want him? It was: why did Wenger go there? Why would a football coach in his prime, who had won the French Championship and led his side to the semi-final of the European Cup, move to a league in Asia which was barely two years old? It was a bold leap into the unknown for Wenger, who had left tiny Monaco, a playground which has a beach, harbour and casino to go to work in the most industrialised country on earth, a nation of 126 million on three big islands, a land of vast factories full of robots, of spa towns built around sulphurous hot springs, of white-faced geisha girls and sushi delivered by scooter boys, of mist-filled valleys which only occasionally revealed the magnificent scenery?

The stink of corruption, of course, in part drove him away from his homeland, but fundamentally Wenger is a teacher who always wants to learn more, a man with a curiosity about other cultures, an interest in disciplines outside football and an ability to look outwards and forwards. Clearly, he is a singular personality, a man marching to the beat of his own drum, and at that time he had a postgraduate mentality about his career. He realised that this was an opportunity to learn, to broaden his horizons, which might never come again, so he took it.

Wenger joined Grampus Eight in January 1995. Two weeks after he arrived he was contacted by Werder Bremen president Fritz Bohme, who wanted him to replace their Bayern-bound coach Otto Rehhagel. Once again the timing of a possible move into the Bundesliga was wrong. Wenger said later, 'I had to tell them, sorry, but how can I leave Grampus Eight when I have only just arrived?' Bremen's general manager Willi Lemke, who flew to Nagoya with Bohme to talk to Wenger, paid him some extraordinary compliments. 'Arsène is almost too good to be true,' he said. 'You would not expect somebody like him in a business like football. He is such a respectable, decent person.'

One of Wenger's players during his first season in Japan was Masaru Hirayama, a college defender who had joined Grampus Eight in the summer of 1994. A knee injury soon ended his pro career and he went to work at Keishin High School in Fukui, where he now teaches social studies and coaches the school team. Hirayama said that he learned a lot in the short time he was with his French mentor. 'Wenger pulled the club from the bottom to second place in one year,' he said. 'I watched the team keep winning as Wenger coached. He is an able manager, very charismatic. He was amazingly considerate too, and would give personal advice to each individual player.'

Another who recognised the quality of Wenger's impact on Grampus Eight was Dr Christopher Hood, a British academic living near Nagoya when the J-League started in 1993 and who had begun to follow the club when Gary Lineker was signed. 'If there's ever been a case proving how important a manager is,' he asserted, 'then Arsène Wenger's time at Nagoya Grampus Eight is it, because he went in there and he didn't really change the playing squad a great deal but turned their fortunes round overnight almost. And once he left, again without great changes in playing personnel, the team slumped. It was so obvious that their success was down to him personally. So I think his attitude must have fitted in with the Japanese people and players and he must have also been able to control the non-Japanese players in the team, because sometimes they can be the harder players to control. They tend to be well-established players and sometimes get a little bit arrogant and need to be put in their place now and again. I dare say Wenger was quite good at doing that. If you can control Stojkovic you can control anyone. He certainly managed to get the best out of him.' Hood claimed Grampus Eight were a highly entertaining side. 'They were regarded as a very attacking team and a very effective force.'

As someone who has lived in the country and studied it, Hood believed that foreigners who are work-obsessed, like Wenger, can function very well there and enjoy themselves. 'I think Japan is a country that suits people like that. If you look at the people who study in Japan they tend to be, on the whole, quite loner-type figures, people who like to be able to mix with their own friends when they want to be with friends, and completely shut themselves away when they want to be shut away. Japan very much suits that mentality. There's not so much pressure on people always to be mixing and doing things. It's the sort of country where you can be yourself and do what you want to do. In some ways that's surprising because it's always thought of as a conformist society, but I think in Western countries, although we always talk about individualism over here, there's a lot more pressure to conform and go along with what other people are doing. Whereas in Japan you can step back and do what you want to do.'

Steve Perryman hugely enjoyed his experience there after a difficult first six months. Perryman had originally gone to Japan in 1996, to Shimizu S-Pulse as assistant manager to Ossie Ardiles, after managing Brentford between 1986 and 1990, saving Watford from relegation, and a brief spell in Norway managing Start. In 1999, when Ardiles resigned to join Croatia Zagreb, Perryman took over as manager. 'You've got thinking time in Japan,' he said. 'I read somewhere that Wenger said that Japan gave him back his faith in soccer, and I know what he means by that. You work abroad, I suppose it could be anywhere, but for me in Japan, I felt such a surge of energy. You get rid of all the things that are dragging you down. Trips up the motorway and back for six hours. You just concentrate on soccer and that's the beauty of living there.'

For Perryman, as for Wenger, there was the realisation that working in other countries brings out parts of the self that are obscured or suppressed by one's native culture. His twenty-month stay in Japan forced Wenger to explore qualities in himself that were not needed in France, or not available to him then. He later said that his time at Nagoya had made him more calm and composed, and he regarded that as crucial to his development as a manager. He was an immigrant who did not know the language and that made it easier to ignore distractions and focus his energy on what was important: working with his team and winning matches. Japan was also the perfect place for experimentation with tactics and set-up. 'In Japan it was easier to bring in something because professionalism was young,' he recalled. 'Everything was new – they accepted that – and it was more easy to change things. Here in England you have more than a hundred years of history. Any time you want to change something, you must convince everybody, because of the history.

'In Japan I learnt a lot about myself and how I could be,' Wenger added. 'I was very fortunate to have an experience whereby I was still working in football but outside the European mainstream. I had a lot of letters, but I could hand them over for someone else to deal with. I could not understand what people were saying to me or what they were writing in the newspapers, so I did not have that to worry me. I realised that football was what I enjoyed, the rest was just people's opinions. So since I came back into European football with Arsenal I take the same approach. I concentrate on the football, on training the team. I can be happy doing that. The rest is not important so I don't let it affect me.'

Wenger made it clear that at that time his own private agenda was more important to him than a high-profile job in Europe. 'Certainly that decision and my work over there created less of an impression than if I had been coaching Bayern. But as far as my personal and professional plans are concerned, I brought back a lot of satisfaction and a lot of pleasure.' He remains convinced that quitting Europe was a sound decision, and a very educational one for him, although his life in Japan was somewhat monastic. 'I learnt there how to take hold of something by letting go. That's beneficial at any level. When I got back I was much more lucid, more detached, more serene. I had the impression of having passed a couple of years in a convent where I devoted everything I had to my work.'

Perryman concurred with Wenger's views on the Japanese experience. His main source of job satisfaction came from his players listening carefully to him, wanting to learn the game, whereas footballers in Britain are more stale and cynical. 'I don't think the English professional puts in too much overtime or too much of his own thought. I think it has become a bit too humdrum and normal for them.' Where Britain has dumbed down, and behaviour has deteriorated, Japan has a culture where teachers and leaders are respected for their knowledge. 'The players give you their eyes and ears because they're happy to play for you. When I take the kids to school, they walk up to the teachers and formally bow and greet them.'

Perryman talked about Japan and about Wenger on Sky's *Soccer Extra* in January 2001. During that programme he made it clear that, despite the presence of Brazilians such as Dunga and Jorginho, the general standard of football in Japan was well below that of Europe. Most of the Japanese players, he said, are young and naive; 'Overall, the top in Japan is mid-Division One.' When asked if Arsène Wenger was still held in high esteem there, he said, 'Yeah, he's a god there. He did a good job at Grampus Eight, took over a struggling team, lifted it all up. Stojkovic, the big star there, was under-performing and he got him playing again, to everyone's delight. Just reorganising it. Being Wenger, he's got a comment about everything: the way the league should be structured, when you should play, when you should rest. He led them down every street, really. Which they needed, to be fair.'

Perryman also pointed out that the English style of man-management, with aggressive shouting in training and in the dressing room, is utterly alien to the Japanese, where the pride of the individual player cannot withstand a bawling out in front of his team-mates. That scenario, so common in the world in which Alex Ferguson and George Graham grew up and worked, is a non-starter in the J-League. If the coach screamed abuse at a footballer he would be so humiliated that he might go AWOL for three weeks. 'There is a vast difference in culture. You cannot pin a player one to one in a team meeting. Get them in the office one to one, absolutely no problem, say what you want and they take it that you're trying to help them. In an English team meeting, you would need to do it, because if you didn't do it the other players would think: you're soft; he's missed the point, he's left him alone. You have to do it, everyone expects it. In Japan you don't do that. It's in private. Of course, in team meetings you're making your general points all the time.' The phlegmatic Wenger was made for the part. Japan's culture suited his supportive, conciliatory style of man-management. He is able to control his temper in almost every situation, and since he hates shouting at his players anyway, working in a country where calmness is regarded as a strength rather than a weakness was ideal for him.

I have an e-mail pal, Katsumi, a 36-year-old football fan who travels to Europe occasionally on business. He was in France during the World Cup in 1998, and on the day after the England–Argentina quarter-final in St Etienne he bumped into Arsène Wenger on a train and was amazed when Wenger asked him, in Japanese, 'Where do you live?' Katsumi said, 'He changed Grampus quickly and totally. While he was in Nagoya he picked up several talented young players, including Hirano, Mochizuki and Oiwa. The three contributed a lot to the team and were selected for the national side. But once he left Nagoya in 1996, the team started breaking up. The club called in Portuguese coach Carlos Queiroz, but soon he was replaced by Japanese coach Tanaka, an assistant of Wenger. Nagoya supporters still dream of the Arsène days. He is a legendary person here in Japan.'

# 3. BOOZE AND IGNORANCE

*There is no doubt in my mind we are blinkered and backward as a sporting nation.*

Peter Hill-Wood, Arsenal chairman

At some English clubs in the early nineties players did not even bother to warm up before a game. They were allowed to sit around in the dressing room, reading newspapers and watching the horse racing on television, until ten to three. Heavy drinking was also widespread among footballers, who always claimed they could 'sweat it out' at training the next day. Jimmy Greaves and George Best drank like fish, after all, and still played like gods. It was just bonding, fraternity, solidarity, footballers socialising together for the sake of team spirit. Boys will be boys.

Striker Mick Quinn, a bright Scouser who played for Newcastle, Coventry and Portsmouth, used to love a night out with the boys. When Quinn was at Coventry he was on the plump side of stocky and the fans nicknamed him Sumo, but he scored the first hat-trick of the Premiership at Highbury and Ian Wright, no less, told him it was some of the finest finishing he had ever seen. Quinn, now a racehorse trainer, loved pop music, playing cards, gambling on horses and getting blotto. 'If Tony Adams is an alcoholic, I should be dead,' he told me in 1996. 'It's a load of bollocks. He's a heavy drinker, but what footballer isn't? And Tony is blaming a semi-final defeat by Germany in Euro 96 for driving him back to the bottle? While Gareth Southgate, the guy who missed the penalty, is sleeping at night? I think Tony's got to sort his head out.'

Arsenal players seemed to make more than their share of news headlines, as opposed to sports headlines. In 1989 Paul Merson had been fined £350 for drink-driving and failing to stop at an accident, and he was banned from driving for eighteen months. Merson and Steve Bould were later disciplined by the club after drunken, rowdy behaviour at a sponsor's dinner-dance at the Swiss Cottage Holiday Inn. Tony Adams, the captain, used to lead the hard drinkers in a regular session at Ra Ra's, a private club in Islington, and those booze-ups, like everything else in football, were based round the fixture list. If Arsenal did not have a midweek game they usually had Wednesdays off, so Tuesday night was the best opportunity to go out and get bladdered. These gatherings, as Adams later admitted, became known as the Tuesday Club.

Trouble was almost inevitable from time to time, especially in the close season. In May 1990, Paul Merson, Nigel Winterburn and two other players were sent home from a club tour of Singapore following a late-night drinking session. Late that year Adams was jailed for drink-driving even though the incident had happened in May, just after the season finished. His trial was postponed three times, the authorities obviously deciding to use his conviction as a high-profile example to frighten drinkers over the Christmas/New Year holiday. The implied message was: if we can put Tony Adams in Chelmsford prison, we can put you in as well.

The shenanigans did not stop there. In October 1993 Adams and Ray Parlour were accused of yobbish behaviour when a fire extinguisher was set off, drenching diners at a Pizza Hut restaurant in Hornchurch, Essex. Scotland Yard confirmed that police had received five complaints of assault. Adams and Parlour were among a party dining in the restaurant on the Thursday evening after England's 2–0 World Cup qualifier defeat by Holland in Rotterdam. Police said that some of the diners alleged that one of the players used a table knife to remove the pin from one of the restaurant's extinguishers, and that a second player then picked up the extinguisher and began spraying water round the room.

In August 1994 Paul Merson was under police investigation when he left the scene of a car crash in Mill Hill. His Land Rover Discovery had collided with a Nissan Micra, a wall and finally a tree. Both cars were badly damaged and witnesses said that Merson vanished before police arrived, leaving a friend to face questions.

Three months later Merson sold his 'my gambling/cocaine/booze hell' confessions to the *Mirror*. It was predictable that Tory MPs in particular would demand his prosecution for drug abuse. Sir Nicholas Fairbairn, the former Solicitor-General for Scotland, said it was 'appalling' that Merson should be paid by a newspaper for admitting to substance abuse. Merson's revelations caused the usual uproar: big club, young footballer, played fourteen times for England, tragically gone off the rails, set a bad example to the thousands of impressionable young people who idolise him. Police said they wanted to interview Merson, who at the time lived in a mock-Tudor house near St Albans, but he had gone abroad with his wife Lorraine and their two young sons, Charlie (three) and Ben (eighteen months). The Football Association, meanwhile, insisted that disciplinary action should be secondary to Merson's rehabilitation.

Merson had first snorted cocaine in a Hertfordshire pub toilet after drinking nine pints of lager. He claimed that the buzz helped him to overcome his shyness. Like Tony Adams, he was a binge-drinker; furthermore, and unlike Adams, he gambled every day. When an ankle injury stopped him playing football he became bored and gambled even more heavily. His debts began to mount, so he started snorting more coke to cheer himself up. It was a classic vicious circle.

That same month, November 1994, Ray Parlour was involved in a serious fracas at the south-coast World Holiday Centre in Bognor Regis, Sussex. Arsenal had no game on the Saturday because England were playing Nigeria at Wembley the following Wednesday, so he and some mates had driven down to Bognor for a night out. Someone smashed him in the face with a glass during a brawl and he needed four stitches in a large gash above his left eye. It was a typical footballer-in-punch-up incident, and the *Mirror* gave it the usual tabloid treatment: RAY PARLOUR ALMOST BLINDED IN NIGHTCLUB BRAWL sang the headline. A witness said, 'He was in the Manhattan revue bar and the row started when someone bumped into him. People started squaring up to each other and then all hell broke loose. It really all went off when Parlour came out with the line "Don't you know who I am?"' Friends whisked Parlour away from the club before security men could question those involved, but he was forced to withdraw from the England under-21 squad as a result. When a fan bumped into Parlour outside the ground on his way to the Arsenal box office and saw that he had a big stitched-up gash on his eyebrow, the fan said, 'Jesus, Ray, what happened to your eye? Did you do that playing football?' Parlour replied, 'I wish.'

The following summer, in May 1995, Arsenal went on an end-of-season tour to Asia where they played three games. After their final match in Hong Kong several players went out for an all-night drinking session in the Wanchai girlie bar district, where Parlour was said to have drunk twelve pints. A taxi driver was preparing his car for the Sunday-morning shift when Parlour made his way towards the vehicle, threw prawn crackers on to its bonnet and punched the driver. The man's nose needed five stitches. Parlour pleaded guilty to assault at the Eastern Magistrates Court. His lawyer, Adrian Huggins, told the court that Parlour could remember nothing about the incident, but that he nevertheless wanted to apologise to the 65-year-old driver and to the people of Hong Kong. He was fined 2,000 Hong Kong dollars (about £170), but was later fined more than £5,000 by the club. Inevitably there was talk that his future as a player at Arsenal was in jeopardy.

As this story was hitting the headlines, the *Sunday Mirror* dredged up witnesses who had taken speed and Ecstasy with John Hartson in Ibiza, even though the alleged incident had taken place just before he was transferred to Arsenal from Luton Town for £2.5 million, a deal which made him the most expensive teenager in British football history. 'He hadn't been to sleep from the night before,' said the witness, 'and he was still buzzing off his head. He was asking about "Es". He knew what was what. I can spot an amateur a mile off. He had money falling out of his pockets and had loads of women around him purely because of the football thing.'

Despite the headlines, it was not just Arsenal players behaving badly. Hundreds of pro footballers reckoned that a good booze-up was a reward for winning a game, and the best way to drown their sorrows if they lost. All clubs had drinkers, many had heavy drinkers, but most managers tended to turn a blind eye until the law was broken, which it often was.

Mick Quinn served three weeks in Winchester prison for driving while disqualified. He told me, 'Footballers think they can go by the grace of God and enjoy birds, booze, betting and everything else. Half the time they seem to be able to do whatever they want, to be above the law. I was shell-shocked. All of a sudden, from living in a four-bedroom detached house I was cooped up in a twelve foot by twelve foot cell with criminals. It was not a modern, open prison. I was banged up in a Victorian regime for 23 hours a day. I was let out for three twenty-minute walks every day.'

There were, however, dissenting, sensible, practical voices in the wilderness, minds open to the healthier regimes operating on the continent. Back in 1993 I did an interview with Roger Spry, the conditioning coach Ron Atkinson had taken with him from Sheffield Wednesday to Aston Villa, and he happened to mention a scientifically-minded manager at Monaco who treated footballers like finely tuned athletes. At first I thought the man's name was Arthur Venga.

At that time Ron Atkinson was the king of 'personality' bosses, famous for his flash suits and gold jewellery but shrewd enough to employ Spry and Dave Sexton, the most invisible major figure in English football, as first-team coach, showing Dalian Atkinson and Dean Saunders how to make clever runs for each other. Spry is a former kick-boxing champion who has worked with boxers and golfers as well as footballers. He says it is difficult to describe his job to people. 'They say, "What d'you do?" And I say I'm a conditioning coach. They don't realise that you're like a mechanic: you've got to get your player in tip-top condition. You have to oil him, you have to feed him and prepare him. It's a holistic thing.'

This lack of knowledge about conditioning depressed Spry, and he worried about the long-term prospects for English football while it was dominated by the FA and by club managers whose minds were closed to continental training methods. He had worked outside England and could see the difference in approach. 'I worked with two of Norway's players when I was with Start in Tromsö, right up in the Arctic Circle. A friend of mine, an English guy, Stuart Baxter, had invited me over. I was there for almost six months. Then I was offered a job in Portugal, so I went there.' The J-League had just started in Japan, and Baxter, who was also disillusioned with English football, went out there to coach Sanfrecce Hiroshima.

One conversation I had with Spry was in June 1993, just after the fiasco in Oslo when Graham Taylor's England team blundered to a 2–0 defeat at the hands of Norway in a World Cup qualifier. Spry, a neighbour of Taylor's in Sutton Coldfield, was angered by that shambles. 'In England everything's based on effort and commitment. That's fine against fools, but when you play against people who have superior technique and are willing to match your courage and commitment, they're gonna wipe the floor with you. It's often an embarrassment to be an Englishman abroad. We're so far behind, we're ridiculed. But we're so insular that we don't even realise what other football nations think of us.'

Spry said that lucrative television deals had begun to generate more money than ever in English football, but that the game here was still built on a shallow foundation of limited players whose technical development had been woefully neglected. 'Every other country in the world, bar none, has had an influx of foreign coaches. But people still say "That wouldn't work over here." But what is the most traditional English game, apart from football? It's rugby league. Ten years ago rugby league was dull, dire, full of fat guys running around like headless chickens, lots of effort but no technique. Then the Australians started to come over and all of a sudden the game started producing exciting stars like Ellery Hanley and Martin Offiah. And people say, "This is a totally different game!" But *why* is it a different game? Because of an influx of foreign ideas.'

Spry mentioned a Czech manager who had failed in England, Josef Venglos, who was in charge at Aston Villa in 1990/91. 'We need special people to come into English football, with special personalities. No disrespect to Josef Venglos, because he's a very good coach, but he's had the same problem in every country he's gone to. He's too nice a guy to ruffle feathers. The one thing you don't need in England is a shrinking violet. You need someone to come in with all guns blazing and say, "What you've been doing is crap! We're doing it this way from now on!" '

At that time Spry was preparing to address a symposium in Helsinki on the development of youth players. He said that England had exported coaches for decades, but never imported them for fear of losing a club's precious 'Englishness'. In the early to mid-nineties, with the game in something of a crisis, it was time to wake up or join Austria and Iceland in the European Third Division. 'It's time for a revolution in English football. It's totally lacking in imagination, innovation and creativity. It's got to be done. When you see Norway, a small country, streets ahead of us in technique, fitness, commitment, everything, it's tragic, really. But the time for talking, for feeling sorry for ourselves, has gone. We've got to say, "Right, let's do it! There are the knowledgeable people available, let's get them together and do it!"'

In his own area of expertise, Spry said that English football was decades behind. Many people in English football still did not realise that conditioning enhances skills and prevents injuries. If the body is not flexible enough to make certain shapes, the ball cannot be controlled properly, and many injuries are caused during a game when the body tries to make shapes it should have been making a hundred times a week in training. 'I used to find it sad. Then I found it frustrating. Now I just get angry, because all these claims that we have the fittest footballers in the world are rubbish. That is the biggest fallacy in world football. By continental standards we are unfit. Players assume in this country that you can mess around in training, abuse yourself all week, and it will be all right on Saturday. It's the it'll-be-all-right-on-the-night syndrome. It's totally ridiculous. It doesn't work. The best foreign players do all their talking during training, on the pitch, not to the press.

'I've worked with Brazilians, Frenchmen, Spaniards, Portuguese, Kuwaitis and Australians, and every single one of them has been surprised at how quickly skills can be learnt. Some of the Villa players are doing things they didn't believe they could do a year ago. Not because they're incapable of doing it, but because no one had ever shown them. From a very early age players should be encouraged to be bilateral. Everything should be developed equally, both left and right. The South Americans learn to use every part of the body that's legal. If we see a British player backheel the ball we say, "Ooh, look at that!" Over there they say, "If it's legal, learn how to use it." How many players have you ever seen in Britain pass a ball with their knees? I've seen our players control it with their chest, and then with their foot, which takes a helluva lot of time. You can, as the ball comes to you, just swivel and play the ball with your knee. Many South Americans can play the ball thirty metres with their knees, accurately, in one flowing movement. And it's not because they're more technically gifted, it's because they've got more parts of their body in the right condition to give them that range of movement.

'Our whole game is based on linear running. A lot of their conditioning is based on short, sharp, explosive movements, repeated over and over again, with or without the ball. That's the very big difference. A lot of my friends, particularly the Brazilian coaches, have said that the thing that they've got as a nation is teachable, and the thing that we have is not. That never-say-die attitude is one of our greatest strengths. They are very, very frightened that one day the British will train continental-style, because they say that with our attitude plus that potential ability, we'll be unbeatable.'

Spry admitted that real progress towards modern methods at an English club would be impossible without a very brave, forward-thinking chairman. The trouble is, he added, most chairmen want success yesterday. He had not been surprised to see Arsenal soundly beaten 3–1 in a November 1991 European Cup tie at Highbury by Benfica, whose coach was Sven-Goran Eriksson. 'I've talked to Arsène Wenger and Sven-Goran Eriksson about having an international exchange of some of their good young players. Can you imagine the benefits if three of AC Milan's players came and spent a month at Villa and three of our players went over there? What an incredible learning experience! Or even better, what if AC Milan said to me, "Roger, come and help with our training for a month and we'll send our coach over to Villa for a month." Or I could go to Monaco or Marseilles or River Plate. For the good of the game those ideas should be explored.

'I know that Wenger goes from Monaco to the AC Milan training ground regularly and he's welcomed with open arms. There is so much fear in this game. If someone who really knows what they're doing comes in and you don't know what you're doing, and you've been bullshitting and bluffing for fifteen years and getting away with it, when somebody with real knowledge walks in everybody thinks, "Jesus Christ!" '

I conducted several interviews with Roger Spry over a three-year period between 1993 and 1996, but neither of us could have guessed then that a fitness revolution would indeed come to England in 1996 and that it would be launched by his pal from Monaco. If Arsène Wenger had read every detail on the Highbury crime-sheet, the full list of misdemeanours by his players, he would not have believed it. He would have asked, 'Can a team that has won six trophies in eight years really be such a gang of boozers, gamblers and outlaws?'

# 4. 1996/97: THE SEASON OF ANALYSIS

The Arsenal AGM is a small piece of theatre which takes place every year at Highbury at noon on the first Thursday of September. The club had been so stable over many decades that nothing much usually happened at this meeting, apart from the approval of the accounts, the re-election of the directors and a few tame questions – sometimes, veterans claimed, from 'plants', people primed to say certain things to provoke certain responses.

But the 1996 AGM was the most stormy in living memory, notable for Peter Hill-Wood's explanation of Bruce Rioch's sudden departure and Jarvis Astaire's revelations about David Dein's frustrating summer. One shareholder caused an uproar by asking why Dennis Bergkamp had been signed for £7.5 million when his friend, a solicitor and agent, had been offered the Dutchman for £5.5 million. The ensuing debate made it clear just how difficult it is to sign talented footballers in a highly competitive European transfer market.

Directors are always nervous when they change managers since managers vary a lot in ability, and hiring a new one is the most important decision they make. A competent manager can keep a team ticking over, a good manager can improve a team, and a very good manager can win trophies. But all managers can lose their way, all can suffer bad luck, and all take big risks when they buy players.

The meeting began with Hill-Wood making an opening address, as he does every year, and the disposal of formal business. Hill-Wood is a City gentleman who worked for Hambros bank, has an American wife and spends a lot of time in New York. The AGM can be the most nerve-racking day of his year.

'In view of events of the past fortnight,' he began, 'I will explain more about our decisions and their timing. When Bruce Rioch joined us we agreed on a different role for the manager. As time went on he seemed to become less than happy with his role. He didn't sign his contract until very recently, although it had not been altered since last February. We felt that Bruce didn't share our vision for the future of the club, and after a series of discussions over some months the board reached the decision that he was not the right man for our job. You know that he took us into Europe, for which we thank him very much. I would have to agree that the timing of Bruce's departure was both inconvenient and undesirable, but there is no ideal time to release a manager. Much has to do with finding a replacement, and of course activities in the transfer market to strengthen our squad.

'We have acted in the best long-term interests of the club. We have identified a replacement of considerable international reputation who has agreed to join us. We cannot announce his appointment officially as we have given an undertaking not to do so. All being well, a statement will be made very shortly and we expect to have him with us by the end of September.

'The two major changes in the manager's area of responsibility are, first, the transfer negotiations, and second, youth development, which we felt needed a radical overhaul. We have recently appointed Liam Brady as head of youth development. He's very experienced in all football matters both in Europe and in the UK. And we hope we will soon get back to the old days when more of our star players were homegrown.

'The first change I mentioned regards our operation in the transfer market. The way it works is that the manager identifies the players he wishes to buy or sell, and the responsibility is given to David Dein and Ken Friar to do the deals in conjunction with the manager, in what are often very complex financial arrangements. Much has been made of the so-called failure of this system in the past year. It cannot work if the players identified by the manager are, for one reason or another, unavailable to us. And I think it is fair to say that although every player Bruce proposed to the board was pursued, overall his list proved to be impractical. In a very short time we have acquired two new players, Patrick Vieira and Remi Garde, both of whom were signed in time to qualify for this year's UEFA Cup. No doubt there will be more to follow during the coming season. The club has significant funds at its disposal to purchase quality players, but we will not break the bank on one superstar. We all know that there are three or four more pieces of the jigsaw to be put in place.

'The board has taken these steps in the best long-term interests of the club. We are confident that we are planning for a bright future ahead. In the meantime, Stewart Houston has shown that he has the full support of the players, and the performance in our first two games was, I thought, excellent, with everyone showing total commitment. That's all I have to say. I'll now be happy to take questions.'

A shareholder said, 'I'd like to ask Mr Fiszman, who is now the main shareholder, to give his view of the future of this club, and whether there are funds coming into the club.'

Nobody had expected Danny Fiszman to speak on any such matter. Hill-Wood quickly replied, 'I did say that we have substantial funds available, so that, I think, answers that question. Mr Fiszman doesn't have anything to add to that.' There was some ironic laughter. Fiszman, a diamond dealer brought up knowing the value of security and anonymity, is one of London's most invisible millionaires. Sightings of him are rare, comments even rarer.

The board was then asked to spell out their short-term objectives for the club, over the next two years. 'The short-term ambitions are to get the right squad together and win another trophy,' Hill-Wood replied. 'I don't think we had a particularly bad season last year. We finished fifth – fourth equal in fact. We got into Europe. But I don't think anybody in this room would think that the squad we have is actually going to challenge Manchester United just at the moment, so it needs to be strengthened and we hope that it will be. This club needs success. We all want it, none more so than the board of directors. If you look around the stadium, it's a magnificent stadium. We've spent about £40 million over the past ten years on it, we've got the best pitch in the land. Things aren't all bad. We want them better. The board are accountable and we take our responsibilities very seriously, we try our best. Sometimes it doesn't prove good enough but I promise you we will continue to try.'

Another shareholder changed the subject. 'The club has been subject to a campaign of vilification from the tabloid press which I find, as a supporter of over thirty years, extremely upsetting. The club seem unable to counter the fact, fiction or innuendo which is reported almost daily in the newspapers. A company that has a turnover of over £20 million should be much more adept at handling the media and I would suggest that you employ somebody who is capable of giving the correct information, so that the supporters and shareholders know the facts.

'There are other points which require unequivocal answers. One is the Bergkamp transfer. I know for a fact that Bergkamp was offered to this club for £5.5 million. The person that offered him to the club was told, a day before the transfer, that Arsenal were not going to sign him because he was going to break the wage structure. I would also like to know if a former employee of the club, who works now as an agent, was paid commission by the selling club on overseas transfers. I'd also like to know – and I wrote to you about this, I don't know if it's correct or not – about a rumour that he got £35,000. Why was he only sacked last week? Can we have direct answers to the questions and no fudging because I am extremely hurt by what's going on in the media. We love this club. People are not here today to hear the club accounts, we are here out of love for this club.' This emotive speech was greeted by loud applause. The shareholder was encouraged to continue. 'It's a big part of my life and I know that everyone who has made the effort to be here feels the same way. We want straight answers. We want to hear decent things about the club. We want to pick up a newspaper, like we used to do, and be proud to be an Arsenal fan.' There were cries of 'Hear, hear!'

Hill-Wood said, 'So far as the handling of the press is concerned, we do give them facts as we are able to give them, and they interpret them in different ways, often in not very helpful ways. We are considering the appointment of a PR man, a press officer, and I think your suggestion is one we take very seriously. So far as Bergkamp is concerned, I was not aware of what you said. I'm not doubting you, but I personally was not aware that he was offered to us at £5.5 million. When he was finally offered to us he was a lot more than that.'

David Dein seized the microphone and stood up. 'I know who you're talking about. Your very good friend Mel Goldberg did not do the deal. The deal was directly completed with Inter Milan. I played a part in it, Ken Friar played a part in it, and I have to tell you this: we could not have bought Dennis Bergkamp for one single penny cheaper than £7.5 million. That is a statement of fact. He could easily have gone to Barcelona, never mind what your colleague thinks he could have achieved, because in the end he did not do the deal and could not do the deal, because Inter Milan – and we have letters to prove the fact – were not selling for £5.5 million. That's all I've got to say. If anybody here would like us not to have bought Dennis Bergkamp for £7.5 million they should say so now. We could sell him for twice as much.'

This prompted some shouting and heckling. Dein spoke again. 'I take it as an offence that you are questioning our integrity. Every last cent went to Inter Milan and we were delighted to have pen put to paper on his contract because we thought it was an excellent buy. He could have gone elsewhere for more money, but he chose to come to Arsenal. That is the bottom line.'

The shareholder who'd asked the Bergkamp question then said, 'He is the only good buy we have made since Ian Wright, but the point remains that he was offered for £5.5 million –'

'By an agent who could not consummate that deal,' the vice-chairman cut in. 'How do I know? Because I did the deal personally, with Ken Friar, with Inter Milan. That's the bottom line. Not somebody who says I could have got him cheaper because he couldn't do the deal.'

Dein was applauded warmly for that. People were enjoying the aggro, which went far beyond anything veterans had ever seen at an AGM.

Hill-Wood got proceedings back on track by picking up the thread about Arsenal's relations with the press. 'They are very good at their job. They're very good at making you say things you probably shouldn't say. They collar the players at the most unlikely moments when they're probably not on guard and we can't, I'm afraid, gag them totally. We try and advise them to be cautious about what they say, but they don't always manage to do that. These press reporters are very clever. They trip me up periodically and they trip the players up. There's not a lot we can do about it. It's often the same players because some of the players are sensible enough not to say anything while others are a bit talkative. When we have a press officer hopefully that will take some of the sting out of it. I get called, and I know Mr Dein does and Mr Friar does. We get calls at all times of the day or night. If we could divert those to one central point, which is exactly what the Football Association have done and I think the PR that they've got has improved greatly, I think it would improve with us as well. So it's a very sound suggestion.'

Jarvis Astaire, the Wembley director and boxing promoter, his mind obviously still on the Bergkamp outburst and transfer issues generally, stood up to say that although he was not an Arsenal supporter, he was a shareholder and close friend of David Dein. Astaire said he was 'nobody's poodle' and had not been set up to defend Mr Dein or anybody else, that he had remained a shareholder for thirty years because he had always respected the club. Like many of the older people present he had grown up regarding Arsenal as the MCC of football, an institution where stability, probity and sportsmanship were highly valued. 'I am therefore in a position to tell you first hand that during the course of Euro 96 this summer I spent most days in the company of Mr Dein attending matches. And because we were close together, and he had his phone with him, or he was in my car while I was driving, he took me into his confidence to a large extent.

'He did try desperately to obtain the very few players who were available. He was frustrated on a number of occasions when the names of some of the most prominent foreign players came up, including those who have signed for other clubs, because Bruce Rioch didn't feel happy or confident enough to have those players join this club under his management. There is not the slightest doubt about that. I am making a statement of fact. I have no axe to grind. I can tell you that there was one player that the manager was happy about, and that's Seedorf. I was present when Mr Dein had a number of conversations, very difficult conversations, with Sampdoria about trying to sign Seedorf, but by that time, by the time the manager agreed that he wanted him, Real Madrid had already done a deal verbally, and the deal went through and that was the end of it. But I can assure you that there was tremendous frustration felt by Mr Dein about the lack of confidence and imagination on the part of Mr Rioch.'

Since there had been stories in the papers speculating about the imminent arrival of a certain French manager from Japan, people wanted to know why the chairman was still keeping everyone in the dark about his identity.

'I don't think anybody's in the dark,' Hill-Wood said. 'It's been one of the worst-kept secrets of the year. It's just that we did give an undertaking. It may sound odd to you when everybody and his uncle knows who is coming, but I can't say formally.'

A shareholder countered, 'Speaking as a lawyer, an undertaking to whom, Mr Chairman?'

'An undertaking to Mr Wenger and to his –'

This slip of the tongue meant that the rest of the chairman's response was drowned out by the sort of laughter often heard in the House of Commons during Prime Minister's Questions.

'It's a technicality,' said Hill-Wood.

The meeting ended soon after that.

So this was the state of London's number one sporting institution in September 1996. Arsenal was a football club which had enjoyed eight years of stability and success followed by eighteen months of trauma and turbulence. Their most educated fans were still furious with the cowardly way in which George Graham's sacking had been handled. They were also very disappointed that Bruce Rioch had signed no new players and deeply embarrassed by the avalanche of bad press.

## WELCOME TO ARSENAL, MR WENGER!

*Sooner or later a continental manager is going to break through and have success in England.*

Don Howe

The Frenchman from Japan arrived in England to find that the champions were Manchester United and the biggest star in the

41

country was Eric Cantona. His former Monaco player Glenn Hoddle had just started as England coach with a 3–0 World Cup qualifier win in Moldova, Ray Wilkins had resigned at QPR, John Major was Prime Minister but the director of the club he supported, Matthew Harding, had just given a £1 million donation to Tony Blair's New Labour. George Graham had been in the wilderness for nineteen months, but when Howard Wilkinson was sacked by Leeds Graham was appointed manager the following day, 10 September – the day on which Arsenal lost 3–2 at home to the young Wenger's favourite team, Borussia Mönchengladbach, in the UEFA Cup. Nine days after Ray Wilkins left QPR, Arsenal caretaker boss Stewart Houston quit Highbury to go to Loftus Road. On the very same day Tony Adams admitted he was an alcoholic.

Arsenal's Peter Hill-Wood was probably the first chairman to own up publicly about England's old-fashioned football culture. On the subject of Wenger's appointment, he said, 'This signals a new era for us. I believe Arsène Wenger is going to be a great success and drag football in this country into the twentieth century. There is no doubt in my mind we are blinkered and backward as a sporting nation. Look at the British results in Europe, they were not good, including ours. We keep telling ourselves we have the best league in Europe, but it is not true. We need to catch up with the continentals and we think Arsène is the man to help us.' Wenger said, 'It is my dream to take over a club in a top European league and if I didn't take the opportunity now it may never happen.'

Arsène Wenger was the first Frenchman to manage an English football club. His first official day at Highbury would be 30 September, and he would be in charge for the Blackburn Rovers game twelve days later. He was believed to be on a salary of £2 million spread over a three-year contract. He met the players for the first time at the training ground on Monday, 23 September, the day after his press conference, and watched them work with Pat Rice. 'I know how I want them to play,' he said. 'Now I just have to wait and see if they can adapt to that. I am not in a hurry to buy players. It is not the best time to buy at this stage of the season anyway. The teams with good players don't want to sell and they are overpriced. And first I want to give the players here a chance. I want to watch them more. We are third in the league and the results are not too bad. We have a good team. But the squad is quite small if we have to play in everything – Europe, Premiership and cup competitions. If we stay in the UEFA Cup maybe we will have to bring in someone new.

'I spoke to all the players for about five minutes and told them I would be speaking to them individually after the Sunderland game on Saturday, so I can get to know them. I won't take over until next week so I just observed what was going on in training. I want to give confidence to the players first. I am someone who needs challenges. I like to win and I try every day to be better than the day before. I have a lot of failings but if I have one quality it is that I like to give.'

First impressions can be deceptive, but Wenger seemed to be a formidably intelligent man who talked about facts. He took the time to digest the important facts and built his views on those facts – a healthy sign. Opinion is cheap, but professional football is a game of goals and assists and clean sheets. It is, above all, about results. Results are everything. Results win trophies, results make and break careers. Results create big games, big seasons, big money, big opportunities. Wenger also had a cool head. One tabloid had quoted the 1995 World Footballer of the Year George Weah as saying, 'Arsène is the best coach I have ever played for and I would love to play for one of his teams again in the future. He brought the best out of me as a footballer. I owe all my success to him.' Wenger simply said that signing his former protégé from AC Milan was 'impossible'.

He spent that first afternoon studying videos of the Borussia Mönchengladbach game with Pat Rice. 'My first impression is that the players here are aware of what they must do in Germany,' he said. 'The experienced players know it will be difficult but they are used to battles. I believe we can get a result. We were unlucky in the home game with Dennis Bergkamp's injury, but we created a lot of chances. Borussia are also a strange team. One week they win 4–0, the next they lose 4–0. If Pat asks me about something I will try to help him. He will be in charge of the team and make the decisions, but I feel it is important to be here this week. I will be an observer. I will be in the dressing room and on the bench, nothing more. I'll only give my advice if he asks for it. He knows the club, he knows English football, he knows the players very well and he is a pure Arsenal man. I will not become the manager until next Monday.'

It was a bizarre twist of fate that the Frenchman from Alsace was joining Arsenal just as they were about to visit Borussia Mönchengladbach, the German team whose thrilling counter-attacks had first fired his imagination. History was against Arsenal, who had never come from behind to win in Europe after losing a first leg at Highbury. Tony Adams, a substitute for hamstring victim Lee Dixon at Middlesbrough the Saturday before, was starting his first competitive game for eight months after two knee operations. He had not been named in Glenn Hoddle's squad for the World Cup qualifying tie against Poland on 9 October.

The starting eleven for the Borussia game, in 3–5–2 formation, was the side that finished the game at Middlesbrough, which Arsenal had won 2–0: Seaman; Bould, Adams, Linighan; Keown, Vieira, Merson, Platt, Winterburn; Hartson and Wright. This makeshift team was deeply unbalanced, with four centre-backs and only one good midfield player, Vieira. Despite that handicap Ian Wright scored the first goal just before half-time after Hartson had headed on Merson's free-kick. It was his fifteenth goal in seventeen European games, but then Stefan Effenberg slid a pass behind Linighan for Juskowiak to make it 4–3 on aggregate. Early in the second half Merson made it 4–4 with a twenty-yarder into the top corner, but Effenberg restored Borussia's lead after 75 minutes, then Juskowiak scored again to seal Arsenal's fate.

Wenger had watched the first half from the stand and spent the second half on the bench. Pat Rice, ebullient as ever, tried to put a positive spin on the defeat and said that Wenger had suggested a couple of changes. 'One of them was to go to a back four and add extra width to the attack, and of course I took his advice. We've come out of this with a lot of credit and will bounce back in typical Arsenal style.'

It was clear to all that Arsenal's famous rearguard, which had conceded twelve goals in the last six games, was crumbling. Chris

Davies, in the *Daily Telegraph*, reported that Arsenal's 'success in recent seasons has been based on the most solid of defences. Age is catching up with most of the back players and Wenger, who is said to prefer a back four, will no doubt make a commanding stopper a priority. Andy Linighan's weaknesses were again cruelly exposed by Borussia's speedy forwards while Arsenal had nobody with the touch and vision of Stefan Effenberg, the game's outstanding performer.'

Wenger obviously had some work to do. Former Arsenal manager Don Howe, among others, realised that 'Players judge a manager on whether he knows football. The players will want to hear him talk about football. If he comes across as having good football intelligence there will be no problem. Sooner or later a continental manager is going to break through and have success in England, and if Wenger gets success the Arsenal supporters will accept him like anyone else. Supporters want to see their team win.' Glenn Hoddle reminded Arsenal fans that Wenger 'has an English mind but also a German mind, which is very disciplined'. He said that the Arsenal players would find the new manager honest, straightforward and approachable, but ruthless too if a player stepped out of line. 'That's when the German side comes out.'

Wenger himself seemed buoyant after the defeat in Cologne. 'My challenge is to mix the English style to a more continental way. Also I am conscious that I have to win over the supporters because they don't really know me and I am foreign. But if they reject me it will not be because I am foreign. They will reject me if I don't do a good job.'

## OLD GUARD TRY NEW IDEAS

*Other teams noticed that we were still flying after eighty minutes, and when Tony, Martin, Wrighty and I were on England duty the other players started asking what we were taking.*

David Seaman

According to David Seaman, Arsène Wenger arrived and did exactly what Roger Spry said Josef Venglos should have done at

Villa. He said: 'Right, we are doing it my way from now on!' In *Safe Hands*, his autobiography, Seaman wrote: 'Arsène made it clear that there would be total change straight away. There was no messing about. He told us, "This is how I run training and this is how I expect you to eat and look after yourselves." He said we could not carry on eating what we had been used to stuffing down ourselves, as it was no good for us as professional athletes.'

This was, in fact, an over-simplification of what happened. At first the new manager asked the players to train in the afternoons as well, but they refused to do that. So Wenger, whose credibility was low after he had made them switch to 4–4–2 at half-time in Cologne when they were winning 2–1, decided to compromise with a longer session in the morning. A masseur, Mark James, was employed for the first time and the players now had lengthy warm-downs after training and matches. Wenger said, 'I like players to relax with massages and hot baths. I believe they are helpful, physically and psychologically.' He had studied physiology and was an expert on flexibility, nutrition and the best ways to protect a player's body against fatigue. He knew how muscles worked and had also studied plyometric training, an advanced technique which involves jumping, bounding, one-legged hopping, skipping and other exercises which are specific to a particular muscle. Jumpers, sprinters and hurdlers train by doing multiple jumps over a series of obstacles such as low hurdles. These exercises, aimed at strengthening the lower body, can only be done by athletes who are already strong and well conditioned. They add power to existing strength. Arsenal's training ground at London Colney, which they shared with University College London, had antique facilities such as big white baths and a canteen worthy of a Second Division club, so Wenger immediately moved their training base to Sopwell House, a nearby hotel which had a gym, a pool, a jacuzzi and a good restaurant. The players now changed at Sopwell, took a coach down to the training pitch, then came back to the hotel. Sopwell had been used by Croatia, Portugal and many other visiting football teams before matches at Wembley.

The players found that their diet had been revolutionised. Steak, chips, scrambled eggs, baked beans, sugar and junk food were forbidden. Wenger brought in dieticians to explain the benefits of pasta, boiled chicken, steamed fish, broccoli, raw vegetables and lots of water. He also flew in Philippe Boixel, the French national team osteopath, every month to work on the realignment of the players' bodies, and the biochemist Dr Yann Rogier talked to them about the value of dietary supplements such as vitamins and minerals. The players began to receive vitamin injections and to take tablets, including creatine, an amino acid produced naturally in the liver and kidneys which is mass-produced artificially and widely sold in tablet or powder form at health-food stores. Creatine replenishes energy in the muscles and reduces fatigue, so it is most beneficial to sprinters and footballers, who do brief but intense bursts of running. It had been used by British Olympic athletes in Barcelona in 1992. Wenger, however, made it clear that the supplements were optional.

David Seaman noticed that the innovations had an immediate impact on the whole Arsenal squad, whose levels of energy and concentration were now much higher. 'Other teams noticed that we were still flying after eighty minutes, and when Tony, Martin, Wrighty and I were on England duty the other players started asking what we were taking. They copied what we were doing and carried on with it when they went back to their clubs, and most of them said they felt better for it. When this got back to Arsène, he made a point of warning us not to tell the other players exactly what we were doing and taking. At that stage this was all new to the English league and he wanted to keep our edge for as long as possible.' Wenger's training techniques were the distillation of two decades of research, practice, observation and careful thinking, so he must have been annoyed that his methods had been revealed to his rivals in such a careless manner.

Work on the training pitch became more scientific, with fewer long runs and cross-country runs but much more timed running in the form of bleep-tests, where players run back and forth while an electronic device emits a timed signal. Wenger believes that players can over-train, so he made it clear that from now on sleep, rest and relaxation would be very important.

George Graham had never allowed journalists or broadcasters to watch Arsenal's training sessions, and Wenger kept up this tradition. In *Addicted*, his best-selling autobiography, Tony Adams stated that Wenger liked to keep his training methods to himself, but he did reveal that sessions sometimes lasted only 45 minutes: 'stretching and a warm-up, then a ten-minutes-each-way small-sided game and finish with a run round the pitch'. Seaman confirmed that Wenger was out on the training pitch with them every day and always knew exactly what he wanted his players to do. He always had his stopwatch with him and was a martinet about the timing of their work (the word 'martinet' originates in France: Jean Martinet was a seventeenth-century army drill-master notorious for his brutal methods). 'Everything is geared to his watch,' Seaman wrote. 'He knows how long any training or tactical discipline should last and will stop it right on the button. Sometimes he drives us mad. We could be playing an eight-a-side game on a smaller pitch with a bigger goal. The score is 2–2 and it has been a really good, tight game but, when the time he has allowed for it is up, he will always step in and stop it. We all say, "Let's go on until the next goal wins it," but he never changes his mind. We have to stop and move on to the next exercise. There is no arguing with him.' Wenger had a fitness coach working with him, but Adams believed that the manager knew professional footballers inside out and could tell whether a player was fully fit just by watching him run. 'He is a thinker, a listener, and he cares a great deal about the welfare of players,' said Adams.

Wenger's first game in charge of Arsenal was on 12 October 1996 at Blackburn, and that was when he first introduced his players to the stretching exercises which were to become an important part of their lives. 'He called us all down to the hotel ballroom,' Adams recalled, 'and put us through the routine for half an hour. There was some joking among the boys, who were all pretending still to be sleepy and putting on the tiredness, because we probably feared change. But just because it was different didn't make it wrong. It helped that we went on to win the game that day and now it is second nature to us.'

The way Wenger treated his players as people was related to the way he treated them as footballers. He saw football as a game for adults and young adults, so instead of telling them exactly what to do on the field he gave each player the responsibility for his own game, which allowed a more exciting and more varied style of play to evolve, with defenders like Bould and Adams encouraged to bring the ball forward far more than they ever did under Graham, who only wheeled the big men up for set-pieces. Dennis Bergkamp was another who responded positively to these new ideas. He had been sulking since Bruce Rioch, the manager who signed him, had been sacked, and had stopped going into the players' lounge. Bergkamp hated boozers, so Wenger's approach was a breath of fresh air for him. Whenever the Dutchman had smelt drink on the breath of team-mates in the morning he made a point of hounding those players in training matches, giving them a hard time to make them wish they had not indulged the night before.

Wenger was unbeaten after his first four Premiership games against Blackburn, Coventry, Leeds and Wimbledon, but everything was still new to him. He learned something every week: what each player could do in training, whether he could reproduce it in matches, how often he could do it, and whether he did it more often home or away. He watched his players carefully to see how brave, how skilful and how determined they were, and he surveyed them with a fresh, unprejudiced eye, making an inventory all the while, gathering a definitive dossier of information on the basis of which next summer's big decisions would be made. He was making small, specific judgements but also an overall judgement about Arsenal's style of play. Would a different style be more effective with this group of players? If so, how quickly could that new style be created? Will new players be needed? If so, how many? Can the club afford them?

In terms of media relations, Wenger worked with Clare Tomlinson, who had joined Arsenal from the FA after Euro 96, and they decided that he would do press conferences but not give one-on-one interviews to English journalists. Wenger came with no baggage and he decided to travel without baggage, without favourites. He was still trying to figure out the English game and assess the challenge posed by other Premiership clubs anyway, and he had not known any British reporters when he was a player. That sensible approach protected him in the early days when his English was not as good as it is now, buying him time to figure out what the media needed and wanted. That decision has never been reversed, even though most other Premiership managers do interviews as well as press conferences.

## MANCHESTER UNITED 1 ARSENAL 0

*They are so disappointed, so frustrated. I also learnt that they have solidarity when they lose. Maybe David Seaman felt he made a mistake but everybody was all right.*

Arsène Wenger

After a couple of months at the helm Wenger realised that his main rivals were going to be Alex Ferguson at Manchester United, Kevin Keegan at Newcastle, Brian Little at Aston Villa and George Graham at Leeds.

Ferguson had arrived at Old Trafford in 1986, the same year in which Graham arrived at Arsenal. Graham had soon built the powerhouse midfield of Marwood, Davis, Thomas and Rocastle, which showed Ferguson what was needed to win the league. Once, at Highbury after a game, Ferguson had marvelled at the tackling and running power of David Rocastle. 'What an effort the boy Rocastle puts into his game,' he said, pointing out that such hard work by the tenacious Rocky was of great benefit to Lee Dixon, who played behind him.

When Wenger first came to Old Trafford Ferguson was just embarking on his second decade in charge, but United had suffered a disturbing sequence of results. They had lost 5–0 at Newcastle, then 6–3 at Southampton before coming back to Old Trafford to play Chelsea, who beat them 2–1. So, coming into the game with Arsenal on 16 November, the champions had conceded thirteen goals in their previous three games, and Roy Keane was suspended. The young David Beckham had taken his place in central midfield. The game was played in front of

55,210 people, the biggest crowd in the history of the Premiership.

The real action opened with Cantona playing a superb pass across the penalty area, picking out Beckham, whose instant shot hit the post with Seaman well beaten. Bergkamp then put Wright in on the left, but his touch was poor and he had to chase the ball as it ran into the box. Schmeichel raced out, feet first, grabbed it and then jumped up, enraged, suggesting Wright had kicked him. Fierce words were exchanged. Referee Graham Poll cautioned Wright but replays suggested that the striker's outstretched right foot had not connected with the Danish goalkeeper. It looked like Schmeichel's histrionics had got the fiery striker a booking. Seaman had earlier been injured when Solskjær's boot caught him in the chest – he was found to have a cracked rib.

The only goal, when it came in the middle of the second half, was the most untidy, self-inflicted goal Arsenal would concede all season. Giggs closed down on Dixon, who half-volleyed a wonky backpass, and Seaman made a pig's breakfast of his clearance. He should have kicked the ball into Row Z or let it go out for a corner, but he chose to stop the ball with his foot and kicked it straight to Nicky Butt, who jabbed it across the open goal towards Poborsky. As Winterburn intervened the ball hit his arm and dribbled over the line. A farcical goal to concede.

'We lost the game on details, offensively and defensively,' the manager said afterwards. 'In the big games you make one or two small mistakes and you pay for it. That's why we are unhappy today. Because we have the feeling that we could have done more and come back with at least a draw.' He was, however, impressed by Arsenal's team spirit, even in defeat. 'They are so disappointed, so frustrated. I also learnt that they have solidarity when they lose. Maybe David Seaman felt he made a mistake but everybody was all right.' The Frenchman placed huge emphasis on this *esprit de corps* and would continue to do so for the next five years. 'With the internationalisation of the game today, you have many foreign players in the team, and you do not always have the right spirit. You have to find a real balance. If you bring players in, you have to make sure they have the right spirit.'

## ARSENAL 3 SPURS 1

*The real revelation of a player's character is not in his social life but in how he plays. In my social life I can hide my real personality . . .*

Arsène Wenger

After six weeks and seven games the manager did a press conference before his first North London derby and his thoughts represented a half-term report on the players he had inherited. When one reporter mentioned Patrick Vieira's creative touches, the manager said something interesting. 'What is creative?' he asked. 'For me, being creative is scoring goals. That is why, for me, beauty is efficiency. It is not about making nice movements. The crowd love him because he does the right thing at the right moment, not because he's beautiful to watch. I see players who do wonderful things outside a match but once in a match they are disasters because they cannot do them when they are needed.'

Wenger was at his most professorial during a discussion of the alcoholism and behaviour in general. 'The real revelation of a player's character is not in his social life but in how he plays. In my social life I can hide my real personality, but when I'm playing I show really how I am. It's important for me to win while respecting the rules. Sometimes if a player is really dirty on the field but outside in life he is so nice, at important times in his life he will become like he is on the field. When you argue with the referee you are not concentrating on the game and you lose two or three seconds. I know that sometimes a player needs to release his frustration. It depends on the personality. Maybe Ian Wright sometimes needs to say something in order to be better in the next move. But it's better to have a high level of concentration. Look at how we lost at Manchester United – a small thing.'

He pointed out, however, that he had been very impressed by the professionalism of his players. 'I have a deep respect for my squad. We have an experienced team. Some people say that we have an old team but the mental side must still be young because these players are ready to take on anybody to win games. For me, being a professional is not just playing once a week, and playing well from time to time, it's trying to be at your best every time. For this you need a strong mentality. For a professional player, it's not normal every day to get up in the morning and say, "OK, let's go on with the fight." You need a special attitude. Winners are those who are able to do it. When you have players like I have who have been doing it for ten years, that means there is something special inside them which makes them want to win.

'I am surprised by the technical quality of the defenders. English defenders had a reputation for just kicking the ball. You should come to training and see that our five defenders are technically good. Tony Adams and the other ones are able to play. They last so long because they have the quality. If they had only physique they couldn't last.'

Arsenal needed to be at their best on 24 November because they had not beaten Spurs at Highbury for five years. There had been some scuffling stalemates when the sides were managed by those old cronies George Graham and Terry Venables, who used to come in to face reporters together, thereby making sure that the press conference was also a goalless draw. This time Wenger was pleased to see Dennis Bergkamp, his star player, inspiring the Gunners to victory.

The Dutchman won a penalty early on when Clive Wilson fouled him in the box, and Ian Wright converted. It was 1–0 at half-time. Wright missed several chances in the second half before Andy Sinton hit a shot which rebounded from the base of the post, hit the head of the diving John Lukic, and crossed the line for an unusual own-goal. The rest of the game was tense, but some good football was played. Arsenal scored twice in the last three minutes to win the match. Bergkamp flicked on a Paul Merson throw and Adams, charging forward, hit a shot which went in off right-back Steve Carr. Then Merson found Wright on the right side and he hit a long cross beyond the far post. As the cross came down on the wet, slippery grass, Bergkamp killed the ball with one devastating touch, knocked it five yards past Carr, burst across the startled defender and smashed his shot past Ian Walker. Carr tried to grab him round the waist but he was a scarecrow, a man of straw, against the explosive force of the Dutchman, who had decided where he was going before the ball had even bounced. Dennis Bergkamp had administered an outrageous *coup de grâce* by passing the ball to himself. It was a classic goal which decided the game and lifted the ecstatic North Bank fans from their seats in salute. The handsome 3–1 win was the highlight of the season so far.

Beating Leeds 3–0 in October had put Arsenal top of the table, but after losing at Old Trafford they had dropped to third. Next up, on the last day of November, were league leaders Newcastle at St James's Park.

Injuries to key players are a big part of every manager's life and Wenger now found that he was without Seaman, who was to miss nine Premiership games with that cracked rib, and Bergkamp, who had strained a thigh muscle while warming up at Anfield for a midweek Coca-Cola Cup tie which Liverpool had won 4–2. So Arsenal had lost their last two away games and now had to face a trip to Newcastle with John Lukic in goal and John Hartson partnering Wright. On the day, Arsenal were rescued by a fine performance from Paul Merson, who often carries the ball more than Bergkamp does.

A very unusual incident occurred early in the game which could have put Arsenal off their stride. A ball was played down the field towards the Arsenal penalty area. Tino Asprilla was ten yards offside, strolling back in his nonchalant way, and when the long ball came towards him he allowed it to bounce between his legs, leaving it for an onrushing Alan Shearer, and obliging Tony Adams to run round him. When Adams and Shearer barged each other, Adams was sent off by Graham Barber for a professional foul.

But it was Arsenal who took the lead when Hartson made a pass down the left side and Wright craftily allowed big centre-back Darren Peacock to reach the ball first, then knocked him off balance with a neat nudge. He crossed to the far post where flying wing-back Lee Dixon scored with a diving header. Dixon had always liked steaming into the box and what made this one fun was that David Ginola, his old adversary from the Paris Saint Germain ties in the Cup Winners Cup, had failed to track his run. Ginola, however, soon replied with a good cross and Shearer rose above Hartson to head the equaliser. Wenger was entitled to wonder about the marking. Since Bould and Keown were on the field, why was neither of them marking the England striker as he went for the kind of header ten million English football fans had seen him score fifty times? The organisational intelligence of Adams was missed.

The winning goal was a jammy one, but Wenger probably felt his team deserved some luck after having had Adams so harshly dismissed. Merson dribbled straight down the middle of the field and tried a 25-yard shot which hit Ian Wright on the ankle and broke into his stride. Wright deftly slipped the ball past the advancing Srnicek. So Arsenal had played for over an hour with ten men and beaten the league leaders to go top of the table. Overall, Wenger was delighted with his team's form. Unfortunately, this victory at St James's Park was as good as it got because a 3–1 win over Southampton on 4 December was their only victory in five Premiership matches that month.

As 1996 drew to a close, Arsenal were still very much an English side with eight Englishmen plus Bergkamp, Vieira and Garde. Of those three, the first two were key players, as was illustrated on 28 December during the game against Aston Villa at Highbury, where the first goal in a 2–2 draw illustrated their attacking potential. Vieira, back in the side after missing three games, took the ball off Savo Milosevic and poked it towards Bergkamp, whose through-ball put Wright in. Mark Bosnich did not come out, so Wright had time to get his head up, check the bottom corner and fire past the keeper's right hand. Wenger admitted that his side could not sustain their game in the second half of that match because Garde, Bergkamp and Parlour had not had enough competitive football recently. He talked about maintaining a high tempo and finding a balance between getting balls forward quickly and keeping possession. Clearly, his favourite style of football was not as patient as that favoured by Bruce Rioch. He did not like too much pretty possession play, preferring quick penetration – slicing through the heart of the opposition's defence as soon as possible. This conception of the game was Milan-influenced, which is hardly surprising given all those trips he made to their training ground while at Monaco. Wenger favoured powerful, skilful athletes who could press ferociously, win the ball and pass it quickly into dangerous areas.

## HARTSON GLIMPSES TRANSFER THROUGH RED MIST

*I think we outplayed them tonight. Tactically, I think we got it right. I thought they ran out of ideas in the last twenty minutes.*

George Graham

When Arsenal played Middlesbrough on New Year's Day 1997 they won 2–0 with goals by Bergkamp and Wright, a victory which kept them in second place. Both goals came from mistakes and John Hartson was sent off in an incident which seemed to sum up his self-indulgent life.

Hartson had already served a three-match ban earlier in the season and had come on as a 64th-minute substitute for Bergkamp. Within two minutes he had thrown the ball away after a tackle on Bryan Robson, Boro's player-manager. Referee Mike Reed gave Hartson a yellow card for that, but a minute later he swore at Reed despite not being involved in the play at that time and was shown the red card.

Wenger had just gone four straight games without a win, his worst sequence since taking over, and he badly needed three points. Arsenal were 2–0 up and his irresponsible centre-forward had been sent off only three minutes after coming on, leaving his team-mates to play twenty minutes with ten men. A better side than Middlesbrough might have saved the game, especially when a penalty was awarded not long afterwards. Fabrizio Ravanelli, who had been felled by Steve Bould, sent his spot-kick into the North Stand via the crossbar.

Inevitably, Wenger was asked after the match about his team's deteriorating discipline. Was four red cards in the last eight games a worry?

'It's fifty per cent,' the manager joked.

But that's not the kind of consistency you want, is it?

'That's right. I think maybe some red cards I can understand. But it's less understandable when you speak with the referee.

Because we had a red card with Steve Bould at Liverpool, Tony Adams at Newcastle and even Ian Wright. It's a game, it happens; it's a reaction, they played the ball. It's always understandable. This one, I first must check what happened with the referee and with John Hartson. It was not in the game.'

Ian Wright's second goal was his 166th for Arsenal and the 200th of his career. Wenger said this was a great achievement. 'It's a symbol of a big career. I think 200 league goals is fantastic. It's really incredible.'

A steward then came in and handed Wenger a pale blue sheet of paper – a copy of the referee's report.

The *Sun*'s Brian Woolnough asked, 'Does it say there what he called him?'

The reporters giggled, but Wenger said only that Hartson's first yellow card was for a foul and the second for foul and abusive language. 'Too many red cards,' he conceded, 'but I cannot condemn the behaviour of my team because, as I explained to you before, the three red cards we got before we didn't deserve.'

Middlesbrough was a valuable win, but Hartson would now miss another three games. Wenger continued to give nothing away regarding his own feelings about the Hartson dismissal, but it looked as if this particular red card could have long-term significance for the Welshman.

The next three games were all against Sunderland. Hartson played and scored in a 1–1 draw in the FA Cup on 4 January; the tie was replayed at Roker Park on the 15th and the Gunners won 2–0. In between those two games Arsenal faced them in the league and lost 1–0. They beat Everton and West Ham after that, and then, on the first day of February, George Graham showed his old team how to keep clean sheets.

This goalless draw at Elland Road was a prequel to the FA Cup fourth-round clash at Highbury three days later. On that day Graham made sure he did not lose at his old club by employing defensive methods which had won both domestic cups for Arsenal in 1993. Rod Wallace scored the early goal, then roamed around in the Arsenal half with Brian Deane, holding the ball up well as various players broke in support at great speed. Graham had put the quick, tenacious Gary Kelly on to Merson and Gunnar Halle on to Wright, with Carlton Palmer trying to shackle the more skilful Vieira in midfield. Merson worked his socks off, but was hard pushed just to keep possession of the ball let alone make a good dribble or pass. Parlour and Dixon, two players with great drive, made no impact on the right because every Leeds player was as quick and determined as they were. Hartson came on at half-time, hit the post with a header and missed another two chances in injury time. So in two games against Leeds Arsenal had failed to score. Without Bergkamp the goals had simply dried up. Wright, who was having a bad spell anyway, missed his classy passes.

The match, although a disappointing stalemate, provided observers with a chance to compare Graham's personality with Wenger's. Graham, self-regarding as ever, used the first person singular rather than the plural. The Leeds team seemed to be a vehicle for his ego just as much as the Arsenal team was for Wenger's, but the Frenchman seemed more modest and democratic about it. Graham is one of the best tacticians in British football but a lot of his tactics are about nullification, about stopping football being played rather than playing football. He is the sultan of stopping, the nabob of negation. Wenger prefers to believe that the pursuit of excellence will produce the right results as well as enjoyment for players and supporters.

'I thought first half we played very well,' said Graham. 'I thought Arsenal looked a bit jittery at the back, a few set-pieces, a few moves. I thought we'd maybe pinch a few more goals in the second half. They played into our hands really, bringing on John Hartson. I think they started going long ball. The last half hour I think it was very easy for us. Although it was very tiring physically, I thought we handled it well.' He explained his team selection and tactics with no hint of an apology.

'Radebe phoned in this morning, he had the flu. He was really ill. I really needed him to either pick up Merson or Wright. So that was a big problem. So I had to push in Kelly from the right wing, bring in young Harte at full-back. It messed me up a little bit. But I actually thought they coped very well. I thought Kelly on Merson was absolutely outstanding and Halle was probably the man of the match. We had to adapt to a very physical side. I think we outplayed them tonight. Tactically, I think we got it right. I thought they ran out of ideas in the last twenty minutes.'

Wenger thought Leeds had defended well but Arsenal had missed chances. 'I think we had a bad start, an unlucky goal against us, and after that we tried to play to keep the ball on the ground. We tried to play quite well, maybe with not enough mobility in the first half. In the second half when John Hartson came on we could not keep the patience to keep the ball on the ground, and tried very hard to play long balls to put the Leeds defence under pressure. We couldn't find the right balance between playing long balls and keeping the balls on the ground and having patience. But the team gave everything. They fought like crazy until the last minute so we can say, once again, that Arsenal was Arsenal, with the fighting spirit.' He admitted that his team had hit far too many long balls. 'But we had many chances, when John Hartson hit the bar and the post, and if he had scored we'd have said the opposite. So if you don't score you are wrong.'

Nine days later Wenger sold Hartson to West Ham for £3.2 million. The transfer divided the fans. Some said it was Arsenal's best result since beating Parma 1–0 in the 1994 Cup Winners Cup Final, others that the club would have got the same money for him come the summer. Clearly, a coach who admires fast, slim footballers could never have enjoyed the sight of Hartson, a lumbering carthorse of a player, on the training pitch every day. He was also a boozing bachelor who was fond of junk food, and a gambler who allegedly put Paul Merson's bets on for him after Merson told everyone he had given up gambling. Hartson symbolised the bad old days of English football. What was the point of teaching what Wenger had begun to teach and then keeping a walking, talking contradiction on the payroll?

A few months later Sky commentator Martin Tyler made an extraordinary comment to me about the goalless Premiership game at Elland Road. He reckoned he had pinpointed the moment which had convinced Wenger to sell Hartson. 'There was a pass on for Ian Wright, who had come on; there was a break on, and it needed a cool first-time ball on a very dodgy pitch. But John took an extra touch, and when he played it Wright was offside. John was playing safe rather than stab it and have it go off his sock.'

When Arsenal went to White Hart Lane on 15 February it was probably the first time both teams had ever played with three centre-backs. A dull 0–0 draw was no surprise. The surprise was that Rosenthal and Iversen contributed more to the game than Wright and Bergkamp, who were tentative because they had not played together for nearly a month. Spurs' keeper Ian Walker only had to make two saves, one from a volley by Bergkamp, the other when he tipped round a Keown header. Wenger admitted it was a fair result and said both defences played very well, especially John Lukic. When asked about Wright and Bergkamp, he said, 'I think both showed a little bit of lack of competition. For different reasons. One because he was suspended for three weeks, and the second one because he was injured and came back and had just one game. Ian Wright had just one game in five weeks. And of course that is very important for the strikers. A midfielder can play, but a striker – you need to be sharp to make a difference.'

Wenger was proving to be a pragmatic character, a positive thinker, someone who had a firm grasp of the arithmetical possibilities from his remaining fixtures. Football, like politics, is the art of the possible. Wenger was disappointed that his team had wasted a chance to go top of the table, but he remained bullish about their prospects. 'Mathematically, we are in a good position,' he said. 'We are there with twelve games to go. We play seven at home, five away. Everybody comes to Arsenal and it's not so bad. We played at West Ham and Leeds and Tottenham, three difficult games. We won at West Ham and played two draws at Leeds and Tottenham and made five points out of three away games, so it's not so bad.' He talked about 'decompression' following the midweek FA Cup defeat against Leeds, which was a very tense night for everyone.

Arsenal had recently been linked with a seventeen-year-old French striker who wanted to leave Paris Saint Germain, so I asked Wenger, 'Are you trying to get Anelka before the transfer deadline?'

Wenger smiled wearily and said, 'It's impossible. We will try to bring somebody in before the transfer deadline, that's for sure. But if you ask me if we are close I'd say no. But we cannot be far away because the deadline is not far away.'

Arsenal's next match was at Highbury against Manchester United, for which Eric Cantona was suspended. Wenger said, 'I feel every time, every game, it's a game we must win. But this one maybe even more. We have to think that if we play well, if we give everything, if we have the support that we will have, I'm sure, at Highbury, we have a chance to beat Manchester.'

## WRIGHT JUMPS ON SCHMEICHEL'S LEG

*There are things that happen in every game of football.*

Arsène Wenger

One of the talking points before the game on 19 February was that Ian Wright, who was in sight of the club's all-time scoring record, had never scored against Manchester United in a league match, and he had publicly accused Peter Schmeichel of making a racial remark after their flare-up three months earlier. The referee for the game was Martin Bodenham, who was notorious for letting a lot of fouls go unpunished, which usually meant an open, exciting, free-flowing game.

Wright missed two chances in the first eight minutes. The first was a one-on-one with Schmeichel, the second a diving header where he missed the ball by two inches. Roy Keane was captain of United for the first time and his partner, wearing the number ten shirt, was David Beckham. When Gary Neville played a ball down the right Tony Adams was deceived by the bounce and Andy Cole fired a low shot neatly past Lukic. Then a Giggs–Poborsky–Cole move ended with Solskjær making it 2–0.

Adams went off at half-time, Stephen Hughes came on, Arsenal switched to 4–4–2 and Hughes soon smashed a shot against the post. The rebound went to Bergkamp, who touched the ball instantly to Wright, and he rammed it into the net. It was a sublime demonstration of lightning reflexes by both players, but the flag was up for offside. Then Hughes started another move, Merson played the ball in behind Irwin, Parlour crossed low and Bergkamp hit an unstoppable shot between Schmeichel and his near post.

By this stage, with the score at 2–1 and having missed those two early chances, with a third shot unluckily deflected off Ronny Johnsen's leg, not to mention the disallowed goal, Ian Wright was an incident waiting to happen. So when he sprinted after a through-pass and Schmeichel came out of his penalty area feet first and the whistle went for offside, Wright kept on running and jumped two-footed on to the United goalkeeper's outstretched leg. It was spectacularly dangerous play, easily the most outrageous Premiership foul of the season, and it had Alex Ferguson catapulting off the bench in fury. Amazingly, Bodenham did not even give Wright a yellow card, so he must have had a very poor view of the incident.

Schmeichel played on after treatment, and then Bergkamp hit a beautiful early cross to create a wonderful chance for Wright. It was a ball he could, and probably should, have chested down, but he chose to go for a stooping header which he mistimed, the ball bouncing tamely into the ground. He clearly did not want to chest down the ball in case Schmeichel came at him feet first again. So Manchester United beat them for the second time that season. Scottish managers were beginning to be a problem for the Frenchman. George Graham's Leeds had shut down and beaten Arsenal that month, and now Alex Ferguson had handed Monsieur Wenger his first Premiership defeat at Highbury and moved clear at the top of the table, five points ahead with a game in hand.

One of the unwritten rules in football is that a manager does not attack his own players in public. Every manager expects loyalty from his players and in return for that he defends them, so after the Schmeichel assault Wenger naturally tried to pour oil on troubled waters. 'There are things that happen in every game of football,' he said. It was a ridiculous comment, but Wright had put him in the embarrassing position of having to defend the indefensible.

Wright's wretched period continued with a story about his affair with Tina Hodgson, a waitress at TGI Fridays in Mill Hill, North London. The *News of the World* headline had read SOCCER STAR WRIGHT CHEATS WITH BURGER BAR BEAUTY. Wenger did not, of course, involve himself in the private lives of his players, but Wright's embarrassing publicity was harming the team. He had not been the same player since the story came out and he had not scored in his last four games. He still needed eleven goals to beat Cliff Bastin's record, but it was now obvious that he would not do it before the close of the 1996/97 season. Wright was a huge star, a crowd favourite, but he was becoming less reliable. His private life was splashed all over the tabloids and he was more undisciplined than ever. He would soon be starting his tenth domestic suspension at Arsenal in five and a half years.

On the day of the Arsenal–Wimbledon game, Sunday, 23 February, Wright's problems worsened when the *People* produced another scoop: IAN WRIGHT SCORES WITH BBC GIRL. It seemed that Wright, who had always been bubbly, quotable and amusing, had been seduced by showbusiness. He had become a luvvie, more of an actor than an athlete. Venetia Williamson-Noble was a 26-year-old Radio One researcher he had met at the previous year's Brit Awards ceremony at Earls Court in London. The couple had begun to see each other secretly, but were later seen together at nightclubs. In December 1996, Wright went to the *Top of the Pops* Christmas party at the BBC studios in Elstree, Hertfordshire, and she had been his after-match guest in the players' lounge. Wright's wife Debbie admitted that she and Ian had not been living togther as man and wife for a year, but that they still loved each other and were trying to work it out.

On a more promising note, it was announced that Arsenal had completed the signing of Nicolas Anelka, the young striker from Paris Saint Germain, only days after Wenger had pronounced it 'impossible'. Another boost for the club was the selection of Patrick Vieira for the France squad, an honour which was well overdue.

There were just eleven league games left when Wimbledon came to Highbury, where Arsenal were always going to struggle without Adams and Keown. Their three centre-backs that day were Scott Marshall, Remi Garde and Steve Bould, and there was a misunderstanding as soon as the first long ball came over. Lukic came out, Garde let the ball bounce then headed it back, but the ball went for a corner. Arsenal cleared the corner weakly to Neil Ardley, whose cross was volleyed in by Vinnie Jones for the only goal of the game.

In February *Match of the Day* screened their Goal of the Month competition as usual, but for Wenger's men February was the Month of the Goal. They had recorded no league victories and scored only one goal, by Bergkamp in the defeat at Old Trafford. Wenger betrayed a hint of grouchiness. After the Wimbledon game he complained that it was 'not a regular championship' if some teams had more time to recover from their previous games than their opponents. This was a valid point, but one that was never mentioned by British managers. Our domestic league is a rough-and-tumble competition where everyone always says: be first, never say die, never complain, take each match as it comes and do not worry about whether things should be organised more fairly.

On 6 March referee and ClubCall man Kenny Goldman told me that his friend had just refereed the Arsenal–Norwich Combination Cup game. Anelka's registration had come through during the first half so he was allowed to go on, and he looked very good, even though Arsenal lost the tie 3–1. The gossip that week was all about Ian Wright's head being messed up by his marital misdemeanours. Could this talented French kid replace the fading goalscorer? If so, how soon?

In March Arsenal beat Everton, Nottingham Forest and Southampton by the same scoreline, 2–0, then on the 24th they lost 2–1 at home to Liverpool in a match notable for Robbie Fowler's sportsmanship in attempting to persuade the referee not to give a penalty when he had tumbled over David Seaman. Fowler missed the penalty, but Jason McAteer scored from the rebound. In April they disposed of Chelsea and Leicester, but then stuttered with 1–1 draws against Blackburn and Coventry, while Kevin Keegan's Newcastle, the attacking team which leaked too many goals, finished in fine style with two wins, two draws and four clean sheets. The highlight of Newcastle's run-in was their 1–0 win at Highbury on 3 May. Arsenal picked up a final win against Derby on the 11th but ended the season in third place, level on points with Newcastle (second) and Liverpool (fourth) but losing out on a place in the new Champions League to the former on goal difference. Brian Little's Aston Villa and Ruud Gullit's Chelsea finished fifth and sixth, seven and nine points behind respectively.

Arsenal had matched the champions, Manchester United, on the road, both clubs winning nine away games, but they had lost crucial home games to United in November, Wimbledon in February, Liverpool in March and Newcastle in May. They had also lost twice to United and to Liverpool, and neither had they managed to beat Aston Villa. Wenger knew that in the 1997/98 season he would need to win those games against his closest rivals. He would need to beat Manchester United, Liverpool and Newcastle at Highbury. And such victories would of course have a value beyond the arithmetic, since it is vital, in all sports, to beat your biggest rivals. It would be an easier job if Wenger could just figure out how to improve his team, so he asked himself a few fundamental questions. How can we score more goals? How can we win those awkward home games against Aston Villa, Liverpool, Leeds and Manchester United? How can I get more out of Bergkamp?

The most difficult question was: Who should I let go? David Platt had started 27 Premiership games in midfield but had not been tackling. He functioned quite well within the team unit but played as if he had a glass knee. In a team playing power football, trying to win the ball early, this was a major flaw. One recalled a rather ominous remark by Sven-Goran Eriksson, Sampdoria's coach when Platt was there, which was hardly reported outside Italy. He had said that Platt's knee injury did not necessarily have to be career-threatening. Discerning fans rated Platt a bad signing at £4.75 million, an ageing crock.

Aside from Platt, Arsenal's style of play, with Bergkamp and Merson doing the creative stuff, passing to each other when they were not feeding Wright, had been working fairly well – as long as Wright was scoring. In 1996/97 he scored 23 goals in thirty starts and five sub appearances. Unfortunately, Bergkamp had scored just nine from open play, Merson only six. The manager had seen all the matches and had watched all the videos, so he knew that Merson usually passed to Wright, his mate. He decided that Merson and Bergkamp were too similar, and that Merson's presence in the side reduced the impact of his most creative attacker. Arsenal's style of play was still based on the 3–4–2–1 formation Wenger had inherited from Rioch, which Tony Adams had persuaded him to retain for the rest of the season. But that system meant that too much time was spent feeding the flanks, not enough feeding Ian Wright.

Wenger realised that this was a turning point in his Arsenal career, a time when he had to build carefully and re-motivate his key players, especially his most gifted player, Dennis Bergkamp. He said, 'He's 27, and I told him at his age you become a huge player or you go backwards.' Wenger had challenged his star in a very clever way. He was saying: the next five years can be your best, you can be a genuinely great player if you want to be. The following season promised to be very interesting. As Manchester City manager Malcolm Allison once said, 'Coaching is not about what players you've got. It's about what you get out of the players you've got.'

# 5. 1997/98: THE SEASON OF THE DOUBLE

At 2 p.m. on Tuesday, 17 June, Arsenal called a press conference which told us a lot about the ambitions of the new manager and the quality and type of footballer he wanted on board from now on.

Wenger was wearing a beige suit and had a new, very short hair cut. He was especially genial and charming when I had a word with him before the reporters came in and settled down. He said that Luis Boa Morte, the young left-winger he had just signed, had missed the final of that summer's under-21 Toulon Tournament through suspension, not injury.

The manager was joined on the stage by David Dein and two of the new players. Dein, briskly businesslike and brimming with bonhomie, said simply, 'I'm delighted to welcome Emmanuel Petit, who has interrupted his holiday to come over, and Marc Overmars, who signed for us yesterday.'

Emmanuel Petit was blond with a pony-tail. He was wearing a sky-blue suit made of soft towelling-type material like that used for an infant's baby-gro, a see-through shirt and a medallion. He looked like a Californian soap star – the body of an athlete, the face of an actor. Was he hard enough for the Premiership, or was he another Frank Leboeuf? Overmars wore charcoal pinstripe trousers, matching waistcoat and a white T-shirt. This was a formal meeting, a big turning point in his life, but his manner was relaxed and cocky. The most frequently quoted transfer fee for Overmars was £7 million, but the true figure was just over £5 million.

Wenger said that the club's basic challenge was to improve the structure of the squad by bringing in some new players and younger players. 'We also wanted players who are used to winning, used to the pressure in the big clubs, and who are winner-types. I think Emmanuel Petit and Marc Overmars have proved before that they are used to being in clubs where you have to win, and that's very important to us. They play in positions where we wanted to sign some players. On the other side we also signed some younger players like Boa Morte from Portugal and a young German player called Alberto Mendez, and of course Gilles Grimandi, who is a defender who played also in Monaco. That's the five purchases we have made in recent times. It's not all over yet. We might still bring in one, maximum two, players.'

Dein echoed the manager's enthusiasm. 'Marc Overmars is a big signing for us, as indeed is Emmanuel and his colleague Gilles Grimandi, who is still on holiday. All five players will be reporting for training at the beginning of July. So it is exciting times at Arsenal Football Club.' He also pointed out that since Wenger had taken over nine months ago ten players had left the club and as many had joined, emphasising that all the new players were on four- and five-year contracts without any escape clauses.

Wenger then waxed lyrical over his new Dutchman. 'Marc Overmars is a player of class. He has qualities that are very difficult to find now. He's a winger-type who can go in the space, is a good dribbler, and we needed this type of player. We had a problem this season [1996/97], especially at home. Don't forget that we were maybe the best away team but we lost the championship at home. I think we needed more power and more speed at home, and more penetration. I think Marc has won everything until now. He's won the European Cup, the World Club Cup, and championships, but he's still very young and ambitious – 24 years old is the best age for a football player. The four or five years he has in front of him are the best ones, and that's why I went for him.

'They're adaptable players. For example, Petit can play in every position on the left side, in midfield, central or on the outside, or in defence. When I started him in competition he was a central defender on the left side, but he's a technical player and he went into midfield. I think both Marc and Emmanuel are very adaptable in a 3–5–2 or a 4–4–2 system. We will take the best option. But in my choices it was very important that they would be adaptable in different systems because in modern football you need some-times to change the system for one or two games. Basically, we would like to go to a 4–4–2 but it's not decided.'

Overmars confirmed that he had talked to Bergkamp before making his decision. 'I spoke with him a few times, of course, about the club. He said many good things.' He was then asked whether Arsenal had tried to sign him a few years ago. 'It started with a meeting with Mr Dein two years ago. At the time I was playing with Ajax and winning all the prizes. I think I'm now a good age and I feel very good about this transfer. I think the time is right. As Mr Wenger said, we'll play a little bit different. I like it because of the space; with my speed and quality I can use it very good here. At Ajax you've got your own position and you have to keep in your position, so this will be a little more space and freedom, and I like it.' Overmars confirmed that he was fully recovered from a serious knee injury and Dein said that he had just played thirty games for Ajax.

One key issue that summer was whether Wenger would sign any British players. There had been talk that England's left-back Graeme Le Saux was leaving Blackburn, whose board said he could go when a club paid £7.5 million for him. Wenger said he would not pay that sort of money and the *Mirror* reported that a swap, David Platt plus £5 million, was a possibility, although it seemed unlikely that Blackburn boss Roy Hodgson would fancy that deal. Platt was absent from Arsenal's pre-season friendly in Strasbourg on 25 July, said to be watching his horse run in another part of France. Le Saux eventually went to Chelsea – for £5 million.

Wenger continued on the squad strength theme. 'If you want to have an interesting role in the championship you need a bigger squad than we had last season. We were lucky because we had many players over thirty, and not many injuries. But we had Tony Adams out from January to June, only on seventy per cent of his possibilities, and David Seaman out for nineteen games. And we were out of the UEFA Cup and quickly out of the FA Cup. I think that's why we need a bigger squad than we had last season if we want to be more ambitious. It's very difficult to admit, but sometimes I was glad we weren't involved in more competitions because we just didn't have the players to play every three days.

'We have two departments at Arsenal now who work very hard to improve the quality inside the club, the youth department and the professional department. In the professional department I think Arsenal had the best players between 28 and 35 years old. But between 20 and 28 the best players are at Manchester United and at Liverpool. We had no choice, in this age category, but to go abroad. What was crucial was the spirit. That's why we wanted to get in winner-types because of the specific Arsenal spirit, which is a winner-type who will never give up. Emmanuel and Marc are these type of players. The spirit is more important than the nationality. I think they will fit in and integrate well because of their qualities.'

Wenger was asked to justify his 'no choice but to go abroad' view. 'It just says that the best players between 20 and 28 are at Manchester United, Newcastle and Liverpool. We are ambitious. When you are ambitious you always want the best quality. If we had equal quality in England we wouldn't go abroad. But the quality is important for us because we have a big ambition. When you go abroad you look for the spirit of the players. If the spirit of the players is right and the ambition is right, then you don't say, "I won't take these players because they're not English." The good quality players between 20 and 28 are already at the big clubs in England. McManaman, Fowler, Campbell – look who plays in the national team. All the younger players who play in the national team are not at Arsenal. It's very difficult to get these kind of players. So when you have the ambition we have, and you want the quality of players we want, you have to go abroad.

'For me, when you change more than three players in a team, you always take a technical risk because you change the deep structure of the team and the deep balance of the team, mentally and technically. So we have taken a risk, but we would have taken the same risk – maybe a little bit smaller because you don't have the adaptation problem – by buying just English players. When you take more than three new players you always have a problem of unbalancing the team, or creating a new balance in the team. But we had no choice. We couldn't just go on and on until the team dies.'

These were sweeping generalisations coming from a manager who had worked in England for just nine months, particularly the comment about having no choice but to go abroad, which was utterly dismissive of all the players in the lesser Premiership teams, not to mention any hidden potential within the Nationwide leagues. Wenger was, in effect, saying that there were no decent left-wingers in the Premiership (except Ryan Giggs), no good young stoppers (except Sol Campbell) and no skilful forwards (except Steve McManaman and Robbie Fowler). Still, he was being realistic when he implied that he could not hope to sign those players as their prices would be prohibitive and their clubs would not sell them anyway, let alone sell them to Arsenal. Even if those players were for sale, they might not want to play for a French manager.

Emmanuel Petit was obviously looking forward to a new experience. 'The football in England, for me, is the best in Europe. When I was young I saw the football in England. I think it's better than in Italy, France and Spain because it's spectacular, it's funny and it's a game. That's why it's very good for me to play here.'

Overall, the day was a hugely promising moment in Arsenal's history. David Dein was like a dog with two tails, which was hardly surprising since signing these five players had been a lot more fun than last summer's manic phone calls from Jarvis Astaire's car.

Meanwhile, young Nicolas Anelka was headed for the Far East to take part in the under-20 World Cup being held in Malaysia in July that year. The French side was coached by Gerard Houllier, who had said before the tournament that his team could win it. Thierry Henry was the captain of a gifted side which included Stéphane Dalmat, David Trezeguet, Peter Luccin and Mikael Silvestre, but the French players found it very difficult to adapt to the heat, especially in their first game against Brazil, which they lost 3–0. Anelka did not respect Houllier's tactics, so the manager was furious and dropped him for the next match. France beat Mexico in that match to reach the quarter-finals, but Henry was injured and did not play against Uruguay, against whom Anelka missed a penalty. France went out, Argentina beat Uruguay 2–1 in the final, and the Republic of Ireland finished third. Anelka hated being blamed for the failure of the team, so he was in a really negative frame of mind when he returned to England. Arsenal programme editor Kevin Connolly reckoned Wenger only gave Anelka the number nine shirt to cheer him up before the new season started.

When the 1997/98 season got under way on 9 August, Wenger had by then managed Arsenal in thirty Premiership games, had met all the opposing managers and sized them up, and seen their teams play on television and video many times. This new season was his first complete campaign and the first in which he had detailed knowledge of his opponents and an intimate understanding of the resources at his disposal. He had already worked with Petit and Grimandi at Monaco, and he knew that Overmars was intelligent.

## BERGKAMP'S PURPLE PATCH

*It was the best hat-trick I've ever seen.*

Martin O'Neill

By the end of July the whisper from the Arsenal training ground was that the atmosphere was very good and the squad was vibrant. My friend Alexis Grower's accountant pal Lionel Martin, who handled Emmanuel Petit's house purchase and mortgage, said all the players were buzzing. Lambros Lambrou, the young solicitor who interviews the players for the club programme, said that Dennis Bergkamp was fired up and talking about winning everything in sight. One wondered, though, how Ray Parlour felt now that his manager had signed Overmars, Boa Morte and Mendez, three wingers. Paul Merson had been sold to Middlesbrough for £5 million, so would Parlour be next on the transfer list?

There was no such doubt hanging over Tony Adams, who was still a very important part of Wenger's plans. He now felt he had a very understanding manager who was helping him to get his private life back in order. When Adams was young he was a warrior-leader, constantly winning fifty-fiftys and high balls and scoring vital goals in semi-finals and derbies, playing like a man with a rage to win. He was a footballer's footballer. Defenders admired him and forwards respected him as a formidable opponent. Unfortunately, Adams would miss the first month of the new season through injury.

As promised, Wenger changed his system to 4–4–2 and things went well in August. Arsenal started with a 1–1 draw at Leeds, where Ian Wright scored, and then Wright scored both goals in a 2–0 defeat of Coventry at Highbury, both tap-ins, one from a misjudged Richard Shaw back pass. He now needed only two more goals to beat Cliff Bastin's club record of 178, which had stood since 1946.

Two points were immediately obvious about Wenger's dynamic new style of play. The first was that it was designed to make the best use of his three most talented players, Vieira, Bergkamp and Wright, allowing for maximum penetration by the two strikers. Secondly, however, it looked as if Bergkamp and Wright would have to score all the goals because Parlour and Overmars rarely got into shooting positions. Neither of them had track records as goalscorers anyway.

Arsenal's third game, on 23 August, was at Southampton, where both Bergkamp and Wright were tightly marked by Francis Benali and Ken Monkou. Thankfully, Overmars scored the first goal. The winger's strike was a big relief to Wenger, who did not want to be over-dependent on his front two for goals, especially as Wright was injury-prone and often suspended. David Seaman was at fault for the equaliser, failing to come for the cross which Neil Maddison headed in. Remi Garde also had a shaky match at right-back – the return of Lee Dixon was needed. And in Adams' absence Ostenstad gave Grimandi a lot of trouble. Wenger was forced to bring on reserve Scott Marshall to handle him. If there was a turning point in the match, it was when Benali stood on Bergkamp's foot off the ball, then stood on his foot again. On the second occasion the Dutchman grabbed Benali's head and threw him to one side like a rag doll, then started playing like a man possessed. Arsenal won 3–1, Bergkamp scoring twice.

The mistake by Seaman was worrying. Had his bottle gone? Seaman had already enjoyed one great season at QPR and five great seasons at Arsenal, so he had made his mark, won a championship and three cups. What he had done against Millwall in the League

Cup in 1993, against Sampdoria in the Cup Winners semi in 1995, and against many other teams, was magnificent and stayed in the fans' memories. In one game at White Hart Lane he saved four shots from Gary Lineker that would have been goals against any other keeper. In countless big games he made a difference because he had more presence than any of his rivals. One-on-one he was superb, standing up and making strikers work very hard for their goals. He made catching cannonball shots look effortless, and he also had very long arms. The QPR players had admitted that in shooting practice he used to sicken them by saving shots nobody else could have reached. Seaman was England's number one goalkeeper, but recently he had gone through a divorce, had suffered some injuries, and Euro 96 had made him a national hero. He capitalised on that, started to live the celebrity lifestyle, guided by his new wife, who became his agent, and at the same time he began to look vulnerable on the field. He had had a poor season 1996/97 and there was a feeling that he might never be the same player again.

Arsenal's next game was at Leicester on 27 August, with Ian Wright still needing those two goals. Leicester had just won at Liverpool and drawn 0–0 with Manchester United, and they shared an extraordinary, pulsating match in which three of the six goals scored came during injury time. The scorers were Bergkamp (9 minutes), Bergkamp (61), Emile Heskey (84), Matt Elliott (91), Bergkamp (94) and Steve Walsh (96).

In the sixties and seventies fans always talked about George Best, Bobby Charlton and Peter Osgood 'turning it on', but by the nineties football was such a tight team game and there was far less scope for one player to dominate a match. But Dennis Bergkamp certainly turned it on at Filbert Street. He was, in this mood, untouchable and unplayable. His first goal came when Overmars shaped to cross into the box, instead pushing a pass back for Bergkamp, who hit a right-foot floater into the far corner. Vieira put him through for his second, a stabbed shot which spun up off advancing keeper Kasey Keller and dropped in under the bar. After that Arsenal let Leicester back into the game. Platt had failed to reach a clearing header for Leicester's first goal, but he redeemed himself deep into injury time by picking out Bergkamp with a long pass for the Dutchman's hat-trick. Bergkamp juggled the ball with hypnotic skill before scoring what everyone thought was the winner. And then Leicester came back to make it 3-3.

It was apparent to all that Wenger had made Bergkamp a better player, a hungrier, more aggressive competitor. He had played for his country in Euro 92, USA 94 and Euro 96, but there was no tournament in 1997 and the summer break had obviously sharpened his appetite for the game. Martin O'Neill was gracious enough to admit that Bergkamp's 'was the best hat-trick I've ever seen'. Another hat-trick awaited the Dutchman: incredibly, the top three in the August Goal of the Month competition on *Match of the Day* were all Bergkamp goals.

Ian Wright had not been himself at the Dell, and during the Leicester match he had four chances, two of which he would normally have scored. Anelka replaced him for the last thirteen minutes. After the final whistle a frustrated Wright did something very stupid: he ran forty yards from the bench in order to confront referee Graham Barber about the amount of injury time he had allowed. Barber pointed to six goals, six substitutions and an injury to Lee Dixon to explain the six-minute extra minutes. Wenger may have thought, 'If Ian gets a ten-match ban and fails to score in the next couple of games, this Cliff Bastin distraction could go on until Christmas!'

Adams was still missing and everyone knew that if he had played rather than Grimandi, Leicester would not have scored three goals. But it was too soon to write Grimandi off, since all foreigners take time to acclimatise. Petit was improving already.

The 1997 AGM was a very quiet meeting, with David Dein absent on UEFA business, and everyone wanted to know whether the club was staying at Highbury. Peter Hill-Wood said, 'We are not moving, we want to stay here, we are looking at sites we might go to in five years' time, but it is far too soon to talk about that.'

Arsène Wenger charmed everyone again. He said he could not sign a top, top striker to play when Ian Wright was suspended because top, top strikers cost £15 million, but we think Anelka will be a top striker. He said he thought the team was playing some good football, but the new players would take time to settle in. Someone asked: 'Are you going to go off and coach France?' He said: 'No, I've already turned that down.' One shareholder proposed a motion that negotiations to extend Wenger's contract be started not next week, not tomorrow, but now, in this meeting. Someone else said, 'Ian Wright's always in trouble, why don't we sell him?' That suggestion was loudly booed by the majority of shareholders. So, overall, the AGM was gentle, routine stuff, nothing like last year's ructions. Stability had returned to Arsenal FC and that was vital. In football, the club is very important, although nobody ever talks much about the club because they always talk about the team. A good club will often produce a good team, and a very good club will sometimes produce a very good team. But if a club is badly organised, and divided off the field, that will show in the team's performances. What happens behind the scenes at a football club always shows on the field. The next game was at home to Spurs and it was a fierce, fast noisy 0–0 draw in which Arsenal played some excellent football and hit the frame of the goal three times. Spurs skipper Sol Campbell stood up, never went to ground, never allowed Wright to turn him in the box. He was a colossus, especially after being booked early on. After that he was on a knife-edge, one slightly late tackle away from sending the Highbury crowd ballistic, demanding his expulsion, but he continued to make brilliantly timed tackles against two sharp strikers. Wright missed two good chances and Bergkamp was booked for a bad tackle on Campbell. He had also been booked at Southampton and Leicester.

Even though Arsenal had not beaten Spurs, Wenger must have been pleased. For a side with three new players – Overmars, Petit and Grimandi – they were performing well. But a few questions still nagged: How would they handle being a goal down? And how could they raise the tempo if they were already playing at 100 mph?

## WRIGHT FINALLY BEATS BASTIN'S RECORD

*What motivates me is an ideal of thinking how football should be. And to try
to get near this way of playing. And to try to improve all aspects of my
personality that can help me get near this ideal way of playing football.*

Arsène Wenger

In the second week of September Ian Wright went off to Wembley
with Seaman to play for Glenn Hoddle's England against Moldova.
He scored twice in a 4–0 victory. Three days later, on 13
September, he played against newly promoted Bolton, who could
not handle Arsenal's whirlwind tempo. Wright scored a hat-trick
in a 4–1 victory. After scoring his first goal he raced away to
celebrate, pulling up his shirt to reveal a specially printed Nike
T-shirt which read 179 JUST DONE IT. He had got over-excited,
though, flaunting the T-shirt after the strike which *equalled* the
record of 178 goals. The record-breaker, however, was not long in
coming.

Bolton's manager Colin Todd admitted that Arsenal's high-
tempo style had overwhelmed them. 'We tried to slow the game
down,' he said, 'but when we regained the ball we gave it back to
them in our own half, which caused us problems.' When Wenger
came in after the game I asked him if he thought Ian Wright more
relaxed after the Moldova game. 'Yes. It helped him a lot. He was
calm in front of the goal. It brought his confidence back, maybe
eased the pressure off him a little bit because he had not to wait a
week for the game with everybody thinking "When do you break
the record?" It's like when sometimes you see a tennis player when
they have only one point to finish a game.

'We had a bad start, we were 1–0 down, it could have made the
team nervous but we were lucky to come quickly back and go into
the lead very quickly. The image I would like to keep is the joy of
the whole team when he broke the record, along the line where
everybody came to congratulate him. It just shows that everybody
in the team was concerned by it and that shows how well he's
accepted by the whole team and how happy everybody was. It's a
historical moment for the club because maybe we will have to wait

a hundred years for somebody to beat the record. He's a quick thinker, a quick brain in the box, and he has the physical power to react. His second quality is that he's an explosive player, but he's very quiet and calm in front of goal at the right moment. And that's very rare. Usually the explosive players are very nervous in the finishing. And that is one of his qualities. And his third quality is mental: he wants it. He has the appetite. He has a huge one.'

Why did you take him off?

'It was one way to give him a celebration. The game was won and he deserved it. The second thing was he has played on Wednesday and he has to play on Tuesday, so I wanted to spare him some minutes and also to give a little bit of a chance to Anelka.

'I think international level has made him aware that he has not only to score goals but to play for the team. Ian Wright scored two goals against Moldova but he also made one for Gascoigne and he's shown at international level he's not only a goalscorer but a complete player now. He'll feel he has achieved something but it won't make him quiet or release his appetite. He will stay like this his whole life. He wants to be successful. Now I think in his mind he wants to make two hundred, then more. That's the way champions are. They always want more. They want to go further. They're hungry.

'When you want to be successful in life you have that for ever. I believe that some people with a weak motivation can have a strong one for certain periods of their life, but if you are strongly motivated for something you keep that for your whole life. What motivates me is an ideal of thinking how football should be. And to try to get near this way of playing. And to try to improve all aspects of my personality that can help me get near this ideal way of playing football.'

What was your first impression of Ian Wright?

'That he was funny. That he was alive. Frankly, that was the impression of the whole team. The team, together, were all happy.'

Has working with Ian Wright changed you?

'It's difficult to say. I think I'm today better than ten years ago in my job, but I'm not sure. Because I tried for ten years to improve every year. I really think that having an experience in Japan helped me to adapt to different people, totally different to how I think you should behave. Maybe ten years ago I would have thought, "This guy's really crazy", or I'd have been a little bit harder with him, or been less tolerant.'

How long can he go on?

'Nobody knows. But at his age you have to think short-term because your body can let you down a little bit, or you get an injury. Today you could say two years, maybe. But nobody knows. I explained that to the older players, that they cannot think three or four years ahead, just go from year to year. Always the most difficult part of the job is to take decisions like that. You might have thought that two years ago it was the right moment for him to stop already. Now he plays well.'

Wenger said that he had never let a player go who had done well later, admitting that he had not been ruthless enough at times when it came to decisions like that. He said it was hard, when a player had fought for you for seven or eight years, to suddenly tell them they had to leave. 'It's not easy, especially when they still play well. And sometimes you have to anticipate that because you feel, if you're in a big club, you can't take the risk of the team going down if two or three players cannot perform any more like you want. It depends on the characteristics of the player. Take Patrick Vieira now. When he's 33 he might have problems getting the ball back. But while he may not win the ball back as he does today, he will play much better with the ball, so that's why the decision is difficult. He could still be efficient for the team, but not as a ball-winner. So you have the problem of balancing the whole team when you take the decision.'

Arsenal's next game, on 16 September, was a UEFA Cup tie in Greece against PAOK Salonika. The Gunners were now unbeaten in six games, but would be without Bergkamp for this match because Greece was just too far to drive. Before the match *The Times*' Brian Glanville asked Wenger if he would be using Anelka and the manager replied, 'There's a chance, yes.' It was an important remark. At that stage the eighteen-year-old Frenchman had not yet started a game for Arsenal, and Wenger had to choose between sticking with a 4–4–2 playing Anelka alongside Wright, or playing safe with David Platt in a five-man midfield. George Graham would have packed the midfield and ground out a draw, but Wenger gambled on Anelka.

Just three months earlier Wenger had talked about flexibility, about changing the system for one or two games, but before this match he probably thought: 'Why change it for one match? I have just changed from 3–4–2–1 and brought in new players, so is it worth changing the system again just for one match? If I dump my new 4–4–2 framework I will be throwing away eight weeks' hard work. I fancy us to score one goal against anybody. So I'll keep the system and bring in Anelka for Bergkamp. I have to show faith in Anelka and I have to be seen to pick him, otherwise people will say I have not replaced Hartson and I only have two strikers.'

On the night Arsenal played carefully and fairly well for an hour, then Salonika scored and the Greeks started to play well themselves. Seaman made an awesome save, clawing away a free-kick which was going into the top corner, but Ian Wright lost the ball too much, missed Bergkamp's passes and could not combine with Anelka. There was no rapport there, no understanding at all. Ultimately, Wenger's 4–4–2 looked too rigid because it lacked Bergkamp's creative vision and skill. Vieira and Petit looked too similar in the middle of the park and Wright did nothing except get booked for dissent, miss a half-chance that fell slightly behind him, and shoot just wide with his left foot when Overmars set him up. Overmars produced Arsenal's best effort, clipping the outside of the post. Salonika's best player, Frantzeskos, ran inside Winterburn, just onside, and scored after 61 minutes to give PAOK a 1–0 win. Winterburn had stepped up perfectly, but Bould was blocked from doing the same thing. The Spanish referee had been excellent and very few refs could have spotted that minor obstruction.

It was this game, perhaps more than any other, which illustrated what a mixed blessing Ian Wright was in 1997. That night might have crystallised Wenger's thinking about his star striker. Wright, a finisher of genius rather than a footballer of genius, was now dividing the fans and the critics. He could be electrifying but also clueless, sometimes both in the same game. Wenger the tolerant man-manager could forgive his man's aberrations, but Wenger the analyst would have looked at the immediate needs of his team and seen that although Wright was still scoring goals, he was giving the ball away more than ever. The team had been geared to him for too long and had become unbalanced. If another player played badly Arsenal could still win, but they now found it virtually impossible to win if Wright played badly because he gave the ball away so much. Wenger might have summed up the Ian Wright conundrum as follows: he sometimes plays well and scores. But, more often, he plays badly and scores, or he plays badly and does not score. He never plays well, does not score, and Arsenal win anyway. And he never plays badly, does not score, and Arsenal win anyway. So, if Wenger was the analytical thinker we believed him to be, he could only draw one conclusion from the available facts: Ian Wright was a menace, a Liam Gallagher to Bergkamp's Noel, a lout who grabbed the headlines while the quiet man wrote the songs.

The game in Salonika showed, once again, that Arsenal did not pass the ball well without Bergkamp. Like any great team player, Bergkamp improved the play of those around him. A good team is always balanced, and Bergkamp balanced Arsenal. He made the team swing. When he was absent the attack was like a door hanging off one hinge. Another obvious conclusion to draw: the squad was still too thin. One striker would not fly, the other would not keep his mouth shut, the third was a moody novice. With Bergkamp removed from the frame, Wenger needed another half-striker who could carry the ball and play Wright in a few times. Merson used to do that job, but Wenger had sold him to Middlesbrough.

The next match, on 21 September, was at Chelsea, which gave supporters a chance to compare Wenger with another foreign manager, Ruud Gullit, who had joined the club as a free-transfer player from Sampdoria in May 1995. He was just 33 when he took over as player-manager, and he had quickly signed Gianluca Vialli, Frank Leboeuf and Roberto di Matteo. But if we judge managers by what they do rather than by what they say, Arsenal was a much healthier club than Chelsea. Gullit, in his first job, was an impatient chequebook manager who bought current internationals on top wages, a policy which started when he and Mark Hughes joined the club. Wenger, the experienced manager in his fourth job, was more patient, signing unknown youngsters, a couple of solid pros, and Overmars.

His approach was that of a perceptive Chief Scout, someone who makes development deals which address current needs while also investing in the future.

The actions of both coaches in the transfer market had made clear and interesting statements. Ruud Gullit's signings sent this message: I will probably not be here long, so I want to win trophies now with stars who know how to win trophies. Arsène Wenger's signings sent a different message: we need a younger, more athletic, more skilful team that can take us into the next century. Compared to Wenger, Gullit was really just Ron Atkinson with dreadlocks.

The game at Stamford Bridge was the first time that season Arsenal had had a chance on the Sunday to make ground on Manchester United, Liverpool and Blackburn, all of whom had drawn the day before. In fact, it was a winner-goes-second match, but the Gunners were lethargic early on and Gustavo Poyet scored from a corner. They raised the tempo immediately. Vieira passed to Wright, who headed to Bergkamp, who produced an ice-cool finish past Ed de Goey, and when Wright later flicked the ball up, a Michael Duberry header fell to Bergkamp and his left-foot shot bounced in for 2–1. Chelsea came back with a Zola equaliser from a Mark Hughes cross that Seaman would have caught three years earlier, and then Nigel Winterburn scored a sensational winner with a 25-yard shot. Ian Wright was hardly in the game. When he did get the ball he usually lost it.

Apart from the continuing brilliance of Bergkamp (on the Sky Sports *Super Sunday* programme he won man of the match with 91% of the viewers' votes), Wenger was delighted to see Petit having his best game so far, making some good passes and becoming stronger as the game went on. When Arsenal went 1–0 down Petit almost immediately made a burst forward into the box. The pass never came but the idea was right, evidence that Petit was a winner type, as Wenger had claimed. Arsenal were now second in the Premier League, Chelsea three points behind but with a game in hand. Wenger had now been at Arsenal for a year. He must have been pleased that his side had shown a very competitive attitude and had reacted well to their first defeat of the season in Greece. They had also reacted well to going a goal down at Chelsea, raising the tempo and equalising quickly before going 2–1 up. Wenger must have believed that the PAOK tie was retrievable in the second leg.

The main feature of the season so far, of course, was that Dennis Bergkamp had improved so much. He was getting more of the ball now and had better players round him. And why was he getting more of the ball? Because Merson had mostly passed to Wright, his mate. Then Overmars arrived, became Bergkamp's room-mate, and passed to him much more than Merson had done. Remarkably, Bergkamp now had seven goals in seven Premiership games – and four yellow cards. He was fired up all right, maybe too fired up. Continuing at this rate he would get twenty yellow cards by the end of the season – and 38 goals!

## BERGKAMP'S PURPLE PATCH CONTINUES

*I'm a long time in the job. In two or three days you can quickly destroy what you've built up for a long time. We just have to keep humility and try to go to the next game, and start again.*

Arsène Wenger

The West Ham game at Highbury on 24 September was the night when Ian Wright was honoured with an elaborately choreographed ceremony which showed that football had now officially become showbusiness. Four white boards were placed in a square in the centre circle with the words IAN WRIGHT WRIGHT WRIGHT, and four lines of kids stretched diagonally to the corners of the ground wearing the shirts of every club Wright had scored against, including the European sides like Paris Saint Germain and Auxerre. The two teams came out without him, then the hero came out on his own to deafening applause. It was like Sky Sports hype for a

Naseem Hamed world title fight. All that was missing was the announcer's voice saying, 'And now, ladies and gentlemen, would you please welcome, from Croydon in Surrey, in the blue corner, wearing the white shorts, the lightweight champion of Egoland . . . Ian Wright, Wright, Wright!' Chairman Peter Hill-Wood gave the cuddly superstar a silver cannon in a red velvet box, and they posed for pictures with Junior Gunners as the fans cheered his greatest goals playing out on the Jumbotron screens. When nets containing 179 red balloons were opened it began to look as if the kick-off would be delayed, but the razzmatazz suddenly stopped and stewards ran on to dismantle the boards.

Then the match started, and the Dutch master was razor-sharp, slicing through the Hammers like cheesewire through Cheddar. Bergkamp was electrifying in Arsenal's 4–0 win, reminding us that the most exciting thing in football is a big man with skill and pace. Inevitably, Wenger was asked if he thought this was Bergkamp's best-ever display for Arsenal. 'You like to say yes every time,' he replied, 'but I think the whole team played well and we had good speed in our game, it was more fluent. The fluency of the game was good. It was not all easy because West Ham gave us some problems in the air in the first fifteen to twenty minutes where we were a little bit too stretched, but after that every time we came out we looked dangerous. We could score goals with our chances and we had some very good moments in the game today.

'Dennis is a playmaker and a striker. He's a mixture. He's a player who is in a perfect position as a second striker. If you put him in midfield he'll lose too much strength to work and will not be efficient. But when he is in a free role as a striker, he likes it, or a free role in midfield – you feel he always knows which position is the biggest threat to his opponent. Sometimes it's up front, sometimes he's in between the lines, sometimes he's in midfield. He has the experience now to know where he is always dangerous for the opponent. He's a playmaker and an important link between midfield and attack.'

Can Bergkamp get any better?

'Yes, I would say yes. There's no limit for improvement for every player. He lost his concentration a little bit in the second half.'

'Did you tell him that?' I said. Some reporters giggled quietly and Wenger did not answer the question – which answered the question.

Did you consider resting him the second half?

Wenger smiled and said, 'We cannot rest him. But it's good to see that when we had to change some players, the players who came on played well in the collective pattern we want to play.'

Brian Glanville of *The Times* then asked whether Wenger thought the team depended on Bergkamp too much.

'It is a worry, of course. I don't want to deny the importance of Dennis Bergkamp in our team, but I think in Greece we did not see the real Arsenal team. Not only was Bergkamp missed, but we missed the whole team.'

Was this the best performance since you've taken over, or the best first half anyway?

'Maybe, maybe the most fluent one. And where we had the most speed in our ball circulation. That's what we try to improve; we don't manage always to do it. But the team was close to what we would like. But I still think we can improve. In every sector we can win the ball quicker, we can be better off the ball, we can have more accuracy in our passes in the last 25 yards, we can be stronger in the set-pieces. We have a lot of work to do.'

And we thought George Graham was a demanding coach. His team had just played with superb flair and efficiency, sliced a decent West Ham side to ribbons and won 4–0, but the manager was still saying there was a lot of work to do. But, Wenger continued, 'for us every game is difficult. When you win the games you have the feeling that you've done well, you have the confidence. Without the confidence you cannot play. Against us, against Arsenal, every team will try to fight and try to give its best. What is concerning me is not the other team but my team. That my team goes into the game trying its best and trying to play the best football we can.'

Brian Woolnough of the *Sun* asked him to elaborate on a comment Wenger had made about the players enjoying themselves.

'When you love the game, that's what first brings players to football. When you're a professional player sometimes the fact that you play professionally, it becomes too much like work, you lose a little bit of this appetite. When you lose that you're a little bit less good. Everybody always says "You have to win, you have to win." Of course, we know it. But it's not because you know that you have to win that you win. It's best, first of all, to love what you do. And if you want to love what you do it must not be compulsory, it must be something you want to achieve and that you enjoy.'

These comments pointed up the difference between Graham and Wenger. Both are serious coaches, but the importance of player enjoyment never seemed to loom large in Graham's thinking at Arsenal. He wanted to keep his job, and the best way to do that was by winning trophies, so he always told the players that they were in the results business rather than the entertainment business or the pursuit-of-excellence business. The priority was winning because a winning team needs no apologists. For Graham, winning meant never having to say you are sorry. Wenger's aims are more ambitious, more risky, perhaps more fragile, because his Arsenal team reaches for the stars. His players, re-humanised by the holistic training techniques and made to feel more valued by big pay rises, would always take more of the credit for any trophy they won under Wenger than they ever did under Graham, who was always the biggest star at Highbury. He made sure he earned more than the players and he made sure that nobody threatened his power. He could be a master of disinformation when he wanted to be – naming, for instance, suspended players in his squad on a Friday night – but Wenger is a master of transparency who seems to tell you almost everything.

When Wenger was asked whether he thought his team was now doing better than he had anticipated at this stage of its development, he replied carefully by emphasising the fragility of a team, a mood, a winning sequence. 'I'm a long time in the job. In two or three days you can quickly destroy what you've built up for a long time. We just have to keep humility and try to go to the next game, and start again what we did tonight, and try to improve what we did tonight. Sometimes you try and it doesn't work. We could be disastrous at Everton in the next game. What is important for me is that we have a consistency since the beginning of the season.

That shows that we have a quality, and even if we play badly in one game, what we've done until now won't fall away. We've shown in seven, eight games that we had the quality in every game – not always in ninety minutes, but you could see, you could feel the desire to play together.' As he said this last sentence, Wenger rubbed his fingers together, as if feeling the quality of cloth.

I said, 'The players put a lot into the Chelsea game and a lot again tonight. Can you keep that up physically twice a week for eight months?'

'No, I would say no. That's why a strong team is there in March and April. We have our weak moments physically throughout the season, that's why the collective game, the organisation, is important. You cannot play the whole season at the speed we played in the first 45 minutes. It's good to have a collective base for when you are physically a little less strong so you don't lose too many points.'

Anyone new to a Wenger press conference would have put the Frenchman down as a straight shooter who gives genuine answers to questions. Clearly, he would not over-praise his team in September – no coach would. But he was happy enough. His team had already done enough to make the period up to Christmas interesting for themselves and for the fans. The big question was: how long could Bergkamp maintain his dazzling form? Lambros Lambrou had reported in July that he was fired up, and he was still flying at the end of September. His performances were absolutely phenomenal. Lambros said after the West Ham match, 'What impressed me most was in the second half when he cut in from the left, outpaced everyone in a sprint across the field and hit a dipping shot just past the post. That showed how strong he is and how motivated he is.'

Lee Dixon was injured for the game at Everton on the 27th and Grimandi again struggled at right-back, but Wright and Overmars put Arsenal 2–0 up. Then Everton came back with two goals early in the second half. It was not the best preparation for the return with PAOK at Highbury the following Tuesday, Arsenal's fourth game in ten days. Overmars was not fully fit for that match and Wright again kept losing the ball, but victory looked possible after

Bergkamp swerved inside his marker and scored with a wonderful shot, side-footed low across the keeper. Unfortunately, they never really looked like scoring again and the tie was drifting towards extra time when Seaman booted a goal kick straight to a Greek player on the halfway line. Two passes later Vrizas beat Adams and produced a classy finish to equalise. It was not even October and Arsenal were out of Europe already.

They began to concentrate on the title race with a vengeance. Barnsley were thrashed 5–0 on 4 October, but afterwards Wenger spoke about how traumatic being knocked out by Salonika had been, and that in his opinion it showed at the start of the game. 'I had problems to recognise my team in the first fifteen minutes because nothing was going well. For fifteen minutes I thought maybe the shock had been bigger than I thought it was. And after that of course Dennis brought us back into the game, and then it was a little bit easier.'

Wenger had taken Wright off after he had scored and put Anelka on, but the teenager had a frustrating time. So I asked: Is Anelka trying too hard to impress? Does he just need to be calmed down?

'I try, I try. He just needs one day to come on and to touch his first ball and to score a goal. It's strange because he's not a goalscorer type, he's a team player, much more than a usual striker. But you have the feeling when he comes on now his only obsession is to take the ball and run at everybody and score his goal. And that's where he's wrong. But he's young. You had a bad impression of him today. He has not shown ten per cent of what he's capable of doing.'

Bergkamp, yet again, had put in a stunning performance, running the show and scoring two goals. Was there anything left to say about the Dutchman?

'He's among the best players in the world. It looks so easy for him to score goals. And his goals are so spectacular because most of his goals are from outside the box. He scores goals like a midfielder. And he doesn't need three touches. All his goals are two touches or one touch.'

Brian Woolnough asked whether or not Bergkamp's dislike of the spotlight off the pitch was more apparent this season.

'Yes, but he's much more under the spotlight this season than last season or the year before because everybody would like him to explain why he scores so many goals and why he plays so well. But I enjoy it when a player keeps a constant focus on what is important, which is his game and his life. Sometimes when you are like Dennis now you can go somewhere different every night, but he doesn't do that. So I enjoy him very much. Because he knows what is really important in his life, and he does it well.'

Is there anything he can't do as a footballer that you'd like him to do?

'I think he could improve his heading, and he could sometimes get more in the box. Sometimes when we have a break he makes his run towards the ball instead of going up into the box. Because when he makes his runs behind defenders he's very strong physically and I would like him to score five or six goals a season with his head. Because, if he wants to, really, he's a good header. But he doesn't like it. So when you look at the percentage of goals he scores, it's amazing, for a striker, how many goals he scores outside the box. He has been educated in Holland, and in Holland people play always on the ground and combine always on the ground. You look at Ajax, where they score most of the goals on the ground, so they are not educated to score in the air. But he's not bad in the air.'

Does he tend to take it easy when Arsenal are winning 4–0?

'That's a problem of all the talented players – they have to fight against that themselves. But it's not obvious concerning Dennis because he likes perfection. The problem for Dennis at that stage of a game is that he wants to do things that are too difficult sometimes. He likes to be so perfect that he sometimes misses goals because he tries some difficult things. But you must understand that it's rare in games and in the season that the players can do the things they enjoy in the game, so when you're 4–0 up and 5–0 up there are moments when you get a little bit more freedom.'

Which players are in his bracket?

'Among players today, Zola. He is the same type of player but Dennis is stronger physically. But Zola at 28 was a Dennis type. A little bit more activity in midfield, but a little bit less a goalscorer

89

than Dennis. In his early career, Roberto Baggio was the same type of player: efficient, not really a striker, not really a midfielder, but efficient in scoring goals, difficult to mark, not good in the air, but very skilful. And Cantona, but Dennis scores more goals than Cantona, and maybe runs a little bit more.'

Why was Bergkamp not more successful when he was playing in Italy?

'You cannot play well when you're unhappy, that's for sure. But why was he unhappy? It was two things: he couldn't settle down and he was in a team which didn't play the football he likes. He went from a very offensive team to a very defensive team at Inter. He came from Ajax, where they play with two wingers and two strikers, and went to Inter, where they play with man-to-man marking, with a sweeper, and him on his own up front – so that wasn't the best team for him. Because Dennis, when he has something in his mind, he's very difficult to change. He's intelligent. He knows what he wants. He wants to win the games.

'To have a balanced life makes it always easier for the managers. It may be harder to gain his confidence when you come at the start, but a player who comes every morning and has had a good sleep and has good family relations, it's easier than someone who is never at home and is not happy at home. But for me the most important thing is not the private lives of the players, it's not my concern. For me it's how much they love their job, and he loves his game. That's why he's a great player. It's always the same. You can speak about a player, but at the end of the day, does he really love to play? Does he really love the game? Could you call him tomorrow to come and play a game with friends? If he has that, for me, that's a characteristic of the big player: he loves to play.'

Although he never used the term, Wenger had just summarised the modern era of the half-striker, an animal which evolved because creative players were kicked out of midfield. When Milan's Arrigo Sacchi and copycat coaches turned midfield into a war zone with fierce pressing, playmakers in that part of the field became virtually obsolete. The invention had to come from the last third of the field rather than the middle third. And on the evidence of the last two months, Dennis Bergkamp was the supreme exponent.

## STRUGGLING WITHOUT OVERMARS

*Arsène is a wonderful example of an open-minded approach. I think he's done a fantastic job for the cause of other foreign coaches.*

Martin Tyler, Sky Sports commentator

The 5–0 thrashing of Barnsley had seemed like a perfect night for Wenger, but something important had gone almost unnoticed: Overmars had been injured and he would miss the next three Premiership games. Significantly, Arsenal would not score in any of those games.

First of all, though, the nation turned its attention towards Rome where England needed only to draw with Italy to qualify for the World Cup in France. It was in the Italian capital that Glenn Hoddle made a conceptual leap by playing Ian Wright as a defender, showing the kind of realism and tactical imagination Wenger had lacked in Salonika. Hoddle realised that England would not have the ball very much during the match, so he played just one up, Wright, and told him to chase defenders for ninety minutes. He knew a goalless draw would do, so he adopted a George Graham approach.

Rome was a night of immense tension – but it turned out to be a huge tactical success for Hoddle. Paul Gascoigne, returning to the city where he had played for Lazio, had lost his pace but retained his skill and strength, and he shuffled, turned, teased, played short passes and slowed the game down all night. He gave a masterful demonstration of keep-ball and this, added to Wright's fiery, aggressive closing down of the Italian backs, held England together.

Three nights later, on Tuesday, 14 October, Wenger picked a reserve team to play Birmingham City in the Worthington Cup. Only Lee Dixon of the regular starting eleven played (as captain), the team was Manninger; Dixon, Marshall, Grimandi, Upson; Mendez, Vernazza, Platt, Hughes; Wreh and Boa Morte. It was 1–1 after ninety minutes, but through the drizzle the 28,000 crowd watched Arsenal cruise home in extra time with goals by Boa Morte (his second of the night), Platt and Mendez.

Bergkamp played at Crystal Palace on 18 October but Hermann Hreidarsson, a strong Icelander, blotted him out in a 0–0 draw. The Dutchman picked up his fifth yellow card of the season and was now suspended for three games. Nineteen-year-old Luis Boa Morte, who had looked sharp against Birmingham midweek, was Overmars' replacement, but he did not look a Premiership player. He was quick, brave and skilful, but immature, a headless chicken.

Before the Aston Villa game on the Sunday of the following week, featured on Sky, I had a conversation with commentator Martin Tyler, whose apparently laid-back style disguises a tightly focused footballing intelligence and a wealth of detailed knowledge. Tyler's last match at Highbury had been the annihilation of Barnsley. He had interviewed Bergkamp and the manager on camera. After the Barnsley game, I said both to Dennis and to Arsène Wenger that I felt that Dennis, at this moment in time, was the best player in the world. Which is not a statement that I would make lightly. Arsène said, "Maybe there's somebody in Africa that we don't know about, but I know what you're saying. Yes, I can't think of anybody who's playing better. I know some Dutch commentators who follow Dennis very closely, and they believe we've added to his game." Tyler said that Bergkamp was now a better player because he had become more aggressive, but that it had cost him his place in three forthcoming games against Derby, Manchester United and Sheffield Wednesday. 'He's been sent off since he's been here, he's got this suspension. Clearly, this fantastic purple patch can't go on for ever, but there's no reason why it can't go on for another ninety minutes. If I was Brian Little that is what would be concerning me.

'There was a piece in *France Football* with Wenger. My French isn't that wonderful, but I think he was saying, "I want to improve the attacking side of our play. We are gonna let in more goals because of it, but we're already scoring more. That's the way I believe in."

'Petit's been an excellent signing. He played for France against South Africa for the first time in a couple of years, so it's been good for Petit as well as good for Arsenal. Overmars has been slower into his stride. Much has been said about him having to learn the role in left midfield, rather than play as a wide attacker. He's still a very exciting addition. He's had a very serious injury and you always worry about players coming back from that, but he's done enough in patches to suggest that he can play at a wonderful level.

'Arsène is a wonderful example of an open-minded approach. I think he's done a fantastic job for the cause of other foreign coaches. There's the difficulty of coping with the football lifestyle in England, with so many games, and the dressing-room mentality. Mickey-taking is a very important part of the culture. You've got to be cute enough in the language, and radiate the right respect. The impact that he's made is really incredible. And Arsenal is now the place to go to. It's now the fashionable boutique. Before it was a good functional product which would never let you down.

'I do subscribe to the view that had they bought short-term in January/February they were genuine candidates to win it last year. And they had a very good chance of finishing second for the Champions League. But on their recent European form they might not have got past the qualifying round if they'd finished second. That's the only negative I can think of in Arsène's year.'

The Aston Villa game ended goalless; Bergkamp, Wright and Parlour were all off form. The Dutchman had been suffering with flu during the week, Wenger told us later, and Parlour's wife had had their second baby on the Friday night. In the goalless draw against Spurs on 30 August Arsenal had hit the bar three times, but in this game they only hit the frame of the goal once, with a Vieira volley off a Bergkamp free-kick. Wenger was still using Anelka judiciously as a substitute. As long as he brought him on as a sub, and gave him 25 minutes, Anelka was a new player. Wenger was desperate to give him every chance to succeed while at the same time protecting him. The Villa match was notable only for the dismissal of the luckless Petit for laying hands on the referee. The official actually ran into him, so the resulting contact should not really have been deemed a push. Wenger said the club would appeal against this red card.

At the post-match conference a journalist asked, 'Are people starting to rumble how you play?'

'Guess what we want to do? Yes, maybe. But we have to find a way where we can put them under pressure more, and maybe work more on our movement off the ball. And when you see a player like Boa Morte today you see that he has some potential, but you also see that he misses experience, he misses movement off the ball, coming at the right moment – that's where you can sometimes win the game.'

When will Overmars be back?

'Next Saturday. We could have played him today but we were scared of a setback. Next Saturday at Derby, or maybe, at the latest, Manchester United.'

I asked, 'If you get a couple more nil-nils would you consider changing the formation from 4–4–2 to another system?'

'I would rather change the organisation of the team if we conceded goals. Because we were maybe a little bit too offensive. But I don't think it's because of the organisation that we don't score goals. We still have a very good attack, we've scored 27 goals even if we haven't scored in the last two games. It's due to the fact that some players are tired, don't look fresh enough. And we miss Overmars. It happens. You always have periods in the season when you don't score as I would like to score.'

Are you worried by the discipline?

'The best discipline is to score goals. We didn't score in the last two games. There's different kinds of discipline. There's a tactical discipline. If we hadn't been disciplined today we would have lost the game. There is a discipline with the referee, but I don't think we complained more to the referee than Aston Villa did.'

Did you talk to the referee?

'I have never talked to an English referee since I am here.'

'Why not?' one reporter came back.

'He'd get booked!' said another. Everyone laughed, including Wenger.

'I'd get the red cards as well. After the game – what can you change after the game?'

Wenger's overall approach had now become a slight worry because he seemed to see the game mostly in terms of speed, fitness and pressure. Would the fittest, fastest team win the championship? August, September and October had now gone and only time would tell whether the French professor was right.

But there were still question marks over Ian Wright. He was now a third of the way through his seventh season at Arsenal and Wenger could see that his team was very much limited by what Wright could and could not do. When Bergkamp scored against Salonika, Wright ran away to the crowd himself when he should have gone to congratulate the man who gave him the passes for most of his goals. He had done the same thing before: in Paris in 1995, when John Hartson scored against Real Zaragoza,Wright sprinted away towards the Arsenal fans as if he had scored himself. Perhaps, in his own mind, he had. Wenger could now tell in the first ten minutes what kind of game Wright was going to have. Early in the Villa game he must have groaned inwardly when Wright miscontrolled a pass from Boa Morte, letting it bounce behind him – Wright was going to have a stinker. Of course he could still nick a goal when he was playing badly, but Wenger needed more than that. Glenn Hoddle had done him no favours by picking Wright for the England match in Rome because that had taken his mind off Arsenal.

Wenger switched his team at Derby on 1 November, dropping Boa Morte after his two bad games against Palace and Villa, bringing back David Platt and putting Petit wide on the left. He picked Anelka with Wright again, as in Salonika, but it did not work. Arsenal controlled the first half happily enough without making a chance, Wright hit the bar with a penalty in the second half, and they ended up losing 3–0. On days like this, Nicolas Anelka, Christopher Wreh and Luis Boa Morte did not look as if they deserved to be on the same pitch as Dennis Bergkamp, Tony Adams and Patrick Vieira; many fans doubted whether they would ever prove good enough.

However, there was hope that patience would pay off with Anelka, who was still only eighteen. Michael Owen was well into a fine first season at Liverpool and he was nine months younger than Anelka. But Owen lived at home, had no worries, played most games and was only sometimes on the bench, whereas the Frenchman was still adapting to a new city and a new club. Still, if Wenger was right and Nicolas Anelka was a major talent, another George Weah, the patient, developmental approach was the right one. He might get five years and a hundred goals out of Anelka before selling him on to a club like AC Milan for £20 million.

So Arsenal had failed to score in their last three games without Overmars. When he returned to the side at Highbury against Manchester United on 9 November the Premiership champions were beaten 3–2, on a day notable for Anelka's first league goal, just eight minutes into the game. Overmars cut in and shot, as he did so often. The ball rebounded off Gary Neville towards the corner of the penalty area where Anelka retrieved it and, from the edge of the box, sent a high-velocity shot inside Schmeichel's near post. It was a thunderbolt which would have been a great goal against any opposition. Against Manchester United, it was sensational. Ian Wright, who was his ineffective partner that day, had been trying to beat Schmeichel for years and this kid had done it first time out. After this goal we began to glimpse the real Anelka. Much more relaxed now, he seemed to cruise around the pitch, elegant, skilful, able to change gear effortlessly, almost like a young Ruud Gullit. That afternoon, for this eighteen-year-old, the sky seemed to be the limit.

Vieira also got a goal, one made in Essex: a Parlour corner headed on by Adams, then a power-drive from the edge of the box which flashed past Gary Pallister's back and into the goal off the underside of the bar. When Ian Wright fouled Henning Berg a short while later some Muppets in the crowd began to chant, 'Ian Wright, Wright, Wright!' (With fans like that, it was no wonder he lost the plot so often.) But United did not roll over. Teddy Sheringham scored two brilliant goals before half-time, losing Grimandi to score with a typical header for the first, and then, after a flick-through by Giggs, beating Seaman with a superb low shot into the corner.

The match stayed at 2–2 from the 40th minute to the 82nd, when Wright set up Wreh for a shot which deflected off Gary Neville; Schmeichel, on the deck, clawed the ball off the line and Neville cleared for a corner. Parlour took it, and Platt, out-jumping Beckham, sent a stunning header into the top corner. It was by far his best goal for Arsenal.

## ARSENAL 1 BLACKBURN 3

*The last half hour was the worst since I came here.*

Arsène Wenger

When Arsenal played Blackburn on 13 December at Highbury it was business as usual when Marc Overmars scored the first goal. The roof started to fall in when Jeff Kenna hit a cross and Tim Sherwood nudged Dixon away, leaving Jason Wilcox to equalise. Then Chris Sutton climbed above Keown in midfield and headed on Tim Flowers' kick down the middle, Kevin Gallagher raced towards the penalty area, Adams came across but did not tackle, and the Scot hit a stupendous dipping left-foot shot over Seaman to make it 2–1. Another simple pass down the middle released Sherwood one-on-one with Seaman, who came late and feebly failed to claim the ball in front of Sherwood's boot. The ball went loose, and with no defender anywhere in sight Sherwood had time to make it 3–1 and complete the rout. The absence of Vieira, who was on the bench, proved highly significant. The last time Petit had been partnered by Platt, a fortnight before against Liverpool, Arsenal lost 1–0.

Wenger must have been as shocked as everyone else to see Tony Adams dominated by Chris Sutton. Adams was the strong man who had seen off every centre-forward in the league – John Fashanu, Les Ferdinand, Alan Shearer, Graeme Sharp, Mark Hughes, all the strikers who could jump, back in, hold you off, nudge you before the ball arrived. Nobody could outpower Adams, although a tough striker might occasionally battle out a draw with him. He had been the rock on which the team was built. They had won six trophies with him in the side and few fans seriously believed that Arsenal would have won any of them without him. But now he seemed a hollow shell, unrecognisable from the indomitable warrior the fans knew and loved.

It looked as if Arsenal were a team with just two gears: top and overdrive. They attacked at high speed, scored first, and then needed to score a second goal. The style Wenger had created played to his strengths, but on this occasion they were Blackburn's strengths as well. The irresistible force met an even more irresistible force. Arsenal were simply overwhelmed by a team playing power football with more power than them. In the past twelve years they had sometimes been beaten by defensive teams and skilful teams, but they had never been out-bombarded before.

Roy Hodgson was understating the case when he said his men had done a good afternoon's work. 'At half-time I thought we'd played reasonably well in the first half, but we went a goal down from our free-kick, a ball headed back into midfield and kicked over our back four who were maybe a little bit high there. And Overmars this time got his run perfectly right and Tim, unfortunately, having got it right the time before, got it wrong and we're 1–0 down. But I didn't really think we were out of the game. I thought if we kept playing the type of football we'd played in the first half maybe the chances would come. They did, and luckily we took them.'

Arsenal had now lost four of their last six Premiership games. Apart from the Derby and Liverpool defeats, they had also lost 2–0 away at Sheffield Wednesday on 22 November. The victory over Manchester United and a 1–0 win at Newcastle, whose minds were on their forthcoming Champions League tie against Dynamo Kiev, were crumbs of comfort. Wenger had been seething after losing to Liverpool, although it was not too apparent unless you watched his face very carefully. Two weeks later, after the Blackburn débâcle, he was even angrier – and this time it was much more obvious. He still spoke rationally after the match, but his fury went far beyond anything he actually said, even though what he said was strong and true enough. 'It was a fight,' he said. 'They lasted longer in the fight than we did. The last half hour was the worst since I came here.'

So one naturally wondered, would Wenger now sign some younger players who could play ninety minutes rather than an hour? Or would he slow Arsenal's game down and give his side a couple of extra gears? Did this team have the craft to slow the game down? The next game, on 22 December, was against Wimbledon, another physical team. Would he bring back three centre-backs? With results going the wrong way Wenger seemed a slave to 4–4–2, to formation, shape and pace. He seemed too scientific, not intuitive enough, not enough of a gambler, not flexible enough, someone who stuck stubbornly to his own rules come what may.

Later on the day of the Blackburn match it was announced that there had been another Ian Wright incident after the game. A few weeks earlier, when Wright had broken the club's goal record, some fans had chanted for their hero below the window of the dressing room, which overlooks the street, and Wright had conducted their cheers and thrown out his shirt, or some such souvenir. Now they were jeering him and Wright, incredibly, insulted the fans from the same window.

Wenger had now been the manager for fifteen months, but he had bottled the Ian Wright situation, had not yet unloaded David Platt and had not started to rebuild the defence for the future. Wright had become less productive with every game that passed and the back four was falling apart in front of his eyes. Overmars had under-achieved, and while Petit had a great engine he still did not look like a world-class midfield player. Parlour was a good competitor who had improved a lot, but could he improve much more? Wenger had uncovered one unquestionably great player, Patrick Vieira, while Remi Garde and Gilles Grimandi had been competent at best.

However, the Blackburn defeat, and the team meeting which followed, was the catalyst which turned Arsenal's season round. The senior players said that the foreigners were not giving the back four enough protection, so Wenger asked Petit and Vieira to play more as anchormen, with Petit, the more experienced of the two in that role, playing deeper while Vieira pushed forward to add his forceful presence in attack. Sometimes, though, Petit went forward and Vieira stayed back more – it depended on the opposition and the state of the game, and Petit was to prove himself very good at reading those situations.

The game against Wimbledon, a Monday night Sky game, had to be abandoned halfway through at 0–0 owing to a floodlight failure, the third Premiership blackout that season. Sabotage by a Malaysian gambling syndicate was later blamed. The game was rescheduled for later in the season, so Arsenal's first chance to bounce back after being bombed into submission by Blackburn came on Boxing Day against Leicester, the team that had stubborn-ly refused to succumb to that Dennis Bergkamp hat-trick back in August, which now seemed a very long time ago. But Wright, Overmars and Bergkamp did not seem to be on the same wavelength. Bergkamp's form had faded since he had returned from suspension, although he did place a free-kick on Platt's head for the first goal. Then Bould lobbed forward and Steve Walsh, Ian Wright and Matt Elliott raced for it, Keller came out of his goal, and Walsh volleyed the own-goal of the season high over his goalkeeper's head. Then Seaman idiotically dribbled past Heskey and lost the ball to Cottee, who passed to Izzet, who set up Lennon to knock in past Dixon on the line, but Arsenal just managed to hang on to the 2–1 win.

Wenger had said that he needed goals from midfield, but anyone who watched Arsenal carefully could see that the front three usually shot on the run and only passed to each other. They almost never passed to Parlour, Vieira or Petit. There was very little play round the ball, no passes laid back for 25-yard shots, not much passing in the box and no real variety, just rapier-quick thrusts and many passes forward, not sideways. It was an entertaining style of play which created a lot of chances, but it was one-dimensional and it meant that the midfielders only scored from set-pieces.

Wenger, however, asserted that this win against Leicester would help Arsenal get back to their normal way of playing. He then sent Adams to Cannes in southern France for intensive rehabilitation work. There was a rumour that the captain had been back on the booze the night before the Wimbledon game, which he did not play in, so he might have been sent away to dry out although the official story was that his ankle was not right, an injury which had upset his body's balance and caused a nagging back strain. There was even a suggestion that he might retire at the end of the season, or after the 1998 World Cup.

Ray Parlour was the best player on the field two days later at White Hart Lane in a 1–1 draw, and Grimandi had his most solid game so far. Keown managed to snuff out Jurgen Klinsmann, who had returned to play under Christian Gross and save Spurs from relegation, and at the other end Anelka was unlucky with a shot which hit the post. Arsenal dominated the second half without creating much. Alan Nielsen scored for Spurs, then Ramon Vega equalised for the Gunners, Parlour's shot deflecting off him past Ian Walker, his third own-goal of the season. One was still wondering whether Wenger would change his two-gear approach, but Wenger, interestingly, reckoned his players had recovered their confidence. Maybe, but could they dominate their last fifteen games as they had dominated their first fifteen? The players would naturally be more tired from January 1998 onwards and teams knew what to expect now. So when Arsenal played them again would they not just defend deeper, make the game last longer, wait for the storm to blow out after seventy minutes then score goals when Wenger's elderly defenders were wobbling?

By the end of 1997 Arsenal had played twenty, won nine, drawn seven and lost four. The same results again would mean a third- or fourth-place finish, so a pronouncement by Wenger at this time was worrying. He said that he hoped Ian Wright would stay for the next two years and see out his contract – a comment which must have have been just a polite soundbite. If Ian Wright was still at Arsenal in 2000, Arsène Wenger would not be. In January 1998 Wright was due to start hosting his new television chat-show on LWT. Did the manager approve of this new distraction?

Arsenal's FA Cup third-round tie was against Port Vale on a wet and windy day. Vale played 3–5–2, soaked up pressure and used the ball cleverly in their occasional counter-attacks, while Arsenal hit far too many long balls at Bergkamp, who most of the time was either offside or unable to reach the ball because it was overhit or windblown. They rarely looked like scoring in a 0–0 draw, but the Coca-Cola Cup fifth-round tie at West Ham on 6 January worked out neatly for them. Seaman made a silly, clumsy challenge on Kitson to concede a penalty, but Hartson hit the post from the spot. After that, Wright and Overmars scored. Arsenal scoring first meant that Petit did not have to do anything except chase and tackle. At that stage in his first season Petit was still mostly a presser, better when the other team had the ball, so the situation suited Arsenal's midfield.

Then tabloid reports said that Benfica were very keen to sign Ian Wright, but the timing seemed bizarre – except, perhaps, from

Wright's point of view. That is, if his point of view was: Got my record, got my place in the history books, got my silver cannon, cheerio!

## GRAHAM'S BACK-HANDED COMPLIMENTS

*I thought they would have really been up there with United. I don't know why, it's not for me to say. I thought they'd be challenging United a lot closer.*

George Graham

On 10 January Arsenal played Leeds at Highbury. Marc Overmars, who was beginning to show signs of being a better player than he had been so far, scored the first goal, Jimmy Floyd Hasselbaink equalised, then Overmars grabbed the winner.

After the game George Graham was at his most mischievous, tossing out back-handed compliments and wind-ups. 'When you get a team like Arsenal who have got outstanding individuals,' he said, 'and you can keep them quiet for three-quarters of the game, and all of a sudden one of them comes to life, that can win the game for them. I think that's what happened.'

Did you try to sign Overmars?

'Yes.'

At Leeds or Arsenal?

'At Arsenal. We couldn't afford him at Leeds.' Graham laughed at his own joke. 'He's not taken off yet, has he? I don't think so. When you've got that talent, you can be quiet for long periods. They've got him, they've got Wright, they've got Bergkamp. They were a lot more physical today, Arsenal – I thought they did well in that department. I thought it was a difficult game, first half. Arsenal were up for it physically and I think we matched them quite well. The ball was in the air too much. I thought Seaman was putting us under pressure with long kicks all the time – it reminded me of my days here. Not all of them, some of them. For me, we only saw the real Arsenal in the last twenty minutes after they scored. I thought they looked a bit nervous. But we didn't capitalise on it. We showed them too much respect.'

Bill Pierce of PA Sport asked, 'You said at the start of the season they had the players, didn't you?'

'I thought they would have really been up there with United. I don't know why, it's not for me to say. I thought they'd be challenging United a lot closer. With the quality they have, a lot of quality.'

I put the first two questions to Arsène Wenger.

George Graham said he thought Arsenal were up for the physical battle today – do you agree?

'Yes, it was of course a very physical battle, we expected that. I think they came here to frustrate us. The players were up for the battle, every ball was a fight. First, I think we could cope with that. Secondly, we did master our nerves and didn't speak too much with the referee, and didn't forget to play football. Sometimes it's difficult to have a fight because you forget to play.'

Were you worried that all the Benfica publicity would affect Ian Wright's performance?

'No. I think he played very well. I was not really worried. The answer is always on the field, not in the newspapers. And I think he has shown how great his spirit was, and for me he played a great game today.'

Has Ian told you he wishes to stay at this club?

'He cannot say to me every day when I see him that he wants to stay at the club. But he didn't say to me that he wants to leave.'

Is Overmars coming good now, at last?

'For me, he's a great player. Like many great players you expect always more than they produce. But you look at the players in the winger position in the midfield and you look at how many goals he's scored since the beginning of the season, and how important the goals were – who is the player in his position in the English championship who's scored more goals than Marc Overmars? And he works very hard for the team. Of course he takes many risks, and sometimes he loses the ball when you think he shouldn't have lost it, but when he manages to go through he's always a threat. I think he had some great games at the beginning of the season, then he was injured and he was out for three or four weeks, and it took him some time to come back. He didn't play well for a while because he had a kick on his laces on his right foot.'

His instep?

'His instep. And he couldn't kick the ball with his right foot. Since two weeks only he can do it again. And since those two weeks he's played much better. Because I had always the feeling that he does not put his foot in at the right moment, or doesn't go in the box. And you cannot understand why he didn't do it, and suddenly he discovers he can do it again.'

I asked, 'Is that why he stopped taking corners?'

'Yes. We took him out of the corners because he couldn't kick the ball.'

Has he got over his big injury?

'I think so. It is one you never can forget about, because I had the same kind of injury. In the specific position where you were injured, you always try to avoid this position. Because it is in your mind. But in every other aspect he's recovered. Listen, it's difficult to find, all over the world, players who play on the sides and are young. He's young, he's 24. He has won everything – the European Cup, the World Club Cup – and can run without the ball. He has great movement, he understands the game, he can run with the ball, he can work for the team. He has the speed.'

Bill Pierce asked: 'Petit's perfomance?'

'I was pleased with the performance of Petit today, and I must say, as well, at West Ham. It was a continuity of what he did at West Ham.'

Is today's win special because it's George Graham?

'He's welcomed by the fans because he's done very well for the club. That is normal. For me there's no special animosity. I just would like to do as well. And of course it's important to win our games at home in front of our fans. No, I cannot say that it's anything special on that side. I just had the feeling before the game that it was a very, very important game for our Premier League position because we had a win against Leicester, we went away to Tottenham, we had the two cup games and then we came back here against Leeds who are threatening our position at the top of the table, among the first four or five. I thought that for us to win at West Ham was important and to build on that with another win was crucial for the team. I think we have shown today that we can do it.

'It takes some time for players who come from foreign countries to adapt. They are surprised at the beginning. They come and say, "That's not football!" And I think when you go abroad you have to adapt and show that you can cope with it. They are at the stage where they are showing that they are doing it. You see players like Petit who at the beginning of the season would have lost his nerve much more than today. Now he knows what is expected of him. Because some players who were considered to be physical in foreign countries, and come here, they still have to go up a step to be at the English level. I'm surprised sometimes now when I watch continental games, that I get bored. Even if technically it's better. You just miss the intensity, you get used to it here. And when you look at a game on TV or if you go abroad, you think, "What's going on here? It's not alive." The passion is so big here, the commitment so high. You adapt, or you have to go. And the referees permit more than abroad. If you watch games in Italy, for example when players in the box go down, it's a penalty. Or every tackle, especially in the air – they allow much more here in the air. And here in the air the fights are much more important. It takes some time for the players to adapt.'

You seemed very calm during the game.

'When I was younger I was much more excited on the bench. But now I have some problems to get quickly up.'

Naturally, everyone laughed at this.

Were you surprised when the referee did not book anybody in the first fifteen minutes?

'No, it was a relief for me because we have some players who have three or four bookings. We had all the bookings early in the season, and so we have already had our suspensions, and the teams who have better behaviour have them now. We had our suspended players in November and they will have them in January and February.'

Brian Woolnough asked, 'Do you get the impression that Dennis is suffering because he's not scoring? His body language suggests he's very frustrated with himself.'

'I think he's improving in the last two games. He needs a goal now. If you score ten goals and suddenly you don't score any more, you get frustrated. But now in nearly every game he's man-marked, and really man-marked, with defenders holding him. Referees here are not used to man-marking.'

I said, 'Can you work on a style of play which gives him the ball facing the goal?'

'Yes. If the whole team is technically very good, it's easier to give him the right ball in the right space. But it's not always easy. Here at Highbury the pitch is narrow, so there's less space to play to him. Dennis is a winner and he's much more influenced by the results of the team. In our first twenty goals, eighteen were scored by Ian and Dennis. Other managers are not stupid. They say, "We'll stop them, then who will score?" I was always worried about that. If you have a third player, and a fourth player, who can score it gives always more room to Bergkamp, of course.'

Again the question about Ian Wright's future was put to Wenger – has he asked to leave?

'No.'

If he asks you on Monday, will he be allowed to go?

'No.'

He seemed to give a farewell wave to the fans. It looked a bit like goodbye.

'That's your interpretation.'

Mike Walters of the *Mirror* joined in. 'He often waves to the fans, we accept that. But this looked like a deliberate thank you and goodnight.'

'Goodnight maybe, but goodnight is not goodbye.'

Woolnough again: 'Is he in your long-term plans?'

'Listen, he has a two-year contract. You cannot be in the position we are in the middle of the season and let your strikers go away and not have people to replace them.'

Would you be prepared to let him go at the end of the season?

'I can't answer this question, I can only answer short-term questions. But short-term for me, it's difficult to say. I still think one day he will go, but he should not go to Benfica now. Because for me Ian Wright has to play in the World Cup, and to play in the World Cup he must stay in England. I have to defend the interests of our club. It would be irresponsible. If you think like that, you could take any player anywhere, even if he's under contract. That's not feasible. Football is so different when you go to a foreign country, you need some time to adapt. That's just too dangerous.'

But will Wrighty play in the World Cup?

'If he battles like today, and at West Ham, he will go, I'm sure.'

Woolnough persisted: 'Have you discussed this whole thing with him?'

'No. What was really important for me was the game today. When we have some time off, maybe we can talk about his future. For the moment we need the concentration of everybody.'

Do you have a good relationship with Ian?

'Yes, but he's a player. When he doesn't play well, the relationship is less good. When he plays well, it's good. That's normal. But overall, I'd say I'm very happy with the relations I have had with him since I've arrived.'

Then Martin Thorpe of the *Guardian* picked up the line of questioning. 'Have you told him leaving now will harm his chances of playing in the World Cup?'

'No. I will have a chat with him about this story because it came out in the press. But it's like that with Ian Wright. Tomorrow maybe Manchester United wants to buy him. I don't know what his priorities are, I don't know what is his desire. It depends what is your priority in life. I think the biggest priority is always to play at the highest level. And money should always be the consequence of the quality of your performances. Listen, I'm not a businessman, I'm a football manager, so what interests me is sport, and much less money. I haven't seen great players who do not make money today. It existed twenty or thirty years ago.'

I said, 'Does he have to get permission from the club to host a television show?'

'The television show?'

'You're the first guest!' Woolnough quipped.

'It depends, if it doesn't interfere with his training.'

'Can somebody be a regular television star and a Premiership goalscorer at the same time?' I asked.

'Not a regular one, no, but he can have one TV show if it doesn't take up too much time.'

Attention then turned to the club captain. Is Tony Adams fit now?

'He's come back from France. He was at the game today and he looks great. All the tests he had were positive. He came back in a very positive mind. He will train normally on Monday.'

That night, the Arsenal–Leeds game was featured on *Match of the Day*. When the highlights were over, viewers were treated to final proof that Ian Wright had completely lost the plot.

Jon Champion: 'Clarify your position. That's hard work and goals at Arsenal? Not Benfica?'

Wright (looking ridiculous in a big floppy black hat with a Nike swoosh): 'Well, wherever I'm playing, that's how I'm gonna do it. I've always tried to do that.'

Champion: 'Wherever you're playing? Does that indicate a doubt in your mind?'

Wright: 'I wouldn't say it's a doubt in my mind. I couldn't lie and say it's something that doesn't interest me. It's a fantastic opportunity at this stage. It's something that I would have definitely looked at. But the door was closed on it early doors and I couldn't really do anything about it.'

Wright, who usually grinned and flashed his gold tooth, seemed depressed, sounding like a defendant in the dock. He shrugged and said he would have liked to go but 'Everybody knows how much I love Arsenal.'

For Wright to try to walk out in January while the team was still in the hunt for three trophies was evidence that he did not love Arsenal. It was amazing to hear him say on BBC television that he wanted to go to Benfica but the club had told him he could not go. His words made him seem greedy, ungrateful, petulant, submerged in self-pity. Ian Wright Wright Wright had got it wrong wrong wrong by turning into everything a professional footballer should not be. And he had obviously not yet given up on his hope that Arsenal would let him walk away. His sullen grumbling was perhaps the most disgraceful interview ever aired on *Match of the Day* and Wenger must have watched it and wept. He must have thought, 'Excuse me, Ian, there is nothing to discuss. You are under contract for the next two years. And I'm going to put your

I-wanna-go-to-Benfica interview on a tape loop in the Arsenal Museum and label it HOW NOT TO CONDUCT YOURSELF AS AN ARSENAL PLAYER.

Wenger never said what he really thought of his striker's selfishness, but he rarely picked him after that. In fact, Ian Wright never scored another goal for Arsenal after that interview.

In the FA Cup third-round replay at Port Vale on 14 January, Bergkamp took a pass from Grimandi 25 yards out and, with almost no backlift, sent a sublime shot floating into the top corner. Wright tweaked a hamstring, Vale equalised and the tie went to extra time and penalties. Arsenal won the shoot-out 4–3 after Islington-born Allen Tankard sent his spot-kick over the bar.

Noel Whelan scored the first goal for Coventry at Highbury three days later, but it was the pacy Darren Huckerby who posed the biggest problem. Seaman hurt his hand when he tipped over one blistering shot from Huckerby (he chipped a knuckle and missed the next thirteen games) and then Keown pulled a hamstring chasing him. When Paul Williams unwisely headed back to goalkeeper Magnus Hedman, Bergkamp intercepted to score his first Premiership goal since early October. And the Dutchman was instrumental in his side taking the lead, touching the ball back to Lee Dixon whose shot deflected to Anelka, who buried it. Vieira had been booked early on for clattering into Huckerby, and when Coventry took a free-kick on the left Vieira inexplicably jumped like Michael Jordan as the ball sailed towards him and slapped it with his left wrist. Referee David Lodge awarded a penalty and gave Vieira his second yellow card for swearing at him. Dion Dublin converted, and the game finished 2–2.

In the FA Cup fourth-round tie at Middlesbrough on the 24th Arsenal moved on comfortably enough with a 2–1 win, both moves for the goals started by long passes from Adams to Anelka. Taking the first of them, Anelka found Bergkamp who flicked the ball through for Overmars, whose shot beat Schwarzer all ends up. The goal was so good that even Anelka smiled and congratulated him. The second came from a textbook counter-attack after a Middlesbrough corner: Adams hit a long, high clearance to Anelka on the left and his crossfield pass picked out Parlour, who took one touch and buried his shot. This was the geometry of demolition and Wenger must have wondered why on earth it had been such a struggle against Port Vale. Bergkamp, once again, had shown himself a master at releasing other players at pace. And in this team of speed merchants, Parlour was beginning to show that he too could accelerate from box to box in less time than it takes to pull the pin from a fire extinguisher.

Keeper Alex Manninger made the game closer than it needed to be with a rush of blood to the head at the other end. When Mustoe hit a long ball down the middle, Manninger raced ten yards beyond his penalty area, and Merson cruised round him and hit a shot which sweetly bisected Bould and Adams before rolling into the net. Merson had scored 98 goals for Arsenal in 427 appearances and now he had scored one against them. Adams teased Manninger about this aberration for years afterwards: 'You're not gonna give me a heart attack today, Alex? You're not gonna come flying out past me, are you?'

## TEN WINS IN A ROW

*I deeply feel that the team was never as low as people said, but we were at a dangerous moment when the team could have gone both ways, and where we needed small but important victories.*

Arsène Wenger

Tony Adams looked strong, fast and determined against Chelsea in the Coca-Cola Cup semi-final first leg at Highbury on 28 January, nothing like the hollow man we had seen in the 3–1 tanking by Blackburn. This was the real Adams again. Arsenal won the match 2–1 with goals by Overmars and Hughes.

'Big match, big performance?' I asked Wenger. After a year and a half I had started to talk like him.

'I thought so, yes. It was a big performance, but a big performance where the right score should be 4–1, I would say. I had nearly the same feeling at Middlesbrough where we created many chances. We did it again tonight and couldn't take our chances. But collectively the performance was good. I had really the feeling that at 2–0 we could kill it. Not by one, but by two or three more. I still think if we had scored the third goal we could have scored more, because they were struggling at the time. And after it was 2–1 they had hope again, it was more difficult. We were a little bit selfish in the last twenty minutes around the box – we had some people in better positions. But overall I'm pleased with the quality of our game.'

Wenger would soon regret those missed chances. In the second leg at Stamford Bridge on 18 February Petit was momentarily distracted, fiddling with his ponytail, when Chelsea scored two of their goals in a 3–1 win. Had the Frenchman's golden locks been securely tied, as they were later, Arsenal might well have ended up landing the domestic treble. The 2–0 win over the same opposition in the Premiership on 8 February was at least some consolation.

In the meantime, Manchester United, who had been on top of the table since October, had faltered slightly. On the last day of January they were beaten by Leicester when Tony Cottee scored at Old Trafford. Arsenal were at home to Southampton that day. The first half was scrappy, but then Manninger made a fantastic save from a Matthew Oakley shot and three goals in seven minutes gave the Gunners a 3–0 win.

United's slip-up was what everyone at Arsenal had been waiting for, as Wenger was quick to acknowledge. 'First our victory is important. But the fact that Manchester United lost at home gives more chances to everybody. Before the game nobody could believe that they would lose at home, because they looked invincible until now. But they have their bad time now. They've lost now a few games in the last four, I think they've lost three. I always said it's maybe over to win it but not over for second place. But now it looks open for everything.'

Going on to talk about Arsenal's improved form, he said, 'I think the unit is stronger, and tactically they understand each other better. I think as well some players needed a bit of time to settle down and adapt to English football. Gilles Grimandi sometimes looks lost, but in the last two games has played well. With so many new players it takes time.'

Will Ray Parlour play for England in the forthcoming friendly with Brazil?

'It would really be the surprise of the season, the biggest improvement of the season. Nobody would have said before the season started that he would have been an international in February, but on the other hand it would be one game more for him. He deserves it. He had another great game today. And he looks like improving on his final ball. His work rate is fantastic. But of course international is another step. But, if he doesn't make it in the short term, in the long term it must be his ambition. In the World Cup, or after. He's only 24 years old, Ray Parlour, so he can be in now. But in the next World Cup, for sure, he must be one of the players.'

Wenger was also delighted that Adams' spell in rehab seemed to have worked so well. 'I think that's the best I've seen Tony since I'm here. He looks really sharp again. Not only today, but on Wednesday at Chelsea, in his movement. He is not handicapped any more, he really looks like a player, all his movements are back. He still has problems in his back. He must always do his rehabilitation work and be very careful in his postures. He's an organiser, and I think he lost that a little bit when he wasn't physically ready. And now he has it again. He speaks to everybody, and reads the tactical problems on the field. That's why he's very important. When you are not right yourself you cannot care about other players on the field. When you get up every morning and you cannot walk, you cannot feel like jumping around and kicking the ball.'

Is Manchester United's monopoly of the Premier League now getting a bit boring?

'Yes, but it's important that the best team wins the championship, and if they're the best team we shouldn't want them not to win it just because it's Manchester United. It's open. The team that has so far gone through the season without any bad times is Blackburn. If you look at the tables they are the team that's lost less games than anybody else. They are the most consistent team since the beginning of the season in the championship. Because until now they have had no bad time. I expect them to have one. But mainly I expect us not to have another one. If you'd asked my players a week ago, they'd have said, "No, we've got no chance to win it." But if you win your games and Manchester United doesn't, after a while everybody thinks, "Why shouldn't we do it?"

'United went to Chelsea and won 5–3. And three weeks later they've lost three games, nobody knows why. That's how unpredictable football is. I'm not excited because I still think some teams are in a better position. We are still eight points away from Manchester United with a game in hand. We have to win this game, but we'd still be five points behind. That means they must lose two more, and we must win these two. But you never know. If they have a real bad time and we have a real good time, it's not impossible.'

In early February ClubCall man Dickon Geddes spoke about a Swedish striker Arsenal had wanted. 'Right at the end of my piece I said to him, "Arsène, there's a rumour that Andreas Andersson was here on Friday. He passed a medical, then Arsenal pulled out and he signed for Newcastle." Arsène just smiled and said, "Yes, he did sign for Newcastle." Which is as near to an admission as you'll ever get.'

Between 15 and 25 February Arsenal played Crystal Palace three times, needing a replay at Selhurst Park to get through to the FA Cup quarter-final. On 8 March they met West Ham at Highbury in that quarter-final and drew 1–1. Wenger hated the extra burden of these replays. 'For me the most important thing is the championship. So every time we play one more game it reduces our chances to be fresh in the championship games. So I cannot be happy. But on the other hand, in the quarter-final of the FA Cup you cannot calculate – you have to give everything to go through.'

In the Premiership Arsenal were going along steadily enough. Chris Wreh scored a fine goal to give them a 1–0 win at Wimbledon on 11 March, and then came the big game at Old Trafford, where Overmars delivered yet again, scoring the only goal from a flick-on by Anelka on 79 minutes. Those six points, and especially the win at Old Trafford, proved to be the turning point in the title race, psychologically as well as arithmetically.

In the West Ham replay at Upton Park on 17 March Wenger started Anelka and dropped Wreh, who had started in Manchester. Bergkamp had a night of frustration where everything he tried to do for 35 minutes did not work, and then as soon as something did work he was fouled. He played a one-two with Anelka and was going for the return pass when Steve Lomas held his shirt, so he lashed out fiercely with his left arm, smashing Lomas across the mouth, and was sent off. Anelka scored with a flashing shot just on half-time, but Hartson got a late equaliser. When the game went to penalties, Hartson and Abou hit the same post, and Manninger saved from Berkovic, leaving Adams to score the winner. Arsenal would now play Wolves in the semi-final on 5 April.

On 28 March Sheffield Wednesday arrived at Highbury. It was the first warm Saturday of the year and by this stage of the season all the remaining matches were vitally important, the margin for error almost nil. After a wretchedly nervous first five minutes, when Arsenal could not string two passes together, they annihilated Wednesday, creating several good chances before Overmars floated a perfect ball forward to give Bergkamp a side-foot past Pressman from seven yards. Wednesday improved in the second half but Seaman, back after his knuckle injury, did not have a shot to save. Ron Atkinson commented, 'First half, they outpowered us completely and gave us a right good tanking. We were very lucky to be only 1–0 down. Second half, we made a better fist of it, carried the game to them a little bit more. At one stage I thought they had fifteen on the park.'

Wenger's thoughts were now almost exclusively on the title race. 'If you look at the championship, we lost only four games and in January we were the only team with Manchester United and Blackburn. Since then they have lost, but we couldn't win away. The difference between Manchester United and Arsenal in January is they won more games away than we did. So we have reduced the difference by winning at Wimbledon and Old Trafford. So what has become important now is to win the home games and try to get more points away.'

Overmars had another great game against Wednesday. So why was he looking so frightening?

'He's a world-class player. He was a typical winger at Ajax. In Holland they use the wingers to create space for the midfielders, and that means they are in and out of the game. When he came here I gave him a different role where he was much more involved in the midfield, and I think that psychologically it took him some time to adjust to that. Physically it's much more demanding. He's very disciplined, he works very hard for the team, and every time we have the ball he makes his runs forward. So he has a very demanding physical role. So it took him some time to get used to that. In Holland, when you play at Ajax you know that in eighty per cent of the games, if you play at sixty or seventy per cent of your potential you win it. In England that doesn't exist. At Ajax, when they played PSV and Rotterdam, they had to be up for it. But when they played Nijmegen or Roda it was good enough to be at seventy per cent. To get used to fighting every game took him some time.'

Unlike George Graham, Wenger invariably owns up when experiments have not worked out, as he did when he was asked if Overmars could play on the right.

'No, that's really terrible. That's why I bought Boa Morte. One of my ideas, to give an option to the team, was that at home we could play with Boa Morte left and Overmars right. But he doesn't like at all to play on the right side.'

When he talked again about Tony Adams and his problems, Wenger managed to avoid mentioning the words 'booze', 'drink' and 'alcoholism'.

'Tony is thirty years old and he's always pushed his body too far. Since he has changed his way of life he has learnt to cope with his body and know himself much better. And now I'd say he knows when to push on, and when you go out of the game. He's improved a lot by knowing himself much better. He's a strong character and I think he's a very intelligent man. And tactically he's a great reader of the game, so he always knows what's going on on the field and what's wrong. So for a manager he's a very big support. He's a better player with the ball than I thought he was. All the defenders are better players on the ball than I thought they were, Bould as well, Keown as well. Of course Dixon and Winterburn, you know, they had to be able to play. But on the ball the central defenders are better than I thought. When you're a manager you're lucky if you have good players. If you have good players and leaders, it's a privilege. Because most of the time you have to fight to convince them, and that's why you like experienced players. They know what to do, they know how to react, so if your link with the manager is good, you're stronger.'

Wenger went on to say that he had a lot of respect for what Tony Adams had achieved in his private life, predicted that he would have a successful World Cup, and reiterated his faith in his players generally. 'I deeply feel that the team was never as low as people said, but we were at a dangerous moment when the team could have gone both ways, and where we needed small but important victories. In this kind of period, when you see that your confidence has gone, and you have to fight to win your confidence back, to have experienced players is good. Especially at Arsenal, a club with such a big pressure, where you always have to win. And if you don't win, everybody asks why. You need strong characters like Adams, Bould, Keown, Winterburn, Dixon, Seaman. That's very important in the bad periods of the season.'

This was very much a year in which Wenger's first team picked itself. Everyone knew what his best eleven was, so when key players were missing it was obvious. In any team there are four or five core players and the absence of any of them can be damaging, but Arsenal had the mental resilience and organisation to survive those absences, and that was something Wenger was very pleased about.

'We had many games without Seaman, we had many games without Adams, we had many games without Keown – he didn't play for three months – we had many games without Dixon, and we went through all that. Petit was out for a while, Vieira was out for a while, Parlour was out· for a while; Overmars was out, Bergkamp was out, Ian Wright is out. But every time we found the spirit and the strength to get over that. That is what we have to do. We have done it before, gone through it. And that should give us the strength, especially as we are in a not too bad period now.'

Was Wright's hamstring a worry?

'I'm more concerned about Ian Wright than about his injury. When Ian Wright is going well you must put him in jail to keep him out of the game. His impatience, his love of the game, is a big asset when he's fit. But his enthusiasm when he's injured is terrible for him. He thinks he can come back and play when there's no pain. We need to be over-patient because he's impatient. He's pushing you every day. When he wakes up the next morning and doesn't feel any pain, he thinks he can play the next day.'

What about Bergkamp's suspension?

'We can keep him sharp. Last time he had a three-game suspension it lasted five weeks. This time it is only two weeks. I'd say he can keep himself physically fit and keep his concentration although that's hard when you're not playing.'

A Chris Wreh goal at Bolton on 31 March made it four Premiership 1–0s in a row, and there were some decidedly manageable fixtures coming up. Before that, though, there was the small matter of an FA Cup semi-final. Tony Adams did a typically candid press conference before the match against Wolves at Villa Park, during which he explained how Wenger had helped him to rebuild his career. The *Mirror*'s John Dillon wrote that the skipper's transformation was like the Frankenstein story in reverse: Wenger had inherited a monster and turned him back into a man. 'He has great knowledge and insight into people,' Adams said. 'It has helped to extend my career when it could have been over. He's pointed out things that have improved my self-awareness and made me think a lot more about how I play. It makes me wonder how I did things before. It was probably just on instinct. He gets his point over very well. He is a very, very intelligent man, although it may appear that he's aloof because he is detached. But he's a nice guy. It's just that he's standing back and watching all the time. People who are filled with fear and insecurity may take that the wrong way. They panic because he is scrutinising things and weighing them up. But he has no fear. He's not insecure, so he can be honest about things.'

Adams could also be honest since he had already confessed everything – about how his Sundays used to be all-day booze-ups during which he might down twenty pints of Guinness, how he kept a crate of cheap champagne in the boot of his car, how he was embarrassed by his blackouts and bed-wetting, how he smashed glasses on his head to amuse his mates, how he could not remember knocking his bedroom door completely off its hinges one night at the England hotel. After Wednesday night games at Wembley he sometimes stayed up all night, on one occasion stumbling into Arsenal's training ground early the next morning and telling physio Gary Lewin, 'For God's sake, don't let the gaffer see me like this!' But now the dark days of the eighties and early nineties were behind him. 'The way I was going, I was dead. As far as I was concerned, there was no football left in me. But together we have given Tony Adams the chance to play on. Me and Arsène – the pair of us have done it.'

Adams could not remember big chunks of his past life, but oblivion was no longer an option for him. He said that if Arsenal lost to Wolves it would hurt, but he would not be trying to escape the reality of it by going down the pub. On the contrary, 'I'll feel the joy more sharply if we win. I have different ways of enjoying things nowadays when in the past I knew only one way. When you abuse alcohol, you suppress everything – good feelings as well as bad. My recollections of our past successes are patchy. I don't regret anything, but for me it's pretty simple now. I can sense the pain and the pleasure. And it's real.'

In an interview with *L'Equipe*, translated on to a website by Liz Ireland and headlined MY STRENGTH IS IN MY SERENITY, Wenger made it clear how he felt about Adams and his fellow defenders. Money could not buy the kind of commitment shown by players such as Adams, Bould, Dixon, Winterburn and Keown, and he valued the loyalty they showed to the club, to him and to each other. They knew they were part of something special, and they wanted to play together for as long as possible for a club and a manager who had treated them very well. 'In England,' Wenger reminded his fellow countrymen, 'there is a deep morality on the part of players. There simply aren't any mercenaries there yet! The jersey means more than anything. It's simple: at Arsenal, I work with five players who have spent more than ten years at the club. And when we discuss their contracts, the first thing each of them says is, "I'd like to stay, if I can." '

Against Wolves at Villa Park it was Chris Wreh, the erratic Liberian, who again scored the only goal of the game to put Arsenal into the FA Cup Final. Their opponents in that final, Newcastle, visited Highbury on 11 April and found Nicolas Anelka in awesome form. He took a pass from Wreh, dummied Stuart Pearce and rifled his shot into the far corner for the opening goal. Then he stabbed in at the far post after Parlour had burst between Batty and Pearce and crossed from the right. Then Vieira cruised forward from the centre circle and hit a thirty-yard thunderbolt into the top corner to make it 3–0. This was an intimidating preview of the final for Newcastle and their fans. When Warren Barton latched on to a ball over Bould's head and finished superbly, it was the first goal Arsenal had conceded in nine Premiership games.

At Ewood Park two days later, Dennis Bergkamp returned from suspension and destroyed Blackburn, who were 3–0 down after fourteen minutes. A Remi Garde throw went off the head of Henchoz to Bergkamp, who took one touch and rammed his shot across keeper Alan Fettis. That was after 75 seconds, his fiftieth goal for Arsenal. Soon after that Bergkamp released Parlour in a similar position and he fired through Fettis for 2–0, then Parlour scored again.

Since the teams had last met just before Christmas, when Ian Wright was fading, Arsenal had become defensively sounder, and they were now able to attack from deep positions with devastating directness. Blackburn found this out when they took a free-kick and the ball was headed out by Petit to Winterburn, who launched a seventy-yard pass down the middle of the field. Anelka left everyone trailing in his wake, headed the ball on and dummied the keeper before scoring from close range. It was 4–0 at half-time. Amazingly, it started to snow and an orange ball was brought out. Kevin Gallagher went on to volley a very sweet goal, but it was little consolation. 'Before the game we were very focused, very concentrated, very professional,' said Wenger, revealing what everyone could have guessed.

It was clear that the Anelka of April 1998 was a totally different player to the Anelka of October 1997. He looked powerful, confident, fast and was a great turner, able to stop on a sixpence inside the box and unbalance his marker. It was just a shame, in hindsight, that his excellent first goal for the club against

Manchester United back in November had come when Arsenal were struggling. When the team improved in the new year, Anelka took off and never looked back.

This demolition of Blackburn was repeated against Wimbledon, Arsenal playing the football of champions to win 5–0. Adams sent a booming header into the net from Petit's inswinging corner in the eleventh minute, Chris Wreh scored the fifth in the 89th. In between Overmars had released Anelka on the left, spurted forward to support and surprised Neil Sullivan with a low shot across him. Anelka exploded forward again to set up Bergkamp to make it 3–0 in nineteen minutes. In the second half Seaman came out of his box and hammered a long pass to Bergkamp, and from that Anelka and Overmars set up the long-awaited first goal by Petit. On the same day Manchester United were held 1–1 at Old Trafford by Kenny Dalglish's Newcastle, so the bookmakers now had Arsenal odds-on for the title.

After the Wimbledon victory, Wenger said, 'The joy and the excitement of the players to play together was what came out of that game. The pace we had in the game, our quick passing, always looked dangerous. The Blackburn game gave us more confidence offensively, because we had many games when we won only 1–0, 1–0, 1–0 and always had the feeling that one day we could concede a goal and we would not win it. Then we scored three against Newcastle, then four against Blackburn, and that maybe released the feeling that we only rely on defensive efficiency.

'We still have a difficult programme: five games to play, three away and many players away this week with the national sides. That's always very disturbing. We play at Barnsley and this game is very, very important for us. It's the only important game for us because it's the next one. We are focused and we know how difficult it will be. But I think they are just concentrated on enjoying what they do together. That's what comes out of the game when you watch it.

'Anelka was not happy after the game because he didn't score. But I was very happy with him because he's showing us, from game to game, that he's improving. His power, the holding-up of balls, bringing other players in is better. He was tremendous in the first half. With Bergkamp, him and Overmars we have such pace it's always very difficult for defenders.'

Wenger again spoke of how proud he was of the spirit and perseverance his squad had shown through the bad times a few months before. 'We never gave up. In our worst period in the championship we kept the desire to do well and to improve. We came back very slowly into this championship with some small results, some draws, and slowly back into it by winning 2–1 or 1–0. And we had many cup games. But if you look at our run since Blackburn, we had some good results in the Coca-Cola Cup and some good results in the FA Cup, and in the championship since then we have done very well. The miracle is that everybody who came in did well. And that what we've done so far is more the result of a squad than of individual players. Matthew Upson is nineteen years old. It's the first time he's played in the back four in such an important game and he does well.'

Brian Woolnough asked him to elaborate on the sense of 'joy' he had mentioned.

'It comes from confidence and it comes from early goals. Also from an acceptance of a common way to see the game and how to play it. When the players meet anybody during the week, they get told, "You have to win, you have to win." Since I've been in the job people say to me, "You have to win on Saturday." We know it. We know we have to win, but to win you have to enjoy what you do first, and to have the same approach and the same way to do things. The game is not only work. It's work because you have to do it every day, and if you don't enjoy it you cannot bring out in the game what you could feel today.'

Are you surprised it's all going so well?

'I'm never surprised to do well. My ambition is to do it. What we can say today, five games before the end, is that it is still possible. The way to do it is to try to do well at Barnsley and keep the way we played today. I think the championship in England is more difficult than anywhere else, maybe. The commitment is higher than anywhere else in the world. Listen, last night I had the choice between Cannes against Nantes on French TV and Middlesbrough against Manchester City in Division One. And after half an hour I switched to Middlesbrough–Manchester City. Because there was more passion around the field.'

I asked, 'When you won the league with Monaco, was it a home game or an away game?'

'We won the league without playing. It was the night before and our competitors lost, so we won the league without playing, with six games left to play.'

When asked if he had studied Arsenal's history, Wenger said he knew something about it but had resolved to do things his own way.

'When you're a manager you can only be efficient if you respect your own view of football. Could I go on like Arsenal played before? I just wanted to do things my way, but keep the strong points, and try to keep my own feeling of football. You must be a little bit lucky when you change things because you need to be successful. In a big club like this you must be successful because there's always a big force to push you backwards to do things like they did before. If you do things differently and you start to lose, people say to you, "Listen, my friend, let's do it like before and let's be efficient first." So the change must be very slow.'

Is Anelka enjoying it now?

'He's an introvert type. It took him some time to feel relaxed. I always was concerned. I always kept believing in him because there was a tremendous difference between what he did in training and what he did in the games. For me, it was more of a nervous problem. And he's slowly getting rid of it. He had the feeling that he doesn't play enough, and that if he plays and is not successful immediately he'll be out of the team again.'

Woolnough then asked the really important question, and this time Wenger, unusually, did a Geoff Boycott. He just played a straight bat and knocked the question firmly back down the wicket. It was a small but significant exchange.

Will it be hard to leave Anelka out now if Wright's fit?

'I'm here to solve the problems we have now. For the moment we don't have that problem.'

But Wright has to play for Arsenal to go to the World Cup?

'I think so. Usually a striker and goalkeeper are special positions. They rely a lot on confidence. If every time a striker plays and thinks he has to score or he's out of the team, I don't think you're helping him. I think Anelka will play in Sweden on Wednesday, and if he does well he has a good chance of playing in the World Cup. My interest is the club. I have only to consider Arsenal, not England. If I can combine their interests I'll do it. If Ian Wright is the best striker available at that moment he will play.'

Arsenal were now top of the table for the first time since October and needed to win just three of their last five games. Petit was interviewed on *Match of the Day* and said, 'I think against Blackburn we played our best first half. But for the moment we play good football, we are very confident, we don't lose, and we enjoy to play together. You can see it on the pitch and it's really fantastic.'

Wenger also spoke, saying that the mental attitude and focus was right but, as usual, he took nothing for granted. 'At the moment things work well. I think the integration of foreign players and the mixture between English and foreign is right at the moment. Basically, the individual attitude of every player is right inside the club, and that's why maybe they are doing so well. Because they are good players, and they respect the collective way we want to play. And that's why we are efficient.'

Dennis Bergkamp had scored twice against Barnsley at Highbury the previous October, and he produced his trademark goal at Oakwell: just outside the area, left side, minimum backlift, a right-foot shot curling round the keeper's dive and going just inside the post. It was his 22nd goal of the season. Then Overmars cut in from the left side, took Platt's pass on his body and went through to make it 2–0.

Arsenal now needed only two more wins, which made the Derby game at Highbury on 29 April a very nervous occasion. When Christian Dailly tugged Anelka's shirt in the box, he fell, the referee pointed to the spot, Bergkamp took the kick and Poom saved it. Then Bergkamp went off with a hamstring injury. The decisive moment came when Overmars tackled a defender outside the box, perhaps illegally, and the ball went loose to Petit, who smashed it low into the net for the only goal of the game.

That priceless strike set up the climactic day at Highbury the following Sunday against Everton, who were in relegation trouble and in no state to compete with Arsenal's pace, pressing and movement. The force was with Arsenal that day. Their momentum was irrepressible, elemental, tidal, unstoppable.

Wreh started the game with Anelka and the first goal arrived after just five minutes when Petit curved in another inswinging corner. Adams jumped above Bilic, who headed into his own net. Later, Petit was flattened by a two-footed tackle from Don Hutchison, and while he was down Overmars raced away to make it 2–0. The Dutch winger then scored a phenomenal and electrifying third goal, picking up the ball in the centre circle, zooming past Dave Watson and shooting low across Thomas Myhre to clinch the game and the title. Thousands of ecstatic fans jumped out of their seats and Arsène Wenger held the grinning Pat Rice in a fierce embrace. The Frenchman had finally lost his cool and grabbed his assistant in a bear hug that said: We've done it!

Then Tony Adams went galloping through on to a Bould pass and thumped the ball into the net with his left foot. For Adams the title-winning night at Anfield in 1989 had been an epic once-in-a-lifetime drama, but scoring this goal in this stadium in this game at this moment was sheer bliss – and from a pass by big, bald Bouldie. He will never forget that moment.

Wenger, calm again amid the hysteria after the match, said, 'Maybe it's the biggest satisfaction in my career until now. I'm very happy because we had a combination of exciting, entertaining football and efficiency.'

George Graham had always said that the BBC's Alan Hansen was the only pundit who ever gave Arsenal any credit. He had won titles with Liverpool and knew what it took to become champions. This time Hansen said, 'It's been a combination of English grit and determination and foreign talent. And it's bedded in together perfectly.' He then summed up Arsenal's season by saying, 'You get on a roll and you think: "Hey, we're invincible here." And I think that's what happened in the last ten league games.' Sir Alex Ferguson later admitted in his best-selling autobiography that this Arsenal charge had made them worthy champions. 'In the home stretch, they had put together a sequence of ten straight victories and only a truly special team could have done that in a league as tough as ours,' he wrote. 'They had notable quality in every department and Arsène Wenger deserves immense credit for integrating his English and foreign players into such a cohesive, powerful and highly motivated unit.'

In George Graham's 1989 and 1991 teams, some of the running power was at full-back, Winterburn and Dixon up and down the touchlines like yo-yos, putting in crosses. Now, in 1998, the running power was all in midfield and attack, and the full-backs stayed back a lot more. Now, Wenger had Patrick Vieira, a giant gladiator, partnered by Manu Petit, two technical masters of skirmishing and interception, two players who did the work of three, aided by the powerhouse breaks of the indefatigable Ray Parlour, all of them able to release a left winger who was, in effect, a striker. The first time a Petit through-ball put Overmars in for a goal we should have twigged it: Overmars was the new Ian Wright. He scored more goals than he made – sixteen in his first season in a new team – but he started his runs from different positions so we all thought he was a left winger. Or maybe, just maybe, he was a left winger the first time Premiership teams played against him, and when they played Arsenal again he had become a striker. By the time they had figured out that puzzle Overmars had added a Premiership medal to his extensive collection.

One could only wonder about Wenger's real attitude to Ian Wright now. He had not grasped the nettle straight away because Wright was still the big star, still a good goalscorer, and a comparable younger striker would have cost far more than the club could afford. But at the close of the 1997/98 season, Wenger had watched the games and studied the videos and he could see that Arsenal had become a much healthier and more efficient team without Wright. With him they were more vulnerable because games revolved around his form: Did he score? Did he miss? Did he lose the ball 29 times? His style of play was the same as ever – sometimes electrifying, often erratic.

One of the reasons Wenger had sold John Hartson was his dislike of target men. He had talked about hitting too many long balls against Leeds and he decided to remove that option and concentrate on what his team was obviously practising during the week. In football, the three principles of play are possession of the ball, supporting the ball, and penetration. The style of play Wenger created in 1997/98 emphasised the first and third principles at the expense of the second. There were not too many support runs into midfield, or into the last third, and not too many passing options, so there were few square passes. His brand of attacking football was more like fencing – full of sudden, fierce thrusts which were very well-aimed and very well-rehearsed. So it had proved hard to contain Arsenal, except by outpassing them (as Liverpool did) or outpowering them (as Blackburn did). The Blackburn trauma had been the turning point, and the return of a fit Tony Adams in mid-January was an immense stabilising influence on the rest of the season.

Petit was, we came to realise, a tremendous strategic player and it was his footballing intelligence, combined with that of Adams in defence and Bergkamp in attack, that allowed Arsenal to play the game so fast and so penetratingly. It was mostly narrow football suited to the narrow Highbury pitch, with players being supported by high-powered runs infield from Parlour and Overmars. Bergkamp already had a rapport with Overmars, and he developed a rapport with Parlour, who started to read where Bergkamp wanted the ball and where he wanted him to run. Both the 'wide' players were, in fact, narrow players, avoiding the touchlines a lot of the time, and both of them found it easy to link with Bergkamp, who was very astute in seeing where they were and where they were going. Overmars liked coming inside partly because he had smashed up his knee on a rock-hard December pitch when going outside a defender near the touchline, and Parlour liked it because he had never been a flank player anyway. In the Arsenal youth and reserve teams Parlour had always been in the middle, tackling, scrapping, winning the ball and running with it. He wanted to be in the middle of the action now, not watching it. Waiting around for a pass was not his game and never would be.

Basically, Wenger had put a new engine into an old machine. But it was the mixture of French horsepower and Dutch science that was so unique: Overmars and Bergkamp could suddenly drift into good positions to receive the ball and a lot of match-winning goals had flowed from that. Bergkamp was, with his countless assists and his sixteen league goals, better than ever, but the man who had unquestionably made the difference was Overmars.

Close study of the stats reveals this clearly. Arsenal did very badly when Marc Overmars was not playing. They missed him more than they missed Bergkamp, Adams or Vieira. No other winger in Europe could have joined Arsenal, settled into English football and scored twelve league goals to decide so many games. Dennis Bergkamp was PFA Player of the Year, and that was fully deserved, but reporters who voted for Footballer of the Year should have given that award to Overmars, not Bergkamp. His goals made the Double possible.

## THE DOUBLE

*When he leaves Arsenal, his legacy will be felt for many years. I am proud to see him so popular in England.*

Max Hild

The FA Cup Final on 16 May looked like being more an extended lap of honour for winning the title than a normal final. With or without hamstring-victim Dennis Bergkamp, Arsenal were always going to beat Newcastle, who had finished the season thirteenth and 34 points behind them.

Within a few days of the title being won chairman Peter Hill-Wood had said the club wanted to offer Wenger a five-year deal at £1 million per season, which would make him the highest-paid manager in English football. 'Arsène has done a fantastic job and we'll sit down with him after the FA Cup Final and discuss whether he wants to extend his contract. I think we would be talking about a long-term deal and I would be delighted if he signed for five years. The way I feel right now he can stay here as long as he wants. I'm sure this is just the first of many championships for him.' Petit, however, said he was convinced Wenger would accept the French national team job eventually, but hoped he would first want to win more trophies at Arsenal. 'Knowing the kind of man he is,' Petit said, 'I believe he will see this as just the start.'

Meanwhile, Wenger had ordered the team to stay focused. 'The important thing coming up to a Cup Final is to keep up the momentum, so we must keep trying,' he said. He admitted, however, that he was already planning next season's Champions League campaign. 'Even when we were walking round the pitch in front of all those happy people, my first thought was about the European Champions League,' he said. 'I know I must keep those people happy. That means taking things on another step, winning the championship again and the Champions League – an even higher challenge. You must switch that quickly. It's why this job drives you slowly crazy. You never have time to enjoy the present.'

Before the final, Wenger said he would only play one style of football and nothing else. He admitted being very dogmatic about that and even recommended that other managers should be as stubborn as he was. 'Every manager can only be successful if he gets his team to play the way that he holds deeply within himself. When I came to the club I didn't consider too much what had been the style before, although I was aware of the tradition and heritage. I knew that the only chance we had of being successful was by playing how I felt we should. That's why we played the way we played. I respect what happened before because the club was successful. But we played the kind of football we did because it was the way we could be successful. I would not change my philosophy.'

It was at times like this, with so many celebrations going on, so much publicity, so much hype around the FA Cup Final, that Wenger's focus and detachment were invaluable. He was still able to concentrate fully, and he compared himself to a racing driver. 'When you watch somebody driving a Formula One car round a Grand Prix track you ask yourself why he's not scared, how he can do it. But when you ask him, he'll tell you it's because he just concentrates on what he has to do, thinks about the next curve. When you are a football manager, it's the same. It's hard to get away from the environment around you, but you learn that you have to do it. I've got to get with the business of winning it, that's my job.

'You're a manager because you love to win. That's the only thing that lets you survive. I believe that every career is made of winning and losing. But the people who learn from losing win more than those who don't. The quality of the players and their spirit is the most important. Even if you're a winner as a manager, you won't be unless the players are winners too. As soon as it is over, I will be looking ahead. Maybe that's why my job drives me on all the time too much – I don't remember what I did five years ago. No matter what happens at Wembley, I will be looking in front for the next one.'

On the big day itself, Ray Parlour took the bull by the horns and carried the game to Newcastle with a series of powerful runs. Arsenal's pace and defensive determination were phenomenal, even if their passing, without Bergkamp, was patchy. The match as a whole demonstrated, perhaps better than any other, that Wenger's particular trip was not so much finding players with greyhound pace but building a team's entire style around pace. The Petit–Overmars connection was always vital when Bergkamp was not playing since Arsenal needed to use the pace of Overmars in runs off the ball.

Teams are accustomed to defending against dribblers, but when a dribbler makes a good run off the ball and a team-mate finds him with a forty-yard pass, the opposition defence is usually split or seriously stretched and the keeper is often exposed to a one-on-one. When a Petit pass from the halfway line found the speeding Overmars, he stabbed the ball through the legs of keeper Shay Given before tumbling over him. His pace was important, but so was the timing of his run.

Few teams have ever been less nervous, less threatened, than Arsenal were that day while holding a 1–0 lead. But Newcastle did have a good spell: a Dabizas header clipped the top of the bar and Shearer went past Adams and hit a shot against the post. One wondered, just for a moment, whether Arsenal were a one-hour team. But then Parlour found Anelka somewhere on the hairy-scary border zone between onside and offside, there was no flag and Anelka flew towards the goal like a red and white arrow, scoring with a scorching shot. At nineteen years and 63 days he was the third youngest goalscorer in an FA Cup Final.

After a long, long season Arsenal were still showing huge hunger, fierce desire and the ability to score devastating goals.

Parlour still made a burst past Pistone and slammed a shot against the outside of the post; the game was already over, but not for him. This FA Cup Final performance showed that Wenger had evolved a very, very strong concept: a ball-winning machine that feeds supercharged strikers. Power football played relentlessly with huge authority at a very high tempo.

For Wenger there had been far more satisfaction in winning the league, of course, but the FA Cup Final is one of the world's biggest matches, watched by hundreds of millions of football fans all round the world. There was one unknown and unnoticed Frenchman at Wembley who enjoyed the victory too, and that was Wenger's special guest on the big day, the 69-year-old Max Hild, who had now retired after twenty years as Strasbourg's coach and general manager. Hild had been Wenger's guru, the biggest influence on his career. A few days later the Arsenal manager said, 'He stimulated my interest in the coaching side of football. He made me think about the game and I'm delighted he was able to be at Wembley on Saturday.'

A month earlier Hild had done an interview saying that Wenger's part-German heritage had proved invaluable to him. 'Alsace used to be part of Germany and Arsène has the rigour, discipline and sense of order for which Germans are known. He has an intellectual side and has never lost his spirit of inquiry. It doesn't always serve him well though. I told a director of AC Milan that Arsène would make a first-class coach for them, and he told me, "No, he looks too much like a schoolmaster to us." It is true that Arsène is an educator by nature. His greatest joy, like mine, is to discover young talent and make sure it flowers. It was an enormous risk to take kids like Anelka and Wreh from French football so young and transplant them into the English game. But Arsène had the patience and confidence to make it work for Arsenal. Vieira, another youngster, was barely known in England, yet Arsène had the nerve to make him one of the most important elements in his team.

'There is another important factor with Arsène. I first taught him how taking care of the body meant so much. He has deepened what I taught him by widespread reading and consulting experts in sports medicine. Now he is a master of his subjects. What and when we eat and drink is vital, so is rest. How else can you explain the remarkable transformation of Ray Parlour this season? He is now a fantastic athlete and Arsène has shown him the way. You might laugh when I tell you that muscle injuries can come from not eating the right food, even from not having the proper dental care. But Arsène knows it is no joke. He brings science to the job of preparing his players. He remains what he was when I met him, a student with a passion for football.

'When he leaves Arsenal, his legacy will be felt for many years. I am proud to see him so popular in England. He has no time for hobbies. When he returns home from an Arsenal match, he replays it on video to make a more objective analysis. I used to take him fishing. It's not really his thing, but he still wanted to know every tiny detail of how it was done and how all the equipment worked.'

Just for a few days, though, Wenger had earned the right to take it easy and bask in the glory of a well-deserved Premiership and FA Cup double.

# 6. 1998/99: THE SEASON OF ANELKA

Football clubs are driven by ambition, tradition and rivalry, so for each club there is deep meaning in beating certain other clubs. At the start of the 1998/99 season Arsenal were Double-winning champions, they had thumped Manchester United 3–0 in the Charity Shield with goals from Overmars, Wreh and Anelka, and the players felt that they could now win the Champions League before United won it. That motivated them more than anything else. It was a huge incentive.

During the close season Wenger had sold Ian Wright to West Ham for £750,000, thereby placing a huge amount of faith and trust in a relative novice with greyhound pace and great potential. David Platt had retired. New signings included Argentina's World Cup right-back Nelson Vivas from Lugano in Switzerland for £1.6 million and teenage left-back David Grondin from St Etienne for £500,000. Wenger had also made a bid for midfielder Ronald de Boer, who said, 'Arsenal have made a low bid but of course they are going to make a low bid. They are not going to show all their cards at the start. I am going to leave Ajax, that's for sure, and I know Arsenal are very interested and I would like to play there. It's a nice club, nice management, and it is very well organised.'

Although the new season offered the stimulating challenge of the enlarged Champions League, it was business as usual first in the Premiership. Arsenal beat newly promoted Nottingham Forest at Highbury in their first game on 17 August, then drew their next three games 0–0, against Liverpool, Charlton and Chelsea. Liverpool were being co-managed by Roy Evans and Wenger's friend Gerard Houllier, whom he had advised to go to Liverpool. Clearly there was a lack of executive bottle at Liverpool, where Evans did not command the respect of a group of scallywags who were under-achieving every season. The 1996 FA Cup Final had made it clear that the culture at the club was decadent. Both finalists had hosted press days at their training grounds before Wembley. At the

Liverpool press day the players had larked around, while the Manchester United players had taken their media duties seriously and given sensible interviews. Journalists who went to both events did not give Liverpool a prayer, especially when they saw the cream Armani suits that Ruddock, McManaman and company were wearing on the big day. United had won 1–0 with a goal by Eric Cantona, and half an hour later some of the so-called Spice Boys had been seen laughing in the banqueting hall. Roy Evans had kept his job for the next two years, and now, incredibly, Houllier, a former manager of the French national team, was being asked to share the reins.

After the Liverpool game on 22 August, Wenger said, 'Those who played in the World Cup Finals are not yet sharp, so this was a point gained. We could have scored early on and late on, but we didn't and that is why we lost two points.' He was referring to missed chances by Parlour and Bergkamp.

## THE 1998 AGM

*It's always a bit of a struggle between tradition and innovation. Tradition is what I would like to keep here. The very strong spirit of the English players.*

Arsène Wenger

The 1998 AGM turned out to be a love-in starring Arsène Wenger and a spectacular collection of glittering silverware. On display from around 11a.m as shareholders gathered for the usual noon kick-off, set against a wall of scarlet baize, were seven trophies: the Premiership, the FA Cup, the Charity Shield, the FA Premiership Youth League, the Southern Junior Floodlit Cup, the Women's FA Challenge Cup and the Women's League Cup. Grinning shareholders posed in front of the cups while friends took photographs.

The event inside the North Bank Stand was slickly stage-managed. Hundreds of gold-painted chairs were arranged in rows with a central aisle leading to the altar, to make it feel like a place of worship, a cathedral. There were TV monitors every ten yards down the hall, and audio monitors so that everyone could see and hear clearly. David Dein, one of football's most energetic yuppies, was obviously determined to send out all the right signals: success, prosperity, enjoyment, technology. Yet, alongside that, Arsenal still seemed like an old gentlemen's club because it was fronted by chairman Peter Hill-Wood.

At noon the directors walked in to loud applause and cheers – what a buzz for the hero-executives! It was astonishing stuff for a formal shareholders meeting. AGM veterans said it had never happened before. The eight men, mostly wearing black or navy suits, sat down: Danny Fiszman on the left, then Arsène Wenger, Ken Friar (as usual at the chairman's right hand), Peter Hill-Wood, Dein, the Carr brothers and David Miles.

Back in 1995, when the directors came out after George Graham had been sacked just five months before, they looked as if they were about to face a firing squad. Hill-Wood, fidgeting nervously, said the club's lawyers had instructed him not to talk about Graham because it was sub judice, which caused great disgust and unrest in the room because no one believed that the Graham sacking, which did not go to court, could be sub judice at that stage. At the 1996 AGM, just a few weeks after Rioch had been dumped four days before the first league game against West Ham, the flak had started flying immediately. Now, backed by so many glittering trophies, the directors knew that 1998 was as good as it would ever get. Still, they could not have expected to be cheered on to the platform.

Hill-Wood, standing while the others were seated, whizzed through the formal business in about five minutes: acceptance of the accounts, the reappointment of auditors Kidsons Impey, the welcome to new company secretary David Miles and the re-election of directors. It was a case of 'Carried unanimously, thank you!' every time. Hill-Wood is likeable because he does not come over like a high-powered executive. He is old money, a banker who loves a gin and tonic, a trustworthy custodian of a deeply loved sporting institution. He never pretends to have all the answers at his fingertips, which is part of his charm. When closely quizzed by shareholders on a particular point, he will often get the answer from Ken Friar.

'It's a pleasure to be standing in front of the silver vaults,' said Hill-Wood. 'I think it's unlikely that any of us will see this again, so you'd better feast your eyes on it!'

The shareholders who spoke were mostly educated middle-class men, and they spoke well. But none gave his name.

One said, 'When will the stadium issue be resolved?'

'I wish I knew,' replied the chairman. 'The preferred route, as I think you all know, is to stay here.'

Another shareholder said, 'I may be old-fashioned, but I'd like to say that the manager is the most important employee of any football club, and it does concern me when I read in the press that at a number of clubs players are actually paid more than the manager. I'm absolutely appalled by this. I wonder whether you can assure me that Mr Wenger is the highest-paid employee of this football club? I certainly feel he ought to be. If he's not, why?'

Before Hill-Wood could reply to this, Wenger made a gracious, open-handed gesture towards the speaker and said, 'My agent!' People laughed loudly. Indeed, they laughed so loudly that the seriousness of the question, and the answer, became almost irrelevant.

'From the board's point of view,' Hill-Wood began, 'we believe that Mr Wenger is reasonably well paid, and he has committed himself to us for a further period of time. And I think he is satisfied with the salary. I agree with you. The most important task for the board of directors, in my view, is to appoint the best manager. I think we can genuinely say that we got something right.'

There was then a question about the Ticket Registration Scheme from a man who was registered, had got a ticket for the FA Cup Final but had not got one for the Manchester United game. Ken Friar explained the arithmetic: Highbury holds 38,000, there are over 20,000 season tickets, and 6,000 tickets had to be given to Manchester United fans. That left only 12,000 seats, but there are 15,000 fans on the registration scheme. The ground is simply not big enough.

One shareholder picked up on this and asked, 'Mr Chairman, there were reports that you made a bid for Wembley Stadium. Were they true? If it was made, can you give shareholders an indication of how it would have been financed?'

Hill-Wood replied, 'Yes, we did make a very genuine offer for Wembley. This was made up of a number of ingredients. There was a substantial cash payment that would have come from the bank, and through a method of securitisation, if you understand that term. Securitisation is where you sell up front a known stream of future income. So that was one method. We would have had to issue some more shares, which we would have done. And the balance was made up of delayed payments which were guaranteed but which were paid over a period of three or four years.'

Someone else then said, 'I'd like to ask Mr Wenger a question if I may. One of the biggest financial gains in the last year was the way he acquired Nicolas Anelka from Paris Saint Germain for a minimal fee. He's obviously worth a lot more money now. We are now spending a lot of money on our youth team and our youth development system. How are we going to stop people doing to us what Mr Wenger did to Paris Saint Germain? Secondly, I've read in the press over the summer that we have tried to buy various strikers. Could he tell me which ones he tried to buy and which stories were rubbish? And are there any plans to buy a striker before Christmas, in time for the second half of the Champions League?'

Hill-Wood turned to Wenger. 'Would you like to answer that now or later?' Wenger said, 'I can answer now.' There was loud applause. 'You know that, concerning Nicolas Anelka, there is a European rule that stipulates that football is a job like anything else, and if you are at the end of a contract, whether you are 18 or 20 or 24, you can move to a different country. That's why Nicolas Anelka was free. It's exactly the same for players who are eighteen and at the end of a contract. That means they could move to France. So you just try to compete financially. At the time I was told Nicolas was unhappy. He wanted to leave Paris; he would have gone to Madrid or Barcelona. That means they had lost their player. And maybe because I was French he came and became one of our players. We have no protection for our players going abroad if they are not under contract.

'Concerning the transfer market in the summer. When I arrived here two years ago we had a fairly good team, but we needed some younger players to rebuild the team. After four or five months of observation I came to the conclusion that it was not possible to improve the team by buying English players, just because the best young players were at Manchester United or Liverpool, so we had to go abroad to buy the players. I think we did reasonably well getting the players at what I believe was a reasonable price last season. We won trophies and we went into the market again. My first idea was to buy English because I still think it's very important for a club like Arsenal to have a British spirit, and to keep the basis of the English players and the spirit of the English players. And that's what we spoke about.

'It's always a bit of a struggle between tradition and innovation. Tradition is what I would like to keep here. The very strong spirit of the English players. I would say that innovation is to bring in some players who can bring different qualities and that's why, maybe, we were successful last season – because the mixture was right. My first target was stability. That means my first target, in the middle of the season, was to keep the players we had. Because, like you said, Anelka, Overmars, Petit, Vieira, Christopher Wreh, they're all young, they're all between 20 and 25. And the only way to protect yourself from the Bosman rule is to get them on long contracts. And today I'm very happy because we have a good team, and we have all our young players on long-term contracts, at least five to six years. That means we have good protection concerning the value of our team.

'Of course when I say stability I didn't imagine that Ian Wright would want to leave. But I knew he was close, one or two years away from his end, and that we had to buy a striker. And that it would be difficult for him to sit on the bench and not play. The second thing was that David Platt stopped, and that was very late. It happened on 7 July. So when he stopped his career we were in a situation on 8 July where we had to find some new players. Ian Wright, it happened just before the end of the World Cup. He signed for West Ham on 12 or 13 July, so it was late too. We went for strikers, most of them were foreign strikers. None of them was for me at the right value. The second problem we had was that I couldn't imagine bringing in a player who has achieved nothing, and he's better paid than the players who have achieved the Double.'

Wenger was interrupted by loud applause at this point.

'Unfortunately, we didn't make some deals because of that. When you phone up and you're Arsenal, the price of course is very high. But mainly we didn't want to go over the wages we have at the moment. I didn't want to destroy the spirit. So at the moment we are still in the market. I still think we are short and that we need to buy two players. We need to buy one striker, but it has to be the right one. And maybe one midfielder, a creative midfielder because we have so many games to play, and so many targets this season. We want to be the best. The competition is very hard but as long as we keep our quality we can do it.'

Wenger was then asked why he had sold Isaiah Rankin, a reserve striker who had gone to Bradford City for £1.3 million.

'Because he had in front of him too many players who were in a position to play in the top team. He was impatient. I thought that he wouldn't naturally make it this season, and he needed some first-team games. He was one of the players where if you keep him, he drops; if he drops, his value goes down and he isn't happy and he hasn't improved. If you are sure that he won't play for you this season, you give him a chance to make a career somewhere. If he makes a good career somewhere else, I'm very happy for him.'

This was applauded too.

One shareholder then mentioned his new contract: 'Mr Hill-Wood said ten minutes ago that you have committed yourself to the club.'

Hill-Wood replied for his manager. 'Mr Wenger has committed himself to a further four years.'

This bit of news brought deafening applause.

'Mr Chairman,' said another shareholder, 'to administer even the mildest of rebukes to a man who is responsible for the monumental achievement of winning a Double in his first full year as a manager would be churlish in the extreme. However, that said, might I respectfully remind those responsible for running the club that the almost equally great achievements under George Graham, of winning the championship in 1989 and 1991, were both followed by a year of under-achievement, due in large part to a failure to strengthen the squad.'

Hill-Wood said simply, 'I hear what you're saying.'

The next shareholder said, 'Mr Chairman, coming along today, with my wife, she said, "What's it gonna be like today?" I said, "It's gonna be wonderful, it's gonna be a party, we'll be rolling around in the aisles." I first supported Arsenal in 1941, I've supported them ever since and I've never seen an array of silver like that. So why don't we have a dance in the aisles and celebrate?'

This unexpected suggestion brought cheers and more loud applause. There were a couple more questions, and then the feel-good festival was over. The tribe had convened, had heard words of wisdom from the big chiefs, and now they just wanted Mr Wenger's autograph. The 1998 AGM had been a small triumph of magic theatre, a conjuring trick by directors who had come out to parade in front of a dazzling, blinding collection of trophies. Most proud winners stand behind their silverware, but the Arsenal board sat in front of them and simply disappeared. It was quite clever. None of us would ever see eight men hiding in front of seven trophies again.

## LENS, KIEV AND PANATHINAIKOS

*Panathinaikos played much better at Wembley than they did in Athens. In fact every team that has come to Wembley to face us has lifted their game because every team loves to play there.*

Arsène Wenger

Arsenal recorded their fourth draw in a row at Leicester on 12 September, then turned their focus on the club's first ever Champions League game, to be played in the Stade Felix Bollaert in Lens where, less than three months earlier, England had beaten Colombia 2–0 in a World Cup group match. The Gunners played excellent football on the night but were let down by their lack of punch in front of goal. Bergkamp and Anelka missed five or six good chances and an Overmars strike in the 51st minute was not enough to win the game. Wenger took Bergkamp off near the end and put on Garde, an extra defender, but Smicer's corner was flicked on at the near post and Vareilles equalised in the 90th minute. The body language of Tony Adams suggested that he thought the goal was a mistake by Seaman. It was a disappointing start to the European campaign.

Arsenal showed their true ability in the next game that Sunday, turning on the style against Manchester United at Highbury and staging a rerun of the Charity Shield. When Beckham hit the target with a fierce free-kick which any other keeper would have tipped over, Seaman just held the ball nonchalantly above his head. Then Hughes flighted a free-kick perfectly and Adams got there ahead of Schmeichel to head into the net. And when Overmars released Anelka just before half-time Schmeichel saved his first shot, but he buried the rebound for 2–0.

Referee Graham Barber then sent off Nicky Butt for fouling Vieira on the edge of the box, even though he was not the last man, and when Beckham bottled a fifty-fifty with Winterburn, vanishing in a puff of smoke, the Clock End began to sing, 'Can we play you every week?' Designer Dennis was shaping the game freely now, slowing it down, speeding it up, slipping Anelka in, making moves that were triangular, rectangular, spherical, cylindrical, any shape you wanted, while Overmars toyed with Neville and Berg. At one point the crowd gave Vieira a standing ovation when he chased back into defence, mopped up and cruised away with the ball. New signing Freddie Ljungberg, who had recently impressed playing for Sweden against England, then made his home debut. He came on for Anelka after 79 minutes and scored his first goal from a pass by Bergkamp, lobbing the ball neatly over Schmeichel. Small, energetic, brave, resourceful and versatile, Ljungberg looked a steal at £3 million.

Alex Ferguson admitted afterwards, 'Arsenal were far better than us. Wanted to win it far more than we did. And I don't like saying that as manager of Manchester United. They were prepared to give fouls away to win the match. We were tiptoeing into tackles.' Wenger said, 'It reminded me a little bit of the Everton day when we won the title.'

The following Saturday Sheffield Wednesday beat Arsenal 1–0 at Hillsborough in a game notorious for Paolo Di Canio's push on referee Paul Alcock and a Martin Keown red card, which was later rescinded. There was also a tunnel incident involving Patrick Vieira, who was later fined £20,000 by the FA .

Wenger was trying to sign Nwankwo Kanu, on loan from Inter Milan until the end of the season. Kanu was 22 but had already had an astonishingly dramatic career, having been discovered at an under-17 World Youth tournament in Japan in 1993, when he scored six goals and was voted player of the tournament. Nigeria's plane had to overnight in Amsterdam after the competition and Ajax officials met Kanu at the airport and signed him. He played with Marc Overmars, who became his friend and gave him lifts, since he was too young to drive. Kanu won three Dutch titles with Ajax and played in the 1995 Champions League Final, coming on as a substitute against Milan in Vienna on a night when the other sub, Patrick Kluivert, scored the only goal of the game. A year later he captained Nigeria in the Olympics in Atlanta, when Nigeria beat Brazil and Argentina to win the gold medal.

He was signed by Inter for £1.3 million that summer, but a heart valve defect was detected and Inter president Massimo Moratti paid for him to be flown to a Cleveland clinic where he had pioneering surgery. He recuperated in California, but when he returned to Inter the club had changed its style, coach Gigi Simoni preferring to play defensive football with Ronaldo and Zamorano up front. Kanu hated defensive football, and although Moratti pleaded his case with Simoni, he had played only one game in the 1997/98 season and wanted a move. It seemed a huge gamble by Wenger.

Remi Garde deputised for Parlour for the Panathinaikos game at Wembley on 30 September, but looked apprehensive. It was the biggest game of his career. The game featured about twenty minutes of sparring – a couple of punches were landed, but there were no knockdowns – and after an hour one wondered whether Arsenal would be the first ever Champions League club to draw all six games. Then the keeper spilt a corner and Adams rammed it in for 1–0. Soon after, Keown headed in a Petit corner for 2–0. Anelka starred in some breathtakingly fast counter-attacks after that, but the Greeks got a goal back when Asanovic hit a free-kick which deflected to Maud, who headed in from five yards.

The next European game was Dynamo Kiev at Wembley on 21 October. For Wenger, it was exciting to pit wits with a legendary coach like Valeri Lobanovsky, who had created Kiev's wonderfully cerebral teamwork by using the same system for thirty years. He regarded it as one of the most interesting matches of his entire career, and if Arsenal could beat Kiev at Wembley it would be something of a quantum leap forward for the club. It would change the way Europe saw Arsenal. It would change the way Arsenal saw themselves. And it might even change the way Wenger saw Arsenal. But he knew that Kiev were one of the best eight teams in Europe, and he knew he would be facing them without Vieira and Petit, who were suspended.

On the night, Kiev were temperamentally as well as tactically disciplined. They defended deep and cleverly, and rarely fouled except in the last third to prevent a shot or killer pass. Their defenders were very cute at pushing up to narrow angles to pinch the ball or catch a striker offside, and their shape was so good that you did not notice how much running they did. They broke using two or three passes, often one-touch passes, and the whole team just rolled along with automatic movement into the right spaces.

Shevchenko, a slim powerhouse, took only four minutes to rob Overmars, zoom infield and attempt a shot. Early in the second half he smashed a dipper just past the base of the post. Then he took off on a preposterous run from the halfway line, nutmegged Adams, and forced Seaman to come out to him. Later on he chased Keown and shoulder-charged him off the ball, something you never see.

As Arsenal huffed and puffed against a mass of white shirts, who often nicked the ball and broke at awesome pace, Wenger could see that Kiev were the better side. But the better side does not always win. Shevchenko played a one-two with Bialkevich, went through and buried his shot, but the goal was disallowed – wrongly, as replays showed. Within sixty seconds of that, something remarkable happened: Lee Dixon outpaced Rebrov on the right, hit a superb cross to the near post and Bergkamp scored with a diving header from eight yards. One-nil to the Arsenal!

Anelka was still too immature to be a match-winner in the Champions League. He had been shooting from thirty yards, standing around in offside positions and overhitting passes, so

Wenger took him off, brought on Nelson Vivas and moved Overmars forward. When Overmars rounded keeper Shovkovsky, Luzhny managed to kick the ball off the line.

Arsenal's front six had been poor, apart from Parlour, but it looked as if their defence and a bit of luck had won the game – until the last minute of normal time when Bialkevich put the ball across the box and Rebrov equalised. There was no flag and the goal stood. In Lens, Wenger had taken a striker off when Arsenal were winning 1–0 and they had conceded a late goal. The same thing had happened again.

At an unusually chaotic press conference, Wenger said, 'I've heard their first goal was onside but the second was not regular.' On the Bergkamp goal, right after the disallowed goal, he said, 'You can never say when you score a great goal that it's unfair.'

Kiev were clearly the superior team. They had more skill, more possession, more shots, more corners and fewer fouls. They had smothered Overmars and outnumbered Arsenal in every part of the field; it was always four against three, three against two, two against one. And their two strikers, Andrei Shevchenko and Sergei Rebrov, were world class. The brave, dynamic little Rebrov, an ethnic Russian who had chosen to play for the land of his birth, Ukraine, was the scorer of so many late goals that the fans called him 'the Rescuer', while Shevchenko, a phenomenal footballer with a big engine, had proved to be bold, fast, creative, direct and as greedy as great goalscorers usually are.

Arsenal travelled to Kiev on 4 November for the return match without Bergkamp, Overmars and Adams. They were never going to win the tie, especially since Kiev, amazingly, had to win to stay in the competition. Anelka had also dropped out with a septic toe, but this made little difference, given his form in the first game. The side was: Seaman; Dixon, Keown, Bould, Winterburn; Parlour, Vieira, Petit, Vivas; Boa Morte, Wreh. Hughes and Grimandi were on the bench. Wenger was bluffing three positions, the two strikers and Vivas, but he watched a brave eight-man performance in which Petit, Vieira, Parlour, Dixon and Winterburn strove commendably.

The turning point came when Keown was outpaced and mugged by Rebrov. He should have put both hands in the air and let him go, but he allowed his shin to clip Rebrov's heel. Rebrov, of course, went down, then got up to score the penalty. Vivas had passed to Kiev players with uncanny regularity throughout the first half and was the man beaten when Golovko made it 2–0, and then he tripped Bialkevich when he was going nowhere and gave away a free-kick. Shevchenko was always going to hit a right-footed shot round the wall, so Seaman should have had a four-man wall with a big, brave man on the end, like Vieira. Instead he had a three-man wall with little Vivas, who ducked, and the ball flashed into the net for 3–0. Hughes, as sub, got a goal back late on.

Arsène Wenger was two strikers short. It was that simple. He went into the Champions League with only one proven striker, Bergkamp, who did not fly, and one exceptional novice, Anelka, so he was always going to be one injury away from trouble. With this strike force supplemented only by Overmars, Arsenal were struggling. It looked as if Wenger, a risk-taker when it comes to the development of players, was determined to turn Anelka into another George Weah. He was gambling that Anelka could learn enough in the first 25 games of the season to become a star in the second 25 games. The best way for him to learn quickly was to play every game. If he was in and out of the team he would learn slowly because he would be taking one step forward and one step backwards all the time. In 1997/98 Overmars had taken the pressure off Bergkamp, and so had Wright, but now, with Wright gone and Overmars more of a known quantity, the pressure was on Bergkamp again. He had to nurse Anelka, score more goals himself, and in a post-World Cup season that was asking too much. Wenger knew his strike force was threadbare, and he must have dreaded the situation that arose in Kiev. He should have signed two strikers to replace Wright and Hartson, but maybe he did not have enough money or could not get the players he wanted.

The Lens game at Wembley on 25 November turned out to be his biggest disappointment of 1998. Arsenal lost the game 1–0 because Petit was suspended and Bergkamp and Vieira had been injured the previous Saturday against Wimbledon. As a consequence, Arsenal lacked power and confidence. Adams was also a casualty: he had been playing with pain-killing injections but he was in agony and did not come out for the second half.

The team had overcome the absence of key players before and become champions, but this game, against a resourceful young French team, was a bridge too far. They missed four good chances and were outplayed overall. The 8,000 fans from Lens lit up the night in their orange and yellow colours, standing throughout the game, pogoing in unison, clapping rhythmically, singing lustily and having a high old time behind the goal. They were rewarded after 72 minutes when Smicer cleverly beat Dixon on the right and crossed low to the far post, where Debeve scored from three yards. The Arsenal defence had done their job but the linesman had not – Debeve was offside. England's champions were on their way out of the so-called Champions League with only one win in their first five games.

Two players were sent off in injury time by Swedish referee Anders Fisk. Parlour tried a one-two with Vivas, Rool obstructed him and Parlour lashed out, kicking the Frenchman in the chest. Then Dixon tangled with Vareilles, fell over and got Vareilles sent off. UEFA reviewed footage and suspended Dixon, which meant he would miss Arsenal's first European game the following season. It was very, very unusual for Ray Parlour to kick a player off the ball, even when provoked, and virtually unprecedented to see Lee Dixon feign injury. Those two incidents showed the pressure, the rage, the frustration, the intense disappointment which all the players felt, and which Wenger also felt. The Gunners had been outplayed by a lively, spirited small-town club from France. The second half, in particular, was abysmal. Had we ever seen an Arsenal team play with less belief?

Still, Wenger knew that the Champions League, like everything else in football, is a learning curve. No club wins it without being in the quarter-final or semi-final the year before. The competition is a very awkward, testing series of games against variously talented opponents in various cities in various weather conditions. You hope to start in phase one in your first year, progress to phase two a year later, then try to get into the quarters and semis. That process takes three or four years.

Managers suffer when the goals dry up and Wenger was suffering now. By the end of the Lens game, his attack had kept four clean sheets in a row. He had fielded a reserve team against Chelsea at Highbury in the Worthington Cup on 11 November and been hammered 5–0. Then came a goalless draw with Tottenham at Highbury and a 1–0 defeat away to Wimbledon. Overmars had now gone eleven games without a goal.

On the Friday after the Lens game Wenger told the Sunday reporters, 'My job is not to show anger or frustration, but to arrive at a logical analysis of what happened and try to work out why. There is no normal reaction any more in football. When you lose, it is always too negative. When you win, too positive. I try to give small problems small importance and the right importance to the right problems.' He insisted he had known all along that November could be a difficult month because Petit, Vieira, Bergkamp and Overmars had all been involved late into the World Cup. For those players, the problem was partly psychological. 'If you are winning games, you don't think you are tired. You feel well. But if you lose, you're tired – even if you do everything right physically.' He then admitted he felt guilty about the Champions League failure. 'I try to think, "What did I do wrong?"'

Wenger stepped up his efforts to sign Kanu, who was said to be demanding a £900,000 loyalty payment from Inter, who in turn wanted a 'buy back' clause in his Arsenal contract. Wenger naturally refused to give Inter that option. He was taking a calculated risk, but if it paid off and Kanu proved to be a match-winner in the Premiership, he did not want anybody else to benefit.

The bitter disappointment after crashing out of the Champions League so early proved hard to shake off, and performances dipped after the Lens defeat. So far in the Premiership Arsenal had played fourteen, won six, drawn six and lost two. At home to Middlesbrough on Sunday, 29 November, they conceded a goal to Brian Deane inside six minutes, and when Boa Morte came on for Wreh he was booed on to the field. Rarely, if ever, had an Arsenal substitute been booed on to the field. The crowd, unlike the Spurs crowd, was well known for being patient and forgiving with young players, but the team had so obviously run out of ideas and performances that ninety minutes was beginning to seem like three hours. When Lee Dixon hit a shot over the bar from thirty yards, the fans booed again. Somebody said, 'Hill-Wood's just walked out in disgust!' – presumably disgusted with the supporters' reaction, not with Dixon's shot. Middlesbrough brought eleven players back to defend, the crowd lapsed into nostalgia by chanting 'Ian Wright, Wright, Wright!', then, in the final minute, Anelka equalised, slamming in a shot off the underside of the bar. An agonising day for Wenger, but the late goal had at least earned a point.

December started with a 0–0 at Derby, followed by a surprise 3–1 win in Athens in the dead Champions League game against Panathinaikos, for which Wenger fielded a very young team which included teenagers Paolo Vernazza, David Grondin and Matthew Upson. The Greeks had four chances in the first half, but the four goals were scored in the last half hour, three of them by Mendez, Anelka and Boa Morte. Wenger said that Wembley had motivated their three opponents and that this was a factor the club had underestimated. 'Panathinaikos played much better at Wembley than they did in Athens. In fact every team that has come to Wembley to face us has lifted their game because every team loves to play there. What is disappointing to me is that we know now we could easily have won this group and gone through to the quarter-finals. But we dropped four points by conceding a last-minute equaliser in Lens right at the start of the competition, and another against Dynamo Kiev at Wembley. We were also beaten by an offside goal by Lens.' His biggest regret was that Arsenal had failed to win that first game in Lens. 'We learnt that in these games you get very few chances, and if you don't take them, you don't win.'

Since the directors had felt some guilt about inconveniencing their most loyal supporters by asking them to travel to another stadium in another part of London to watch their team, they had sold thousands of tickets at only £10 each. The *Daily Telegraph*'s John Ley did a piece pointing out that crowds of 73,000 had brought receipts in the region of £800,000 per game; failing to qualify for the next phase of the Champions League, however, had cost the club at least £5 million.

## FERGUSON CALLS ARSENAL 'BELLIGERENT'

*Gerard is an open-minded and passionate man. I am the opposite: stubborn and stupid. But sometimes stupid behaviour makes you win.*

Arsène Wenger

When Dennis Bergkamp scored twice at Aston Villa on 13 December and Arsenal went in at half-time 2–0 up, Wenger must have thought his team had turned the corner at last. But then Dion Dublin turned the game upside down and Arsenal walked off 3–2 losers. Wenger had always maintained that you needed experienced players, especially when results were not going well, and it was two of those, Bergkamp and Overmars, who did a lot to help Arsenal get their season back on track over the next few weeks.

Reports now stated that Real Madrid wanted Wenger to replace their Dutch coach Guus Hiddink. The papers made much of the fact that Wenger had so far failed to sign a four-year extension to his contract which would keep him at Arsenal until 2002, but he insisted that this was a minor matter. 'I've told everyone many times that my word is my signature, and it's been that way for the twenty years I've worked in football.' He said the contract discussions were about 'small, small details' which would be agreed within a week or so.

Early in the Leeds game at Highbury, five days before Christmas, Wenger might well have begun to fancy the Real Madrid job when Anelka crossed from the right wing. The cross went past everyone in the goalmouth to Bergkamp at the far post, but the ball went right under his left foot. Wenger had seen balls go past Bergkamp, go beyond him, go behind him, go over his head, but he only saw the ball go under his foot once every two years, if that. Was this going to be another one of those days? Wenger had suffered far too many of those days lately – Wimbledon, Lens, Middlesbrough and Derby were the kind of days he wanted to forget. He sat there watching his team play without rhythm and fluidity for 28 minutes. Then Anelka flicked on, Bergkamp was one-on-one, and he poked the ball in for 1–0.

Leeds had certainly been the better team until the goal, but now Arsenal hit a groove. Overmars skipped easily past Halle and crossed for Anelka, who shot wide; Bergkamp put Petit through but his flick went over the bar. Early in the second half a slick move ended with a terrific left-foot shot by Vieira for 2–0, Hasselbaink replied with a cannonball, perhaps the hardest shot to go past David Seaman since Juan Esnaider's thunderbolt in the 1995 Cup Winners Cup Final, and finally Petit made it 3–1. Wenger had at last seen his team play as he thought they should play.

When West Ham came to Highbury on Boxing Day they made Ian Wright captain against his old club – and this seemed to inspire Anelka. We had never seen him in this mood. He was hyper-aggressive and super-confident, playing with real venom and tremendous two-footed skill. For once, everything about him was right. His body language screamed a simple message: Give me the ball and I'll score! Overmars made it 1–0 after eight minutes and Anelka was so compelling he seemed certain to make it 2–0. Why was he suddenly playing like this? To show Ian Wright who was the main man? But then Anelka picked up an injury, which was rare for him. Physio Gary Lewin went on to treat the ankle, but it was serious enough for him to have to leave the field after half an hour.

There was no further score, and afterwards Wenger was full of praise for Petit. 'He brings a balance. He knows when to drop back and he's the one who can find Nicolas and Marc. He sees openings very well. He can run for hours, he's a winner, he's an ambitious guy – and he's very consistent. The World Cup gave him more confidence.'

It was true that Petit had been phenomenally consistent for a long time. He had had a great year in 1998, and then he sustained it. He had taken his Arsenal form into the World Cup squad, earned a regular place in the team, scored in the final against Brazil, come back to London as a world champion, and, unlike others in France's team, taken his World Cup form into the new season and carried on playing brilliantly for Arsenal. At his old club, Monaco, Thierry Henry and David Trezeguet had barely bothered to raise a leg.

Two days later Patrick Vieira was sent off at Charlton and the newspapers had another field day about Arsenal's disciplinary record – which, admittedly, was unique. This was their eighteenth red card since Wenger's arrival 27 months earlier. More disturbingly, it was their fifth red card of the 1998/99 season, and it was only just after Christmas. On average, Arsenal were having a player sent off once a month.

Referee Uriah Rennie had made himself the star of the game by issuing seven yellows, Charlton's five cautions including one for Eddie Youds, who should have been sent off for a violent tackle from behind on Bergkamp which ended the Dutchman's participation in the match before half-time. Six minutes into the second half Vieira was looking to run away from Neil Redfearn when he impeded him, so he swung his arm back and caught Redfearn on the shoulder. Rennie sent him off. Three minutes later Mark Kinsella felled Parlour in the box and Overmars scored from the spot. Arsenal held on for a 1–0 win.

In the FA Cup third round on 4 January 1999, Arsenal were drawn away at Preston and Manchester United played Middlesbrough. Alex Ferguson met four Sunday reporters for an interview on the day after his 57th birthday and took the opportunity to make some very rude remarks about his nearest championship rivals. He talked about Arsenal's 'belligerent' style of play, saying that some Arsenal players liked 'a scrap'. He added, 'When they're not doing well in a game, they turn it into a battle to try to make the opposition lose concentration. The number of fights involving Arsenal is more than Wimbledon had in their heyday.'

Arsenal went 2–0 down at Preston, but then came back to win 4–2 with goals from Boa Morte, Petit (two) and Overmars. After the game Wenger described Ferguson's attack as 'clumsy' and said that every Premiership team should respect the others. 'We always try to play football,' he said. 'You do not win championships and cups by fighting. We respect every team and let the referees do their job on the field. I think we have to give a good image to the game, and it starts by respecting every other team. What he said does not bother me at all and I do not want to make a fuss about it. I think it was just a little bit clumsy on his part.'

Wenger admitted that Preston had dominated the early stages and said that the match had been close. 'Preston played like world champions for the first twenty minutes. They were quicker and more aggressive than us. It was like a poker game for them. They gave it everything early on and gambled on getting a lead they might be able to maintain. If they had got three they might have done it because I could not see us scoring. We came very close to making our exit tonight. We were two goals down by the time we woke up. And then I thought it might be one of those nights when their goalkeeper was the hero.'

Meanwhile, Alex Ferguson was telling reporters that he had sent a letter of apology to Wenger. 'Arsène Wenger has a right to be annoyed over this matter. I have already dropped him a note explaining the situation and I offered him the apology he deserved. It is not my policy to criticise teams and the way they play. People go on about it all being psychological warfare, but that is far from the truth on this occasion. I was stitched up and feel I have been betrayed.'

The matter did not rest there. Joe Lovejoy followed up his original piece in *The Sunday Times* a week later by strongly denying that Ferguson had been 'stitched up'. He said that the Manchester-based reporters were frightened of Ferguson and treated his quotes like tablets of stone. He noted that Ferguson had named biased referees, grasping agents and one player who was 'the biggest cheat in football'. Many Premiership managers talk off the record in this way, but Wenger never does so he never creates the opportunity for such misunderstandings to arise. Lovejoy made the point that, had he chosen to report Ferguson's remarks in full, the United boss 'would have been in serious trouble with m'learned friends'.

Wenger had always talked in a measured manner on every subject that came up in football, but the one topic that infuriated him (and still does) was systematic fouling against his players. When Vieira used an arm to free himself from the attentions of Charlton's Neil Redfearn, he had been sent off. The manager, as usual, defended his man vigorously, but this time he did it in a more emphatic way than ever before. He called Redfearn 'a cheat'. 'Do you know which player has committed more fouls than anybody else in the Premiership this season? I'll tell you who – Neil Redfearn. The people who sponsor the Premiership compile statistics on these things and his record is the worst. Just imagine what people would be saying now if that was an Arsenal player. And Dennis Bergkamp has spent ten days on the treatment table because of a dreadful tackle by another Charlton player. But again we never hear anything about that.'

Charlton boss Alan Curbishley joined the verbal war, and then the FA became involved through their new 'compliance officer' Graham Bean who said that the 'undignified squabble' must stop or misconduct charges could follow. Wenger said, 'I had a phone call from Graham Bean. I was surprised. I am surprised by the kind of job he is supposed to do. After the incident involving Patrick I was asked a question and I just said Redfearn was a cheat on that occasion. I just gave my opinion. He can call me fifty times and I don't know why I should change that view. We live in a democracy and Alan Curbishley has every right to have a different opinion. It doesn't change my respect for him. I didn't feel that, at any time, I attacked him or Charlton. At first you are surprised at all the attention. After that you wonder if you are right or not, then you get fed up with it and after that you ignore it. That is the stage we are at now.' Wenger said there was a danger that managers could lose freedom of speech. 'I can accept that sometimes some managers are fed up with Arsenal. You don't expect to say we are the greatest and the best all the time. I don't ignore critics. I think criticism is right sometimes, but I should be able to say what I believe is right. I don't know how Mr Bean can stop me saying what I believe is right unless he puts me in jail.' And on the subject of Alex Ferguson's apology, he said, 'If he has written the letter it must have been sent by horse because I haven't received it. But the comments didn't upset me and I accept what he said. We don't expect presents. If you are good enough you win, and if you are not you lose. That is why the game against Liverpool is so important. We need to beat Liverpool and we need to win our home games to stay at the top.'

Arsenal were at home to Liverpool on 9 January and desperately wanted to improve their poor record against them. In nine Premiership meetings between the teams Liverpool had lost just once, with seven wins. Roy Evans had bowed out in November and

Gerard Houllier was now in sole command. 'Arsène is a good football man and a good friend,' Houllier was reported as saying, 'and whatever happens we will stay friends.' Wenger, in turn, made one of his most enigmatic comments when he said, 'Gerard is an open-minded and passionate man. I am the opposite: stubborn and stupid. But sometimes stupid behaviour makes you win.'

Wenger had always wanted to sign Robbie Fowler, who would have benefited from a fresh start and would have enjoyed playing with Petit, Bergkamp and Overmars, but Houllier regarded Robbie almost as a son. Whether Fowler and Michael Owen were compatible was always in doubt, so Houllier might have been tempted to break up the Spice Boys and rebuild his team around Owen. He could have begun to finance that by selling Fowler to Wenger for £15 million, but it did not happen.

The match itself was wholly forgettable. With Bergkamp still injured as a result of the Youds assault, the erratic Boa Morte played up front with Anelka, so it was no surprise that, after a good tussle between Keown and Fowler, it finished goalless.

Arsenal's appeal failed to overturn Vieira's sending-off on Boxing Day, so he would miss the FA Cup fourth-round tie against Wolves on 24 January and two Premiership matches against Nottingham Forest and Chelsea before and after that. Wenger immediately called for an overhaul of football's disciplinary procedures, saying that a panel of experts should adjudicate on red-card incidents. 'After examining the evidence, they would have the power to let the ban stay, decrease or increase it. It would be, I think, more fair, and that's all we want at Arsenal, to be treated the same as everyone else. To call us a dirty side is unbelievable. It seems to us that it is always Arsenal players who are being watched and their every move examined. I would like to see other teams scrutinised in the same way. It might be worth watching a recording of our FA Cup match against Preston and the fouls on our goalkeeper, Alex Manninger. Their players just jumped into him and made no attempt to play the ball. We are not guilty of that kind of foul. Nobody mentioned that, though, which is frustrating for me.'

January was only eleven days old and 1999 had already been a controversial year for the Frenchman, but at least his team was showing signs of being able to score goals again. He had sent Tony Adams to Florida for some sunshine, rest and recuperation, and Adams now came back to first-team action on 16 January at the City Ground, where Arsenal beat Forest 1–0. He had missed ten games since coming off at half-time against Lens. Results improved steadily after his return to the team, prompting his manager to label his captain's injuries as 'a small problem'. 'The only problem for him,' Wenger went on, 'is how long he will want to go on. If he is motivated I think he can go on until he is 37 or 38. At the moment he looks very focused.'

## KANU ARRIVES

*It's the same type of gamble I took with Overmars and I will be happy if we can get the same kind of result. I try to calculate my risks, and with a talent like his, it is not a huge one.*

Arsène Wenger

The day before Adams' return to the first team, Wenger finally landed Nwankwo Kanu, who passed a rigorous medical examination and signed a six-year contract. Arsenal had paid Inter £4.5 million for him. 'He will be a big asset for us,' the manager said. 'He can play as the main striker or off the main striker and has already proved himself at top club and international level. But his problem is that he has had very few chances at Inter because he is behind strikers there like Roberto Baggio, Youri Djorkaeff and, of course, Ronaldo.' There were parallels with Bergkamp's departure from Inter in 1995. He, like Kanu, hated defensive football, and now they were both playing for Wenger, an attacking coach.

But did happy times lie ahead? Anelka gave an interview to a French reporter at Sopwell House on Tuesday, 2 February 1999. The interview came out in *L'Equipe* three days later and was translated, predictably, into a *News of the World* back-page sensation on 7 February. For Anelka had said that Marc Overmars played for himself and never gave him a pass to score a goal. The pair had detested each other ever since Anelka had slagged off Overmars in a previous interview in *L'Equipe*.

At Upton Park on 6 February, after Arsenal had stuffed West Ham 4–0, the players walked off the field. Bergkamp and Overmars applauded the fans, but Anelka did not bother, and for the next game, the following Saturday against Sheffield United in the FA Cup, it looked as if Wenger might rest Anelka and play Kaba Diawara, his boisterous new loan striker who had understudied Sylvain Wiltord at Bordeaux. If Wenger did play Anelka against Sheffield United and he got injured, he would miss the game at Old Trafford on the Wednesday night, and he was already without Bergkamp and Petit for that game.

Kanu was on the bench and fans were intrigued to see him warm up. He was six foot five inches tall, a beguiling beanpole whose feet seemed to have the same degree of ball-control as a basketball player's hands. In an enjoyably competitive game Vieira scored with a header and Marcelo equalised with another header. Then, after 75 minutes, Grimandi got the wrong side of Lee Morris, stretched in the box, fouled him, missing the ball by inches, and referee Peter Jones waved play on when he might have given a penalty. Morris stayed down, injured. When the ball went down the other end, keeper Alan Kelly kicked it out of play near the halfway line. Morris had treatment, then limped off for more treatment. So Ray Parlour threw the ball down towards the corner flag for Sheffield United to collect, as you do, to give back posesssion to the team whose player has been injured, even when it is 1–1 in an FA Cup 5th Round tie with fifteen minutes to go. But Kanu, in his first sub appearance, intercepted Parlour's throw and crossed the ball to Overmars, who raced forward and tapped it into the net.

All hell broke loose. The visiting players protested and the game was held up for eight minutes. Sheffield United manager Steve Bruce called his players off, but Graeme Stuart persuaded them to stay on the field. Peter Jones did not have the power to disallow the goal, so it stood. It was 2–1, and for the rest of the match the 6,000 Blades fans sang, 'Shame on Arsenal, shame on Arsenal!' Those last eighteen minutes were all fear and loathing and dangerous nonsense: wild tackles by Sheffield players, anger from the visiting fans, stewards in fear of a riot. Peter Jones gave every fifty-fifty decision to Sheffield, which made things even more ridiculous.

On some days there is only one question to ask, and when Wenger came in I asked it. 'Did Kanu understand what he was doing?'

'No. He hadn't seen the injured player at the other end. He didn't realise the keeper had kicked it out deliberately.'

Wenger said that Arsenal had offered to replay the game. The FA approved that suggestion very quickly and the story was on PA Sports News by a quarter to six that evening – probably the fastest FA decision of the twentieth century. FA spokesman Steve Double confirmed, 'We have agreed for this game to be replayed. David Davies and Terry Annabel, the chairman of the Cup committee, discussed this situation within half an hour of the end of the game. It is an unprecedented situation. Everybody welcomes the sporting gesture by Arsène Wenger. He is to be congratulated.' The decision seemed to be a victory for common sense, but there was no discussion about what should happen were this kind of 'goal' ever to be scored again. Maybe the referee could consult the linesman, who could give a foul throw, even if it was not a foul throw, which would give possession back to the team which had the ball originally.

Kanu, naturally, was distraught. The man who had won the European Champions Cup in 1995 and Olympic gold in 1996, faced death on the operating table and survived to spend a year in limbo at Inter Milan before joining his little pal Marc at Arsenal, a new club where the manager believed in him so much that he had spent many months negotiating to buy him, had finally made his first appearance but had only been on the field for ten minutes before unwittingly creating a huge controversy.

Four days later Kanu made his first Premiership start at Old Trafford in the pouring rain. Arsenal were outplayed in the first half, and when Parlour fouled Ronny Johnsen just inside the box a penalty was given, but Dwight Yorke fired it wide. Then Kanu bamboozled Stam, Phil Neville tackled him and the ball broke to Anelka, who scored. Just after the goal Vieira was involved in another of his trademark incidents. This time he was beating Roy

Keane when the Irishman grabbed him, Vieira raised his arm in retaliation, and both players were shown yellow cards.

Arsenal's passing became much shorter after Anelka's goal as they tried to keep possession, but United equalised within ten minutes when Andy Cole headed his one hundredth Premiership goal. After that Arsenal had to defend stubbornly to earn a 1–1 draw; they had been outplayed for seventy of the ninety minutes. Vieira, however, had performed magnificently. 'He has everything you want from a midfielder,' his manager said. 'I don't think there is a limit to what he can achieve. It is hard to believe sometimes that he is still only 22.' Wenger also emphasised that Kanu, although he looked individualistic, was, above all, a team player. 'What I like most is his intelligence, the way he is aware of team-mates and always wants to bring them into the game. He does not want to do things individually. To me, he is a great player and he showed his strengths against Manchester United.' One suspected that Wenger saw himself as a Svengali of rehabilitation, that he enjoyed restoring stalled, problematic careers just as much as he liked turning raw young talents into international stars. He continued, 'It's the same type of gamble I took with Overmars and I will be happy if we can get the same kind of result. I try to calculate my risks, and with a talent like his, it is not a huge one.'

Ten days after the big controversy, on a Tuesday night, the Sheffield United game was replayed. The announcement of Marc Overmars' name was vigorously booed by visiting fans, as expected. It was a vivid, compelling match because it had that extra edge. As Overmars dribbled towards the Sheffield punters at the Clock End, they sang, 'One cheating bastard, there's only one cheating bastard!' But the Dutchman was fired up, ready to show them just how good he was, and he began to slice the Blades apart with deadly accurate shooting and passing. Early on Bergkamp played the ball forward, Hughes touched it on and Overmars hit a low left-foot shot under Alan Kelly, a super-clinical finish by the player Wenger had once called 'an efficient guy'.

Bergkamp, who had had four assists the previous Saturday in Arsenal's 5–0 demolition of Leicester City, also looked scalpel-sharp. Overmars hit a Beckham-style diagonal fifty-yarder from the halfway line, picking out Parlour's run, and Parlour cut it back into the box first time. The pass was not quite into Bergkamp's stride, but it gave him space to adjust his body shape and execute an exquisite chip which sent the ball sharply up, across Kelly's dive, and into the far side of the goal. At such moments it is Bergkamp's crowd, Bergkamp's stadium and Bergkamp's pitch. Why else did groundsman Steve Braddock create the finest playing surface in England? So that the ball will run true and such moments of skill will be possible. Braddock's immaculate pitch was Arsène Wenger's invisible player, his twelfth man, rolled and cut and manicured to suit his pace-based style of play.

There was another plus to the evening. Winterburn had come back, Nelson Vivas switching to the right. Playing full-back is a game of angles and good habits, so it is not easy to play left-back on a Saturday afternoon and right-back on a Tuesday night, but Vivas was now concentrating, tackling well, winning headers, passing accurately and looking skilful. A small man, he is very good at back-pedalling quickly to prevent passes being played over his head. When he mistimed a tiny backpass to Tony Adams at one stage during the Sheffield game, the skipper cleared the ball and gave him a little pat on the bum, as if to say, 'Don't worry about it – we got away with that.'

Against Leicester Anelka had scored a hat-trick, but after the game he had revealed something which made fans wonder just how unusual a character he really was. 'I was a little tired before the game,' he said. 'For a week I had been waking up in the middle of the night running with sweat. I don't know why. I had the impression of playing against ghosts. I don't know whether they are dreams or nightmares.'

After the Leicester game Bergkamp said that Anelka was similar to Michael Owen in his speed and finishing. 'I don't see a great deal of difference between them. Nicolas now needs fewer chances to score from. This season he is deadly. We are getting to understand each other more and more. Look at the statistics. He has opened the scoring in perhaps nine or ten games. He has hit crucial goals. You can see his speed and power, and the team is playing to his strengths. He beats goalkeepers with raw power. It is not just his speed, it is what he does when he gets in front of goal.'

Against Sheffield United, however, Anelka struggled all night against sharp, tight marking. On the Thursday we learned that Juventus executive Roberto Bettega had been at the game and that Juve were thinking of offering £20 million for Anelka. What might they have offered had they seen him play well? Would Wenger let him go?

The manager had been causing outrage on the continent by signing promising teenagers like Jeremie Aladière and German youngster Moritz Volz from underneath the noses of local clubs. He defended himself against accusations of poaching and vowed to continue scouting abroad for the finest young players. His view, as before, was that as the wages of established stars spiralled upwards clubs would be forced to concentrate on youth development. 'In my native France and in Germany, a lot has been said about Arsenal's player policy. In my own country the signing of Jeremie Aliadière created a sensation because the French don't want to lose their best talents. The sixteen-year-old players we signed were free agents and several other top teams in Europe wanted to sign them too.'

Anelka scored again in a 1–1 draw with Newcastle on 28 February, and then on 6 March Arsenal ended Derby's FA Cup run with a very late goal. The game had changed completely when Kanu came on in the last 25 minutes, grabbing the winner after a corner in the last minute. Keown's shot hit the Nigerian on the chest and he swivelled and lashed it into the net.

At this point in the season Wenger must have felt that he had assembled perhaps the strongest and most skilful squad of players in Arsenal's history: an English defence that was more durable than Stonehenge, a French engine room, a double Dutch threat in attack, an improving goalscorer who lived on Planet Anelka, and an all-star bench with a sparky Swede, a Nigerian ball-wizard and an Argentinian who was as versatile as a Swiss army knife.

When league leaders Manchester United and second-placed Chelsea drew their FA Cup quarter-final, Ferguson and Vialli said they really did not need another game and Fergie produced one of his classic wind-up remarks, a comment calculated to annoy Arsène Wenger. 'Arsenal are probably in the best position to win the championship after this,' he said. At that stage Arsenal were seven points behind United and three points behind Chelsea! Wenger dismissed the comment, saying, 'Is that his latest joke? Would he like to swap positions with us? I would certainly offer him that if I could.' It had become a point of honour for Wenger not to allow anyone to say that Arsenal were favourites to win anything. They had six of their remaining eleven league fixtures at home, but he insisted, 'It is much tougher for us to win the championship this year than at the same stage last year. Mathematically, we had it in our own hands then, but that is not the case now. The small chance we have is to keep winning our games and hope the other two will drop points.' The season had in fact turned out to be remarkably similar to 1997/98. With eleven games left Arsenal were seven points behind United with a game in hand; a year earlier they had been nine points behind with three games in hand.

Against Sheffield Wednesday on 9 March, Bergkamp was a Rolls-Royce marooned in London traffic, longing for a motorway, and the game was so dull that Wenger made a substitution at half-time, bringing on Diawara for Ljungberg. Diawara hit the post with a shot and then obliged Srnicek to make two brilliant saves. Petit and Kanu came on, and there were only seven minutes left when Petit found Bergkamp with a smart free-kick and he hit a shot which bounced past Srnicek at last. Overmars then picked out Kanu, who banged his shot high into the net, and went on to run sixty yards with the ball to set up Bergkamp for 3–0. Wenger was buzzing – three goals in five minutes, another three points, another clean sheet and another masterclass in demolition. He told reporters that the success culture within the club had inspired his new players, Kanu and Diawara. 'It's infectious,' he said. 'There is a pressure from the group to do well. For us it is important to do what we enjoy well, and when you come from outside and feel that, it's easier because there is a positive feeling about the game. They never know when they're beaten and refuse to give up. There's a lot of great characters in the team. You are a winner or not a winner, and if you are a winner, it's important for you to win throughout your whole life. They try to give everything to win and as long as they have a chance, they fight for it.'

Arsenal were now second in the Premiership. They won at Everton on 13 March, and a week later met Coventry at Highbury, where Kanu came on for Anelka after 76 minutes and made a priceless goal ten minutes from the end. He nutmegged Bosnian centre-back Konjic, then stumbled as Barry Quinn stretched into a tackle, just touching the ball away from Kanu. The Nigerian fell but still managed to shovel the ball square to Overmars, who fired a shot low into the corner of the net.

Once again Kanu had arrived and changed the game. Against Derby he had scored the winner in injury time and against Wednesday it was goalless when he came on for Anelka and Arsenal had ended up 3–0 winners. There was nobody like Kanu in the whole country, maybe the whole world. He divided seconds into nanoseconds, yards into inches. He reinvented geometry, seeing angles that did not exist for other players. Bergkamp was an elegant power player but not a great dribbler in the box, and when Anelka dribbled in the box he saw nothing but the goal. Kanu, however, seemed to create the game from moment to moment, could see team-mates and pass to them while dribbling in the box. He was the complete opposite of Anelka and therefore a perfect substitute for him. When he came on it really was a case of 'And now for something completely different'. Kanu was good at what Anelka was bad at.

At the press conference I asked, 'What is it about Kanu that allows him to come on and pick up the pace of the game and do something every time?'

Wenger smiled and said, 'Intelligence and class.'

Are you tempted to give him more than a fifteen-minute runaround when he's fitter?

'Yes. We work hard on his fitness because he was out of the game for a long time. And he knows that as well. He works very hard at the moment in training, and we work on specific things. But you can see that this player, fit, can play in any team.'

Wenger was also delighted by Ray Parlour's goal in the win over Coventry. Tony Adams had lashed a long clearance up to Bergkamp; he had passed it square to Parlour, who had accelerated, swerved inside David Burrows and hit his shot with the outside of his right foot across Hedman into the far corner. He said that new England coach Kevin Keegan should feel very positive about Parlour. 'I think he's ready to play. He has shown again today that he can adapt to different positions. He's strong technically now. I'm very pleased with the goal he scored today because of the way he finished, he wouldn't have done that a year ago. He's calmer in the box, composed in the box, and less nervous in his finishing. I believe as well that he's the kind of player who lasts in a season. Because he has such tremendous stamina. When other players start to be tired he still keeps up with his same performances, or even improves. The more he plays, the better he is.'

Wenger's assessment of Coventry was generous. 'They cannot go down. What I've seen today, they cannot go down. Because they can frustrate everybody, they run like crazies. All eleven are very resilient. I was quite impressed by their passing ability. They missed maybe a second striker, like Whelan, and Boateng. I don't think they will go down.'

Bergkamp and Overmars missed the game at Southampton on 3 April after playing for Holland, which infuriated Wenger. 'Overmars has blisters after playing on hard ground and Dennis has returned with flu after being away. We had fifteen players away on international duty this week, so you cannot expect to come through without some casualties. But we have lost two significant players and you can see now why I do not like international matches being played at this time of year. They could have a different arrangement for international games. I do not think they should be played in March or April. It is everybody's concern, not just Arsenal's, because all over Europe championships are coming to a climax so every match is hugely important.'

At The Dell Kanu started his first game as Bergkamp's replacement, but the game finished 0–0 and he missed a second-half sitter when Anelka set him up with a square pass. He side-footed his shot and Benali blocked it on the line. Then Mark Hughes almost won the game with a diving header, but Seaman made a world-class save. 'We are very disappointed,' said Wenger afterwards. 'This is two points dropped.'

There was more bad news at the training ground, where Alex Manninger had been injured saving a shot from David Seaman. Wenger said, 'At first we feared Alex had a fractured wrist and that could have threatened his career. It is not as bad as that, but he will be out for the rest of the season.' John Lukic, who was 38, would now be on the bench.

The narrow win over Blackburn on 6 April brought Arsenal to within a point of Manchester United on a day when Bergkamp scored and Martin Keown was sent off for lashing out at Chris Sutton. The *Guardian*'s David Lacey picked up on this latest infringement. 'This could be the moment when Arsenal's perennially poor disciplinary record catches up with them. Emmanuel Petit, arguably their most influential player, will miss the semi-final through suspension following his third dismissal of the season. Arsène Wenger's two-and-a-half years in charge at Highbury have consistently offered the paradox of cerebral football let down by the hole-in-the-head school of indiscipline, even if Keown's flailing arm on Tuesday night was prompted by worries about his sick son ... Red cards continue to sprout among Arsenal's performances like poppies in disturbed ground. When Wenger philosophises about his players and lists their qualities he comes across as the head of a science faculty enthusing over the examination results while down the corridor the students are about to blow up the lab for the umpteenth time.'

The point about Petit was important, since Arsenal would miss him at Villa Park on Sunday, 11 April, just as they had missed him in the decisive European game against Lens at Wembley back in November.


## BERGKAMP'S PENALTY

*The two teams are very close to each other, it was a smashing game, and in the end the luckiest won.*

Arsène Wenger

For the manager who loved competition, the FA Cup semi-final was the defining moment of the 1998/99 season. His team still had a chance of winning a back-to-back Premiership and FA Cup Double, and no English club had ever achieved that. Back in 1991 Arsenal had become the major force in English football by overtaking Liverpool, then Arsenal were themselves overtaken by Manchester United, the biggest club in the country. Alex Ferguson made them the best team and their consistency in the nineties set the standard to which several clubs aspired. The Arsenal–Manchester United rivalry was therefore intense, and had been given an extra edge by a few well-publicised spats between Wenger and Ferguson.

This FA Cup semi-final was the biggest game of the English season and a contest of many dimensions and many duels: North versus South, Scotsman versus Frenchman, Stam versus Bergkamp, Keane versus Vieira, Giggs versus Overmars, Schmeichel versus Seaman. League leaders against defending champions for a place at Wembley. United had not beaten Arsenal for two years, but they were unbeaten in 21 games.

The game kicked off with Vivas in midfield for the suspended Petit, and Nicky Butt playing instead of Paul Scholes, who was on the bench. Gary Neville fouled Overmars twice in the first two minutes to earn the first yellow card. Vieira won a foul off Keane and then won a tackle with him. Nicolas Anelka hovered on the halfway line like a bullet waiting to be fired. He had scored twice for France against England at Wembley in February and had also scored six goals for Arsenal that month. He had also started four games against Manchester United and scored a goal in each; his presence, his potential, seemed to dominate the early minutes. Could he score the first goal? Could Arsenal launch him on one of those turbo-charged sprints?

When a Bergkamp pass finally released Anelka, Roy Keane chased him and made a crucial pass back. Then Cole fed Giggs and his shot flashed inches past the angle of post and crossbar. The game soon developed into a pulsating contest, with Jaap Stam outstanding as he made a great tackle on Parlour and blocked an Anelka shot. Schmeichel made two fine saves, tipping over an Adams header from a corner and stopping a Bergkamp rocket after Stam had cleared a corner.

Then Roy Keane had a 'goal' disallowed. Giggs beat Dixon and made a fine cross, Yorke headed on and Keane rifled his shot into the net off Keown. The linesman gave offside against Yorke earlier in the move, a deeply misguided decision which was very lucky for Arsenal.

Vivas, already on a yellow card, tripped Keane early in the second half and was lucky to stay on the pitch. United were dominating now and Anelka was peripheral, drifting around, dawdling, walking back from offside positions so that some Arsenal attacks had to slow down. Anelka had not yet scored in the FA Cup campaign and did not look as if he cared. He had decided to sulk, and Wenger must have been amazed and disgusted to see him outsprinted by Ronny Johnsen a couple of times. Pace has to be driven by desire. If you really want to win, really want to score, really want to get past defenders, you find another gear, but Mr Moody did not fancy it today.

In extra time Vivas stuck his elbow into Butt's face after the ball had gone and referee David Elleray sent him off. Ten Arsenal players were capable of beating many teams, but Manchester United was a slightly different proposition. Still, they held United comfortably and Bergkamp almost won the game twice in the last five minutes of extra time. His clever short pass released substitute Freddie Ljungberg into the box but he did not shoot first time and the chance slipped away; then he jinked past Keane and Ronny Johnsen, only for Gary Neville to make a covering tackle near the penalty spot. The defending by both teams had been exceptional.

The replay was at the same ground the following Wednesday night and Wenger restored Petit after his suspension. Alex Ferguson switched his attack, bringing in Sheringham, Solskjær and left-winger Jesper Blomqvist, all of whom played well in the first half. After seventeen minutes Beckham played a cute one-two with his mate Sheringham and then curled a 25-yard shot past Seaman. As passions spilt over Elleray dished out four yellow cards in seven minutes: Stam, Keown, Keane and Beckham went into his book. Then Bergkamp equalised after 69 minutes with a shot that took a big deflection off Stam, and four minutes later Keane was sent off for a rash tackle on Overmars, who had come on for Ljungberg.

Arsenal now had their strongest team on the field, the eleven who had won the Double, facing ten men with the score balanced at 1–1. It was a huge opportunity for victory and they almost took it. Ray Parlour had played with more bottle than craft, but in injury time he dribbled straight at Phil Neville in the box, swerved to the right, and Neville tripped him. Elleray gave the penalty. It was clear-cut and nobody protested.

Dennis Bergkamp had missed three of his last five penalties. One of those had been saved only the week before by Blackburn's John Filan, and now he had a penalty to take him back to Wembley for a repeat of the FA Cup Final he had missed through injury a year ago. He stood well back, looking composed, an erect, blond gladiator faced by a dead ball and a great Dane. The game was in stoppage time. If he scored, United could not come back. He ran up, struck the ball firmly to his right – and Schmeichel saved it. What drama!

The Dutchman had played superbly up to that point, and he continued to play well in extra time. He hit a fierce shot which Schmeichel saved. The unmarked Keown muffed a header from Parlour's cross, and when a Petit corner bounced and hit Johnsen the rebound flew towards Schmeichel, who parried it; Butt hooked away. Then a Bergkamp pass just eluded Petit in the box.

In the second half of extra time Patrick Vieira made the most catastrophic pass of his career. His tired crossfield ball was intercepted by substitute Ryan Giggs, who cruised past a desperate Vieira, swerved between Dixon and Keown, accelerated towards the corner of the six-yard box and hit a thunderous shot past Seaman at his near post. This strike, after a sensational slalom through the best defence in Europe, was the finest goal of Ryan Giggs's career because it was spectacular, because it was the most important and because it catapulted United into a position where the mythical treble was now a possibility. The title, the FA Cup and the Champions League were now within their grasp.

When Sky's George Gavin spoke to Wenger after the final whistle he looked and sounded very flat but spoke in a dignified way. 'It is not easy to take a defeat, but what you can demand of your team is that they give everything. They are very sad today of course because it was not our night at all and we were really, I think, unlucky. The two teams are very close to each other, it was a smashing game, and in the end the luckiest won. We had the chances to win. Especially, we had the penalty with a minute to go. So you expect, of course, to win the game. But that's football. We were a little bit unlucky, lost the ball in the middle of the park and Giggs did the rest. There were one or two rebounds for him, but Giggs is a great player. It was a fantastic goal. They have so many qualities in the middle of the park and up front that every ball you lose is dangerous. But there's no reproach. I would just like to congratulate my team. They were fantastic. They are very sad tonight. They have shown again they are a great team. Sometimes you can say that when you lose.'

Can you pick them up for the remaining league games?

'That's part of our job. We want to win, and if you want to win you have, of course, to survive disappointments. And we have to show that in the next game, that we can react. When you lose, of course you're very sad. But, at the moment, it's history. We just have to look forward.'

Alex Ferguson praised the courage and commitment of his team and defended the resting of Cole, Yorke and Giggs for the following week's Champions League semi-final against Juventus, as he had every right to do. He had been a manager since he took over at East Stirlingshire in 1974, and he knew that winning the game always justifies your team selection. 'I think we deserved the win,' he said. 'Over the two legs I think we were the better team. The players· have played in agony to get the victory. Ryan Giggs has injured himself near the end also. There's a lot of pain in there. The two strikers and Blomqvist were magnificent. If I don't play them when they're playing well, when do I play them? Do you wait till you lose a game? No, you play them now.' Rotation had worked well for Ferguson that night, and the subject, already much discussed at Stamford Bridge, would become a big theme in English football over the coming three years as Liverpool, Leeds and Arsenal all became able to afford four good strikers.

Two years later I talked to Sky Sports commentator Martin Tyler about the Arsenal–Manchester United rivalry, particularly the crucial Old Trafford game in March 1998 and the 1999 FA Cup semi-final replay. Television is more important than the newspapers, so managers do the Sky and BBC interviews before they talk to the press. The broadcasters therefore see them immediately after matches when the adrenalin is still flowing, not twenty or thirty minutes later, so Tyler's impressions were illuminating.

'The win at Old Trafford in 1998 was really the key game because Arsenal had never scored a Premiership goal at Old Trafford up to that point. And Overmars was exceptional, which wasn't always the case away from home. But it didn't look as if it was gonna produce a goal. Then it did, and that shot of the Arsenal fans that Sky have used over and over again in the titles, of that demented guy behind the goal where Overmars scored, sums up what it meant to everybody. Then they believed they could win the league. Manninger played brilliantly in that game as well. Not with a great deal to do, but he came out at Andy Cole's feet when he broke away in the first half.

'Arsenal had the Indian sign on United until Dennis Bergkamp's penalty was saved by Schmeichel. I've never seen Wenger more angry after a game than that night. Not just losing the Cup, but losing that edge that they had over Manchester United. They'd had a very good recent record and they beat them again in the Charity Shield. The general feeling around that time was that the best Arsenal would beat the best Manchester United. That seems an extraordinary thing to say now. But through 1998 and 1999 that was what many people believed – if Arsenal got their best team out, which they didn't always do.'

There was a slightly strange, subdued atmosphere at Highbury on Monday, 19 April, everyone still digesting the disappointment of losing the semi-final. Wenger rested Anelka and Wimbledon played more defensively than they had ever done at Highbury, so Arsenal had to play a much slower, more patient passing game based around Kanu, who allowed everybody to link in and have a shot. Arsenal notched up 34 goal attempts, eighteen on target, and won 5–1. They followed that by going to Middlesbrough and winning 6–1, Kanu scoring memorably by flicking Parlour's cross between his own legs and into the far side of the goal. Anelka's reaction to being dropped against Wimbledon was to play out of his skin at Middlesbrough and score twice.

On Saturday, 1 May, Ian Wright surpassed all his misdemeanours at Arsenal after being sent off the pitch just twelve minutes into West Ham's game with Leeds by referee Rob Harris. Wright went straight to the referee's changing room and damaged his clothes. Harris was in his first season as a Premiership official and had showed Wright a second yellow card for 'acting in an aggressive manner towards an opponent'. Two other West Ham players were also sent off. Leeds won 5–1.

The following day, a warm, sleepy Sunday afternoon, Arsenal played Derby, Kanu starting the game with Bergkamp on the bench. Anelka put them ahead from a Parlour cross in fifteen minutes, and after that they emphasised accuracy and possession more than usual, spurting forward as spaces allowed, but mostly playing save-your-legs football, leaving Overmars to jog in the shade of the West Stand. Wenger said his team had suffered a lot from the heat and needed that special strength they had at the back. On Derby, he said, 'They know how to lose 1–0 here. They don't let us score the second goal.'

Wenger had crossed swords with Alex Ferguson and Alan Curbishley earlier in the season, and now, in the last month, he found he had upset Chelsea chairman Ken Bates by making some comments over the weekend about escalating wage bills in the Premiership. Bates was furious at headlines like WENGER ACCUSES CHELSEA OF CHEATING, and he told the *Mirror*, 'He is an idiot for calling us cheats and he's also out of order because, as I recall, when he was coach at Monaco they survived on gates of 3,500 – because they were funded by Prince Rainier.' In his defence, Wenger said, 'I didn't mention Chelsea at all in what I said, or maybe once when I was asked about them and I answered that I did not know if they had an extra income. I also said that if clubs spent more than they can afford then that is nearly cheating, but I didn't mention any particular club. If Ken Bates is thinking of suing me then he must be a very sensitive boy, but I am not worried about what he says.'

## SPURS 1 ARSENAL 3

*A very good game. I thought Arsenal, in the first half, outstanding. On the break they were real, real quality tonight . . .*

George Graham

Arsenal had been holding back during the heatwave against Derby because Wenger had always planned to play high-tempo football at Spurs on 5 May, a night game which would be much faster and fiercer. They put on a superb exhibition of collective commitment, pace and one-touch passing.

After sixteen minutes Petit took off on a powerhouse sprint, controlled Bergkamp's devastating pass with one touch and lifted it over Walker for 1–0. When Bergkamp's pass split Spurs again, Anelka powered through and finished with a flourish, an imperious flicked shot that looked so casual, as if he had done it a hundred times. Spurs were pressing, pressing, pressing, desperately chasing the ball, trying to close the gap in class through sheer energy. Then Vieira put an arm on the dribbling Ginola, who immediately crumpled, and a harsh free-kick was awarded. Darren Anderton's shot from 25 yards was very well placed, bouncing and skidding past Seaman into the bottom corner. Just before half-time Tim Sherwood elbowed Dixon and threw the ball in his face. From the kick-off, Anderton tangled with Vieira, who fell, Sherwood steamed in and, with the ball about six feet away, kicked Vieira in the groin area while he was on the ground. Petit was outraged and got a yellow card in a scuffle. Vieira had treatment for two minutes.

Dennis Bergkamp was also fiery, focused and explosive, playing as he had in the replay against Manchester United. Remarkably, he had already, in an hour, headed the ball more often than he had in all his 26 Premiership games that season. After 75 minutes Kanu came on for the Dutchman, but he only got one kick in eleven minutes until, suddenly, he produced a moment of genius. He controlled the ball on his chest, let it bounce, flicked it up over Luke Young's head and rammed his shot past Ian Walker for 3–1.

The 4,000 Gooners in the corner were celebrating happily enough, singing, 'We beat the scum three one!' and then suddenly pandemonium reigned there, the area transformed into a pulsating mass of jumping bodies and laughing faces. This could mean only one thing: Liverpool must have drawn! The final score from Anfield was indeed Liverpool 2 Manchester United 2, and the over-excited Gooners began to chant, 'Champions! Champions!'

The Arsenal players had given a performance of tremendous steel and nerve. George Graham, the master tactician who had so craftily squeezed the channels at Highbury to dig out a 0–0 in November, had got it all wrong in May because you should never defend that high up against pace. It was suicidal. Arsène Wenger, in contrast, was as satisfied as he ever will be in N17, talking about how thrilled he was with the first-half performance. 'Our passing was excellent, our runs were great, and every time we got through the first defending of Tottenham we were dangerous. So to go back at half-time with 2–1 was very difficult. We needed to be very strong mentally. We came back to the dressing room thinking it should have been 4–0, and it was 2–1. Of course we expected a reaction of Tottenham in the second half. They fought very hard and we had to be strong and well organised in the second half, and wait for our chance. Again we missed chances in the first twenty minutes, but after Kanu came on we scored the third goal. That killed it.'

Do you think you have a psychological advantage over Manchester United going into the last week?

'I don't know. We are consistent for a long, long time now, and we have to keep that consistency till the end. But we are not the only ones who are consistent because Manchester United has lost only three games, Chelsea as well lost only three games. It's difficult to predict now who will win it, and how they will win it.'

But surely it's in your own hands again? If you keep winning, and win by enough goals, you will win the championship.

'That's what we have to try. But don't forget that they have one more game to play, so if they win their games they have more chances to score goals. So that's why I think it's still in their hands.'

Brian Woolnough then asked him if there was a key to the victory over Spurs.

'The key was that maybe they played very high, and we found the space behind them with Dennis dropping off and finding Marc

Overmars, Ray Parlour and Nicolas Anelka with their runs. Because they played in a very high position. So as long as we could find Dennis when we won the ball, and he could feed our strikers, we were very dangerous.'

Graham was generous in defeat but showed flashes of anger when he talked about the first and third goals conceded by his side. 'A very good game. I thought Arsenal, in the first half, outstanding. On the break they were real, real quality tonight, especially in the first half. We got into the game just before half-time with a good free-kick, gave us a lift. I told the boys, second half, to be more positive. Second half, for half an hour, 35 minutes, I thought we did well. I thought we did very well. And then they broke again with real quality players.

'I thought some of the defending tonight was schoolboy. I really did. I thought it was disgraceful. I thought the first goal – on the training pitch I would sort it out in no time. And the last goal, terrible defending. There were too many chances. Arsenal had lots of chances tonight. I thought the back four were not good enough. But I'd give Arsenal credit for assembling a very strong squad there. Not only talented, but physically very strong, so they can take you on. Whatever way you wanna play it, they've got the answer to you.'

## TITLE RACE GOES TO THE LAST DAY

*Our contest with Arsenal is almost over. We've played Juventus, Inter Milan, Barcelona and Bayern Munich this season, but if I had to nominate the toughest side we have faced it would be Arsenal.*

Jaap Stam

There was a rumour flying around that George Graham had said privately that Wenger would quit Arsenal when the legendary back four packed up, but Graham was too shrewd to say something like that in public. Remarkably, David O'Leary had no such inhibitions. Before the Leeds–Arsenal clash on 11 May, the penultimate game of the season, he said, 'Arsène has done a fantastic job but he has a lot of old defenders and there is a risk that they will all go at the same time. People say it's half the team, but for me it's more than that. In terms of resilience and discipline and all those things I learned at Highbury, it is *the* team. Replacing them is going to be a big job and a long job, and it may be that Arsène won't want the challenge of it. That's why I feel that Manchester United, with many more younger players, are better positioned in the long term.'

On the night, Leeds pressed so ferociously that Arsenal had Parlour, Petit and Vieira booked in the first 36 minutes. That was inhibiting, but it was an exciting match, despite the abysmal refereeing of Gary Willard, who took the names of nine players. Keown flattened Harry Kewell with a wild tackle in the box on 45 minutes, but Ian Harte blasted his penalty against the bar, and when Hasselbaink followed up Seaman made a superb save. Two minutes before that Seaman had made another miraculous save from a Kewell thirty-yarder which was flashing into the top corner.

The game changed after Kanu came on for Overmars and made some fabulous passes. Diawara also came on, for Parlour, and went close with a header which shaved the bar. Nigel Martyn saved at Kanu's feet and Jonathan Woodgate headed a Diawara shot off the line. But the turning point came on 75 minutes. Winterburn was lying on his back after a tackle and Alfie Haaland ran over him, smashing his knee into Winterburn's face and demolishing his nose. Doctors were called and play was held up for five minutes before the bloodstained left-back was taken off, to be replaced by Vivas. The delay interrupted Arsenal's rhythm at a crucial time, and after 86 minutes Harry Kewell crossed from the left and Vivas got on the wrong side of Hasselbaink, whose diving header killed Arsenal's title hopes.

Would Hasselbaink have scored that winner had Nigel Winterburn still been on the field? Wenger thought not. 'We made a huge tactical mistake at the far post,' he said. 'Vivas was not well positioned for the cross, but it's unbelievable that we made so many chances and did not score. We are guilty of not taking our chances.'

The Frenchman knew that his team now needed a miracle to retain the championship after their first defeat in the league since Aston Villa on 13 December. He said, 'We have given Manchester United the chance to win it now. I don't expect them to lose against Blackburn tonight and a point will be good enough for them. If they win, then the title will be over because I cannot see Spurs doing us a favour at Old Trafford on Sunday.' But he added, 'Everything is possible, and you have to be optimistic. If I was not optimistic I would not have survived sixteen years in management. But I would have to say that it's seventy per cent certain that Manchester United will get something out of the game at Ewood Park and only thirty per cent for Blackburn having a chance to win it. I would not bet all my money on Blackburn tomorrow night, but you never know. I will watch the game on television and hope. If Manchester United win, we will have to rely on Spurs, and I don't think they will go there and win. I just hope they fight like Leeds fought against us.'

Blackburn had been champions in 1995, but now they were at the foot of the table, having sacked Roy Hodgson and hired Brian Kidd, Ferguson's number two, in December. They needed to win to stay in the Premiership, but in the event they could only hold United to a 0–0 draw.

So the closest title race of the nineties went to the final day of the season, Arsenal trailing Manchester United by one point. Jaap Stam wrote a column in the *Telegraph*, saying 'Our contest with Arsenal is almost over. We've played Juventus, Inter Milan, Barcelona and Bayern Munich this season, but if I had to nominate the toughest side we have faced it would be Arsenal. They have quality running through the side and enormous self-belief which shows itself in their determination to win every game.' Arsenal were at home to Aston Villa, United at home to Tottenham. Would Spurs shock everyone by beating United to win the title for Arsenal? Strange things happen in football, but that would have been the strangest of all time.

Vivas continued at left-back against Villa, but when he suffered an injury Arsenal were totally disrupted. Petit went to left-back, Parlour moved inside and Ljungberg went wide right. As usual they struggled to create openings against Villa's three centre-backs.

In Manchester, George Graham had taken David Ginola off after four minutes because he was injured following (wait for it) a little push in the back from Gary Neville. Did Graham think Ginola might slam in one of his 25-yard thunderbolts to grab the headlines with a goal that would live for ever in the annals of infamy? With Ginola, you never knew. Could he be trusted to shoot over the bar as usual when a chance came? Graham apparently thought not, but of course nothing much, if anything, was ever said about that deeply mysterious substitution.

Back at Highbury, the highlight of the first half came after nineteen minutes when the stadium erupted at the news from Old Trafford: Les Ferdinand had scored! Four words that must never, never be spoken inside Highbury were now being muttered by thousands of people: Come on you Spurs!

Patrick Vieira miscontrolled a couple of early balls and then recovered to become the game's best player. He had a rocket shot saved by keeper Michael Oakes, a header kicked off the line, and later on he powered past Ugo Ehiogu and won a corner off Southgate. After the corner he had two more shots blocked. He had reinvented his partnership with Petit in this game, moving to left midfield to keep in close contact after the Golden Ponytail had been re-deployed at left-back.

David Beckham made it 1–1 at Old Trafford late in the first half, then the Arsenal crowd heard that Andy Cole had made it 2–1. Arsenal, meanwhile, continued to dominate Villa without scoring. Then Kanu came on to conjure a goal yet again, flicking in from three yards after a Petit corner.

So the last day of the season produced what Arsène Wenger had expected: Arsenal had won and Manchester United had won. Suddenly the tension and struggle and drama was all over. After a long, exciting season and some thrilling team performances, the final day turned out to be a victorious anti-climax.

In 1997/98 Arsenal had lost six games and become champions. Now they had lost four and finished runners-up with 78 points, the same number that had won the title a year before. They were unbeaten at home and had the best defence in Europe. In 38 games they had conceded only seventeen goals and diehard Gooners reckoned that phenomenal record the swansong of the greatest defence the world had ever seen.

Wenger was left feeling deeply dismayed that Arsenal had been unable to beat Kiev or Lens, but he was proud that his players had pushed Manchester United all the way in the Premiership. He had continued to play attractive power football, Anelka had developed rapidly, and the style was very exciting and penetrating. Other managers had begun to read his tactics and learned how to nullify Arsenal, so when the team stuttered they looked one-dimensional, lacking creativity, and collective confidence drained away. Then Wenger signed Kanu, who made a goal against Manchester United in his first game in February and became the team's supersub and talisman. If Arsenal needed a goal, Wenger put Kanu on and he usually scored or made one. So Wenger had kept faith with power football with an ace up his sleeve, an alternative, a Plan B – the Nigerian had scored six Premiership goals in five starts and seven sub appearances.

Most serious managers do an audit of their results when the last ball has been kicked, and Wenger must have wished he could have signed Kanu sooner. He had scored his first Premiership goal on 9 March when there were only eleven games left. Had Kanu arrived earlier and started playing in, say, November he would surely have made a difference in at least one of the 0–0 draws against Tottenham, Derby and Liverpool. If not, a single goal in the 1–1 draw with Middlesbrough might have been enough, in the final audit, to make the difference between winning the Premiership and losing it by one point.

Wenger also recalled the defeat at Aston Villa in December after Arsenal held a 2–0 lead and the 1–0 defeat at Wimbledon in November just before the Lens game. 'You are bound to think about these things,' he said, 'but, all in all, the team has performed magnificently. We had a slow start and the World Cup unquestionably affected some of our most important players. But losing the championship so narrowly is like losing a race by a yard.'

## THE ANELKA TRANSFER SAGA

*Real Madrid have not been in touch with Arsenal so there is nothing legal in what they are doing. The player has a four-year contract and any direct approach to the player is illegal.*

Arsène Wenger

Back in April, Wenger had defended Anelka staunchly and shown huge tolerance. 'He is not an arrogant guy,' the manager insisted.

'He is reliable and shy, much more sensitive than people think. I sometimes put myself in his position and he is amazing for a twenty-year-old. He doesn't drink, he doesn't smoke, he is at training every day, he has played nearly every game this season. That deserves a lot of respect.'

But now the young striker said he was very unhappy. In mid-May, when Arsenal were on tour in Malaysia, Anelka said, 'The English press causes me enormous problems on a personal level. As they aren't going to stop, that marks out my road for me. The English journalists are all rubbish. They are frustrated players who never made it as professionals. It is pure jealousy.' Wenger immediately told Anelka to grow up and stop moaning. 'Anelka has no right to complain. The press has treated him relatively well. He has not been harassed or blamed. Invoking the press to justify leaving the club is a bad reason. They will be worse anywhere else. Leaving Arsenal would be an enormous strategic error. Here he is guaranteed the Champions League and is part of a strong team. He still has progress to make. I'm sure that if I chat to him, he will say he wants to stay. I think he's ninety per cent certain to stay.'

In the meantime, Wenger re-signed Bould, Winterburn and Dixon, all of whom were over the age of 35, on one-year contracts. 'I want at least three new signings for next season,' Wenger added, 'because the fixture list is crazy and we will need some experienced players, especially in the Champions League.' He was weighing up a possible £1.8 million bid for Dynamo Kiev right-back and captain Oleg Luzhny, even though that contradicted his policy of not signing players over thirty. The Ukrainian, at the age of thirty, was signed on 28 May. Wenger warned again that next season's expanded Champions League would be very demanding physically because clubs would be playing matches every week rather than once a fortnight. He reckoned that clubs would now need eighteen players of comparable quality. 'No one can really evaluate the influence of a weekly European game on the Premiership. Rotation of the squad will be a necessity. It will be very physically demanding and there will be more competition for places. Oleg is an important addition to our squad. He is a quality defender with vast experience at both international and club levels. He's a top-quality player and the price was right.'

The day after Luzhny was signed, Juventus refused to dismiss reports that representatives of the club were planning to visit London the following week to discuss a deal for Anelka. Their director-general, Luciano Moggi, said, 'I will not deny it but I will not confirm it either. I don't want to say anything as it might cause confusion.' Real Madrid had apparently agreed a £3 million-a-season deal with Anelka and his agents. This seemed a strange call by Madrid, since they already had two young strikers, Raúl and Morientes, friends who passed to each other. How would Anelka fit into that? Madrid were ready to make a £14 million bid, but this outrageous policy of negotiating with Anelka before agreeing a transfer fee with Arsenal left Wenger furious and meant that David Dein was more likely to do business with the elegant Italian Roberto Bettega, who had played with Liam Brady at Juventus in the 70s.

Wenger was, of course, still looking for new players himself. He was said to admire left-back Gianluca Pessotto, midfielder Edgar Davids and winger Thierry Henry, and the Arsenal manager was in Turin to watch Juventus play Udinese in a play-off to decide which club would be in next season's UEFA Cup. Juventus lost out, a dire situation for a club which had been Champions League winners in 1996 and finalists in 1997 and 1998. Wenger had agreed terms for Pessotto the previous summer, only for Juventus to pull out at the last moment.

On Thursday, 3 June, Anelka was with his national team in Clairefontaine, south-west of Paris, and was quoted as saying, 'I'd be surprised if I stayed at Arsenal. Coming here, I said to myself it could be the last time I left London. I think things are going to be settled in the coming days.' Arsenal supporters were told that Real Madrid had begun to talk wages with Anelka's agents three weeks ago, and Real claimed to have spoken to Arsenal. Real president Lorenzo Sanz said, 'It's true that we've started negotiations with directors of Arsenal. We still haven't made an offer so reports of Arsenal rejecting a bid are false. We continue working to bring him here.' But Wenger, who was now understood to want £20 million for Anelka, was talking to Juventus, who valued him at £15 million. Meanwhile, Anelka was saying, 'I want to go to Spain and nowhere else. Italy doesn't interest me. I don't like the game they play there. Spain corresponds more to my style of play. Strikers score more often, there are more spaces in defence, a bit like England.'

On Friday, 4 June, Wenger called for a FIFA investigation into 'illegal' approaches by Real Madrid, even though the results of such an investigation would probably not be available for weeks as FIFA usually handled more than a hundred disputes between players, clubs and agents at any one time. 'Real Madrid have not been in touch with Arsenal,' Wenger said, 'so there is nothing legal in what they are doing. The player has a four-year contract and any direct approach to the player is illegal. We will ask FIFA to look into this. What I should say to Real Madrid is that they should concentrate on solving their own financial situation, which is not very good. Nicolas is an Arsenal player. What is real is that the player knows what he is doing when he signs a contract. The basic thing is to respect the rules. You have to do what is legal. That is what we try to do. We don't expect any presents from clubs. As we speak, Nicolas is at Arsenal. If he is unfortunate enough to pick up a serious injury playing for France today, will Real Madrid pay his money? Of course not, it will be Arsenal.'

Meanwhile, talks took place in London between David Dein, Lazio director Massimo Cragnotti (the son of club president Sergio Cragnotti) and Vicenzo Morabito, the agent acting for Lazio, who had recently received £31 million from Inter for Christian Vieri, although Diego Simeone, rated at £7 million, went the other way as part of that world record deal. Dein and Wenger had decided to use the Vieri fee as a benchmark. By mid-June we were being told that Wenger rated Anelka at £28 million and that Dein had considered Lazio's £21 million cash offer for 24 hours before turning it down.

These hikes in prices were made not just to keep pace with market value, but also, in all probability, because of reflection on the Arsenal manager's part. He had, after all, hugely improved the young French striker through his coaching and advice, and Anelka's form during March, April and May had been awesome at times. Wenger had groomed him into the ideal centre-forward for

*Right* Professor
Wenger of the Faculty
of Football Arts and
Sciences, Monaco
University, April 1994

*Left* Nike star Ian Wright
gives photographers his
golden grin after
swooshing past Cliff
Bastin's goal-scoring
record, September 1997

*Above* Wenger celebrates with Nicolas Anelka, who scored more often than he smiled, November 1997

*Left* 4–0 and ten consecutive victories. Wenger lifts the Premiership trophy after Everton are hammered at Highbury, May 1998

*Right* Only 2–0 to the Arsenal but Tony Adams and Wenger both knew Newcastle had no chance in the FA Cup final, May 1998

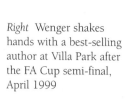

*Above* Ray Parlour and Tony Adams, two fine Essex men who grew up together, eventually (March 1999)

*Right* Wenger shakes hands with a best-selling author at Villa Park after the FA Cup semi-final, April 1999

*Right* A Cocu penalty dive and bad defending left Wenger devastated after Barcelona beat Arsenal 4–2, October 1999

*Below* Gabriel Batistuta's wonder goal kills Arsenal's Champions League hopes for another year, October 1999

*Left* Every footballer can improve, and that includes you, Dennis Bergkamp, March 2000

*Right* Nicky Butt would never admit it but Patrick Vieira is the best player in the Premiership, February 2001

*Below* So Petit did make a tackle against Galatasaray! UEFA Cup final, May 2000

*Left* England's Ashley Cole, the Londoner who has made the number 3 shirt his own

*Below* Immortal, invincible – who knows? But Arsenal made it into the history books with their unbeaten run in 2003/04, playing some of the most inspirational football to have been seen in a long time

2003 — 2004

a stylish power team which played the football Wenger had always dreamt about, football with speed, skill, energy, unstoppable attacks, unplayable strikers – the geometry of devastation, a high-powered football machine with enough momentum to blow the opposition away. Anelka's international career had taken off and he had played for France in a Euro 2000 qualifier in Moscow in October 1998, scoring the first goal in a 3–2 victory, and now he was playing against Russia in Paris. Petit and Wiltord scored but Anelka did not, which was hardly surprising with everything that was going on.

Also in June, midfielder Dietmar Hamann, who had joined Newcastle the previous summer for £4.5 million from Bayern Munich on a five-year contract, took the liberty of telling a German magazine that Arsenal were interested in him. Hamann, 25, said, 'Newcastle know what I want, and that is to leave. I can play Champions League football for Arsenal and that would be better for me and my career.'

Claude and Didier Anelka, Nicolas's brothers and agents, were proving to be utterly intransigent in the continuing negotiations with the Italian clubs and had sent a fax to Highbury saying, 'Nicolas does not want to play in Italy, he will never go to Italy. He wants to go to Real Madrid. That is the choice of his heart.' Claude, 31, was the elder brother, a former aspiring professional whose career was ended by injury. He was a part-time DJ at The Spot, a Covent Garden nightclub, and played Sunday football in North London with club owner David Blackwood. Didier, 29, had business qualifications and had negotiated with Madrid.

When this fax was delivered, Wenger was still trying to sign Roberto Muzzi for £7 million. With Lazio now threatening to withdraw their £21 million offer for Anelka, Wenger and Dein invited the young Frenchman to a crunch meeting in Paris which would decide his future, the Arsenal manager again expressing his shock at the underhand way in which Real's Sanz had courted Anelka. 'They are a big club run by little men. What they are doing is out of order.' Sergio Cragnotti had understandably refused to meet Real's demands for a £6 million payment to 'buy out' their option on Anelka.

Incredibly, agent Marc Roger now suggested that the striker could take Arsenal to the FIFA court for demanding that he observe the four-year contract he had signed only six months ago. Wenger must have wondered what planet all these people lived on. What a way to spend a summer! Still, there was better news when Cagliari agreed to accept £10 million for Roberto Muzzi.

On Tuesday, 22 June, Arsenal issued a statement saying that Anelka would be staying at Highbury. 'In the light of recent media reports, Arsenal FC would like to stress that it is our wish to retain the services of Nicolas Anelka. On Nicolas's impending return from holiday the situation regarding his future at Arsenal FC will be discussed and resolved.' This threat was enough to persuade the Anelka brothers to make a U-turn and agree to sign for Lazio. It looked as if Dein and Wenger had at last won the most squalid transfer battle in British football history.

In the last six weeks Wenger's frustrations had mounted as Anelka refused to speak directly to him or to David Dein while insisting that he would only move to Real Madrid, but now a resolution was in sight. As Nicolas and Didier prepared for their flight to Rome to meet Lazio officials, Anelka was all of a sudden singing a new song. 'Lazio are a prestigious club,' he said, 'and their squad is full of star players. I like their coach, Sven-Goran Eriksson, who has been successful wherever he has worked. I know what a fantastic city Rome is but above all it would be wonderful for me to play alongside Marcelo Salas. I still need to clarify my situation at Arsenal, then I will make up my mind.'

Wenger was by now desperate to complete the transfer so that he could concentrate on finding a replacement. Roberto Muzzi was still a strong possibility, and he still believed that Robbie Fowler could be available if the price was right. But Anelka was still proving elusive. By now it was obvious that Claude and Didier, knowing how persuasive Wenger could be when talking to footballers, wanted to make sure that their younger brother did not talk to the man who had trusted in his talent and made him France's top striker. The player Wenger had described as reliable and shy only ten weeks before was now hidden away in Martinique. In the *Mail on Sunday* on 27 June reporters David

Walker and Bob Cass discovered this and wrote a story under the headline ANELKA ON CHEAP TRIP THAT LEADS TO A FORTUNE, which made the whole story seem like a bizarre soap opera in which three scheming French brothers had made sure they were incommunicado. The Anelkas were staying at Buccaneers' Creek, 'a £56-a-night economy-class hotel' where there were no telephones in the bedrooms, so negotiations had to be conducted solely by mobile phone. This scenario made them seem subversive, as if it was a kidnapping. The brothers continued to talk to Lazio officials, who said a deal was imminent.

Wenger was on holiday in the Riviera, recovering from a knee operation, and he said that Anelka was risking his international career by leaving Arsenal. 'Two weeks ago, I was sure Anelka was going to stay, but today I'm a little more pessimistic because he is showing a real determination to leave us. By leaving us, Nicolas is taking a real risk, knowing that at the end of the season there is the Euro 2000 tournament.'

It was then reported that Real Madrid had pulled out of the chase, and that Lazio could now pay less than the £23.5 million they had offered the week before. A fee of around £20 million was now expected to clinch the deal. On 29 June Anelka was insisting that Arsenal could not complain about illegal approaches made to him since that was how Wenger acquired him in the first place. 'All the clubs do that,' he said. 'Arsenal did the same thing with me to get me to leave Paris Saint Germain. My priority is to join Real Madrid, but if that does not work out, why not Lazio? I prefer that than to return to Arsenal. I would have no problem going to Italy. I always planned to play there one day.'

These shabby events left Wenger in an extremely vulnerable position. July had begun, and the shrewd team-builder who had reconstructed his side so brilliantly two summers before found himself in a situation where he did not have Anelka or a replacement or the money to buy a replacement. He was now said to be keen on Brazilian striker Christian, 23, of Internacional of Porto Alegre.

On Sunday, 4 July, Anelka told the *Corriere dello Sport* that talks over his move to Lazio had stalled, partly because of new interest shown by Juventus and Parma. He admitted, however, that he thought Arsène Wenger a reasonable man. 'He's got the ability to listen to others. He's very fair. He's understood the reasons for my decision. I think that by Tuesday the transfer will all be sorted out. I'm an Arsenal player, but their club officials have to listen to my desires and to respect my wishes.' Of Dein, he said, 'He wants all the money he can possibly get out of the transfer.'

The next day Anelka went further, accusing Dein of thinking of 'money, money and only money'. 'David Dein is keeping this deal from going through because he wants to make as much out of it as possible. We were supposed to complete the transfer on Friday, but Arsenal got late inquiries from Juventus and Parma, so they asked for more time. It does not matter, however, because I want to play for Lazio. Arsenal are a big club, but Lazio have a virtual dream-team, filled with world-class players. It will be an honour to play alongside them.'

By Tuesday there was a new twist: Lazio had offered Arsenal a player plus £20 million. Wenger wanted Marcelo Salas, who was not available; Cragnotti offered one out of Alen Boksic, Fernando Couto, Pavel Nedved and Kennet Andersson.

Former Arsenal striker Alan Smith, who had played with Adams and Dixon in the 1989 championship-winning team, then entered the fray via his *Telegraph* column, lamenting the anti-social personality of Anelka, who always gave one-word answers when team-mates tried to make casual conversation, and the fact that he had no pals at the club apart from David Grondin, the young left-back who had recently been loaned back to St Etienne. He said that Anelka had never understood English dressing-room humour and thought that everyone was taking the mickey out of him. Smith wrote, 'On one occasion last year, as the team bus prepared to depart for an away game, somebody noticed that Anelka was missing. He was refusing to travel. Wenger had to get off and try to coax the player, via his brother, on to the coach. He did eventually succeed but only after listening to Nicolas's gripes about how the entire team disliked him. The times the loner did make it on to the bus, his first move was always to quickly slip on some headphones and watch a film intensely on his laptop. For the next four hours or so his eyes would never leave the screen.'

Early that July, Wenger sold Steve Bould to Sunderland for £400,000. The big defender had another twelve months of his contract to run, but Peter Reid had offered him regular first-team football. 'Arsène has been top class,' said Bould, who was 36. 'He said that if someone came in for me he would let me go if that's what I wanted. It's a chance of regular first-team football. But it was Arsène's fitness regime which has probably extended my career by two years, maybe more.' Bould, when asked, said he was convinced Anelka would be better off remaining at Highbury for the time being. 'I wish he was staying at Arsenal because he is a great player. I believe another two years under Wenger would have done him big favours. It's all about money, though. Football is big business, and who can knock him for what he is going to earn?' The solidarity expressed in that last line might have shocked some fans, but the game had been all about money for a long time.

Anelka's next move was to threaten a legal case that would allow him to join Lazio for no transfer fee, a development that was more extraordinary than anything that had happened so far. His lawyer, Marguerite Fauconette, said that she had discovered an obscure European employment law which would allow Anelka to walk out on Arsenal simply by paying them three months' wages in compensation (around £200,000). However, it turned out that any legal battle would be a test case because that particular European agreement did not yet apply in the United Kingdom.

Arsenal had by now suggested a swap deal involving a fee of £15 million plus striker Alen Boksic as one way to end the stalemate, but Boksic did not want to leave Rome. By this time Roberto Muzzi had said that he would rather join Udinese; Wenger had been interested in Inter Milan's young hot-shot Andrea Pirlo and Greek striker Nikos Maklas, a prolific goal poacher for Vitesse Arnhem who had just been signed by Ajax for £5 million. David Dein, however, was still holding out for £22 million from Lazio, with Didier Anelka saying, 'Nicolas wants to go to Italy and has definitely chosen Lazio for the seriousness and importance of the club. And also for the players who will be around him there. Nicolas wants the best, and today the best is Lazio.'

By Monday, 12 July, Dein was apparently ready to call Lazio's bluff and keep Anelka at Arsenal if the Italians did not increase their bid, although Cragnotti was saying, 'I will be making a new offer to Arsenal for Anelka tonight. We will make a small improvement to the offer but it will be our final offer and if that is not accepted by tomorrow night we will leave the negotiating table.' Dein was confident that Juventus would still top Lazio's highest bid, and since Wenger wanted Thierry Henry, that would be a better deal for Arsenal. Time, however, was running out and all the available strikers were being signed up.

Cragnotti then faxed Dein to inform him that unless Arsenal lowered their asking price of £22 million there was no possibility of a deal being done. The agents, Marc Roger and the Anelka brothers, were insisting on a huge cut for themselves, so Cragnotti was understood to have told Dein that 'the offer of £18 million cannot be modified due to budgetary restrictions and on account of the heavy commission that Lazio would have to pay to the agents of Nicolas Anelka'. The size of this commission was variously reported as £5 million and £6.5 million.

On Thursday, 15 July, lawyer Alisdair Bell, an adviser to UEFA, warned Anelka that he would not be able to walk out of his contract. 'George Michael tried to walk out on his contract with Sony and he wasn't able to,' said Bell. 'That incident is a good comparison to this. Michael demanded the same thing as Anelka is demanding now, and that result was subject to English law, as will this one. Being tied to a record company is like being tied to a football club – you can't just walk out.' Bell believed that if Anelka's move to Lazio did not happen the best he could hope to do was buy himself out of his Arsenal contract.

Anelka versus Arsenal had turned into an extraordinary battle of wills, a game played for very high stakes, but the saga had by now become extremely tiresome for everyone and the club had started to take some flak. In June it had been said that the Anelkas were greedy, but by mid-July people had started to say that Arsenal were greedy as well.

Over the weekend Lazio made their 'final final' offer, which still fell £4 million short of Arsenal's asking price. But this time

Cragnotti cleverly guaranteed to pay Arsenal the difference, in cash, if Lazio sold Anelka before 2003, which reflected Lazio's sensitivity to Arsenal's suspicion that their aim was to make a quick profit in an inflationary transfer market. Cragnotti's personal spokesman said, 'David Dein has been going round all over Europe saying we just want to make money out of Anelka, so we are offering to pay the difference if he leaves.'

Meanwhile, Wenger signed 25-year-old Brazilian left-back Silvinho from Corinthians for £4 million and established a training camp in Lyon to prepare for friendly matches against newly promoted St Etienne on 24 July and Monaco on 26 July. He now had to figure out which of his new players would be in the team and how they would manage without their main goalscorer. Life with Anelka had been difficult at times, but he would be hard to replace. Bergkamp and Overmars were injured for the St Etienne game, so he picked Kanu and Ljungberg up front with Silvinho on the left wing. The full team was: Seaman; Luzhny, Keown, Grimandi, Winterburn; Parlour, Vieira, Petit, Silvinho; Kanu, Ljungberg.

Wenger knew that the threat of Anelka's pace had dictated the shape of many Arsenal games, making them less compressed so that Vieira and the others had more space in midfield. The loss of their speedy striker therefore had a big impact all over the field. If Arsenal stopped attacking at lightning speed and played more passes, they were more likely to lose the ball in dangerous areas and be subjected to counter-attacks at times when they had too few players behind the ball. Indeed, both St Etienne goals in a 2–2 draw came that way. The keeper hoofed a big ball downfield, Luzhny headed forward, Vieira tried a risky short touch to Petit, the ball was intercepted and Aloisio scored. Then Vieira chested a ball and was fouled, Aloisio flicked the ball behind Grimandi and Revelles spun into space and hit a volley past Seaman from sixteen yards. Arsenal were 2–0 down after nine minutes and playing like strangers. Then Petit intercepted and Kanu produced a classy left-foot shot. Kanu then had another shot saved, but Ljungberg volleyed in the rebound. It was a very untidy game in which Parlour, who usually worked well with Bergkamp and Anelka, looked lost. After the goals the contest fizzled out in a parade of substitutes.

For the game against Monaco in Clermont Ferrand Boa Morte was up front alongside Kanu. Unfortunately, half of Boa Morte's passes went to his opponents and the other half were fifty-fifty balls. The game was dozy compared to the St Etienne match, played at sixty per cent of the tempo, but even with a slower game it was difficult for Arsenal to change their style of play. They did not make enough runs to support the main striker – they had lost that habit because neither Wright nor Anelka had passed very much. The team, struggling to adapt to life without Anelka, looked very frustrated. Vieira hacked someone down to earn a yellow card, and there was an incident between keeper Fabien Barthez and Winterburn. Petit made a comment about it and the referee walked across to the bench to speak to Wenger. 'I want you to take Petit off or I will send him off,' the official said. So Wenger put Stefan Malz, his new German midfielder, on for Petit.

At half-time Wenger experimented by putting Grimandi on for Upson and Luzhny on for Parlour, so that the Ukrainian was playing in front of Dixon in a 4–4–2. But now Vieira was having to carry the ball thirty yards when he would have preferred to push it down the channels. The Charity Shield against Manchester United was just days away, and Wenger must have thought, 'Alex Ferguson will love an Arsenal attack without pace. We terrified them in last year's Charity Shield when Anelka turned Stam inside out. But now they won't be scared of us!'

After the Monaco game Wenger issued an ultimatum, telling Anelka to find a new club within two days or return to Arsenal. 'If in 48 hours Anelka has not found another club we will consider him an Arsenal player, that he's coming back home to us.'

By this time the Lazio deal had broken down completely because they refused to increase their 'final final' offer of £20 million. Cragnotti had said, 'Lazio have decided to withdraw definitively from the negotiations to buy Anelka from Arsenal.' Wenger summed up the impasse by saying, 'The situation is very bad for Anelka's career. He doesn't gain anything with this and the club also loses. Arsenal and Lazio are in agreement so the fault lies with the player. What's happening this summer is abnormal because the contracts between players and clubs are no longer controlled by the directors.'

By Monday, 26 July, Ivan Speck was telling *Mail* readers that Anelka would become a Lazio player if he agreed to take a £4 million pay cut over four years so that Lazio could agree to meet Dein's £22 million asking price. The negotiations seemed endless, but nobody had yet asked the $64,000 question: Was Anelka mature enough to make it in Serie A, the tightest, most tactical league in the world? Without the help of Petit and Vieira? Without the passes of Bergkamp? Without the guiding hand of an ultra-sympathetic coach? The whole thing seemed ridiculous, and Arsenal were still, of course, paying Anelka £12,500 a week to behave in this ungrateful and devious manner.

Meanwhile, back at the saga, Marc Roger told *Soccernet*, 'We have yet to reach an agreement on Nicolas's personal terms because Lazio decided they wanted to pay him £4 million less to make up for what they are giving Arsenal. He is thinking things over at the moment. But I am hopeful I can persuade Nicolas to accept the new package Lazio have offered and that a deal can be concluded on Monday night.' The 'new package' was a five-year contract worth around £15.5 million. If Anelka refused Lazio's terms, Wenger would insist on his return to Arsenal, so it seemed certain the player would now back down, even though Roger and the Anelka brothers would have £1.5 million sliced off their commission as a result.

Then, amazingly, Real Madrid came back into the picture with a £23 million bid. Lorenzo Sanz claimed that Arsenal had been persuaded to abandon their complaint to FIFA and meetings had already taken place on David Dein's yacht in the south of France.

# 7. 1999/2000: THE SEASON OF HENRY

The 1998 Charity Shield had been a tremendous triumph, Arsenal thrashing United 3–0, but the 1999 rematch was approached with some trepidation. Wenger found himself playing his fiercest rivals at Wembley with half his team missing. In sweltering heat – the temperature hit 93 degrees inside the stadium – Arsenal struggled to adapt to playing without Anelka, Bergkamp, Overmars, Seaman and Adams. The plan was to feed Kanu and make narrow runs to support him, so Parlour had to cut inside looking for through-balls and Vieira had to use his power to run beyond the Nigerian.

Wenger must have been dismayed by the first hour. Most Arsenal–Manchester United games had been close, but United had been well on top in this one, Dwight Yorke making all the play and giving Grimandi the run-around, teasing, creating, making space, making angles. United had more rhythm, more understanding, more good habits. Then Beckham's dipping free-kick from thirty yards went in off the underside of the bar. Referee Graham Barber did not award a goal, but Yorke followed up to head home anyway.

Wenger could see that his experiment, playing Silvinho as a left-winger in front of Winterburn in a 4–4–2, was not working. The Brazilian could not find the right spaces to receive the ball because United pushed up, crowding the midfield. So he brought Boa Morte on for Silvinho and switched Ljungberg to the left.

The game changed immediately. Ljungberg fed Kanu, who fed Parlour, whose cross-shot hit the inside of the post. Then Irwin grabbed Vieira's shirt in the box, a penalty was given, and Kanu sent Mark Bosnich the wrong way to make it 1–1. Not long after that Kanu played Parlour in and his shot flew in off the far post for 2–1, and Nigel Winterburn, skipper for the day, led the Gunners up the 39 steps to collect the Charity Shield for the second time. It was a big day for Kanu, who had celebrated his 23rd birthday by scoring an immaculate penalty and creating the winner for Parlour. Remarkably, this was Manchester United's first defeat of 1999.

Wenger's post-match press conference began with confirmation that Nicolas Anelka had been sold to Real Madrid, although the contract was yet to be signed. He said, 'I am sure Arsenal will survive without Anelka, but I am not sure what would have happened had we not agreed the deal with Real. We have talked to Real and we are satisfied with their explanation of what went on before. Now I hope it is all over.' So Anelka had officially left Arsenal only fifteen months after becoming the third youngest goalscorer in an FA Cup Final. Conveniently, Davor Suker left Real Madrid to join Arsenal at the same time, for £1 million, and Thierry Henry arrived from Juventus for £8.5 million. Wenger commented, 'It would not be right for me to give you the figures, but I can tell you Suker has taken a substantial cut in wages. This is very unusual.'

The acquisition of this ageing goal poacher seemed like a shotgun wedding: Arsenal needed a striker quickly and Suker needed a club quickly. Suker was a patient predator who worked hard at being invisible and waited for an opening. Could the most passive poacher in Spain adjust to the rough-and-tumble of English football? Wenger had certainly transformed Petit and Overmars, given them new roles, made them look like world beaters, but they were younger. Could he rejuvenate Suker, who had been a problem for all four coaches he had played under at Madrid? Jupp Heynkes had fallen out with him, Fabio Capello had kept pushing him to deliver more, and Guus Hiddink had not picked him much. John Toshack had tagged him 'one of the Ferrari brigade' and then sold him.

Suker had previously played for Dynamo Zagreb and Seville. In 1996/97 he played the first of his 38 league games for Madrid under Capello, who had coached the club only for that season. He scored 24 goals and they won the title, but when Capello left and Heynkes took over, Suker had gone into decline. His stats over the last three years were those of a star who was going through the motions. He continued to play well for Croatia long after he stopped doing it for Real Madrid. He was the top scorer in France in 1998 with six goals, but it is never wise for a club manager to judge players in terms of performance at international level. Most millionaires can raise their game for a World Cup, but what are they like at Sunderland in February?

However, at the highest levels in all sports there is no substitute for experience. Anelka, for instance, had failed for Arsenal in the Champions League because he was far too raw. After his PAOK, Lens and Kiev experiences it was always likely that Wenger would sign experienced players such as Luzhny and Suker, whose arrival at Arsenal showed the way European football was going: the clubs in the Champions League were selling players to each other. Wenger had been severely disappointed by his European results; he had probably looked closely at those failures and privately vowed that such defeats must never be allowed to happen again.

Kanu partnered Bergkamp up front virtually throughout August for the first five Premiership games. Luis Boa Morte, so disappointing in his few appearances, was sold to Southampton for an undisclosed fee. Arsenal beat Leicester and Derby and drew with Sunderland, and then, on 22 August, played Manchester United at Highbury with a back five which contained, for the first time, three players Wenger had signed: Manninger, Upson and Silvinho (alongside Dixon and Keown). Ljungberg was in central midfield, and he put Arsenal ahead just before half-time, but without Adams and Petit one goal was never going to be enough. When Vieira lobbed the ball over Keane's head it went to Scholes, then Cole, then Keane, who equalised. Wenger brought on Overmars for Kanu, and then Suker for Henry, still trying to decide on his best team. Then Parlour lost the ball to Giggs and his shot deflected to Keane who made it 2–1. Both goals had come as a result of losing the ball in midfield and allowing Keane to run beyond the defence – the same problem they had had pre-season against Monaco.

When Arsenal played Bradford three days later, Vieira powered in a header from a corner, Parlour was chopped down in the box, and Kanu made it 2–0 from the spot. It was another short match at Highbury – just seventeen minutes long. The only question for the next 73 minutes was: Would Henry score? He missed one attempt from two yards, but Bergkamp was clearly determined that the Frenchman should break his duck. He had been down this road himself, and he had seen Anelka go down this road as well. Bergkamp knew how vital a striker's first goal was psychologically, so he fed Henry pass after pass after pass. Henry soon had a one-on-one but hit keeper Gary Walsh with his shot, then he cut in and had a shot saved. Wenger was using the second half like a pre-season game, looking at different combinations, checking things he would have preferred to see in July, bringing on Overmars for Henry, Suker for Bergkamp. The score stayed at 2–0, and when Bradford's cheeky Scouse boss Paul Jewell was asked whether Walsh had ever played better, he said, 'I thought he could have saved the penalty and come for the corner.'

Liverpool–Arsenal was Wenger's 150th game in charge. He had won 81 of those games but none against Liverpool, and that did not change on 28 August. Kanu was injured so Wenger gave Henry his first start at centre-forward, but Houllier knew all about Henry, having coached him in France's under-20 team, and he had by now changed Liverpool's culture. They played well and beat Arsenal 2–0.

## THE 1999 AGM

*It's always the same: if you lose a player late, you buy late. If you buy late, you can have problems at the start of the season.*

Arsène Wenger

Thursday, 2 September saw Wenger again sitting at a long desk with the Arsenal directors, this time for a rather dull AGM. The best moment came when a shareholder brought up the subject of the protracted departure of Nicolas Anelka. 'If newspapers are to be believed,' he said, 'Real Madrid are £100 million in debt. How can we be sure we will get all of the five staged payments?'

Chairman Peter Hill-Wood replied. 'I did mention that we have a bank guarantee, or we will have it.'

'You have it, or you will have it?' said the shareholder.

'We will have it.'

'When will that be in place?'

'Tomorrow,' said Hill-Wood. There was loud laughter and considerable applause. Hill-Wood, embarrassed, quickly added, 'That is absolutely true.'

The first hour of the 75-minute meeting was routine stuff: the re-election of Hill-Wood and Clive Carr, predictable questions about relocation, media companies buying stakes in clubs, the state of the executive ladies' loos and the inaudibility of the public address system in the West Stand. Other perennials included, 'Can you stop bombarding us with pop music?' and 'Why don't you show the whole game on the big screens like Spurs and Aston Villa?'

Hill-Wood had to apologise for not being able to give news of progress regarding the relocation of the stadium, although two sites were under investigation. He said it would take four years to build a new stadium and move in.

A shareholder said, 'We went to Wembley last year for the Champions League games, and you've withdrawn the planning application to redevelop Highbury, so it's very clear to all and sundry that the board have made the decision to relocate away from Highbury. I really think they should come out and say this, so that the fans and shareholders are properly prepared for this.'

'It is our preferred option to relocate,' Hill-Wood confirmed. 'We've never really hidden that fact. Saying that we are definitely going to relocate, however, would be rather irresponsible. We don't know that we definitely are.' This was a change from the 1998 AGM, where the chairman had stated that the board preferred to stay at Highbury.

Another shareholder wanted to know if the purchase of Suker and Henry was dependent on the money from the sale of Anelka. Hill-Wood denied this was the case.

'With Anelka going, it was important to get a player in, or two players. One was not dependent on the other. We assumed Anelka was going. You basically buy a player when you can buy them. I think Mr Wenger is looking to strengthen the squad at any moment he can.'

One speaker said that he felt the lunatics were taking over the asylum, for he had read that on no account would Anelka be sold to Real Madrid. 'We don't get the money up front,' he added, 'as a colleague has mentioned earlier. The problem I have with that is that the two forwards were signed three days before the season started, which is not ideal preparation for the coming season. One the manager says is not fit, the other is obviously taking his time to get into the team. I would put it to the vice-chairman, if it wasn't linked to the Anelka transfer, would it not have been better to give said forwards a full pre-season, playing in the pre-season friendlies? Can the vice-chairman answer, please?

David Dein, always combative when criticised, said, 'We did not want to sell him. We did everything we possibly could to get him to remain with the club. He eventually returned to England, he was desperate to leave the club, and we managed to get an auction going between three clubs. We did not want to deal with Real Madrid. However, prior to doing so we made certain stipulations to get them to explain their conduct, which they did to our satisfaction. We had originally made a complaint to UEFA and to FIFA, which is now being dealt with by their officials. I can say no more on that. All I can tell you is that the deal we concluded was in the very, very best interests of Arsenal Football Club. On what we achieved, I would like to think you are satisfied.

'Turning to the new players, the timing of that was really very, very difficult. Trying to make sure a club is willing to sell a player. Very often they are not. We managed to get Thierry Henry and Davor Suker, albeit it was late. But it was important we got those two players.'

The shareholder interrupted. 'With respect, Mr Vice-Chairman, if I can have the right of reply to that. Davor Suker, I'm led to believe, bought his own contract out. He was a free agent who touted himself about for a number of months. It seemed to me and my associates that he was bought very, very quickly, as soon as Anelka was sold. My point to you is, surely it would have been a lot better if these players had been in place pre-season, achieving fitness and getting to know the other players before having to play for the first team in what has been an inauspicious start for the club this season.'

David Dein clearly did not relish being reminded of those months of Anelka aggravation. Speaking with controlled aggression, he said, 'I'd willingly swap jobs with you for one day, so you can see the problems we have to deal with. For us to get world-class players in, very often the timing is not ours.'

Another shareholder noted that while players' wage costs had gone up 60–70% over two years, directors' costs had increased by 300%. 'Is there any particular reason for this?' he asked.

The question again brought loud laughter.

'Well, the principal one,' Hill-Wood replied, 'is Mr Dein. He had a fairly substantial bonus which the Remuneration Committee felt he had earned fully. I supported that, and I don't think it's excessive.'

As usual, Hill-Wood was now impatient for the meeting to end. He does not enjoy being asked questions he cannot answer, and he knows that many of the shareholders are educated adults who have more experience of public speaking than the Arsenal directors. At any moment an accountant, solicitor or barrister might stand up and ask a really penetrating question. Amazingly, nobody asked why Arsenal were going back to Wembley for Champions League games again, when last season's experiment had failed.

The mood of the meeting changed after an hour when one shareholder went to a microphone and said, 'I would like to congratulate Mr Wenger on an outstanding season last year.' This sentiment was applauded immediately by some 400 people, about half of those present.

Hill-Wood then said, 'That's probably an appropriate moment to ask Mr Wenger to say a few words to you.'

This was what everyone had been waiting for. Arsène Wenger stood up and spoke for ten minutes. He was 49 but still had a youthful quality about him, and he came over as a decent, purposeful head boy giving a report to an assembly of grammar-school parents. He proved, once again, to be a master of these set-piece events, someone who knows how to press the right buttons. With a group of players he is persuasive, with a group of journalists he is plausible and informative, and once a year with the shareholders he is warmly intelligent and likeable. He seems to have a lot in common with the shareholders who are, like him, mostly middle-class. His words somehow manage to contain exactly the right blend of honesty, humility and ambition.

'Once again Arsenal has a huge attendance and I must say I enjoy that,' he said. 'That's why I would like to thank you for the huge support you brought to the team last year. Everyone takes it for granted that we get 38,000. I don't because I've worked somewhere before that didn't get that. I personally enjoy it very much.

'We are deeply disappointed that we didn't win the championship last year. We failed by one point, but we made 78 points like we did the year before and lost only four games. The basic target we have reached is to establish Arsenal Football Club at the top of domestic football for three years, as well as we can. It becomes always more difficult because many clubs have big potential in England, and almost everybody buys and tries to improve his team. I personally believe that my responsibility is to work on the short term – that means to make this club very successful every year – and as well in the medium term and the longer term. In the short term, I think we can look back over the last three years and say we've improved our stock, and we've heard a lot about transfers today.

'As the manager I feel responsible to the shareholders to look at the balance, the financial balance. We spoke about Anelka, about Suker. We lost Anelka this season but the financial benefit was great. We could have said, "You have to stay in the reserves for four years, to learn a lesson." But at some stage we had to respect the financial interest of the club today. The pressure to survive at top level is so big that we had to compromise a little.'

Interestingly, Wenger contradicted the chairman.

'To get the other players in, like you said, I'm not scared to say yes, it was linked to Anelka, of course. Why? Because the wages of top-class strikers are very, very big. In my opinion, for a long, long time, Anelka stays with Arsenal.' This was exactly what one had suspected during the Anelka soap opera that summer, that Wenger always hoped to take charge in July after convoluted negotiations had stalled and persuade his protégé to stay another year. 'It's always the same: if you lose a player late, you buy late. If you buy late, you can have problems at the start of the season. Suker was not our target early in the summer, for two reasons. One, he had a contract where he could buy himself out for £1 million. Two, his financial requests were too high. He came down to fit into our wage structure very late. That's why he came to our club very late.

'As well I've heard some questions about the midfield, why we don't have better cover. But there as well I want to be responsible for the longer term. I want to bring young players in. I've done that my whole career. I've put Petit in at eighteen and Thuram at eighteen, and of course they were not like today. But if you want to give a chance to the younger players, you have to have an opening there. That's one reason. Second reason, to find replacements on the international market for Petit and Vieira, for example, is very, very difficult.'

Wenger went on to say that if you have a very good player like Stephen Hughes who has a player like Manu Petit in front of him, and you buy another player, then another, the youngsters will never get a chance. He said that was why Arsenal worked very hard with the youth team, who should provide the basis of the side in the future with the addition of four or five players from outside the UK. In the long term Wenger said he would like a team that is 60% home grown, 40% continental imports.

He then touched on the stadium question and the long-term future of the club.

'This club worked very hard to build a new training ground. It is one of the most advanced in Europe and will help guarantee the future success of the club. We spoke about the ground. When I go out there, I love this stadium, but we are now 17,000 or 18,000 less people than some of our rivals, and tomorrow it will be 20,000 or 25,000 less than them. That means, at the end of the season, a huge difference. And if we want to compete with the top clubs, in the longer term, how can we keep up the pace? 'You talk about Anelka. But if you sit down with Anelka, and tell him: Listen, how much can you get at Real Madrid? If we can pay the same, he might still be here. But at the moment we cannot do it. And that is what we have to find. But maybe at some stage in the future we will be able, if we want, to keep the player.'

He finished by referring to the two recent defeats by Liverpool and Manchester United. 'We had a deep disappointment last week because we lost two games and that's not happened for a long, long time in the same week. And we have to redress the situation very quickly, because last year we lost four games only, and we didn't win the championship. This year we have lost two already.' He also said he would be very proud if Arsenal did well in the Champions League. 'I'd like to thank you once again for your support, and I hope we'll see each other again next year. And we'll be very happy because we've had a successful season. Thank you.'

The French maestro sat down to a storm of applause, and Hill-Wood wrapped up proceedings by saying, 'I think we've exhausted ourselves, and maybe you have too. Thank you very much for your attendance. I hope you've had an enjoyable season. We'll see you all again next year with a lot of silver, I hope. Thank you.'

At the 1998 AGM, after winning the Double, Wenger had answered questions, but that was obviously not on the agenda this time. It may never be on the agenda again.


## FIORENTINA AND AIK SOLNA

*If you keep scoring late, you believe you can score late.*

Arsène Wenger

In September a manager is usually concerned about how his new players are fitting in and which ones can make a contribution to the team sooner rather than later. Wenger had signed a 31-year-old Croatian, a 30-year-old Ukrainian, a 22-year-old Frenchman and a 25-year-old Brazilian. Now that Overmars was fit again it looked as if the Croatian would be the first to claim a regular place.

Arsenal had often struggled against Aston Villa's 3–5–2 system, which stifled the pace of Wright and Anelka, so it was interesting when Wenger gave Davor Suker his debut in a home game against them on 11 September. In a crowded penalty area, where defenders outnumber opponents, they often create a comfort zone for themselves and switch off mentally. Suker had proved himself cute at moving away from a defender at the last moment to create a yard of space for a precise shot or header. In a low-scoring game, which Arsenal–Aston Villa usually was, he might do well.

On the day Suker was tightly marked by Gareth Southgate, the Villa captain, and just as the crowd was beginning to accept that it was a typical Arsenal–Villa game, where the Gunners had eighty per cent of the play but could not score, Julian Joachim got a goal from a Merson pass. But within a minute Bergkamp flicked Suker through to equalise. Early in the second half referee David Elleray penalised keeper David James for time-wasting when he held on to the ball, even though James was carrying a knee injury which prevented him kicking. Arsenal were awarded a free-kick eight yards from goal and Suker rifled it high into the Villa net. James was then substituted. Towards the end Kanu dribbled, fell, poked the ball to Overmars, took the return pass and made it 3–1.

Afterwards, Wenger said, 'We have link players but we needed a goalscorer, and Suker is obsessed by goals. We were dominating games in midfield but couldn't finish off teams. When Davor is inside the box he hits the target, and you can see how he loves to score. He reminds me of Wright both in his play and his attitude.' This was one of Wenger's stranger remarks, since Wright was fast, aggressive and kept losing the ball, while Suker was one-paced, passive and kept possession very well.

Three days later Arsenal's 1999/2000 Champions League campaign began. It looked like a challenging programme, kicking off with Fiorentina in Florence, AIK Solna at Wembley and Barcelona at the Nou Camp. Solna at Wembley was obviously the easiest game of the three, Barcelona away the hardest.

Fiorentina had led Serie A the season before, but then Gabriel Batistuta sustained an injury, morale had collapsed and they finished third. Italians maintain that Florence is a schizophrenic city with unforgiving supporters, a mercurial team and an interventionist president, the film mogul Vittorio Cecche Gori. Coach Giovanni Trapattoni now had a side unbalanced by new strikers Enrico Chiesa, noted for his explosive shot, and Predrag Mijatovic, a tricky, provocative Yugoslav. Their arrival meant that playmaker Rui Costa, the main provider for Batistuta, was being wasted in a deeper role. But then in Serie A many presidents collect stars who upset the balance and harmony of a developing team, a scenario Wenger would have found intolerable. On the night the diving of Mijatovic infuriated Arsenal, but they dominated the game. Overmars gave Ljungberg an early chance which Toldo saved. When the Dutchman put the Swede in with another cross, Toldo brought him down, then got up to save Kanu's penalty and clinch a 0–0 draw.

The next Premiership game was on 18 September at Southampton where Thierry Henry came on as a sub and scored with a terrific shot from just outside the penalty area. It was his first goal for Arsenal and it was a valuable one, since it was the only goal of the game.

Four days later a huge crowd of 71,227 turned up at Wembley expecting to see an easy victory over AIK Solna, who were managed by Stuart Baxter, the man Wenger had wanted as his number two when he joined Arsenal. The team was as expected, with Ljungberg wide on the right and Grimandi in midfield; Kanu, Henry, Silvinho and Luzhny were on the bench with Upson, Vivas and Lukic. In the second minute Overmars hit the best left-foot cross of his Arsenal career but Suker muffed the near-post header. Solna defended cleverly with a solid, compact 4–4–2 system, pushing up to the 45-yard line whenever possible. Nevertheless, Arsenal kept coming. After nine minutes Bergkamp played a pass to Suker, got the ball back in the box and hit the keeper. Then Vieira broke upfield, beat two men and slipped the ball square to Bergkamp as Suker made a run across the centre-back, creating a momentary gap. Bergkamp's pass found Ljungberg, who put Arsenal 1–0 up. After that it was one-way traffic.

Until the second half. Eight minutes after the restart, Winterburn, for only the second or third time in twelve years, was a fraction late coming out, playing Nordin onside, and suddenly it was 1–1. Time was running out when Wenger brought Kanu and Henry on for Overmars and Ljungberg. There were desperate moments towards the end. Two Swedes went clear of the Arsenal defence, looking offside, although the replay showed them onside. The striker delayed far too long, however, and allowed Winterburn to block. Suker produced an ambitious dipper from 25 yards, just over, then his exquisite backheel gave Henry an open goal, but he shot wide of the far post.

Frustration mounted. With two minutes left, Bergkamp began to foul defenders. But then Winterburn hoisted a good ball downfield and Suker headed on to Kanu. The Nigerian was wrestled to the ground by Brundin, but he still managed to hook the ball square to the unmarked Henry, who scored. Solna poured forward after that, and when Manninger punched out a cross, substitute Silvinho won the loose ball and flicked it to Bergkamp, who released Henry. The Frenchman raced away from inside his own half, took the ball right up to the keeper and gave Suker a tap-in. The score looked comfortable, but this was Arsenal's most uncomfortable 3–1 victory for decades. It might also have been the longest 91 minutes of Arsène Wenger's life.

He made five changes for Saturday's game against Watford, another hard-working team of journeymen who battled bravely. Wenger expected his side to score, of course, as the first half, then the second half went on, but when? Ljungberg crossed and Thierry Henry sailed in at the far post and missed the ball completely; then Ljungberg hit a low cross from the byline and Kanu failed to connect at the far post. Two sitters in two minutes. Would Arsenal convert a cross before Christmas? Ljungberg crossed again, and this time Kanu's header hit the post. Then Luzhny hoisted a huge throw to the near post and Kanu netted from four yards. The goal came three minutes from time, but as Wenger said afterwards, 'If you keep scoring late, you believe you can score late.'

## KANU OUTSHINES RIVALDO

*If you realise your ambitions so quickly, you start dreaming about new challenges.*

Marc Overmars

Wenger must have felt he had a chance of winning in the Nou Camp on 29 September, mainly because his defence was so strong. He had said Arsenal must defend collectively, a sensible approach because Barcelona had more brilliant players than any team Arsenal had ever faced in their entire history.

Rivaldo was more dangerous than Shevchenko, Zidane or Batistuta because he could win matches with dribbles, long passes, short passes, long shots, headers, crosses and free-kicks. The Brazilian is tall, strong, durable, awkward and very good in the air, but he is only flesh and blood, and he had looked jaded against Betis the Saturday before, a game Wenger, with his usual thoroughness, would have watched on Sky Sports. Rivaldo could be stopped by tight marking and tough, fair tackling.

In the larger scheme of things, Wenger knew that Arsenal needed time to get the hang of playing against the big boys in Europe. The Champions League is a steep learning curve, and the big question was not so much whether Arsenal could get a point. It was: Can the team handle it? The biggest club ground Arsenal normally visit is Old Trafford and the Nou Camp is twice the size. Would they get stage-fright in Europe's biggest football theatre?

Surprisingly, Kanu, the supersub, started the game and gave an astonishing 93-minute performance. The Nigerian was hungry, brave and immensely resourceful. He foraged, feinted, dummied, turned, jogged and generally made himself available everywhere. He was better than Rivaldo. Sadly, Bergkamp played like a zombie. When Wenger put on two subs, Ljungberg and Suker, he left Kanu on and took off Bergkamp and Overmars. Louis van Gaal also made an unexpected striker switch when he selected the nimble Dani rather than Kluivert, the tall target man. But Dani was anonymous and Barcelona missed Kluivert's power in the second half when Arsenal raised the tempo. Wenger was delighted to see Overmars play his best game of the season so far. He had missed chance after chance all through September and had not scored a goal in his seven games. But he showed, once again, that he has the big-match temperament.

The match had been billed by Wenger as a let's-find-out-how-good-we-are exercise. On the evidence of the first 35 minutes the answer was: not good enough. Grimandi gave away two 25-yard free-kicks and Dixon had to kick a Luis Enrique header off the line. After 35 minutes Barcelona had enjoyed a mind-boggling 71 per cent of the possession. Manninger was flapping and punching, and when he spilt a tame Cocu shot the ball bounced up on to Vieira's thigh inside the six-yard box. Amazingly, Vieira took a second touch and wanted a third, so Luis Enrique came up behind him and poked it into the net from four yards. What a gift! What was Vieira thinking about? He should have whacked that loose ball into Row Z!

Bergkamp, having just witnessed the most idiotic goal Arsenal had conceded since he joined the club in 1995, reacted by kicking Rivaldo. It was an angry, dangerous kick on the ankle and he deserved his yellow card. Vieira also fouled Rivaldo, another yellow card. The Barcelona crowd jeered Davor Suker when he warmed up, howled when he took his white top off and screamed when he replaced Bergkamp after 73 minutes. He had only been on the field twenty seconds when he lunged in late on local hero Guardiola and kicked his foot. Not content with that, Suker chased across the field, allowed Winston Bogarde to clear the ball, then dived in fractionally late so that Bogarde's follow-through connected with his studs. It was a very bad foul and the crowd went ballistic. If Suker was a hate figure before that tackle, he was a demon now. His name went into the book, and Barcelona's concentration went out of the window.

The second half had been a different match, nothing like the first half, but now, suddenly, a third match started. Arsenal were still 1–0 down, but at last they looked capable of winning the game. Then Grimandi elbowed Guardiola when they were on the ground, right in front of the referee, and was sent off. The pendulum had swung dramatically towards Arsenal, but now it swung back.

Then, incredibly, within a minute of Grimandi's red card, Kanu equalised. When Guardiola jumped and missed the ball, Suker nodded it forward and Kanu nudged Guardiola off balance. While this was happening the Croatian readjusted his body position, just in case the ball rolled back towards his left foot. When the ball did exactly that, Suker hit a shot through Guardiola's and Bogarde's legs, wrongfooting Hesp, who managed to parry the ball with his right hand. It popped out to Kanu, who half-volleyed into the corner of the net from eight yards. The game finished 1–1.

Wenger must have been disappointed that half his team seemed to be overawed by the occasion. Manninger did not cope in the first twenty minutes and Bergkamp, Parlour, Vieira and Grimandi did not handle it either. So five of his eleven players did not really cope with the pressure of the event. But he must have been encouraged that they were, eventually, well worth a draw. The next game was Barcelona at Wembley and if Arsenal had an inferiority complex before the Nou Camp they should certainly not have one now. Barcelona versus Arsenal had been fascinating but Arsenal versus Barcelona promised to be pivotal. Not decisive, but pivotal. Because if they could beat Barca at Wembley they could also beat Fiorentina.

Vieira then proceeded to let his team down again at West Ham on 3 October, where Arsenal lost 2–1. He allowed himself to be wound up by Neil Ruddock, was sent off and came back to spit at the defender, which earned him an eight-match ban. He later apologised for his actions and said he was ashamed of himself. Maybe he was still upset about his blunder before the Luis Enrique goal.

The build-up to the second Barcelona game on 19 October highlighted how difficult it can be for coaches to handle superstar egos. A small mystery surrounded an Overmars feature in the *Mail on Sunday* by David Walker, a north-of-England-based reporter who does not normally cover London clubs. Overmars was quoted as saying, 'I went to England to win the league title and FA Cup with Arsenal. That happened quicker than I thought possible. If you realise your ambitions so quickly, you start dreaming about new challenges. My next aims are to win a major trophy with Holland and to win a league championship trophy with a club in another country.' He admitted that his current contract did not expire until 2004, but added, 'When I first joined Arsenal three years ago I asked for a clause so that I could leave for a set fee of £10 million. Arsenal wouldn't allow that. At the time it seemed like a bizarre amount. Now such a fee would be negotiated by most clubs. If I'd had that clause in my contract last summer I probably would have gone. It doesn't matter that the clause isn't there. We'll just see what the future brings.'

What did Wenger make of these extraordinary comments? We may never know, but Arsenal fans were furious. If those quotes were true, Marc Overmars believed that Arsenal could not win the Champions League. Could Wenger accept this? Could he accept that mercenaries rule? Could he accept that Marc Overmars might already want to leave?

Arsenal met Everton on Saturday October 16 and played their best football of the season in the second half and won 4–1. Then they moved to Wembley three days later and played Barcelona. Why were they hammered 4–2? Three reasons: Tony Adams had a bad night, cynical strategic fouls by Barcelona, and exceptional counter-attacks by the visitors. Adams was very unlucky to concede an early penalty when Cocu dived. He slipped on the second goal, then scuffed a left-foot shot into the ground from five yards. He might have done better with two headers.

Tactically, the game was the most interesting contest Wenger has ever lost in England. It looked as if Louis van Gaal had learned more from the Nou Camp encounter than Wenger had, so Barca had a superior game plan and would probably have won without the penalty gift. The way Barcelona played was cool, shrewd and relaxed. They did not support their attacks, did not use overlappers, did not flood the box, and only won one corner against Arsenal's thirteen. Their style was mathematical, geometrical and economical. Very little energy was wasted, very few passes were wasted, and they seemed to have thirteen players to smother every Arsenal move. There was an element of Muhammad Ali rope-a-dope about the night – Arsenal wore themselves out and never saw the punches coming. The pitch seemed to be full of spaces that the Barcelona players decided not to run into because they wanted to save them for later. The game would make for a superb instructional video because the near-misses were as good as the goals: Figo's left-foot rocket, which Seaman tipped on to the post, Figo's header just over the bar from Kluivert's cross on 49 minutes.

Wenger must have been grateful for the enthusiastic support of the Arsenal fans, who were passionate, optimistic and marvellous. No recent Arsenal crowd has been so supportive. When the penalty was awarded they sang 'Seaman! Seaman!' because the keeper had been a penalty-saving hero notably in big games against Millwall, Sampdoria and Scotland.When Luis Enrique made it 2–1 they sang 'We love you Arsenal, we do!' and at 3–1 down they roared 'Stand up for the Arsenal, stand up for the Arsenal!' And they still had enough left to get right behind the team when Overmars made it 4–2 after 84 minutes.

Wenger had had fair warning from Frank de Boer that Barcelona were cynical masters of the strategic foul forty yards from goal. Sure enough, after nine seconds, Guardiola grabbed Kanu, who had dispossessed him, and threw him on the ground. Then Cocu cheated with his dive. Swiss referee Urs Meier was deceived because it was a subtle, understated, elegant dive. He gave a penalty and Rivaldo scored superbly with a shot into the corner. Keown was off the field having treatment behind the goal when Arsenal, shell-shocked and furious, conceded a second goal just ninety seconds later, Figo making a terrific stretch to beat Winterburn and flick on for Luis Enrique, whose finish was perfection. Figo was carded for a foul on Vieira, and when Bergkamp juggled the ball past Abelardo the defender handled and also got a yellow. Reiziger then obstructed an Overmars run, but escaped a booking. Arsenal's four midfield players committed just three fouls in the game, while Barcelona's four notched up ten. Not a huge total, but it highlighted their strategic ruthlessness.

As Wenger stood up from the bench at the final whistle and we saw his face on TV, he looked humbled. Of course, this very testing competition is an education for the club, the players and the manager, so the fans sympathised with Wenger, doubting whether he had ever wanted to play at Wembley. The Champions League is home and away against the best in Europe and Arsenal's choice to play 'home' games away from its own stadium two years running will rank as one of the biggest own-goals in the history of English football.

The Chelsea game at Stamford Bridge on 23 October, the day after Wenger's fiftieth birthday, started badly. Dan Petrescu made the first goal and scored the second, and Arsenal were 2–0 down with about forty minutes to go against a team who were coming off a sensational 5–0 win over Galatasaray in Istanbul in the Champions League.

Most of the match was played in a monsoon, so the pitch was covered with surface water. The first Kanu goal came when Dixon crossed and the ball rebounded from Babayaro to Overmars, who hit a feeble shot from 25 yards that was going wide until Kanu stretched to control the ball with his left foot and toe-poked the ball hard enough for it to skim through the water and beat de Goey's right hand. With this goal, Kanu became the first player to score against Chelsea at Stamford Bridge in the Premiership that season. Then he scored again. Overmars, on the right, crossed left-footed, craftily, to the rear of a crowded penalty area, picking out Kanu, who cushioned the ball at an angle away from the goal, avoiding the nearest defenders, so that the ball rolled towards the corner of the six-yard box. He got to it just before Desailly and buried a right-foot shot at the near post for 2–2. It was reminiscent of Bergkamp's audacious pass to himself to score the third goal against Spurs back in November 1996.

The winner was the best goal ever scored from a bad pass by a striker who wanted to score the goal himself. When Wise made a poor pass Overmars chested the ball to Suker, who was wide right on the halfway line. Suker cruised infield on his left foot, beating Wise; Overmars scooted forward looking for a return pass from Suker, but the Croatian passed wide to Kanu, who was standing near him on his left. It was the wrong pass under the circumstances. It was a pass that had 'You get wide and cross for *me* to score the winner' written all over it. Kanu chased the ball to the touchline, but Albert Ferrer got there first and attempted to clear down the line. Kanu somehow blocked, regained the ball and continued to amble down the left touchline. Incredibly, keeper Ed de Goey charged out of his area and tried to tackle Kanu somewhere near the corner flag. As de Goey came at him left foot first, Kanu jabbed the ball with his right foot against his own left ankle so that it bounced up and hit his right knee. Desailly was by now running back to cover the near post. The Nigerian then took a very delicate touch with his right foot as Leboeuf also ran back to cover the goal. This set-up touch was perfect, but he was a yard inside the penalty area and a yard from the goal-line. It was a hugely unfavourable angle, but Kanu hit a tremendous curving shot which flashed past the two French defenders.

What a moment! What a goal! What a player! What an electrifying hat-trick! Chelsea 2 Kanu 3! Was this the finest late strike among Kanu's many late strikes? Was it the greatest hat-trick in Arsenal's history? Ian Wright had scored some sensational hat-tricks, Anelka got one in the 5–0 demolition of Leicester in February, and Martin O'Neill had said that Bergkamp's hat-trick against Leicester in August 1997 was the best he had ever seen, but Kanu had done more than that. The player Wenger had rescued from oblivion at Inter, the player he had waited a year for, the player he had gambled £4.5 million on had followed up his stupendous performance in the Nou Camp by putting on a one-man show which turned the game upside down. When all seemed lost Kanu had scored three goals in the last sixteen minutes to put Arsenal second in the table, one point behind Leeds.

## BATISTUTA'S WONDER-GOAL

*It's a real regret to me that Arsenal have not yet played to their full potential in the Champions League. We need to establish the club as one of the top teams in that league.*

Arsène Wenger

Arsenal–Fiorentina was the crunch game of the club's 1999/2000 European campaign, and it looked like being a tight, low-scoring chess match. 'They play quite deep and wait for the right moment to strike,' said Wenger. 'I expect to be under pressure, but only for short spells, and then it is intense. They are like snakes, they have spurts and in five minutes they can kill you.' He admitted that his team had yet to earn recognition among the European elite. 'It's a real regret to me that Arsenal have not yet played to their full potential in the Champions League. We need to establish the club as one of the top teams in that league. Historically, that's what the club is missing. You are not a great team until you have done that.'

Wenger might have been expecting to be under pressure, but his players had won most of the important duels in Florence: Overmars had baffled Angelo di Livio, Keown had dominated Batistuta, and Luzhny had overpowered the fiery Jorg Heinrich.

Moreover, Barcelona's pace had been in midfield, Fiorentina's pace was in attack, so the Italians were more conventional – with the exception of Gabriel Batistuta, a shoot-from-anywhere centre-forward, a spectacular player who always goes for power, not placement. He gambles, fires cannonballs, so it is always going to be a sensational goal or a misfired rocket into Row Z – rarely anything in between. His Italian record was an amazing 134 goals in 219 league games.

On the night, Batistuta scored an exceptional goal with what seemed to be his third kick of the match. His first, a nasty late tackle after two minutes, almost broke Lee Dixon's ankle. His second, after 48 minutes, was a ridiculous overhead kick which sailed six yards over the bar. Then, in the 75th minute, the Argentinian scored the goal that knocked Arsenal out of the Champions League and proved, once again, that he is the greatest centre-forward since Marco van Basten.

The move that brought the goal justified Fiorentina's defensive strategy in the match. Vieira broke forward powerfully and promisingly but was tackled by Firicano. Adani hit a crossfield pass, Rui Costa laid it back to Chiesa, who found Heinrich just inside his own half, and Heinrich broke past Vivas and ran straight down the middle of the field as Rui Costa's run took Keown wide on the right. As Heinrich swerved past Adams, Batistuta was hovering onside and wide of Winterburn, on the corner of the penalty area. He stopped the pass with his right foot, and touched it forward instantly with his left, so that the ball went seven yards forward and he had to race Winterburn for it.

When Batistuta spurted forward past Winterburn, he was flying, like Colin Jackson going over the last hurdle in an Olympic final, and he knew he was going to shoot if he got there first. He was stretching but he lashed a volcanic shot through Seaman and high into the far side of the net. It was an awesome example of centre forward play, one of those special moments where an athlete suddenly has access to all his talent, all his power, all his training, all his experience, all his ambition, and makes a mark in the memory.

The whole move was superb – the dribble by Heinrich, the pass to Batistuta, the audacity and precision of the set-up touch, the electric movement – but the goal was astounding because of the velocity of the shot, the narrow angle and the fact that at the time the game was balanced on a knife-edge. It was the greatest goal I have ever seen in a one-goal game.

Afterwards, the articulate Wenger for once struggled to explain Arsenal's failure. He seemed dazed, like a boxer doing an interview ten minutes after being knocked out. 'We lost,' he said. 'We don't know why, but we lost. That's the reality now. We can't change it and we have to cope with that.' So Wenger was still the manager of the biggest medium-sized club in Europe, still frustrated, still just one elusive goal away from joining the big boys.

There were still eight weeks to go until Christmas, and the big story from now on would be the success or failure of his record signing Thierry Henry, who was only a sub in Arsenal's first four Champions League games and an unused sub in the fifth.

Quite simply, Wenger now needed to concentrate on making sure he got a return on Henry, his £8.5 million investment. If Thierry Henry did not score goals, Arsenal might not be in next season's Champions League.

## SEEING RED – AGAIN

*Freddie did not butt me. I don't know how he has been sent off for that. I have no problem telling the FA this.*

David Ginola

Referees have a very difficult job now that television proves them wrong so often. Wenger very rarely adds to the barrage of abuse, but in the game at White Hart Lane on 17 November David Elleray made two big mistakes, and Wenger must privately have despaired when the Harrow teacher sent off two of his players.

He had picked Kanu with Bergkamp again, prompting fans to wonder why he had signed Suker and given him the number nine shirt if he was not going to play him. Suker was the only centre-forward at the club. Did Wenger now think the Croatian was only a twenty-minute player?

Spurs took an early lead when Iversen scored after seven minutes, and Arsenal were losing the key duels. Overmars was well contained by Carr, while Bergkamp was pushing up on Campbell, asking for the ball to feet, backing in, turning, beating him occasionally, but never getting near enough to the goal to do any real damage. Petit made a stupid late tackle on Chris Armstrong and Ginola teed up the short free-kick for Sherwood, whose right-foot shot went round the wall for 2–0. Vieira got on the end of a Petit free-kick after 38 minutes and powered a header in off the post to make it 2–1, and soon after that a mêlée started on the far side of the pitch and Ljungberg was sent off. Then substitute Dominguez teased Keown, the defender lunged in viciously, and Keown was sent off as well. Arsenal lost the match and finished with nine men.

When Wenger looked at the videotape of the Ljungberg red card he could see that the circumstances were quite bizarre. Bergkamp had a a tussle with Campbell, who pushed him over, so Elleray blew for a free-kick to Arsenal. Edinburgh came in for the loose ball after the whistle had gone and kicked it out with his left foot. Ljungberg, standing close, did not contest the fifty-fifty ball because he had heard the whistle go, but Edinburgh, following through, kicked Ljungberg with his right leg and ended up in a sitting position on the ground. The Swede was annoyed by this and pushed Edinburgh in the chest – a mild reaction in the circumstances. Clemence then pushed Ljungberg backwards, Ginola arrived but did not raise his hands, Iversen got between Ginola and Ljungberg but did not raise his hands either, Armstrong came up behind Ljungberg and pushed him in the back, Clemence pushed his right hand in Ljungberg's face and the Swede then put his left hand on Armstrong's throat. Dixon shoved his team-mate away as Armstrong continued with verbals. At the same time as Iversen pushed Armstrong away, a coin was thrown from the crowd and it hit Ginola on the head.

Elleray then sent Ljungberg off for a headbutt on Ginola. A yellow card for a tame push on Edinburgh would have been harsh, but a red card for a headbutt that did not happen was ridiculous. Ljungberg walked away across the field, turning briefly to give the ref a V-sign, and when the bionic eye of the camera followed him into the tunnel he could be seen angrily kicking a door. He had been the victim of gamesmanship by Armstrong, Clemence and

Edinburgh. 'Freddie did not butt me,' Ginola said afterwards. 'I don't know how he has been sent off for that. I have no problem telling the FA this. I was just looking at what was going on and I was then hit in the face by something.' Wenger said, 'Frederik is destroyed. He said he didn't do anything wrong.'

The referee got it wrong again when he gave Keown his first yellow card. Sherwood had played a bad pass to Ginola and the Frenchman was not going for it as Keown made his challenge. Keown did not tackle Ginola from behind because Ginola was never between him and the ball. He was adjacent to the ball, which Keown played. There was probably slight contact, so Ginola dived, trying to con the crowd and the referee. When Elleray, standing only six yards away, called this a foul, Tony Adams and Bergkamp both went ballistic. Elleray had made the game a farce.

Next day, of course, there were big headlines: Arsenal's 26 red cards under Wenger. David Miller suggested in the *Daily Telegraph* that chairman Peter Hill-Wood should be hauled up before the FA to provide an explanation, but Pat Rice did not seem too worried. When Pat was on television on the Monday morning he was shown a photo of Ljungberg making the two-fingered gesture. He was asked, 'What does he mean by that?' and Pat said, 'He was ordering two tickets for the Scotland–England game.'

Like most managers, Wenger lives each game, and the preparations for each game, but for him every match is part of a sequence, a bigger picture. He thinks about the British game, the European game, the global game, and how football reflects the way society is going. However, like any manager, his mood becomes more expansive after a big win. So after Arsenal hammered Middlesbrough 5-1 at Highbury the ideas flowed out of him just as the passes and shots flowed out of his team. He hit some bullseyes when he talked about the stylistic evolution of the Arsenal attack in the post-Anelka period, and how performances depend a lot on fitness. He admitted that the two Dutchmen often perform below their maximum because they are carrying minor injuries which restrict their running and undermine their self-confidence.

Since late 1997 it had been apparent that Wenger loved a certain style of football, a dynamic way of playing which depended on early passes and explosive acceleration. So, day by day, week by week, he had built and tested an Arsenal machine that could win the ball and score two seconds later. He prepared his team to play technical power football, always hoping for the days when they would produce a ninety-minute goalfest like the performance against Middlesbrough, where he saw Overmars score three goals and Bergkamp two. He had often talked about killing the game, and this was one of those days when Arsenal were overwhelming. It was an exhibition of fast, skilful, precise, penetrating football. They certainly killed the game. It was a case of Bang! Bang! Bang! You're dead!

Dennis Bergkamp played his best football since the FA Cup semi-final against Manchester United seven months earlier, making the first goal, scoring the next two and winning the penalty for the fourth. So I kicked off the press conference by asking Wenger about the Dutchmen. Had they found another mood, another level, today?

'Yes, they played very well, but I think overall it was a very good team performance. And I'm very happy for them that they scored because they missed that a little bit. We had a good creative game today – good passing, the right concentration for nearly ninety minutes. We lost it a little bit at the beginning of the second half when we were under a little bit of pressure and lost our game, but I'm quite happy that we had a good, creative game for eighty minutes. The challenge is to repeat it.'

Best performance so far this season?

'Over ninety minutes, defensively and offensively, yes. I think we had some quite good games this season, but we could never put together defensive concentration and offensive efficiency. For example, against Barcelona, at home, I personally believe that going forward we were outstanding, but defensively we were very poor.'

You looked like a hungry team today.

'We looked a hungry team. We looked like a team who had time to think about what happens to them. And who have the intelligence to react.'

Does that performance indicate that you're now at your best?

'No, it's not enough. This team has a huge potential, but we have lacked consistency until now. We found a good level today and we have to repeat that. Consistency gives you a chance to win something. Potential, nothing.'

Pleased with Dennis today?

'Yes, I'm pleased with his runs. It was maybe the first game when he had so many runs forward, behind the defenders. And he looked really sharp going forward. That's why I'm pleased. Because he looks like he has changed his game, and is playing really to go behind the defenders. The mixture he had today, between coming off the ball and running behind the defenders, was right.'

Bergkamp often plays too deep and does not vary his game enough, so I could not resist the obvious question: 'Have you asked him to do that?'

'Yes. He wants to do that as well. He's an intelligent player, and he adapts his game to his physical potential. So when he had some problems at the beginning of the season, and was not feeling as sharp as he is at the moment, he came deeper for the ball. When we don't play so well as a team he doesn't get as many balls behind the defenders, so he comes and tries to build up the game. And last year he was always in a situation where we wanted him to come to the ball, and Nicolas to go behind the defender. And this year we try to mix that with Kanu, and that takes some time as well.'

This was a very significant point. Wenger had just admitted that he had asked Bergkamp to make more runs behind the defence in Anelka's absence because he could do that better than Kanu. Basically, August through to November had been a period of transition in which Wenger had had to decide whether to play Suker or Kanu at centre-forward. He had looked at both and played both and decided on the younger Kanu.

It was suggested that the team had regrouped in the time off for international matches after the Spurs game. Wenger, in response, neither confirmed nor denied this. He simply said that the team was at a stage of the season where they had to react. He said that everybody at the club felt they had lost some games they should not have lost. 'But I think the team realised that they have to show more concentration. Look at our season. We lost at West Ham but we should have won. We won at Chelsea but we were 2–0 down.

And we were 2–0 down at Tottenham after twenty minutes. So we are missing something. I think that is down to concentration sometimes. Not the right concentration when you start the game – maybe you think it will be easier than it is. And I believe that the English Premier League is every year more difficult.'

The *Sun*'s Brian Woolnough asked about speculation that the Dutchmen might move, and noted that Overmars had not yet killed off the speculation himself.

'No, because both players have long-term contracts. Long-term contracts mean that I want the player to stay. When I sign a player for a long time it always means I have a lot of confidence in his quality and his commitment to the club. We have no special problems with Marc Overmars. It was just things coming out in the newspapers . . . that's down to you!'

Is Overmars now back to his best?

'Yes, he's back. Marc had a lack of preparation. He went into the season injured. He didn't play the first games. He's just back to his best now. Tonight you have seen the best Overmars because they've changed three times the player marking him. That's always a sign.'

Is he the quickest player in the Premiership?

'Over the first five yards, certainly. I believe as well that he has the intelligence. And the timing of his movement is intelligent. When you add that pace to the timing of his movement, he is always dangerous. Petit is an important player for him because he finds him, and because he covers him defensively.'

Bergkamp's best game of the season?

'Difficult to say. He had a very good game against Barcelona. But it's the game where he got what I want from him right. That means his runs, the way he balanced his game, was maybe the best, yes. That's what we miss a little bit. So it gets easier for the defenders to push in on every player if they know that you don't go in behind them. So it's easy for them to hold the line if you don't make the runs.'

Wenger almost always talks moderately, never over-reacting, never exaggerating, even when the adrenalin is flowing after matches. He is a natural teacher, always supportive, always encouraging, but always patiently demanding more from his players. Coaches always want more, and although Wenger wants more than most he knows that some Saturdays are a lot better than others. This was one of the best, so his face, voice and body language told the same story: he was very pleased. He had an almost tangible aura of satisfaction about him because, having seen Bergkamp outpace a defence as Anelka used to do, he seemed to be halfway towards solving the biggest problem in his team.

The five goals were proof that this was the best Wenger's Arsenal had ever played without Patrick Vieira. The key point was that Bergkamp and Overmars had pulled their fingers out because Vieira was not playing. They knew they had to do the business. Necessity had been the mother of Dutch invention.

The five goals were also excellent preparation for the start of a fresh European campaign, for the UEFA Cup now beckoned, if Arsenal were really up for it. Eight of the 32 Champions League clubs had now been eliminated from Europe, including AC Milan, and another eight third-placed clubs had parachuted into the 32-team third round of the UEFA Cup in an absurd new format. This gave Arsenal a chance to play at Highbury and redeem themselves with a few victories. There were five Italian clubs in the UEFA Cup – Juventus, Parma, Roma, Udinese and Bologna – and four Spanish clubs – Celta Vigo, Atlético Madrid, Deportivo La Coruña and Real Mallorca – so Arsenal were quite fortunate when they drew Nantes, who were second from bottom in the French league and had lost their last six games. The easy draw was a sign that Wenger's luck had changed because it virtually guaranteed him another four games in Europe.

Arsenal beat Nantes 3–0 at Highbury on 25 November, although the result was better than the performance. On the Sunday, for the Derby County match, Wenger made four changes, the most interesting change being Thierry Henry for Kanu. This meant that Bergkamp and Henry were partners again for the first time since the Liverpool game at Anfield in August, when Arsenal had lost 2–0.

It was obviously a big test for Henry, and when Dean Sturridge scored for Derby after two minutes he really was in the spotlight.

Wenger had left Kanu and Suker on the bench so that Henry could start, but now Arsenal were losing at home and the pressure had doubled. Any chance he missed now would trigger a groan twice as loud as those which had accompanied his misses in previous games. After eleven minutes Overmars made a speedy run from inside his own half and saw Henry making a run from right to left, so he passed forward and Henry hit a first-time shot across Mart Poom and just inside the post, a beautiful finish. So the score was 1–1 and we began to realise that Wenger's changes were not rotation, but an admission that the Bergkamp–Kanu partnership had not really worked against Nantes.

Henry's pace had already elongated the game, forcing Derby to sit back more than they would have done against Kanu, and that gave Petit room to dictate the play, which he did in magnificent style. Overmars spurted forward again and found Henry, who took one touch into the box and fired across Poom for 2–1. So Thierry Henry came good at last and won the fans over. But was it a flash in the pan? Could Henry replace Anelka as a striker who terrorised Premiership defences every Saturday?

What Wenger calls 'our game' is a very fast, precise passing game which is based on explosive choreography, a game which, for the sake of convenience, we might call 'Bergkamp football'. The Derby match was a return to Bergkamp football: direct, dynamic, penetrating attacks. The fact that Bergkamp had a stinker was ironic, but Overmars and Petit played Bergkamp football on a day when Dennis did not.

Only three weeks earlier Wenger had told us that Henry could not time his runs, so his best position 'at the moment' was on the wing. The $64,000 question now was: Can Henry score regularly? Arsenal's attack often failed because the movement was not varied enough and if the attack was to be consistently effective Henry would have to improve because his on-the-ball play was far better than his off-the-ball movement. The Derby game was only the second time Wenger had selected Thierry Henry as Bergkamp's strike partner and he had scored two goals. After four months of experimenting he had at last found his best pair of strikers. But, this being football, as soon as something goes right, something else goes wrong. Bergkamp had gone off with a calf injury and would miss the next eight Premiership games, so Kanu partnered Henry in five of those games. Bergkamp did not partner Henry again till February.

The return leg against Nantes on 9 December was really an appendix to the first leg rather than a real second leg, and the game turned into an entertaining battle which finished 3–3. Wenger was angry with his team for not taking it seriously enough. When the draw for the fourth round was made he found that his next game would be at home to Spanish league leaders Deportivo La Coruña, who were like a Spanish Dynamo Kiev: well organised and technically sound in midfield and defence, giving very little away.

Then, on Monday, 13 December, Arsenal met Blackpool in the third round of the FA Cup. The date was an innovation everyone hated, since the third round had always been played on the first Saturday of January. Blackpool were third from bottom in Nationwide Division Two, and after fifteen minutes it was a massacre, but still goalless. Blackpool struggled to cope with Arsenal's pace, skill and movement and Arsenal struggled to cope with ninety per cent possession. Then, after 23 minutes, Overmars squared the ball to Grimandi who hit a fine shot into the bottom corner, his third goal in three matches. Phil Clarkson equalised, but Adams and Overmars soon made it 3–1. Oleg Luzhny, at centre-back between Dixon and Adams, covered well, headed solidly, passed accurately and ran confidently with the ball when space opened up for him. It was a successful experiment.

Thierry Henry was improving with every game, and he scored in a 1–1 draw with Wimbledon on 18 December, although that was little consolation for the loss of two vital points. However, a quick scan of the Arsenal teamsheet – Manninger; Dixon, Grimandi, Luzhny, Winterburn; Overmars, Ljungberg, Petit, Silvinho; Kanu, Henry – suggested that failure had been almost inevitable. The enforced changes had broken up all the vital partnerships in the team. Any team needs partnerships which cement the side together, and there were five key partnerships in this Arsenal team: Seaman–Adams, Bergkamp–Overmars, Bergkamp–Parlour, Adams–Keown and Petit–Vieira. This match was the first time all five of those partnerships were missing from the team. It was the dodgiest team Wenger had ever fielded in the Premiership.

## ROBBIE KEANE IS FLICKING FANTASTIC

*Footballers are made by their mums and dads.*
Mick McCarthy, Republic of Ireland manager

The game at Coventry on Boxing Day, a Sunday, must have made Wenger wonder why he had not signed Robbie Keane, the talented young Irish international. He must have thought, 'How many times have my scouts seen this boy play?' Aston Villa boss John Gregory had offered Wolves £5 million for Keane, but Gordon Strachan, who had just raised £10 million by selling Boateng and Huckerby, signed him for £6 million.

Arsenal started the match feebly, Petit misplacing passes and overhitting corners, Kanu sleepwalking, and Belgian loan striker Roussel winning balls in the air against Keown, who had just come back after seven weeks out. Then McAllister hit a thirty-yarder which deflected in off Keown's back for 1–0 after six minutes, and Coventry made it 2–0 when their Moroccan international Mustapha Hadji curled a right-foot shot just inside the post. Seaman thought the shot was going wide and embarrassed himself by not going for it straight away, then panicked and ran along his line. Kanu and Overmars had stinkers, but Ljungberg managed to get a goal back for Arsenal.

Then Robbie Keane scored an extraordinary goal to make it 3–1. There was a long free-kick, Carlton Palmer won the header against Petit, nodded the ball to Roussel, who headed down past the rusty Keown, and Keane was on the ball in a flash, flicking it sharply up and across Seaman so that it looped in by the far post. Very few players in Britain could have reached that ball as quickly as Keane did, and none could have flicked it so early, so hard and so accurately. He instinctively did the only thing he could have done to score from where he was. It was a goal made in the womb. As the Republic of Ireland manager Mick McCarthy says, 'Footballers are made by their mums and dads.' Then Suker, just onside, collected a long diagonal pass from Petit, left Telfer on his backside, swerved inside Breen and scored with a left-foot toe-poke across Hedman.

The Keane strike had been the highlight of Coventry's 3–2 win. We all knew that Wenger had wanted Robbie Fowler, who was not for sale, but Robbie Keane had been available – a cheeky dribbler with lightning feet and exceptional movement, an agile volleyer, an aggressive competitor and an electric poacher, very smart at gliding down the channels and bending his runs to stay onside. He can also head the ball and is a natural finisher. Strachan had effectively signed a £14 million player for only £6 million and left Leeds, Chelsea and Arsenal looking stupid. For Wenger, the most annoying thing of all was that Robbie Keane would have been dynamite alongside Overmars and Bergkamp because he is sparky and they are cool. The chemistry would have been perfect. He would have been exactly the right player to replace Anelka, but Arsenal blew it, big-time.

Wenger had now seen his team lose five Premiership games since August, so this latest defeat made Leeds on 28 December a must-win game. The shock team news was that Keown, Dixon and Winterburn were not playing. The back four was Luzhny, Grimandi, Adams and Silvinho. Clearly, Wenger feared the pace and energy of this bubbling Leeds side and wanted to reinvigorate his side with fresh, speedy full-backs. This game marked the moment when Nigel Winterburn stopped being Arsenal's first-choice left-back after thirteen years of astonishingly consistent service.

Tony Adams was soon thundering into tackles and making interceptions like the Adams of old, the fearless, ferociously competitive warrior-athlete, and we immediately knew we were watching an all-or-nothing performance by one of English foot-ball's supreme gladiators, a man who was reaching down deep inside himself to dominate this vital game. Many fans were gobsmacked. They did not know that Adams could still play like this. The way he played that day was a statement which said, 'I want another title before I pack up.' It said, 'Leeds will win this Premiership over my dead body.' Adams was also sending a message to Leeds manager David O'Leary, who played for Arsenal for twenty years and made 722 appearances, a club record. That message might have been, 'You know I was a boozer who pissed the bed, but I'm still playing and I'm still a winner.'

Leeds competed very energetically and aggressively. Vieira was being caught in possession more than usual, but as the game went on he began to improve, giving us glimpses of his steely power. This was a rough, tough game to come back into after such a long suspension. Alan Smith, a pitbull of a player, jumped into Petit, who screamed at referee Graham Poll.

The first goal was scored after 34 minutes when Kanu spun away from Radebe and shot left-footed. Nigel Martyn dived to his left and got both hands to the ball, but Ljungberg stabbed in the rebound. The game had been intense until the first goal, and when Smith kicked Grimandi in the chest, and was booked, one wondered whether it would finish with 22 players on the pitch.

Seaman had nothing to do except punch away a couple of crosses, and as the second half went on Leeds just never got going, while Thierry Henry looked full of running, full of improvisation, very positive. Arsenal made it 2–0 when Kanu gave Henry a great pass and he went inside Radebe and hit a fine left-foot shot – his most explosive goal so far at Highbury, his most Anelka-like goal.

So Wenger saw his new players come through with flying colours. Silvinho had been very quick and sharp, a model of energy and concentration; Ljungberg had had an excellent game – feisty, skilful, productive, riding tackles and recovering, sticking his foot in here, there and everywhere, a jack-in-the-box who ambushed defenders; and Kanu was back to his best form, playing a big role in both goals. Near the end, Thierry Henry had produced a brilliant bit of showboating when he flew on to the ball on the left touchline and juggled it as he sprinted, playing keepy-uppy, kicking the ball six to ten inches in the air as he ran along. An astonishing sight: Henry dribbling the ball in mid-air! It was an incredible and spontaneous demonstration of balance and coordination which made the nearby Junior Gunners laugh out loud. Hooray, Henry! Wenger had also, of course, watched Adams at his best. He had toyed with the Leeds strikers, dispossessing them and accepting their fouls philosophically, shrugging off the kicks and elbows of Bridges and Smith as the fleabites of novices. George Graham had said it many times since 1986, and Wenger had agreed with him: Adams is a colossus.

It was a handsome 2–0 victory over the league leaders, an immensely satisfying one for Wenger. Arsenal had ended 1999 in third place with a win which brought them to within five points of Leeds.


## LIVERPOOL MAKE WENGER ANGRY AGAIN

*Since I've been in football, when you don't win people always say, 'Do they want it enough?' It's the same old story.*

Arsène Wenger

In the FA Cup fourth round on 9 January 2000 Arsenal played Leicester at Highbury, and afterwards Arsène Wenger and Martin O'Neill revealed that all the significant action had taken place before kick-off in this dull 0–0 draw. Wenger said he had originally picked his team without Kanu, and O'Neill said that Emile Heskey almost did not play. It was a reminder that backstage life at football clubs is a lot more improvised than the fans imagine.

All week Kanu had been at the centre of an acrimonious tug-of-war between club and country, and it had been reported that FIFA would kick Arsenal out of the FA Cup if they refused to release the Nigerian for the African Nations Cup. Wenger said, 'I planned to play without him yesterday. Last night I had a chat with the manager of the team who told me there's no way he plays for Arsenal. OK – now we change again because I got the clearance at one o'clock. He was in a Nigerian restaurant last night. He was not even with us because I was sure he couldn't play. So I let him come to join the team at one o'clock.' Martin O'Neill, charcoal-suited and bespectacled, quirky and funny as always, in turn revealed that Heskey had travelled down to London that morning separately from the rest of the squad. 'We went for a walk at twelve o'clock. He wasn't feeling very well at all. I asked him if he could give us 25 minutes in the game. Just as a boost for us all. I said, "Have a think about it. Give me a shout at half past one." I didn't speak to him at half one. I just asked him when we were in the dressing room at a quarter to three. He said: "I'll give it a go." For him to play the whole game, I'm delighted.'

The draw for the fifth round was made before the press conferences, so both managers knew that the winners of the replay would be away to Chelsea or Nottingham Forest. Wenger was asked what he thought of the draw. He smiled and said, 'It's very difficult to go to Nottingham Forest.' Everyone laughed. A grim day at Highbury had ended with a good joke.

At Leicester on 19 January the replay finished goalless again, and Arsenal lost the penalty shoot-out, just as they had at Middlesbrough in the Worthington Cup fourth round on 30 November. Then they beat Sunderland 4–1 in the Premiership, Suker and Henry each scoring twice, which put them in reasonable shape for their next game – at Old Trafford on 24 January.

Many pundits reckoned this game would be a walkover for the treble winners because United, having been allowed to drop out of the 1999/2000 FA Cup, would be refreshed after their working holiday at the Club World Championship in Brazil, while Arsenal had no strikers. But Wenger, a student of the fixture lists, knew that United would be rusty, lacking their usual rhythm. They were poor in Rio, especially against Vasco Da Gama, and they were bound to lack fluency and sharpness. English teams find form by playing matches, not by sunbathing.

Wenger selected two strikers who had not yet played together, Henry and Ljungberg. Sure enough, United were a rabble in front of 58,293 people, the biggest crowd in Premiership history, and the Swede's gutsy attitude paid off after eleven minutes when Henry headed the ball on and he put his head in where Stam's boot almost caught him in the face, kept going, and whacked the ball under Bosnich's body. Arsenal were the better side and should have won, but Seaman missed a punch and Yorke hooked the ball back to give Sheringham a tap-in.

Ljungberg and Henry had done well together, but Wenger did not pick the same pair at Bradford on 5 February. Instead, he brought back Suker. Henry scored but Arsenal lost 2–1 and Suker did not start another Premiership game until the last day of the season at Newcastle. Then there was a problem with the increasingly temperamental Emmanuel Petit, who did an interview in the *Express* talking about how he feared every game would be his last, that he was worried his knee would fold after the next bad tackle. He said Wenger had had a go at him after the Leicester game, questioning his commitment. Petit was a ball-winning midfielder. If he was scared to tackle, what use was he?

Despite talking on the phone to Liverpool manager Gerard Houllier several times a month, Wenger never seems to be at his best after contests against his friend. Arsenal 0 Liverpool 1 on 13 February was a defeat which effectively put the Gunners out of a title race which had, ironically, opened up slightly with Newcastle's 3–0 victory over Manchester United. It was a cruel disappointment for Wenger and he was very sour and bad-tempered after the game. Arsenal had now won only two of their last nine matches. Was Wenger angry with his own players, or was he disgusted that Liverpool had played so negatively? Surely, after their dismal 0–0 draw last season, he had expected Houllier's team to shut up shop if they scored first?

Was it a significant blow for you, Arsène?

'Because we lost the game, of course. I think it was a poor game. That's even more disappointing, on both sides. I personally thought the two sides were poor.' Wenger had never before lost a match, come in and said both sides were poor, so I asked him if Arsenal had done enough to deserve a point. 'I think we deserved a point. Just because we at least tried to play, and tried to break Liverpool down, even if I think we didn't do enough to force it and we were not enough of a threat to break their defence down. I think it can be explained by the fact that we lost Petit at half-time, and by the fact that some players come back after a long injury and are not sharp enough at the moment to be dangerous.'

How deep is any concern you might have about qualification for the Champions League next season?

'It's very deep, because Chelsea's one point behind. Liverpool is three points ahead. It will be very difficult for us.'

Why has it gone wrong?

'I think we had too many players out through the whole season. If you look at the number of games some players have played together it's not enough.'

Kenny Goldman of ClubCall then asked, 'Is it a striker problem?'

'No. It is a problem, of course. But when you lose Kanu in the middle of the season, and Bergkamp is injured, and Overmars is injured, it's an explanation. We've lost three strikers – nine weeks for Bergkamp, six weeks for Kanu and six weeks for Overmars. That just explains that up front we have a problem.'

Who do you think the championship race is between now?

'Manchester United and Leeds.'

Just those two?

'Yes.'

Nigel Clarke of the *Daily Mail* asked, 'Is getting back on track going to provide you with the most difficult task since you've been here?'

'No, I've had difficult periods every year.'

This sounded, at last, more like a typical Wenger reply to a leading question. Clarke continued: 'You've always finished third, first, second – and now you appear to be slipping out of it.'

'Yes, but it's not over. There are thirteen games to go and we will see in the end where we stand.'

Have you considered playing Suker and Henry up front with Bergkamp behind them?

Wenger was very annoyed by this question, which is the sort of thing armchair tacticians talk about. His reply was emphatic: 'No, never. Not for one second.'

Brian Woolnough then mentioned a comment by Ray Parlour after the Bradford game, when he said that Bradford wanted to win the game more than Arsenal.

'Listen, when you lose games you have to accept that negative things always come out. I've no doubt about the state of mind or the commitment of the team. You can always find thousands of reasons but you always have to see what is important. Since I've been in football, when you don't win people always say, "Do they want it enough?" It's the same old story. But I have no problem about that. It's not about commitment, it's about quality. We miss quality at the moment.'

Kenny Goldman: 'You've had more shots on goal than any other team –'

'And we are less efficient. That's down to quality. And the way many teams play against Arsenal. They know how we play, so they just drop back and wait and defend deep, and then if we don't score first we always have a problem. And I think as well we are a little bit impatient at the back because we know that we have a problem, we need to score. So we don't have the patience at the back to avoid making a mistake.'

Wenger never interrupts a question. It was obvious that he wanted this press conference to end very soon. But first he was asked about Tony Adams, who had a toe injury caused by a swinging dressing-room door pushed by Petit. Wenger described his centre-back as 'short physically'.

If he was picked by England on Thursday, for the Argentina game, that would be OK?

'No chance. We live in a crazy world, but not one where the players don't play for the club but play for the national team.'

Clarke: 'Are you saying that Adams is not fit to play for England?'

'No, it's not that he's not fit. It's just not acceptable that he plays for England without having played for Arsenal.'

Clarke: 'So you won't allow him to join up?'

'No chance. Especially for a friendly. It's not like the country has to see if he is good enough. If he's fit in June [for Euro 2000], that is important. But at the moment he cannot play for the national team if he isn't playing for us.'

Jack Steggles of the *Daily Star* asked, 'Was it his decision not to play or yours?'

'It was my decision because I make the decisions. But deeply inside he agreed with that, because he didn't feel ready.'

And that was it. Seven minutes of Mr Wenger reacting to one of his worst days at the office since Blackburn stuffed Arsenal 3–1 at Highbury in December 1997. The good ship Gooner had been torpedoed by Camara's early goal and it was surprising that he did not give Liverpool a bit more credit. Perhaps his most revealing line was 'We at least tried to play', which suggested he was mad at

Houllier rather than his own team. Sky's stats gave Arsenal 65% possession.

It was mid-February and Arsenal were fourth in the table. If Wenger took stock of his resources he might have had mixed feelings because he had already seen the best years of seven of the players who started the Liverpool game. Only Silvinho, Henry, Vieira and Ljungberg could possibly improve. Seaman, Dixon, Keown, Grimandi, Parlour, Petit and Bergkamp could not get any better. Keown would do well to stay at the same level for a year, while Parlour might sustain his efforts for another three years. Silvinho, however, was establishing himself as an adventurous, dynamic footballer who wanted the ball all the time, and Ljungberg had done well against Liverpool. A week later it still looked like a cardinal error not to play him as a striker at Bradford after he had played out of his skin at Old Trafford. Arsenal lacked bite in the box and the Swede was giving them that.

Thierry Henry had also adapted well and learned English quickly, and he was liked by the other players. He had scored eleven goals and was quite good against Liverpool. He startled Westerveld with a thumping shot, powered past right-back Heggem to force a good block-save, headed a Silvinho corner a foot over the bar and had a good shot stopped by Westerveld's foot. Grimandi, too, had been solid. Still a journeyman, still a bit green, still getting done when he should not be, but mobile, durable, brave and a decent passer. Arsenal would have been in mid-table without his efforts so far that season. He had proved after all to be a worthwhile signing.

All in all, though, in mid-February 2000 Arsène Wenger was having a rough time, and the strain was showing. He would probably have been fine without the Anelka saga, but that had been partly his fault. He had thought he could find a way to keep Anelka for another year.

On 26 February Arsenal beat Southampton 3–1 at Highbury. Wenger was calm and businesslike, as usual, but very detached, talking about the match as if it had happened three days ago rather than half an hour before. Intriguingly, he said that constant competition for places was more important than having a settled first eleven.

'That was much more like Arsenal,' said Wenger. 'We had the needed reaction today and the needed performance. Not only because we won, but concentration-wise, spirit-wise, I would say we had what I expected of the team. It was a great test today, not of the ability of the players, but of our desire still to be at the top in our job. And I think we reacted well. I played Ljungberg on the left because I needed him there today. Because Overmars was a little bit short. He's maybe the player who can play everywhere. And he may be the most improved player of the season, compared to last season, when he had some problems to adapt and everybody said maybe he's not an Arsenal player. Don't forget, he's only 22. He has shown since the beginning of the season that he's one of the most consistent players in our team.'

When everyone's back and you've got a full team, will you play your best team in every game?

'No. If you say I'll play the same team every time, no matter how they play, the competition inside the squad goes, and that's not right. I'll play the team that has the best chance of winning the game, and I'll try to create stability in our shape and in the players who play well together. For example, when you play at home, Kanu–Bergkamp works better than when you play away. Because you get more space away and so you need more players who will go in behind the defenders. You need more pace away.'

Arsenal then beat Deportivo La Coruña 5–1 and while the scoreline was a surprise it was not a mystery. It was just one of those nights where everything went right. Bulgarian referee Ouzounov allowed the game to flow and it turned into a thrilling spectacle. Dixon ! Henry ! Djalminha penalty for 2–1! Djalminha sent off! Henry scored again for 3–1! Kanu made it 4–1! A Bergkamp free-kick for 5–1! Ouzounov was conned by Flavio, who dived when Ljungberg made minimal contact, and Djalminha showed his class by floating the penalty down the middle while Seaman dived to one side. The referee was also conned by Grimandi, who over-reacted to a butt in the chest by Djalminha to get the little sorcerer sent off.

The next two games were both away from home in early March. Lee Dixon scored in the 1–1 draw at Aston Villa and after that Wenger had to play a bizarre back four at Middlesbrough: Luzhny, Grimandi, Petit and Silvinho. This was the first time Petit had played at centreback for Arsenal and it was also the last. It was little wonder they lost 2–1. In the UEFA Cup they lost 2–1 in La Coruna, and then they beat Werder Bremen 2–0 at Highbury and 4–2 in Bremen, courtesy of a Ray Parlour hat-trick.

## MORE DUTCH RUMBLINGS

*We missed two chances with Arsenal to win the Champions League. In your career you don't get too many chances to win such a big trophy. Who has the patience to wait for the next time with the same club?*

Marc Overmars

Both Arsène Wenger and George Graham were smiling on Sunday, 19 March after Arsenal beat Spurs 2–1 with an own-goal and a Thierry Henry penalty. Wenger said, 'Thierry keeps doing it. He keeps improving, and he has just to keep fit and to work hard. He shows he has large potential because he has started to improve in the air. He's cool enough to take the penalties and I think he had a tremendous game again today. He is the penalty-taker at the moment.'

Do you feel Grimandi's sending-off was justified?

'It was a second yellow card. It was unfortunate. Gilles didn't want to make a bad tackle. But that happens sometimes when you're tired; you're a little bit late and you get a yellow card. He's a physical player. He's a defender. He has to win the ball for us and sometimes he gets a yellow card. But for me he had a tremendous game against Werder Bremen, and today again. I feel sorry for him that he got this second yellow card, because at the moment he's a very important player for us.'

For Wenger, there is always a big difference between a player who is sent off for a wild tackle or a serious misdemeanour and someone who picks up a second yellow card, which can be for something innocuous.

George Graham, the former king of the Gooners, appeared at the press conference in a navy suit, dark blue shirt and club tie. He had played a memorable role in the sporting life of Europe's biggest city, won six trophies for Arsenal and one for Spurs, but he now seemed to have become a cabaret turn. What is cabaret? Cabaret is when you sing the same old songs again and again and again. Cabaret is an act, but you try to hide your boredom, try to make it meaningful, try to make it convincing, try to make it real.

Was it a close game, George?

'Yeah, I think so. First half we started nice and brightly, a few corners, a few poor efforts on goal from Iversen and Ginola, should maybe have done a litle bit better. I agree with Arsène. I think they looked tired, too many games. They were there to be beaten today. We just couldn't capitalise on it second half. We had lots of possession but didn't really create enough.'

Why did you play Ginola on the right?

'I wanted to see how good a defender Silvinho was.'

How good is he?

'I don't know. I still don't know. David created the chance, great cross and a lovely little flick. If you consider Arsenal's two goals – one's an own goal and one's a penalty.'

Wenger had mentioned the special atmosphere at Highbury that day, but would it still have been special had Spurs not been managed by George Graham? Rivalry is the lifeblood of football, but in terms of the Premiership Leeds, Liverpool and United were Arsenal's rivals now, not Tottenham.

The following Sunday, Wenger must have been shocked by a Joe Melling story in the *Mail on Sunday*, its headline OVERMARS TEMPTED BY BARCELONA CHALLENGE. The winger had made some comments which summed up his point of view perfectly. 'We have missed two chances with Arsenal to win the Champions League. In your career you don't get too many chances to win such a big trophy. Who has the patience to wait for the next time with the same club? Has every player still got the same desire and willpower to win that trophy?' Overmars reckoned he had developed considerably and had become a match-winner. 'At Arsenal I have become a more complete player. I can play as a midfielder now. I can decide matches, I can score goals and I can give the team something extra. But there is room for another ten per cent of improvement. To get that extra I may have to go to another football country where I will experience different challenges.'

Arsenal played Coventry on the day the piece appeared, and a remarkable thing happened at Highbury: Petit started tackling again after months of not tackling, and it made a big difference. They beat Coventry 3–0, but they were still fourth in the league. Arsenal never really got going in a tedious first half, but then they raised their game, Henry scoring his eighteenth goal of the season. Vieira played him in with a superbly weighted through-pass, Henry accelerated, took one touch and swept it confidently past the advancing Ogrizovic. This was real Wenger football: dynamic, skilful, direct and unstoppable. Straight down the middle – Grimandi, Vieira, Henry, bang!

Petit had been pressing Coventry in the first half, even pressing them in their own penalty area, and was flying into tackles. He was involved in everything. In the second half he took a free-kick wide on the right, the ball bounced into a crowded penalty area, hit Shaw and broke to Grimandi, who buried his shot from seven yards. Kanu then waltzed through to collect a Petit chip over the top and delayed for an eternity of seconds before dummying Ogrizovic on to his backside and stroking the ball home sweetly from two yards. In the next game they played Wimbledon and Kanu got two and Henry came on as sub, took a penalty and scored.

After that came the UEFA Cup semi-final first leg at Highbury against Lens, Arsenal ideally needing a two- or three-goal cushion to take to France on 20 April. Lens were missing several key defenders, and when the game started the centre-backs were shaky. The goalkeeper, Warmuz, who was also the captain, was obviously expecting that. So when Petit launched a fifty-yard pass, Warmuz raced out of his penalty area to claim the ball but Bergkamp zoomed past him and scored beautifully. After that goal, Arsenal dominated for the next fifteen minutes, but then Lens improved and matched them for energy with five players in midfield closing down their angles, swarming like bees, pressing the pressers, forcing errors and breaking quite well at times. It was a brave effort in damage limitation to keep Arsenal to 1–0.

Lens coach François Brisson came into the post-match press conference first. A strongly built guy with short black hair and a serious, businesslike manner, he seemed relaxed and satisfied. The reporters talked to him in French, and there was no translation. Then Wenger came in.

Will that be enough, Arsène?

'I don't know. I just think that we were a little bit frustrated coming off. The performance was not maybe our best of the season. The result was not too bad because we kept a clean sheet and could score a goal. But it was very difficult to get our passing together because they played very well, closed us down, and when they dropped physically in the second half we couldn't improve our level any more. They were wobbling in the last 25 or 30 minutes but we had nothing more to give and we couldn't kill the game off.

'Our target is clear: we have to go out there and try to score a goal. But having seen them tonight you can see that it will be difficult. But they have two difficult games now. They play against Metz and against Paris Saint Germain. We have a difficult game at Leeds. We'll see. Psychologically, championship games can have an importance in the second leg.'

It was a quirk of fate that two Premiership clubs who were also UEFA Cup semi-finalists should have to play each other in a league game between the first and second legs of their respective ties, against Lens and Galatasaray. But if Wenger really believed that football is a game of sequences, he would have had no worries as his team bus arrived at Elland Road. Leeds had lost their last five games while Arsenal had won their last six.

The visitors handed the Leeds players bouquets before the game in memory of the two supporters who had been murdered in Istanbul the previous week. It was a scene reminiscent of Anfield in 1989 when the Arsenal players had given the Liverpool players flowers in memory of the Hillsborough disaster, before beating them 2–0 to take the title.

Arsenal produced a powerfully efficient team performance on the Sunday, thrashing Leeds 4–0 and completing seven wins in a row. Wenger had fielded his strongest side so that they would have no excuses for not winning, and they had demonstrated the high degree of ruthlessness needed to sustain unbeaten runs in professional football. Ljungberg had been preferred to Overmars, a landmark selection by Wenger. It was the first time the Swede had been chosen over the Dutchman when both were fit – the manager had obviously seen that Joe Melling interview. Ljungberg was voted Sky's Man of the Match, on his 23rd birthday.

Arsenal then went to Lens and won 2–1 to reach the UEFA Cup Final. Bergkamp and Silvinho were excellent, but Vieira was better than both of them against a fast, aggressive French side who made Arsenal work very hard for their victory. Overall, the UEFA Cup had suited them and they had scored 21 goals in eight games. Thierry Henry, who had not started a Champions League game, had now played seven UEFA Cup ties and scored seven goals. If only he had arrived on 4 June, not 4 August. Arsenal now faced Galatasaray in Copenhagen on 17 May, the Turks having drawn 2–2 at Elland Road.


## TWELVE IN A ROW

*The ball rebounded against his hand, yes. But that doesn't mean they had to concede the goal. It was 35 yards out on the right side.*

Arsène Wenger

Three days after the victory over Lens, Arsenal won 3–2 at Watford. Henry scored twice, but then he missed the trip to Everton on the 29th, where Petit made Overmars the star by picking him out with a series of defence-splitting passes. Vieira, rested, sat on the bench with a face like thunder. The only goal of the game was a vintage 1998 one: Overmars sprinted into the Everton half, chested the ball forward, guided it brilliantly into his stride with his left foot and, with David Weir backing off in terror, hit the ball between Paul Gerrard and the near post. The shot was very relaxed, very fluent, with lots of disguise, the greatest Robbie Fowler goal of his career.

Arsenal had now won ten games in a row, and they only had to keep it going for five more games, against West Ham, Chelsea,

Sheffield Wednesday, Newcastle – and Galatasaray. Every match is a potential banana skin, of course, but ten wins was the best possible confidence-builder for these last five games.

The West Ham game at Highbury on 2 May turned out to be the most controversial of the season. Arsenal badly missed the pace of Henry, who was injured, and Kanu was feeble against Stimac. Five minutes before half-time di Canio put the Hammers a goal up, and it was still 1–0 after 56 minutes, when Wenger made one of his best ever substitutions: Petit for Dixon. Time was running out when Overmars got past Foe and rifled a low shot inside the post. Twenty-one minutes left to win the game. In the last ten Arsenal played fast, fluent, inventive football, and then, in stoppage time, Petit handled the ball on the right side and hit a tremendous shot which deflected off Stimac into the net. Incredibly, referee Paul Durkin allowed the goal, in the face of furious protests from the West Ham players.

There was only one question for Harry Redknapp after the match. Do you feel you've been robbed tonight, Harry?

'Oh, for sure. We were robbed tonight, yeah. It was handball. It was our throw-in in the first place. Luzhny's come right in front of him and kicked the ball out of play. And the linesman's just naturally put his flag that way because he's been doing it all night. And then the ball comes in to Petit and he handballs it.' Not surprisingly, Harry had the hump with Durkin because he had come with a team of 'odds and sods' and reckoned the Hammers deserved better than to lose to a handball in stoppage time.

I had the inevitable question ready for Wenger. Were you lucky tonight?

'I don't think so. Because I believe that overall we deserved to win. And it was an exciting game, a cracking game, with a high pace. West Ham played very well but I believe overall my team has shown a great spirit and great quality and never gave up tonight. In the end you can say it's a lucky three points because we scored in the last minute. But if there was to be a winner tonight it's Arsenal.'

Brian Woolnough asked about the Petit handball.

'The ball rebounded against his hand, yes. But that doesn't mean they had to concede the goal. It was 35 yards out on the right side.'

So that was it. A handball, a late goal, a fiery finish, an angry Harry, a plausible Arsène, another three points, second place, and a bigger, harder game to come against Chelsea and George Weah.

On a very warm 6 May Thierry Henry scored twice against Chelsea, whose minds were on their forthcoming FA Cup Final against Aston Villa. A through-ball from Vieira was misjudged by Leboeuf and Henry rounded de Goey to slot home his 24th goal of the season. Soon after that Bergkamp sent Henry racing through against Desailly. His shoulder-charge knocked Desailly over like a skittle and he scored from a narrow angle through de Goey's legs. Poyet volleyed inside the post with ten minutes left.

Manager Luca Vialli reckoned Chelsea had lost the midfield battle, and that Henry was virtually unstoppable. Wenger said that Arsenal had been expecting a difficult last 25 minutes but their spirit, determination and organisation saw them through. He also paid tribute to Henry, saying he had shown tremendous strength to beat Desailly for the second goal. Television replays explained the incident: Desailly was standing still and Henry was flying, so his speed did the damage, demonstrating a simple law of physics: force equals mass times acceleration. The collision provided an exciting and comical moment, although it was not funny for Desailly, who did not claim a foul, as some players might have done. His handsome face just registered disbelief and indignation.

In the last home game against struggling Sheffield Wednesday on 9 May, it was obvious that the players all wanted to avoid injury eight days before the UEFA Cup Final. Arsenal had already achieved second place in the league (of their twelve straight wins, eight had come in the Premiership), so they started without their three strategic brains: Adams, Petit and Bergkamp.

It was a still, sticky night, unsuited to a high-tempo game, so Arsenal took a long time to score, Henry crossing for Dixon to net the opener after 34 minutes. In the second half Sibon and de Bilde came on as subs for Wednesday, each got a goal to make it 2–1, then Alan Quinn beat the offside trap and went round Seaman far too easily for 3–1. Silvinho was sent on, and his 25-yard shot reduced the deficit, and then Henry made it 3–3. That was the final score, and Wednesday were relegated. Their manager, Peter

Shreeves, said the turning point was Silvinho's goal because its quality had lifted the crowd. With their minds firmly on Copenhagen, Wenger fielded a reserve team at Newcastle in the last league game and Arsenal lost 4–2.

In the build-up to the final, Leeds manager David O'Leary did his old club no favours by saying that Galatasaray were far inferior to them. 'There's only one winner,' he said. 'Arsenal as a team are so superior to Galatasaray. I still have many friends at Highbury and I'm certain Tony Adams will be lifting the cup on Wednesday night. I don't even see it as a close game. I can see them winning by two or three goals.'

## UEFA CUP FINAL MEDIA DAY

*It's been quite unbelievable the way the club's moved on from six years ago. Every single aspect of the club has changed, and I can't emphasise enough how much Arsène's had to do with that. I think he's been a massive influence on the club.*

Lee Dixon

Before the Chelsea game Wenger and his players hosted a media day at their superb Shenley Training Centre. From the outside, the training complex is just a place where footballers practise and park their Porsches and BMWs, but from the inside, it is immediately apparent that Shenley is a serious place of work for serious footballers which cost serious money to build. The high-tech complex was designed to Wenger's specification and is luxurious, reflecting the status of his gifted, multinational squad of players. It is a 2,500-square-metre glazed building which houses a senior squad gymnasium, state-of-the-art medical equipment, and offices for the coaches, physio, doctor and youth officer. A hydrotherapy unit, with swimming pools, jacuzzi and sauna, plays an important part in the warm-down routines and is used a lot on the day after matches. There are ten immaculate pitches including two designed for high-intensity use, with polypropylene strips inserted into the top soil layer to aid drainage and prevent divoting, and two also have underground heating.

When you are there for a few hours everything else melts away and the world is simplified. The working life of the players and coaches is divided into match days and preparation days, each day existing in relation to the match that has just been played and the match that is about to be played. There are newspapers and TV sets tuned to news and sports channels, but they reflect an external reality which is a lot less relevant than the internal realities of who is fit, who is injured, who is playing well in training. A footballer's life revolves around the fixture list, the clock, meal times and travel schedules.

On this media day reporters were welcomed into what is normally the restaurant, a huge first-floor room with glass walls and French windows leading on to balconies down both sides. There were large circular tables, each seating eight people, sofas at both ends and help-yourself coffee, bottled water and Danish pastries. Wenger wore a dark blue suit and did a general press conference and another for the Sunday papers. He said that a cup final can always go either way, unless you are playing a team three divisions below you. 'Some people will say Galatasaray is favourite but I wouldn't say that. We have a fifty-fifty chance. And we just have to go for it. In a cup final you just try to win it.' He said that this season's UEFA Cup competition was full of strong teams. 'You had La Coruña, who can be champions in Spain, Monaco, who will be champions in France, Juventus, who can be champions in Italy, maybe. You had Roma, Parma, Udinese and Leeds. So it was a highly competitive UEFA Cup. You cannot consider it as a consolation trophy if you look at the teams who were in there, and you had all the cup winners as well. It's a great achievement to be there, and if it's taken sixteen years for an English club to be in there again, it's not easy.'

He also spoke again about how going out of the Champions League had been very, very disappointing for everyone. 'Today, when you are at a club like Arsenal, the players feel that if they are not in the Champions League they are not at the top. It's such a big thing now, created by the media, that if they are not there they feel, "I'm wasting my time, I'm not at the top." To achieve something at the end of the season will give the players the feeling that they did not fight for nothing.'

Wenger confirmed that he had not seen Galatasaray himself, but he had sent scouts and reviewed videos and he admitted that sometimes as a young manager he was too obsessed by his opponents. 'You watch them and watch them and re-watch, and you forget about your own team. It's good to concentrate on your own strengths.'

He then talked about the return of Tony Adams in a way that showed his tolerance and ability to analyse character. 'He came back with a lot of other big players and the team feels more secure when he is there. The team felt, with everybody being back, stronger again, psychologically. It was a huge boost to have everybody back. I think when you come out of such a huge problem as he had, you have to find a new balance in your life. That takes time. He has found a new balance in his life. When I arrived he was just trying to get out of the problem and stabilise his situation. It wasn't difficult for me because he's a very intelligent guy. He had a little bit of a rough image and I was surprised to discover somebody who is very intelligent and sensitive. But he had been hiding that behind different behaviour.'

Tony Adams himself – big and rangy with long, untidy hair, wearing a pair of jeans, a striped shirt and a short-sleeved grey sweater – clearly felt a strong sense of duty towards his beloved club. 'Physically, today, I feel well. I've been very frustrated and very impatient. I had a double hernia operation in September and played 25 straight games, and I don't think that was very wise. I should have taken it a bit slower perhaps. So basically over the last month or so I've done a lot of work in the gym and it's been a slower comeback this time. I wish we could play once on Saturday afternoon, three o'clock, once a week – that would be the ideal thing.'

Lee Dixon, in black jeans and navy shirt, talked about the changes in the skipper since he conquered alcoholism. 'I can't speak highly enough about that side of his life,' he said. 'If you knew him before and you know him now, as a person he's totally different and he's a nicer person to be around. A few years ago he wasn't a nice person to be around all of the time. Although he was still a mate, he had problems and we didn't really know how to help him. You can have a conversation with him now about all sorts of things. He's done it all himself with hard work and determination. It just shows the character of the man.'

Only Adams, Dixon and Seaman remained from the 1994 side that beat Parma in the same Parken Stadium in Copenhagen, where they were now due to face Galatasaray, the first Turkish club to reach a European final. Dixon was asked about his memories of the Parma final. 'I remember thinking when the final whistle went, "How the hell have we won that?" Because we got absolutely battered for ninety minutes. We were the underdogs and we played like underdogs, got absolutely hammered and won 1–0.' He reckoned the transformation the club had undergone in the intervening years was mostly due to the manager. 'It's been quite unbelievable the way the club's moved on from six years ago. Every single aspect of the club has changed, and I can't emphasise enough how much Arsène's had to do with that. I think he's been a massive influence on the club. Certainly the club would have moved forward, but whether it would have gone forward at this pace – I don't think it would have been possible under anybody else. The team, the facilities, the stadium, everything, just the professionalism in the way the club's run. Everything's spot-on. If there's any problem, he sorts it out. Simple as that. And he doesn't allow complacency to breed in any part of the club.'

Thierry Henry was as friendly and laid-back as usual, wearing trainers – as all the players did – faded jeans and a light navy jacket over a pale-green knitted cotton top. He was revealing when he talked about Arsenal's pressing style, and about his struggles to score in the first four months of the season. 'Manu and Patrick, when they are in great condition, they can win the ball high on the pitch, and I can make some good runs. We scored so many goals like that this year. Some teams think they can destroy us, but Manu and Patrick can take the ball high around the pitch and we can counter-attack with me or Marc or Dennis or Kanu. So I think we always play like that.'

He said that when he first started to play football he always felt like a striker. 'I lost my confidence when I played as a winger because you have to cross for the striker. At the beginning, when I first arrived at Monaco, I was sixteen years old and I was a striker with the youth team. After, they put me in the first squad and I played as a winger and I started to lose my confidence in front of goal. I played four years. I knew what to do in front of the goalkeeper, but I didn't have that feeling any more. I think this year I missed so many chances, I missed more chances than I scored goals. So it was a little bit difficult at the beginning because all the time Patrick used to tease me. It was funny, but it was true as well. I remember I missed so many chances. Some chances were difficult, but many of the chances I was missing were not difficult. I think playing striker is the most difficult position, along with the goalkeeper. When he makes a mistake it's a goal. With a striker, when you don't score for one game, or two or three or four, you lose your confidence and people talk about you. They say, "He's not fit any more, he's not like before." You have to score to stay confident.'

He was then asked if during this period he had ever gone to Wenger and said, 'Look, it's not working, I must go back on the wing.'

'One day I wanted to do it. I didn't do it because I have a lot of confidence in Arsène. But it was so hard. In my mind it was so hard because I was always in the French squad as a winger. And everybody in Europe used to know me as a winger. So one day I thought, "I have to speak with the boss." Then when I arrived at the training camp I said, "No, it's all right." You know, sometimes you have players who stop when they have a little problem, but I thought, "I'll just have to keep going, and maybe we'll see at the end of the season." The day it clicked was Derby at home. We were losing 1–0 and I scored two goals. I was like a proper striker, I made a run. I can remember, it was Marc Overmars sent me twice in the goal. He gave me the first goal and I scored with my left foot – it was an easy goal. And I made a good run with Marc again. And I started to have more confidence. Sometimes when you score two goals you feel like a striker. So the last time France picked me I played as a striker.'

Such sentiments are common among top strikers, whose jobs consist of goals and misses seen by millions of people every weekend. In a *Gazzetta Italia* interview, Christian Vieri of Inter Milan once said something very simple and very profound on this point: 'Only a striker knows what it's like to score – and not to score.' But it was good to know that before Arsenal's first European final for five years Thierry Henry was now feeling like a proper striker.

## GALATASARAY

*We improved in the second half, but really we could not find our true game today.*

Arsène Wenger

In Copenhagen, Arsenal seemed to be intimidated by the pre-match hooliganism in the city centre and the Turkish-dominated atmosphere in the stadium. Adams and Keown were shaky from the start, and anxiety spread forward into the rest of the team. When Adams headed out early on and Arif volleyed, the ball hit Keown and deflected just wide of the post. Arsenal were on the back foot right from the kick-off and as the first half wore on they seemed to be too diagrammatic, too shape-conscious, broken up into three separate units of defence, midfield and attack, players staying in their boxes fifteen yards apart. Bergkamp was having to forage back among four Turks just to get a touch of the ball on the left side of midfield because Petit never made a tackle, never got into the game. Vieira and Okan were booked for fouls on each other, Overmars was giving a hundred per cent, scrapping with Capone and fouling him, but Petit was a jogging passenger. Overmars managed to recover a Bergkamp flick and drill in a low shot which Taffarel saved at the near post, but Galatasaray dominated possession, which is what happens when you are effectively playing with ten men.

At half-time in the BBC studio, Martin O'Neill reminded the viewers that world-class players can play badly. Ljungberg spoke to Garth Crooks and said, 'It's good. It's 0–0. Because I think Galatasaray are gonna get tired in the second half. Galatasaray have been running a lot in the first half and hopefully they're gonna get tired in the second half. They've been pressing a lot and I don't think they're gonna last for ninety minutes.' O'Neill reacted to that. 'It's a dangerous way to think. That that's how you're gonna win a game – the other side gets tired.'

In the second half a Bergkamp–Vieira move put Parlour into a good position, but his cross hit the near post. Then Hakan Sukur was through and Keown, with a last-ditch tackle, just managed to divert the ball on to the post. Later, Henry hit a fine cross to give Keown a golden chance, but he spooned over the bar from four yards. Arsenal were dominating the game at last, and then, on 74 minutes, Wenger took off Bergkamp and brought on Kanu. To little effect.

Who would score the golden goal in extra time? One shot, one header, one mistake and it would be all over. Arsenal got on top again and looked like winning. Henry had a run, but he shot from a silly angle. Then Hagi dribbled, Adams tackled well, and the ball went loose between them. Adams moved to impede the Romanian's recovery before playing the ball himself, as you do, so Hagi pulled his shorts and grabbed him round the waist. Adams flailed backwards with his arms, so Hagi slapped Adams on the back with his little fist. Spanish referee Antonio Lopez Nieto handed Adams a yellow card and Hagi a red card, and after that Galatasaray just sat back and played for penalties.

During half-time of extra time, Wenger could be seen prowling the touchline with his hands in his trouser pockets. Should he have taken a defender off and gone for broke? Grimandi, strong in the air, full of running, might have given them more presence in the box. Blocked and frustrated in the centre of the park, should he have tried to work the flank more using Silvinho's energetic overlaps? Had he backed himself into a corner by taking Bergkamp off? Did he not need to add to Bergkamp, rather than replace him? What a hellish experience it must be for a coach when the last match of the season, a UEFA Cup Final, becomes a journey to the outer limits of his faith, his ideas, his strength, his nerve-endings. Sometimes the hardest part of being a coach is to do nothing. Anybody can throw new bodies on, but if you keep faith, believe in your players, it often comes right.

Suddenly, the season almost worked out when Parlour hit a fantastic cross from the corner flag. Henry jumped well at the far post and headed down firmly, but Taffarel parried. Arsenal kept coming forward. Kanu swerved in from the right wing and smacked in a shot which Taffarel again parried, this time against Popescu's legs and back to Kanu, whose second shot was saved again by the keeper. A Galatasaray cross from the left byline then skimmed low across Seaman's goalmouth with no takers. Wenger put on Suker for Overmars for the last six minutes. Both teams were exhausted, though, and the last throw of the dice was a Petit free-kick from the right side. He swung the ball into the right area, Adams challenged, but the referee whistled for a push, as he did too often on set-piece plays.

The penalty shoot-out did not look promising as the kicks were to be taken at the Turkish end, facing a wall of noise. David Seaman had done his job well so far but he does not save penalties any more and Arsenal had already lost shoot-outs at Middlesbrough and Leicester.

Ergun took a perfect cool penalty, left-footed, just inside the post, beating Seaman's dive. Davor Suker checked his run and smacked his penalty against the inside of the post and it came out. When Hakan Sukur hit a slick shot high into the net for 2–0 there was bedlam behind the goal. Parlour was now under a lot of pressure from the crowd. But he fired his penalty perfectly into the bottom corner to Taffarel's right for 2–1.

Davala sent Seaman the wrong way for 3–1. Patrick Vieira seemed to rush his run-up, not taking time to compose himself. He hit his penalty hard and centrally and it came back off the underside of the bar. Then Popescu hit a classy shot into the bottom corner to clinch the first European trophy ever won by a Turkish club.

Man for man, Galatasaray had been more up for it than Arsenal. They had defended deep, broken up the rhythm by diving, worked the angles in midfield, played in little triangles and always seemed to have an extra player until Hagi was sent off. Coach Fatih Terim had really done his homework, and had got a swarm of players round Vieira and Bergkamp at key moments. Their pressing was backed up by craftsmanship, players who were resourceful and patient when it came to keeping possession. Terim's tactics nullified Henry's pace and isolated Bergkamp, who nevertheless played well in bursts and was furious when he was taken off.

Arsenal had looked too schematic, too German, with too little play round the ball and not enough support runs close to the ball, not enough improvisation. Ljungberg, with his energy and devilment, might have added a lot from the bench by getting into the box and matching Galatasaray's fiery commitment. Wenger had relied on pace to win it early, and on fitness to win it later on if pace was not decisive, and on supersub Kanu if pace and fitness failed to produce a goal. But none of those three factors was significant on the night. Petit had been abysmal, but Wenger was either too loyal or too conservative to substitute a World Cup winner.

The manager was furious that referee Nieto did not toss for ends to decide where the shoot-out would take place. UEFA officials, in response, claimed that the toss to decide ends for extra time also counted for where the penalties were taken. Wenger said, 'I can't agree with that. The referee may be saying that now but I don't believe it and I think it was unfair. Nobody has seen this toss of the coin which is supposed to have happened. The referee just told Tony Adams that it was what he had decided.'

On the game as a whole, he said, 'We had a not very good first half and in the end lost to a good Galatasaray side. We improved in the second half, but really we could not find our true game today. It is very disappointing because this is the third cup we have missed this season through penalty shoot-outs. We lost in the FA Cup and the Worthington Cup in that way too, and it is very difficult to take. If we had won the penalty shoot-out it would not have made any difference to the quality of our game.'

Wenger was probably the only manager in England who would have said that winning in a cup final on penalties would not have changed the fact that they had played badly. It showed how idealistic he was, how high his expectations were in terms of the exciting, entertaining football he expected his team to play. He really wanted to win that UEFA Cup Final, and he was devastated by the defeat. He later told Philippe Auclair of *France Football* that it took him a week to get over it.

# 8. 2000/01: THE SEASON OF ROTATION

In the summer of 2000 Wenger sold Marc Overmars and Emmanuel Petit to Barcelona for £28 million. Overmars had been a world-class player when he was scoring goals, Petit a world-class player when he was tackling, but Arsenal had been turning into Chelsea because those two players were just not performing in Premiership away games.

The manager again decided to invest in foreign players. On 11 July Edu, the £6 million replacement for Petit, arrived at Heathrow but was sent back to Brazil for having a fake passport. He had a Portuguese grandfather and was eligible for dual nationality, but only after his father had acquired the necessary documents from Lisbon, which might take six months, so he went back to São Paulo and continued to play for Corinthians. This was a severe blow to Wenger. Should he wait for Edu or buy someone else?

He then signed French winger Robert Pires for £6 million from Marseilles to replace Overmars, and Lauren, a versatile Cameroon player from Real Mallorca, for £7.2 million. He also acquired Latvian centre-back Igor Stepanovs for £1 million from FC Skonto Riga, and was looking at Lithuanian striker Tomas Danilevicius from Lausanne in Switzerland.

Tomas was Lithuania's under-21 centre-forward. He had been having secret trials with Arsenal for a week when the club took him to a pre-season tournament in Amsterdam to celebrate the centenary of Ajax. During the match against Barcelona, Silvinho rolled the ball to Tomas, who cleverly dummied Guardiola and rifled a shot past Richard Dutruel. Arsenal lost the game 2–1, but Tomas looked like he might be another Marian Pahars, the lively, brave little Latvian at Southampton. Big players from small countries might be just what was needed by Wenger, who said of Tomas, 'He's fast, he has good presence, he's good in the air and he's scored a great goal.' In fact, Tomas seemed almost too good to be true and Wenger made a bid for him.

The acquisition of Sylvain Wiltord proved problematic for many weeks. Wenger initially offered £8 million, but Bordeaux wanted £15 million. Four years earlier Wiltord had played for Rennes, who had sold him for £1.75 million to Deportivo La Coruña. Before Wiltord had even so much as played a game in Spain he was sold on to Bordeaux for £2 million, with a sell-on clause which gave the Spanish club 35% of any future transfer fee. That clause was due to expire in June 2001, so Bordeaux wanted Wiltord to stay and play another season so they could keep the full transfer fee.

For Wenger and other Champions League coaches the biggest date in the summer calendar was 31 August, the deadline for registration of squads with UEFA. As the deadline approached, Wenger said of the Wiltord negotiations, 'We will make the deadline or not the player.' In other words, he wanted Wiltord before 31 August or not at all. He eventually signed him for £12.5 million just before the Charlton game on 26 August.

Wenger now had a very odd quartet of strikers. The first was the best left-winger in the world, a player so gifted that there had been 26 moments in the season before when he had made scoring look easy, and made people think he was a striker. Alongside Henry was Wenger's second striker, an injury-prone Dutchman who had not been on an aircraft for six years and had only scored six Premiership goals in 1999/2000. The third was a Nigerian whose heart foundation was helping sick kids and who could not fully plug into the reality of Premiership football, where you had to believe that getting three points at Coventry is the most important thing in the world. Kanu also wanted Wenger to pay his huge salary while he vanished to Sydney for a month to play in another Olympic Games – a strange impertinence.

Now that gifted but often problematic trio had been joined by a new Frenchman who should have been a centre-forward who could head the ball. Instead, Wiltord was a five-foot-eight-inch buzzbomb who liked to get the ball in wide positions and come inside and have a shot. So Messrs Henry, Bergkamp, Kanu and Wiltord was an odd firm of strikers, a very unbalanced quartet indeed, and rotating them would prove a test for any manager. Finding one productive strike partnership would be hard, let alone two or three. It had taken many months for Bergkamp to help the great left-winger to score the goals that made Thierry Henry, in his own mind, a striker again.

## PASSIONATE VIRTUOSITY

*I want to make one thing clear: I will never leave Arsenal.*

Patrick Vieira

In Rotterdam on 2 July Patrick Vieira played for France against Italy in the Euro 2000 final. France were within twenty seconds of losing the match when Sylvain Wiltord equalised. Then David Trezeguet scored the golden goal and Vieira added a European Championship medal to his World Cup medal from 1998.

Seven weeks later it was back to business with Arsenal, whose first Premiership game was at the Stadium of Light in Sunderland on 19 August. The team played very well but missed eight chances and conceded the only goal of the game when former Gunner Niall Quinn headed home a cross in the 53rd minute. Seaman bottled that cross, jumping outside the huge Irishman. Vieira had been targeted for special attention throughout, and in the closing seconds, when Darren Williams grabbed him round the waist, Vieira kept running, swung his arm and caught Williams with a back-handed slap on the neck. Williams went down pretending to be hurt and referee Steve Dunn sent Vieira off. Most neutrals thought Williams should have gone as well, especially when the camera caught Williams winking at the Sunderland bench. After the match, fourth official Paul Taylor claimed that he had been manhandled by Arsène Wenger during an argument in the tunnel between Henry and Williams. The *Sunday Telegraph*'s Colin Malam thought Arsenal's opening day a harsh one. 'Sunderland won a match yesterday that they could easily have lost 6–1,' he wrote. 'Just to compound their misery, Arsenal had Patrick Vieira sent off again right at the end of the match. The tall Frenchman, man of the match by a mile, was shown the red card for retaliation when fouled by Sunderland substitute Darren Williams, who escaped with just a yellow card.'

Far worse was in store. Three days later at Highbury, during the second half of the match with Liverpool, referee Graham Poll – who had had a reasonable first half, sending off Gary McAllister for a clumsy two-footed lunge which injured Vieira – completely lost the plot for half an hour. He gave Jamie Carragher a yellow card for elbowing Vieira, then booked Vieira for reacting. Then, three minutes later, Vieira slid in for a loose ball, won it, and was himself deliberately kicked by Dietmar Hamann. Amazingly, Poll gave Vieira his second red card in four days.

At least Arsenal won the game, 2–0 – the first time Wenger had beaten Liverpool since arriving at Arsenal, and the club's first win over the Merseysiders in seven seasons – and Lauren had a fine home debut in Parlour's wide position, scoring, like Ljungberg, in his first game. He won a corner which really should have been a goal kick, Silvinho took it, and the Cameroon new boy knocked the ball in off Adams. Thierry Henry had scored the second goal and was named Man of the Match, but he did not care about that because he was so upset about Patrick. In a live interview on Sky Sports Henry was almost in tears because his friend was being so cruelly abused by opponents and officials. Vieira had cleared his locker and left the stadium before the match finished. He said he was quitting English football.

The next day, a Wednesday, Wenger was charged by the Football Association with 'alleged threatening behaviour and physical intimidation' after the Sunderland game. Under the new guidelines, 'jostling or holding' a match official was punishable by a twelve-match ban and a fine of four weeks' wages. A statement from the club read, 'Arsène is certainly surprised by the charge. He is looking forward to providing the FA with a detailed explanation of events.'

That Saturday, against Charlton, the sympathetic Arsenal fans sang Vieira's name even before kick-off, and they continued to sing his name after the game started. After nineteen minutes, Vieira glided forward on to Kanu's sublime pass and scored by baffling keeper Dean Kiely with a right-foot stepover and a left-foot flick over his body, a Kanu-type goal. Then Charlton's Andy Hunt scored twice and the visitors led 2–1 at half-time, which dampened down the atmosphere considerably until Thierry Henry equalised within forty seconds of the restart. It seemed that Arsenal would surely win now, but a Graeme Stuart near-post volley made it 3–2 to Charlton. Two minutes later Vieira was set up by Kanu again and he fired a 25-yard shot into the bottom corner. Henry scored Arsenal's fourth, then Vieira fed Silvinho, who made it 5–3.

After two traumas in four days which had left him in the depths of despair, Patrick Vieira had come out and played like a super-gladiator. This comeback performance was majestic, a statement of intent, an expression of loyalty, an exhibition of skill and spirit that spoke louder than any words could have done. Wenger's teams for the last five years have always been a blend of warriors and technicians, but that day Vieira was a warrior-technician who played with passionate virtuosity. In football, as in jazz, you admire technique and you admire passion, but it is the combination of the two that is exciting – when they play brilliantly from the heart. There is nothing more thrilling than passionate virtuosity, and that was exactly what we saw that day. In that super-motivated mood, Patrick Vieira was colossal, phenomenal, fictional, a supremely strong anchorman who played deep in his own half but cruised forward like a twenty-first-century Becken-bauer to win the game. No other player in England, no other player in the world, could have started the week with two red cards and ended it with two goals of such quality.

Naturally, Arsène Wenger was delighted. 'I'm pleased that we could win this game after such a controversial week, and as well by the performance of Patrick Vieira today. Because he was outstanding and exceptional. Not only because he's a great player, but mentally his response was great. I think he had a little bit less aggression. One of the positive effects of this whole controversial situation was that today there were less fouls on him. Charlton tried to play football against him. Some people asked me if I thought of leaving him out. And I said, "Never for a minute did I think of not playing him." Because I know how strong this guy is mentally. And he has shown that today. I never thought he would walk out on Arsenal. He's committed to the club. He's committed to the fans. He knows how much people love him here. And how much he has improved since he has arrived here.'

Vieira said later, 'The day after the Liverpool game I spoke to the manager and to Mr Dein. What we talked about was enough for me to keep going and to want to stay at Arsenal. The sending-off was frustrating. I said things straight after the game and that is the time when you are emotional. You can't make an important decision when you are feeling like that. But I want to make one thing clear: I will never leave Arsenal.'

## THE 2000 AGM

*Concerning my future, I'm very happy at Arsenal at the moment. And I'm pleased as well that the directors want me to stay.*

Arsène Wenger

The AGM on 7 September was notable for chairman Peter Hill-Wood's comment that the new stadium at nearby Ashburton Grove would cost £200 million. A few shareholders moaned and groaned, perhaps believing that there was, somewhere, a perfect football club with perfect directors, perfect players and a perfect manager. So when you give them a very good team, a superb manager and ambitious plans for a new stadium, and you hand them a press release as they walk in detailing a £47 million share deal with Granada Media, they will still complain.

So it was fitting when shareholder Martin Wengrow stood up and made some comments which caught the mood of the silent majority, simple words that were as well-timed as Silvinho's Exocet at Stamford Bridge the previous night. 'With all due respect to the earlier speakers, I would just like to say a very big thank you to Mr Wenger for the fantastic quality of footballers he's brought to this club.' Loud applause. 'Also for the fantastic quality of the football that's played. I've never looked forward more to coming to Highbury every week in fifty years than I do at the moment. I'd just like to say that whatever the outcome of the negotiations, thank you very much indeed for being here. I think we all hope that you do extend your contract. I think everybody here, every Arsenal fan, perceives you to be very much an Arsenal person. We sense that the club has got into you as it has us. We'd be immensely proud and absolutely delighted if the directors make every effort to keep you here. I think you can lead us right into this century with loads of success, and I hope it's your last job in football. We love you!'

The applause which followed lasted eighteen seconds. It was the applause of 800 people thanking someone for saying what the earlier speakers should have said.

Wenger then stood up and spoke in his lucid, modest way. 'What can I say after that?' he said. There was laughter. 'Good afternoon, everybody. It's quite impressive to face you. Because usually I can never see you during the whole season. You're behind me, or on the other side in the stand. Judging by your questions you're quite an offensive team.' Laughter. 'I like that! I'd like to thank the gentleman who was so nice to me, but I feel that we can do better. We have to do better and we want to do better. Concerning my future, I'm very happy at Arsenal at the moment. And I'm pleased as well that the directors want me to stay. And I don't see why we can't find an agreement!'

The shareholders were ecstatic. Everyone was dreading going into a new stadium without the guiding hand of Wenger because, at this moment in time, he seemed to be the only man on the planet who could ensure that Arsenal would have a team as good as their new stadium. Clearly, the club would pay whatever it took to keep him, matching whatever he was offered by Milan, Real Madrid or Barcelona. If it took £2 million a season to keep him, or £4 million, so be it.

As the autumn progressed, Wenger was pleased to see his Brazilian left-back begin to score vital goals. Silvinho, a steal at £4 million a year ago, had replaced Nigel Winterburn and was proving to be a special player who could do special things, even if he would never be able to defend as heroically as Winterburn had done for thirteen years. Silvinho's excellent distribution put him on a par with the muscular Roberto Carlos of Real Madrid. However, Carlos is a power player, an elemental force, a rumble of thunder, while the compact Silvinho is a zigzag streak of lightning who can deliver a better final ball.

Against Charlton on 26 August he had scored the fifth goal in the 89th minute, racing on to Vieira's pass, swerving into the box and firing across Kiely in fine style. Against Chelsea on 6 September he had enjoyed an eventful night. He got a yellow card for a foul on Panucci, collided with Luzhny to allow Hasselbaink to score a sensational twenty-yarder, lost Zola for the second Chelsea goal, played Henry in to make it 2–1 and then saved the game when a ball went loose on the edge of the Chelsea box. He pounced on it and smashed a banana shot just inside the post to earn a 2–2 draw. That 86th-minute equaliser meant that Arsenal were now unbeaten by Chelsea in five years.

In Arsenal's first Champions League game of the season, against Sparta in Prague a week after that Chelsea game, he scored in the 33rd minute. Kanu hit a long diagonal pass that Pires chased to the corner flag. Pires then found the Brazilian on the corner of the penalty area, where he was unsupported with nothing on, and Silvinho just skipped inside Mynar, quick as a hummingbird's wing, darted towards the goal, swerved left again and clipped the ball across the advancing keeper Postulka for the only goal of the game.

After that Silvinho did not score in the next fifteen games, but his next goal, when it came during the match in Moscow with Spartak at the end of November in stage two of the Champions League (for which Arsenal had at last qualified), was one of the finest ever seen in that competition, a classic demonstration of how to destroy a sweeper defence with a breathtakingly quick counter-attack. And it happened just 77 seconds into the game. Silvinho won the ball deep inside his own half, played it infield to Pires and then zoomed off on an 83-metre sprint across the snowy grass and icy mud. Pires passed to Henry, who accelerated towards the Russian sweeper and right-back. Henry, four yards outside the penalty area, facing Ananko and Tchuisse, nutmegged them, taking out both defenders with a sublime pass through Ananko's legs which played in Silvinho, who glided round the Spartak keeper, Filiminov, and gently rolled his shot into the net. The best thing about the goal was that the defenders did nothing wrong. It was just a shame that Moscow Spartak beat Arsenal 4-1 that night.

## PIRES, LAUREN, WILTORD

*Tonight is more about Arsenal than the Champions League.*
Sir Alex Ferguson in Eindhoven

Wenger took Robert Pires to Sunderland on 19 August and gave him his first look at Premiership football from the bench, so that the culture shock would not be too great. His 66th-minute appearance as a sub for Ljungberg went unnoticed amid all the controversy of the game, but he went on, after the Liverpool game, to feature in the next four matches against Charlton, Chelsea, Bradford and Coventry.

A right-footed left-winger, the canny Pires was Arsenal's best player at Chelsea in the 2–2 draw. He carried the ball cleverly, passed carefully, held the side together during some rough patches and put two corners on Grimandi's head. Without him Arsenal would have been swamped and beaten. Lauren was also proving to be an energetic, resilient, solid craftsman who could pass the ball early and accurately. He started the game wide right, played well, and also looked good when he switched to right-back.

Pires was improving with every game, and against Coventry on 16 September he was the hub of the team in a 2–1 win. Artful, versatile and consistently constructive, he redefined Arsenal's attacking options, cruising forward, turning Carlton Palmer inside out and embarrassing Marc Edworthy. He hardly wasted a pass all afternoon and set up six shots on goal. Sylvain Wiltord also had some good moments. Ray Parlour looked three yards offside when Luzhny's seventy-yard pass bounced off him, but there was no flag and Wiltord buried a left-foot shot past Hedman. The new striker was chunky and combative, able to twist sharply away from opponents without losing his balance. On Wiltord, Wenger said after the match, 'Once he's in his stride he's very fast, and I believe he has shown the potential. He's quick on the turn, good movement. But he is still lacking fitness. He has no preparation at all at the moment, just two games. He's a goalscorer and he has shown that today – he created two or three chances.'

Are things different now you have four strikers?

'It's very good, especially when you have many games. It is very bad when you have not many games.'

Is Pires the player who can make you great again this season?

'What is interesting is that he has a good mixture between individual and team play. And he could play central as well.'

You've said he could be a possible successor to Zinedine Zidane for France.

'He's the closest I know to being a successor to Zidane. Unfortunately, he's too close age-wise to Zidane, so that will not leave him much time. But I think as well they can play together. That's why I want him to play on the flank. Because he has shown one-on-one he can pass anybody. He's very quick. He doesn't look it.'

What kind of man is he?

'A very nice guy. A happy boy, he's very nice with everybody. He has real team spirit. I wanted to buy him when he moved from Metz to Marseilles and I made a bid. I couldn't get him at that time. Fortunately, I could do it during the European Championship. If I had not done it just before the final it would have been over for us.'

The Arsenal–Lazio game at Highbury on 27 September featured Wenger's most radical team selection ever when he played Bergkamp wide on the right in a 4–3–3 formation. It took 43 minutes to work and everyone had a lot of doubts during that time because Lazio's defensive awareness in terms of covering all the angles around their box was excellent. It looked as if Arsenal would not score in a month of Wednesdays until Kanu crossed high and perfectly, Bergkamp appeared on the left to head the ball down, and Ljungberg swept it past the keeper. After 55 minutes Luzhny intercepted and played a first-time pass to Bergkamp, who powered infield and slipped the ball between Negro's legs, which allowed Ljungberg to go past Lombardo and side-foot the goal that ended the contest.

The other European news that night was that Sir Alex Ferguson had decided to rest six players, including Giggs and Beckham, in Eindhoven with an eye on the Premiership clash at Highbury that Sunday, and United had lost 3–1 to PSV. He said, 'Tonight is more about Arsenal than the Champions League.' Thus Fergie set himself up for looking like a fool if he did not beat Arsenal, and that was exactly what happened on the Sunday afternoon, Thierry Henry scoring a long-range goal with an outrageous flick-up and volley which looped over Barthez into the top corner.

Wenger said that Henry had been very worried about not scoring for six games. 'It was playing on his mind that he didn't score the goals he wanted to score. And sometimes you do something completely crazy; you don't think, you just do it. Maybe if he'd had a one-on-one with Barthez he'd have missed it. When you have a little doubt in your mind, doing something completely unexpected helps you. Just do it, don't think about it. That was important for him. He's never gone through a period where he didn't score. Because he's new in the position it played too big a role in his mind. It's the first time since he's been in this position that he didn't score for a while. It's part of the learning process in this position, for me. I talked to him about it. But you can say what you want – when a player is so desperate to score you can only show confidence in him. They need it to survive.'

The fans were already warming to Pires, whose style is unique because he shuffles and waits and dummies and changes his mind at the last moment. As he carries the ball he is always thinking and rethinking the best pass. He takes his time, reviews his options, and if he does not like them he reviews his options again. Then he makes his choice. So Pires does one thing better than Overmars ever did: he gives his team-mates the time to run into good positions. He demonstrated this on 14 October when he created the winning goal against Aston Villa after 61 minutes. As he cruised down the middle of the field, Bergkamp and Henry scissored, Bergkamp going left and Henry gliding right, the latter taking the ball and shooting early through Alpay's legs and past David James, who was standing tall, not crouching. The game was Pires's comeback after going off with a hamstring against Ukrainians Shakhtar Donetsk on 20 September, a game in which Arsenal had gone 2–0 down but won 3–2 thanks to a goal from Wiltord and two from Martin Keown.

On 17 October Arsenal travelled to Rome for the return against Lazio, who went ahead via Pavel Nedved's fluke-of-the-season deflected goal in the 24th minute. Then, in the 88th minute, sub Wiltord made a long pass down the left wing and Pires, another sub, knocked the ball forward for himself to the edge of the penalty area where, with sublime disguise, he almost ran past the ball. The advancing Peruzzi realised just too late what was coming and was helpless as Pires curved a shot over him and into the net for a handsome equaliser. Rome was a good moment for the Frenchman with the Spanish name to score his first goal for Arsenal, giving Monsieur Wenger yet another reason to be cheerful: his team now had three wins and a draw from four Champions League games. He must have asked himself, 'Why the hell did we play those two seasons at Wembley?'

November was always going to be a tricky month because in the first week two strange games were scheduled, matches which hovered somewhere outside normal sporting reality because they did not have to be won – Ipswich in the Worthington Cup and the dead Champions League game in Donetsk. The Arsenal mindset is all about playing hard, concentrating and winning, so matches you do not have to win are weirdly artificial and mysterious, a parallel universe, a disturbing place where you never go and never want to go. If the full first team does not play, or does not try, is it a real game? Does it count? Is it part of your sequence?

The main team problem at this time was the integration of Wiltord, which was still proving difficult. A striker needs games and needs goals, and, like Anelka in 1997/98, Wiltord could not improve unless he was in the team. Wenger tried to play him as often as he could and paid a price. Wiltord's do-it-yourself style, coming in from flank positions, made him more of a deputy for Thierry Henry than a suitable partner.

There was an unexpected trauma the day before the Worthington Cup tie when reserve manager Georgie Armstrong collapsed at the training ground and died of a brain haemorrhage. Despite this tragedy, the game went ahead. Five reserves made their debuts, Ipswich scored an early goal, Stepanovs equalised with a header from a Vivas corner, and Ipswich got a last-minute winner.

The Premiership game at Middlesbrough on 4 November took place exactly seventeen years after Tony Adams' debut for Arsenal.

Ljungberg was clattered in the box by keeper Mark Crossley, who was harshly sent off, so Marlon Beresford came on for Hamilton Ricard and got his first touch when he picked Henry's penalty out of the net. Nobody realised then that this would be Arsenal's only win in seven games during November.

Donetsk, in the deepest Ukraine, far beyond Kiev, was a city nobody wanted to visit for a sixth Champions League game that did not matter. Keown, scorer of two goals against Shakhtar at Highbury, made two expensive mistakes in a 3–0 defeat, and then learned to his dismay that England caretaker manager Peter Taylor had left the over-thirties out of his squad. Every Arsenal player was at Georgie's funeral in Cambridge the next day, which left Friday to prepare for the visit of Derby, the only team in the four divisions so far without a win. In the swirling wind and rain Rory Delap missed three good chances. Wenger played Bergkamp behind Wiltord and Henry, which did not work and Arsenal were lucky to get a 0–0 draw. Having too many strikers was proving as problematic as having too few, and when he tried Kanu with Bergkamp and Wiltord at Everton on 18 November, things seemed even worse. Weakened by the absence of Vieira, and with Luzhny having a nightmare at left centre-back, they lost 2–0.

Spartak Moscow was the first game of Group Stage Two of the Champions League and a major event in the Russian capital, an 82,000 sell-out where £4 tickets were being sold on the black market for £60. The partially frozen pitch was passed fit just two hours before kick-off, and Spartak responded to Silvinho's goal with a whirlwind of creative movement and slick passes into well-timed runs, earning themselves a handsome 4–1 win which could easily have been 8–1. When the draw was made Wenger had said that Spartak Moscow were 'a very, very good team'. He was right about that.

The game at Leeds on the 26th showed that Henry was uncomfortable with a short passing game. He had been playing in avenues for a year and now Wenger was asking him to play in triangles. Most of Arsenal's triangles were telegraphed, and Radebe and Woodgate saw them coming a mile off. Wiltord dribbled in his own half and lost the ball four times, once before the decisive goal when his short pass did not find Lauren and Dacourt broke forward, was fouled by Parlour, and took a free-kick which looped in off Lauren's shoulder. Overall, though, Arsenal were unlucky. They deserved a draw, but Wiltord and Henry were a long way off from being effective strike partners. Wiltord at least got better as the game went on. Henry got worse.

For the first time under Wenger Arsenal had lost three games in a row, so for the match against Southampton a week later he rested Henry and gave Wiltord a chance with Bergkamp, who can make anybody look good, especially when he is in gladiator mode, roaring all over the field like a Rolls-Royce in overdrive, giving a performance that seemed to say, 'Yes, we have had a shocking run of one win in seven games, but I did not play in five of those games and I'm going to turn this round, starting right now!' The improved passing rhythm suggested that Wenger had put the last five days to very good use. A whole week without having to visit Russia was a big help, and his team had recaptured ninety per cent of their dynamism and eighty per cent of their fluidity. Even so, the winning goal was a long time coming. Arsenal hit the post three times before Vieira's miscued header dribbled in off Lundekvam's shoulder in the 85th minute.

## ARSENAL 2 BAYERN MUNICH 2

*We should have won.*

Arsène Wenger

Arsenal had never previously met Bayern Munich in European competition, so the game on 5 December was a massive opportunity for them, an open door which, should they drive through it, would put the club one giant step up the stairway to heaven. A team which beats Lazio is noticed, but a team which beats Bayern Munich is respected. Bayern, like Real Madrid, are the establishment.

Wenger knew that his rival, Ottmar Hitzfeld, would want a tight game, because in an open game Bayern might get slaughtered. The Germans had won only two of their last eight games in the Bundesliga and had been lucky to scramble a 1–0 win against

Lyon, so their results were better than their performances. Wenger brought Ashley Cole in for the injured Silvinho, showing that he trusted the youngster at left-back, while Luzhny kept his place at right-back. Henry had not scored for six games, and in seven Champions League games so far he had not scored either.

Bayern started by playing some solid keep-ball, but then Vieira won the ball cleverly from right-back Willie Sagnol, spun and passed to Pires, who moved forward on the left side and pushed a crossfield pass towards the penalty area. Henry dummied, Kanu played him in with a disguised pass and Henry swept his shot past Kahn. Arsenal had scored with their first attack. Usually a laid-back player, one of the coolest dudes in football boots, even when he scores, Thierry Henry now raced away to the corner flag like a demented man, screaming his head off, releasing the tension, so much tension, so much frustration. He had obviously been wound up as tight as a spring and now, after this perfectly executed goal, he let it all hang out. His eyes were bulging and he pummelled invisible enemies with both fists as he ran. He was more pumped up than we had ever seen him. Manic? Just a little bit!

Arsenal had taken 42 minutes to score against Lazio (Ljungberg) and seven minutes against Shakhtar Donetsk (Lauren), but now they had breached the defence of the big boys inside four minutes with a stylish goal that must have given immense technical satisfaction to Wenger. The geometry of the move was exquisite, the speed stunning.

Amazingly, after conceding that early goal, Bayern carried on playing negatively as if nothing had happened, refusing to respond by trying to get the goal back, as a British side would do. Their one promising moment came five minutes before half-time when Effenberg produced a moment of EffenVision, launching a stupendous seventy-yard pass from the left-back position. The ball sailed just beyond Keown's attempt to intercept, Adams could not reach it, Cole was sucked infield to cover Adams, and Elber prodded the ball back to Scholl, whose shot swerved a yard wide of Manninger's post. It was their first shot of the game.

At half-time Hitzfeld took off Sagnol, moved Salahamidzic to right-back and brought on Paulo Sergio against Ashley Cole, who had played confidently for 45 minutes. Bayern started the second half at a higher tempo, but on 55 minutes Henry zoomed down the left and set up an awkward half-chance on the edge of the box for Kanu, who guided his low shot towards the far bottom corner. Kahn dived and managed to touch the ball, but it went in. Another excellent goal, another big step towards the quarter-finals, another moment of sublime satisfaction for Wenger. This was how he wanted his team to play. This was the football he loved. Goals of such quality were a vindication of his ideas, his faith in pace, his confidence in slick, explosive moves between sprinting strikers. Kanu and Henry had been rested at Southampton three days before and now both had scored – and they had made each other's goals. Rotation had worked at last.

In his twentieth Champions League game as Arsenal manager, Wenger was now beating the big boys. He had just gone 2–0 up against Bayern Munich and his team looked capable of beating anybody, but just as he was starting to enjoy his most exhilarating European night so far, Salahamidzic raced down the touchline, collided with Pires and fell over. It was a debatable foul, but Effenberg quickly took the free-kick from the right touchline. Vieira, jogging back, turned to find himself slightly out of position, jumped knowing he could not reach the ball, obscuring the view of Luzhny, who was standing behind him. Elber laid the ball back to Tarnat and his shot rifled into the bottom corner for 2–1.

Arsenal had broken one of the most basic rules of professional football by conceding a goal just after scoring. Wenger now had to suffer the agony of watching his team fall apart. For the next ten minutes they were unable to string even two passes together. The whole season seemed to be trembling in the balance.

When Jeremies tanked down the left wing and crossed blind, Keown headed the ball out and Sforza volleyed it forward to Elber, then ran for a flick-on which he could not reach. As he went Sforza brushed Ljungberg and tumbled just outside the box, claiming a shirt-tug. It was one of the most blatant dives of the season so far. Italian referee Stefano Braschi should have waved play on – the replay showed only minimal contact between Ljungberg's hand and Sforza's elbow – but he gave a free-kick.

The wall lined up, Scholl dummied, Ljungberg encroached, Scholl appealed and Tarnat smacked his shot into the wall. Braschi booked Ljungberg and ordered a retake. Unfortunately, Manninger did not read Scholl's intent, for it was he, not Tarnat, who replaced the ball, and everyone knows that the player who places the ball is usually the one who takes the free-kick. Scholl whipped it over the wall and into the corner of the net for 2–2.

After that, Wenger must have been thinking, 'If we had scored the second goal before half-time, or if we had passed the ball around just for ten minutes at 2–0, we would have won.' Near the end Wenger lost his temper with the fourth official, who refused to allow him to shout a message to his players. So the big night turned out to be a roller-coaster ride of thrilling success and dramatic failure, a game which promised everything and delivered, in the end, a bitter lesson: Arsenal and referee Braschi had been mugged by crafty diving.

The events of that evening took a lot out of Wenger, who rolls with the punches better than most managers. When he came into the press conference he looked weary and sounded drained. His voice lacked its usual energy. 'It's very disappointing and very frustrating,' he said, 'because I felt we'd done the most important thing in getting a 2–0 lead. But at that level you know you can't lose concentration. I felt straight away after the second goal, we lost a little bit, subconsciously, concentration – and were punished straight away. I'm especially angry at the first goal because I think it's unbelievable, how we gave a goal away. You could see straight away, the way we cleared the ball, the way we were positioned, that we could concede a goal.'

This was an unusual thing to say, especially given his low-angle view of a free-kick taken on the opposite side of the field, so reporters asked him to elaborate.

It was collective bad defending?

'Yes.'

You could actually see from the touchline, before they took the free-kick, that you were in trouble?

'Yes,' he replied. But he would not name individuals. He merely went on to say, 'That of course gave mental strength to Bayern and we lost confidence. On the free-kick I think we were unlucky. They miss the first free-kick and he gives it again. Then Scholl took it well.'

Brian Woolnough asked, 'Do you think you can still go through?'

'I think we can still go through, yes, because Lyon beat Spartak Moscow tonight. That shows that everybody still has chances. It was, of course, important to win tonight, but crucial not to lose. And in the end we got a point. It looks as if everybody can beat everybody in this group. The most disappointing thing tonight is that we should have won. We got a goal early on, and if you look at how many saves Alex Manninger has made tonight, you will be surprised. I can't remember a real difficult save for him.'

Brian Glanville then asked Wenger if he thought his team had looked demoralised after conceding the first goal.

'It looks a little bit like that. The team has lost confidence straight away. We were still in the goal we scored, instead of being conscious that it was important in the next five minutes not to concede a goal.'

After Wenger was asked a question in German, which he answered in German, Woolnough wanted to know what he had been gesticulating about near the end of the game.

'We had two free-kicks with one minute and thirty seconds to go. We had everybody up in the box and we played a short ball. That is difficult to understand. I just wanted to tell the players to put the ball in the box because in the last minute they can panic and make a mistake and you have a chance, when you have twenty players in the box, to score a goal. And that's all. The fourth official didn't let me do it. It was a little bit ridiculous.'

'You were much better than them until the first goal you conceded,' Woolnough observed.

'Yes. That was the turning point.'

Another reporter said he could not remember the last time Wenger looked so angry and disappointed. Was it getting him down?

'No, I'm not down at all. I just feel that when you see your team giving everything you want them to be rewarded. And it's frustrating when you feel that your players gave everything and got only a point. If you can find a manager in the world who leads 2–0 at that level and is happy when he comes out with a 2–2, I would like to be introduced to him.'

That was his exit line, and in the circumstances it was a good one. Wenger must have known his team were still on a learning curve, and that with a few more tight Champions League games under their belts they might not have contrived to snatch this draw from the jaws of victory. He also knew that Arsenal had been the better side on the night. They had scored two excellent goals in open play, had hit the post and twice had viable penalty shouts in the same attack, for a push on Keown and a clear handball by Sforza, who admitted handling the following day. The best side does not always win, however, and Wenger, a coach for nearly twenty years, had been through many, many games where he had told himself, 'We should have won!' Every footballer and every fan has said those same words. Nevertheless, he was probably seething when he studied the video, which showed how clever and systematic Bayern's gamesmanship had been. They created nothing in open play. They had a few shots wide, but Manninger did not have to make a real save all night. Tony Adams conceded only one foul in the whole game and that was a bad call near the end by Braschi, after Elber had backed into Adams. Adams was furious, tried to pick Elber up, and almost ripped his shirt off. Quite simply, Bayern played for free-kicks throughout the game. But nobody said much about it, which proves that you can fool most of the people all of the time.

Overall, Arsenal's 2-2 draw with Bayern Munich was a night when the performances of each team reflected the personalities and priorities of their respective managers. Hitzfeld was 51 and a pragmatic tactician who was in the results business, not the entertainment business; Wenger, also 51 but nine months younger, was more idealistic, in love with the beautiful game, dreaming of the perfect attacking performance backed by defensive concentration. Hitzfeld must have left Highbury a content man; Wenger, having seen his team lose their shape, focus and nerve, the weaknesses in his side suddenly becoming obvious, was savagely disappointed. In those ultra-tense final seconds he was as furious as we had ever seen him.

In all their European games Arsenal had never really been outplayed, except by Kiev and Galatasaray, and they had chances to win those games. In most of those games there had been a very fine line between success and failure. Wenger knew that Bayern Munich could be beaten, he knew how they could be beaten, and a win at Highbury would have been deeply satisfying. But the year 2000 was about to end and that big victory, that night of satisfaction, was still proving elusive, still hovering just out of reach.

Arsenal were now bottom of Group C with one point from their first two games, but their Champions League fate was still in their own hands. They could still beat Lyon twice and they could also take three points from the Spartak Moscow match at Highbury. But the next match was not until February, so it was time to focus again on the Premiership. Arsenal got straight back into the groove by thrashing Newcastle 5–0 on 9 December.

The press conference after that game reminded us that the restaurateur's son from Alsace had a lot in common with the miner's son from Durham. Bobby Robson is one of the most compelling personalities in the game because he gives you something you do not get from other managers: a sense that Premier League football is still a sport. He really loves a football match, and thinks it is important, but he knows it is only a football match. He was a gracious loser whose enthusiasm lit up the early-evening darkness as much as Ray Parlour's hat-trick had done.

'We got smashed,' Robson admitted. 'It's as simple as that. Once the first goal went in, then the second one soon after that, it was a case of damage limitation. Because Arsenal were hungry. Apart from their quality, excellent quality on the pitch, all over – every single player was a top-class player, and their passing and movement was top class – I just thought they had a terrific desire. And yet all of their goals were not a result of great possession football, where they're making seven, eight passes, and you're chasing the ball and you can't get the ball and then they get through you. They were breaking up our attacks and playing very effective two-pass, three-pass, four-pass movements, with the move being finished on the fourth or the third pass.

'I mean, Adams gets the ball in midfield and hits the ball over the top, Henry gets in behind Aaron Hughes and finishes – two passes, goal. Second goal is a mistake by Griffin. We lost the ball down by the left corner flag, it gets played through, Parlour makes a straight run through between the two young centre-halves, it's a terrific finish. And Kanu did the same for the third goal after half-time. Ball over the top, no clever passing movements, just effective, simple, early football – got in behind our two young centre-halves. And that was the difference: we had two young players learning the game; Henry and Kanu are two gifted, intelligent, experienced international players. It's like you playing against me – you wouldn't win. Parlour's come in, fresh as a daisy, didn't play Tuesday night against Bayern, so he's able to make strong runs out of midfield. We couldn't cope with it. Three times he's done it, three times he's scored. So it's not a game for me to get angry with my players in public. I won't do that. We've lost 5–0, forget about it.'

## ANFIELD AND OLD TRAFFORD

*I have had worse experiences, but the size of the score makes this a very bad one.*

Arsène Wenger in Manchester

The two biggest tests of the 2000/01 Premiership season were the away games against Liverpool in December and Manchester United in February. Arsenal failed both, and the most interesting thing about the failures was that Wenger picked the right team at Anfield and the wrong team at Old Trafford. The 4–0 thrashing in the first game was entirely the fault of the players, while the 6–1 humiliation in Manchester was mainly the fault of the manager. The latter was surprising, since Wenger had mostly been a model of consistency in his team selections, picking his strongest team without trying to do anything radical or clever. He obviously believes that tinkering baffles your own team as much as your opponents because it breaks up rhythms, partnerships, angles, understandings.

When Arsenal visited Anfield two days before Christmas, Liverpool had just won 1–0 at Old Trafford. If they beat Arsenal now they were back in the big time, but if Arsenal beat Liverpool then they themselves were still very much title contenders. Both managers knew it would be a battle so they picked their most aggressive players: Owen instead of Fowler, Murphy instead of Smicer, Ljungberg instead of Pires.

Arsenal started brightly, but then Babbel launched a long throw from the right, Vieira headed out, and Gerrard hit a phenomenal half-volley from twenty yards that flew into the bottom corner. Liverpool had scored with their first shot of the game. Parlour was denied a penalty when he took on Carragher, who fell and knocked the ball away craftily with his arm, and as the first half wore on it was Arsenal playing all the football in an intense game on a soggy, sandy, bumpy pitch. Again in the second half it was all Arsenal for fifteen minutes, Vieira playing twenty yards further forward, but then Heskey made a long run to the left corner, turned Keown, barged him away and hit a shot which Manninger fumbled to give Owen a tap-in. The build-up to the third goal began when Heskey, again using his strength, muscled Parlour off the ball near the centre circle. Biscan played a simple ball to substitute Smicer and he played a cute pass through for Barmby's run inside Silvinho, who stood like a statue and let him go. Barmby clipped the ball neatly past Manninger. Finally, when Parlour let a long ball bounce off his thighs it went to Heskey, who found Barmby, who played in substitute Robbie Fowler for the fourth.

Only time would tell whether this game signalled Liverpool's arrival as England's number two team. Gerard Houllier had won nothing yet, but his best players were all English, apart from centre-back Sami Hyypia, who has now become as important to Liverpool as Vieira is to Arsenal. Hyypia was a reminder that great players at big clubs are invariably spinal players – goalkeepers, centre-backs, midfield anchormen and centre-forwards. Houllier had bought two spinal players, Hyypia and Heskey, while Wenger, after almost five years, had signed only one.

In their must-win games Liverpool usually play very defensively, even at home, hitting long balls up to Owen and Heskey, and their formidable unit of six tall defenders invariably works against Arsenal, who play avenue football, looking to support each other by gliding quickly down central avenues near the man with the ball. So when Arsenal play Liverpool they are usually reduced to shooting from 25 yards, as they were here.

Their next game, on Boxing Day, was against Leicester at Highbury, where Latvian centre-back Stepanovs came in for his Premiership debut. Arsenal were average for half an hour, but then Henry scored from 25 yards and they stormed home 6–1 winners. A 4–0 defeat away had been followed by a 6–1 victory at home – all very up and down, which was very much the story in January 2001 too: a defeat at the hands of Charlton, uninspiring draws against Chelsea and Leicester, a 6–0 demolition of QPR in the FA Cup. At least they were not conceding goals, and that trend continued into February, Arsenal keeping six clean sheets in a row. They beat Coventry 1–0 on 3 February and Ipswich 1–0 a week later, then they went to Lyon and won with a second-half header by Henry. The clean sheets were ended by Chelsea on the 17th in the FA Cup fifth round tie at Highbury, but Arsenal won 3–1, Wiltord coming on as a sub to score two goals. But they could only draw 1–1 with Lyon at Highbury in a game where Edmilson, a Brazilian centre-back Wenger had tried to sign, had a seesaw night. He was nudged off the ball illegally by Bergkamp, who scored, and then he equalised in stoppage time with a booming header.

The team Wenger had selected to face Lyon was Seaman; Dixon, Grimandi, Luzhny, Cole; Ljungberg, Parlour, Vieira, Pires; Bergkamp and Henry. But when he went to Old Trafford four days later, he tinkered, making some changes he should not have made and picking only four outfield players in the positions they should have played in. The new selections were illogical, perhaps the most misguided in his five years as Arsenal manager, showing how easy it is for rotation to become confusion.

The team Wenger fielded against Manchester United on 25 February was Seaman; Luzhny, Grimandi, Stepanovs, Cole; Pires, Parlour, Vieira, Silvinho; Wiltord and Henry. Wenger knew that Arsenal had never won a game in which Wiltord and Henry had started together, but he still dropped Bergkamp. Pires should have stayed on the left to support young Cole, Luzhny should have been at right centre-back to partner the relatively inexperienced Stepanovs, since they had done very well together against Chelsea, and Grimandi should have played in central midfield, where he had battled bravely against Keane and Scholes in the past. The manager knew that Manchester United's off-the-ball movement in attack was the best in England, but he still picked two centre-backs who had never played together. Furthermore, the compromise of playing Silvinho in front of Cole, especially after Wenger had gone on record saying he was not convinced by Silvinho in midfield, was bizarre and self-defeating. And his best option at right-back, in the absence of the injured Dixon, was Vivas, who came on as a sub.

Arsenal might have lost at Old Trafford anyway, but Wenger's selections were unfathomable. The make-up of the team was criticised by many fans, but not by the press, none of whom mentioned his kamikaze line-up. United were always going to score goals against such a side, and the first one came after just two minutes and eight seconds. A Scholes dummy baffled the entire back four, and he returned the ball to the unmarked Dwight Yorke, who let the ball bounce in off his thigh from three yards. Henry equalised after a lovely move, but Yorke scored again when Grimandi played him onside, Beckham hit a magnificent long pass over Stepanovs' head for Yorke to make it 3–1, Yorke left Stepanovs floundering on the halfway line to set up Keane for 4–1, then Grimandi sold himself to Butt, who crossed for Solskjær. After only 38 minutes, the score was Manchester United 5 Arsenal 1. Sheringham made it six in the last minute of normal time.

It was a humiliating experience for Wenger, who had to sit there in a stadium packed with 67,000 people knowing that hundreds of millions were watching on television all over the world, many of them in France. The scoreline equalled Arsenal's worst-ever defeat at Old Trafford, in 1952. They were still in second place but they were now sixteen points behind United – and their hard-earned goal difference had been ruined.

'I have had worse experiences, but the size of the score makes this a very bad one,' Wenger said later. 'Defensively we were too poor. Nobody was communicating, we had no leaders, and there were times when we looked like a youth team. We are not into March yet and it hurts me that the title is already over. It's not good for the league, and I'm not proud of that.'

## TYLER ON PREMIERSHIP MANAGERS

*I don't hear much grumbling about Arsène, whereas there are Liverpool players who grumble about Houllier.*

Martin Tyler

Sky Sports commentator Martin Tyler has a knowledge of Premier League football which is second to none, and he has known all the key personalities for many years. When we spoke in January he said that he had worked on the Sunderland–Arsenal and Arsenal–Liverpool games in August, and he believed Vieira was unlucky on both occasions. 'He's now played twenty matches without being booked. As an aside, it has taken a little bit off his game.

'What is Arsenal's form now? Three wins in the last eleven Premiership games? After the Charlton game on New Year's Day I said, "Are you worried about second place?" Because Manchester United were playing that night. And Wenger said, "Yes, it could be second, third, fourth, fifth or sixth the way we are at the moment."

'There's a feeling that if they hit it off they can wallop anybody. But it's a bit more off the cuff now. It's an obvious thing to say, but if Adams or Keown don't play they haven't got that thou-shalt-not-pass look about them. Silvinho was at fault for the Charlton goal at the far post – he allowed Jonatan Johansson to make up quite a lot of ground to get his head to that. I thought Stepanovs did all right on Saturday against Chelsea, and he has good, brave qualities, and he accepts responsibility on the ball as well, but he's only had five or six games. Stepanovs might not be here if Upson hadn't had that knee injury.

'Ashley Cole does look a prospect, but he was a year too young to replace Winterburn. I'm still not sure whether Silvinho's an Arsenal player, but he's a fine player. Freddie Ljungberg is fantastic, he has got English spirit. It's a dangerous thing to say it's a lack of Englishmen. Overmars and Petit were shoulder-shruggers.

Petit hasn't been replaced, Overmars has. Edu is very good on the ball, but I don't think he will be that sort of player. I'm going from glimpses of him, really.

'We're talking about Arsenal not playing well, and it has been like that for a period now. Arsène was manager of the month for October. In November they lost five games in league and League Cup and Europe. In December they did some silly things but they still put five past Newcastle and six past Leicester. I don't think they've scored the second goal enough. They did win at Middlesbrough with a penalty and they didn't need a second goal against a team who were struggling. Derby they didn't even get one, Everton they didn't even get one, Leeds they didn't get one, but they should have done. And then one was enough to beat Southampton, they blew Newcastle away, should have got more than one at Tottenham for their second-half showing but had to wait till right at the end. They were in it at Liverpool till 2–0. I thought they did all right for an hour and then they fell away – most un-Arsenal-like. We did that game. Two up against Sunderland is the one contrary argument to that. They should have got a second against Chelsea when Leboeuf was paddling about. I would say the second goal has been very elusive for a little while now. But when they get it they're likely to get five.'

We wondered why Lithuanian striker Tomas had not been involved against Chelsea the previous Saturday. Then Tyler mentioned that Jermaine Pennant had been summoned from the youth team in the morning. 'Bergkamp was genuinely sick. He tried to do some running and, being a foreigner, he decided that the most sensible thing to do was not to play. Instead of giving it a go and seeing how he felt. And maybe producing one bit of magic. He definitely was ill. There's no problem with his contract, other than Dutch tax laws. There's some deal about how he juggles figures around to make sure he gets the maximum. He's Sheringham with pace. But, unfortunately, he's not Sheringham with goals.

'That's another point that you should look at. The dependence on Thierry Henry, it's frightening. Bergkamp has two goals in his last 29, Kanu has scored one Premiership goal this season. You don't get many from Parlour, although he gets his occasional good days when he cashes in on the team winning 5–0. But he doesn't win many games 1–0 for you. The bonus has been Vieira, although the Premier League are trying to take a goal off him, the Southampton game. Henry needs a sidekick in there. If you wanted to do one thing to get the team right, you'd get someone in there. The rest would tend to fall into place.'

So we talked about what Sylvain Wiltord had offered so far.

'The football people I know in France say, "Give him time." They think he has got something. He's a personality player and you need that personality to be fostered generally. Not to be seen as a squad player. People have likened him to Ian Wright, but Ian Wright ran on adrenalin, and that adrenalin came from being the main man. Wiltord looks like he's got the ability to be the main man. But Ian Wright would have struggled to be the main man with Thierry Henry in the team, to be fair.'

Tyler went on to point out that Wenger, knowing the age of his goalkeeper and defenders, was open to criticism. 'Seaman will probably be replaced as well. On the goal, he was knocked by Keown, not a Chelsea player. He's not the greatest in those physical situations. I thought he kept goal well actually, apart from that. So the big criticism is that he has not replaced the key elements. Wenger's argument is, "I can't patch the team up, I've got to get the right people. They're not there."

'Petit was a pain in the backside for the manager, and the players. It was so stupid. I was in Amsterdam in August when he came back to play against Arsenal. And they gave him a shirt. All the players signed a shirt for him – and he burst into tears! It was, "I don't know why I'm going!" and all this. And they said, "Oh, you've been a pain in the backside to us, go and enjoy yourself at Barcelona. Thanks very much, but we've now had enough." Marc pretty much the same. He's a Dutchman and the noughts on the end of the pay cheque are important. But for all his jumping out of tackles, look at what Arsenal did when he was here. His ratio of goals to games was excellent for a wide player. And he scored in the important games. He scored a lot of goals and Pires ain't gonna get double figures. They scored 112 goals last season, which David Dein told me was in the top four of all-time for Arsenal. That's two seasons on from the Double. It didn't crumble overnight, but it's in danger. If Arsenal finish sixth this season it's a transitional season.'

Tyler said that back in 1996 and 1997 Wenger had a great edge on French footballers, and that was illustrated by his shrewd captures of Vieira and Anelka. 'But now it is Fulham who are getting the great young French players. Houllier's come in since Arsène came here. It's that much more difficult now. The foreign influence is so strong in our football now that everyone's looking in France.

'Arsène is the most cerebral manager that you could ever want to work alongside as a broadcaster. A most sophisticated and civilised human being, somebody who does nothing but enhance the role of football manager. As far as I'm aware he wants to stay, but this is the crunch, because he's never been under any pressure. Only the pressure to win when you're expected to win. He's never been really under pressure to sort out a losing team. Arsène is getting some criticism now and if you stay there long enough you will. There is a life-span for a football manager, at one club, and he is coming into that territory, isn't he? It's absolutely fascinating. They are a wonderful club, Arsenal, and they are a massive club.' However, Tyler also made the point that Sir Alex Ferguson had been at Old Trafford for fourteen years and there had been some lean periods during that time. 'I think Arsène should be entitled to a lean period. I don't think there's any pressure from within the club. What we're talking about is a media perception of what is interesting viewing at the moment, to see how a masterful manager deals with the ravages of time on the key elements of his team and the fallibility of certain foreign players within the demands of our football. Vieira, you couldn't ask for a better player. Freddie, we've just talked about. It may be that some of the others will come good. It's the blending of it, the chemistry.'

Tyler believes that the big wages players now earn make a fundamental difference to the way managers operate, compared to ten years ago. 'Alex Ferguson could not start his management now, as he is. He was tried and trusted, and he had this reputation, so he could be the Victorian father figure with them. But I don't think anybody could do that now. Not in the Premiership. You can do it lower down. Gary Hill is a bit like that at Dagenham & Redbridge. He's a very strong disciplinarian. Nowadays it's management by personality, by respect. You have to be either very, very good at it, like Venables – he walks into Middlesbrough and transforms it because people know straight away they're learning – or like Peter Reid, who is mentally stronger than anybody else at the club, so nobody else can challenge him.

'And there's management by intellect. I think Wenger's the best example of that. I don't hear much grumbling about Arsène, whereas there are Liverpool players who grumble about Houllier. He is a very imposing person, he's kept himself in fantastic shape. He's totally devoted to it. He is an absolute football nut and that's why he likes it here. Because he's in that culture. In France, that isn't the culture.'

## NO MORE CABARET

*I'm hoping they still want to employ me. I've done a lot of good things, maybe.*

David Pleat

Sylvain Wiltord had played poorly in some league games, dribbling in his own half, losing the ball and shooting wildly from silly positions, but the FA Cup proved to be his salvation. He scored the only goal of the game at Carlisle in the third round, scored twice at QPR as Arsenal romped through, then scored twice again against Chelsea. On 3 March he grabbed his first hat-trick against a weak West Ham side, and then he got an early goal in the 3–1 victory in the FA Cup quarter-final against Blackburn.

Ashley Cole was improving too. On 28 March he made his debut for England in Albania after just nine Premiership starts for Arsenal. Sven-Goran Eriksson's new-look England won 3–1, and the twenty-year-old left-back was struck by a metal lipstick case thrown from the crowd as the players celebrated Andy Cole's long-awaited first goal for his country.

Wenger was in Paris that night to watch France play Japan, and *France Football*'s London correspondent Philippe Auclair did an interview, which he kindly translated for this book. Wenger made it clear that, like Steve Perryman, he had been captivated by the refreshing innocence of Japanese football and that he would return there one day.

'Nagoya got in touch with me,' he recalled. 'I had never been to Japan before. I had worked ten seasons in the French first division without ever taking the time to stop. I knew nothing about Japanese football and my knowledge of the culture of this country was far from perfect. Those years I spent in Japan have been a turning point in my life. Whether we like it or not, European culture is a little one-dimensional. When we go from one country to the other in Europe we don't really feel like we're changing culture. In Japan I was confronted by a completely different culture, by different values, and this at a time when I probably needed it. When one invests himself to that point in football, the only priority is win, win and win. You end up by pushing away the rest of your life. Even if there are cultural differences within Europe, we have lost the power to discern them.

'In Japan I was forced to open my eyes, and to take stock, and to think about the values I had been taught in my youth, and about the life that I had led until then. It was a determining experience for me on a personal plane, but also on a football plane, because I rediscovered the pleasure of coaching. It was as if I had been brought back to the France of the forties and fifties when professional football was only starting and when the players were discovering professionalism. For the first time in my career I was obliged to hide the ball from the players so that they couldn't train. That was something extraordinary, that we are not used to any more at home. But the enriching process has been reciprocal. I built a training centre in Nagoya and it was my inspiration for the one we built at Arsenal.

'Will I come back to Japan some day? The answer is yes. That is absolutely certain. We all have places where we have lived something unique and Japan is that for me. I will go back because of curiosity, nostalgia. Maybe privately, maybe in football – that I cannot exclude.'

Wenger also spoke of the giant strides Japanese football had taken in recent years, but France thrashed them 5–0 and they looked decades away from being able to win a World Cup, even in their own backyard. Wenger knew that, however much he loved the country, he was much more likely to win a major trophy managing Arsenal – or France.

Back in the Premiership at the end of March, there were ructions at White Hart Lane. Tottenham chairman Alan Sugar had sold most of his shares to ENIC, an investment company whose board surprisingly sacked George Graham, days before the Premiership game at Highbury and the FA Cup semi-final with Arsenal at Old Trafford. Southampton manager Glenn Hoddle almost immediately invoked his £800,000 buy-out clause and rejoined his alma mater, ostensibly to restore Tottenham's DNA and bring back style and glory. The timing of Graham's departure was as bizarre as the timing of Hoddle's arrival, raising serious doubts about the competence of ENIC. Did they really think Hoddle could walk in, beat Arsenal, and then beat Liverpool in Cardiff?

David Pleat, Tottenham's director of football and commentating, took over for the league game on 31 March, and a young side packed with reserves competed well against the Gunners, losing only 2–0 as Hoddle watched from the stand. Henry and Wiltord were the strikers against Spurs Reserves, with Kanu on the bench, which suggested that Bergkamp would not recover from his Achilles injury in time for the forthcoming Champions League game against Valencia at Highbury. It looked as if Wenger did not want Kanu to be injured playing in a game Arsenal could win without him, although they never really looked like scoring early on.

In the second half, Wiltord, unmarked, shot two yards over the bar, but Pires scored, at last, after 69 minutes, neatly skipping inside Iversen and blasting his shot low across Sullivan. Kanu, on for Lauren, won the ball in the centre circle to release Henry, who flew down the middle of the field at phenomenal speed, backed Chris Perry into the box, went round him, stumbled and just managed to jab the ball past Sullivan. Despite this defeat, Pleat hoped he would still have a job with Hoddle in charge. 'I'm hoping they still want to employ me. I've done a lot of good things, maybe.'

Glenn Hoddle had just six days with the Tottenham team to prepare for the FA Cup semi-final at Old Trafford on 8 April, and on the day he gambled on the fitness of Sol Campbell, who had not trained after twisting his ankle on England duty in Albania. Gary Doherty put Spurs ahead with an early header, but the body language of Adams and Vieira clearly said, 'We are better than you, and we will win.' The equaliser was not far away. Campbell was off the field receiving treatment when Pires sent a fine free-kick into the box and Vieira got in front of Chris Perry to head past Sullivan. Vieira, fittingly, then launched the move for the winning goal when he broke powerfully forward and played a pass wide to Wiltord, whose low cross was converted by Pires at the far post. The match had been one-way traffic with Arsenal having eleven shots on target against Tottenham's four and nine corners against none. The Spurs Reserves had been better at Highbury than the first team were at Old Trafford.

## VALENCIA'S AWAY GOAL

*We are still in a situation where we can put everything right and have a great season. Tonight is a big occasion because Valencia have proved consistently to be one of the best sides in Europe. If we can win through this one, everything is possible.*

Arsène Wenger

Another Henry goal had ensured a win for Arsenal over Spartak on 6 March, which was just as well because a week later they were inexplicably pitiful in Munich, losing 1–0. They finished stage two level on points with Lyon, but progressed to their first ever Champions League quarter-final on the back of their 1–0 win in Lyon.

Arsenal were up against last year's finalists, Valencia, with the first leg at Highbury. This was knockout football, not a mini-league. Away goals would count double if aggregate scores were level, so a clean sheet would be vital. In Europe, as in the Premiership, Wenger had proved to be an attacking coach but a conservative tactician, although at times he was, perhaps, not conservative enough.

Early on in the game, when Pires placed a corner to the far post, Vieira headed against the bar from two yards – a bad miss. After half an hour Arsenal seemed to have run out of ideas. Seaman had to save with his foot after the giant John Carew went round him, and then, on 40 minutes, Mendieta crossed into the box and the ball squirted out to centre-back Ayala, who volleyed expertly past Seaman. Valencia were 1–0 up at half-time. Would this be Arsenal's first Champions League defeat at Highbury? Dutch referee Dick Jol, one of Europe's very best, was sensibly letting quite a lot go and was guilty of no very bad decisions, but he was having one of those watch-me-I'm-no-homer nights, giving every fifty-fifty decision to Valencia.

For the second half Wenger switched to 4–3–3, bringing on Wiltord for Ljungberg, and Arsenal raised the tempo. Vieira powered past Aimar and Mendieta and fed Wiltord on the left; he cut the ball back to Kanu, whose touch failed. The ball went loose towards Pires, who backheeled neatly to Henry, who banged it in from ten yards for 1–1. Then Vieira, fouled in midfield by Angloma, took a quick, short free-kick to Kanu, Parlour burst on to the ball, skipped sharply beyond Kanu's marker, the huge Pellegrino, with a terrific change of pace and slammed a 27-yard thunderbolt high into the net. Highbury went wild with delight. Two goals in 107 seconds had the old East Stand rocking on its foundations, a slightly alarming new experience for this reporter, who had sat there in an apparently solid structure through dozens of jump-to-your-feet goals.

Five minutes after Parlour's cannonball, Vieira released Henry and a semi-final place looked certain if he could just slip the ball past Canizares's legs, but he swerved round the keeper, had to slow down, and Angloma just reached the ball first. Still, there was no reply from Valencia and this was undoubtedly Wenger's most exciting Champions League win, a quantum leap forward, although the score had left the tie very finely balanced indeed.

Arsenal had failed to support their strikers in the first half, as the manager had said they should, but in the second, when they played high-energy football, pressurising ferociously, it had worked because that is their most effective way of playing. They cannot play cagey cat-and-mouse football like Bayern Munich. Their game is based on speed and energy, skill and momentum, so they are the kings of coming-at-you football but the dunces of wait-and-see football.

Robert Pires was impressed by the support that night, as he told Alex Hayes of the *Independent*. 'What a racket! I've never heard anything like it. The Arsenal fans never cease to amaze me. It's wonderful to play for a club where every man, woman and child screams for you at the top of their lungs.' Last season Pires had been captain of Marseilles, a club with serious administrative problems and a disappointed, hostile crowd, so he was definitely enjoying happier times. 'It's an unbelievable sensation to be standing on the pitch when the whole crowd erupts,' he continued. 'When Ray scored the winner on Wednesday, I thought Highbury was going to collapse. As a Frenchman, I had never experienced that kind of support. That's why I sometimes stand back and just look around me. The intensity is such that I often think the fans are about to pour on to the pitch.'

That week Bayern Munich president Franz Beckenbauer was brave enough to come out and say that German players and coaches were resorting to 'dirty tricks' to fool referees and it was time to stop diving. 'We only have to look over the borders to England, Spain or Italy,' he said. 'There is no play-acting any more. After a foul, players bounce right back up and keep going.' Wenger would undoubtedly have agreed with that sentiment.

Kanu was called up to join the Nigeria squad for a World Cup qualifier against Sierra Leone, scheduled just four days after the Valencia second leg, so Wenger had to ask for him to be allowed to fly out to Africa from Spain. For Arsenal's midweek game at Maine Road on 11 April he played the Nigerian but rested six players. Midfielder Edu had arrived in January, and Wenger now gave him his first start in this side: Seaman; Keown, Luzhny, Stepanovs, Cole; Lauren, Parlour, Edu, Ljungberg; Kanu and Wiltord. Struggling Manchester City, five points adrift of fourth-from-bottom Middlesbrough, were still outclassed. Ljungberg scored after eight and sixteen minutes, Wiltord grabbed Arsenal's second goal in between, and Kanu added a fourth after 36 minutes. Arsenal now had sixty points, thirteen behind Manchester United but seven clear of Ipswich and Leeds. City manager Joe Royle said,

'We're not giving up, but they were awesome. They gave us a spanking. On that form they could win the Champions League. They were on a different planet to us.'

On the Friday Wenger said he had no plans to spend heavily on strengthening his squad in the summer. 'Knowing the difficulties players have adapting to the English game, I would like to keep the same team. The new players have adapted well now, although it took them some time. They have found their confidence and there is a balance about the team. I would like to see that carried through into next year. I will sign only one or two players. Not more. And I am happy with midfield and up front. We are quite solid there.' He was more preoccupied with retaining his current players. 'It would be frustrating if anybody wanted to leave now. I think everyone is happy and will want to stay here. I want to keep everyone. The key to it, of course, is making sure we are in the Champions League again next season. That is why our remaining league games are so important.'

Arsenal were second in the table, had reached the FA Cup Final and were in the quarter-final of the biggest tournament in Europe, if not the world, holding a 2–1 lead from the first leg, but some people were still complaining that it was a transitional season. 'I hope I have many transitional seasons like this one,' said Wenger.

'The Champions League is a huge ambition, personally and for the club, and once you are in the quarter-finals the competition is open to everybody. We were lucky to go through because our minds were not right in Munich, but the fact that Valencia scored an away goal against us at Highbury means we have to play and be positive in Spain. You have to show character. You have to stay calm. We cannot play for a nil-nil. That way, we would get punished. I will play with at least two up.' During this interview Wenger also revealed that Vicente, Valencia's nineteen-year-old left-winger, was a player he had tried to sign last summer. 'He came here with his agent and I was very hopeful we would get him, but in the end the fact that he comes from Valencia was probably decisive in signing for them. Either that or they made him a slightly better offer.'

The Maine Road walkover may have lulled Arsenal into a false sense of superiority for their next game against lowly

Middlesbrough on 14 April. Edu had a traumatic home debut, scoring an own-goal after 33 minutes. Silvinho scored a second own-goal, then Hamilton Ricard scored early in the second half. A team which had managed only two shots on target had won 3–0. It was Arsenal's first league defeat at home for fourteen months and their worst since the Premiership's opening day in August 1993, when Mick Quinn scored a hat-trick for Coventry. The defeat also allowed Manchester United to celebrate their third consecutive title. 'Everything seemed to go against us,' Wenger said afterwards, 'but that can happen when your concentration is not right. My worry is finishing second in the table, and now that looks much more difficult. We could have gone seven points clear of third place today, but now the gap is only four and Leeds, Liverpool and Ipswich can all still catch us.

'I congratulate United,' he added. 'What they've done is remarkable. We have to accept that they are a better team. Everybody wants to beat them but they already have a good team and a big financial potential to buy even more players this summer. It's going to be difficult to catch them. It's boring for you and frustrating for me, but it's a fact. Once United had the title in the bag they could relax and it became easier for them to win. The difference was in October and November when we slipped away. Just because United dominated doesn't mean everyone else is bad. But the table doesn't lie. We were too poor away from home.' Wenger then made an untypically defeatist comment, saying that Sir Alex Ferguson's retirement need not signal the end of United's domination. 'I don't think Ferguson leaving will stop United, as long as they can keep the players they have at the moment and buy right. That is the most important thing for them, although the other teams can improve, you never know.'

Wenger took his team to Spain a day earlier than usual to prepare for the match, the most vital of Arsenal's season so far. 'We know our defenders will have to be at their best,' he said. 'You know we will need a big game from David Seaman and something similar from Martin Keown and Tony Adams. Because without that you have no chance, and they know that. We have to show our potential and our quality. We are not a defensive team, though.

Our team is frustrated if it can't get out and play. We are still in a situation where we can put everything right and have a great season. Tonight is a big occasion because Valencia have proved consistently to be one of the best sides in Europe. If we can win through this one, everything is possible.'

It was a great motivating line, and it needed to be. In recent years the Mestalla Stadium had become the most impregnable football fortress in Europe, the home of a very proud and consistent team. Valencia's Champions League record was played fourteen, won ten, drawn four, lost none, 26 goals for and just seven against. It was going to be very tough, and unfortunately, on the night, Arsenal were not quite good enough. The game was close, though, and at the end of the first half Arsenal's steady performance had silenced the 48,000 crowd. Wenger had not started Kanu, who had missed three chances against Middlesbrough three days earlier. What did that tell us? Did it mean Kanu would not be at Arsenal next season, or that his mind was already in Sierra Leone? It was still there to be won early in the second half, but Wiltord and Henry did not click. Valencia had Ayala's away goal in the bag, so it was always likely to be Fiorentina revisited – a very tight one-goal game.

This second leg was 0–0 for 74 minutes and Arsenal did not show enough initiative in those 74 minutes. In the 75th, Angloma hit a hard cross, dipping towards the near post, and Carew sent a header bouncing down across Seaman, who reacted late, still got a full hand to it but only managed to push it into the net. It was 2–2 on aggregate, but Valencia were through to face Leeds, who had beaten Deportivo La Coruña 3–2 on aggregate.

Overall, the 90 minutes showed the limitations of Wenger's straight 4–4–2 selection. Most teams who play 4–4–2 depend a lot on crosses, but Arsenal did not hit crosses because Wiltord and Henry play avenue football, dribble-and-shoot football. If you do not cross the ball, you need a creative half-striker to link the play, giving time for midfielders to make supporting runs, and Arsenal did not do that enough. They defended intelligently, but attacked stupidly. As usual, far too much depended on Thierry Henry.

The bonus on the night was Ashley Cole, who got close enough to make Carew shoot wide from a promising position in the first half and, just before the goal, completed a seventy-yard dribble before being obstructed by Angloma. In the final minutes, when Adams was playing centre-forward and Valencia broke three against three, Cole took the ball off Zahovic with a tremendous covering tackle in the box when Keown was beaten, just as Winterburn would have done. He was now, clearly, a better defender than Silvinho. Arsenal had lost a quarter-final but found a left-back.

At the pre-Everton press conference that Friday, Wenger said that he would be signing new players in the summer, but not massive names. Five years on, Wenger was still the straight-shooting corporate gentleman he was in 1996, still willing to shoulder all the responsibility. 'We have a good game,' he said, 'but maybe not good enough. I accept that. There are lots of ingredients. It's up to me to make the right changes.' Valencia had been his 53rd match of the season, and there is nothing as instructive as 53 competitive games to help you clarify your strengths and weaknesses. Typically, though, he also cited the need for stability, pointing out that the Bayern Munich team which had just beaten Manchester United contained eight of the same players who had lost to United in the 1999 final in the Nou Camp.


## THE CARDIFF COLLAPSE

*As soon as Michael scored it was a different game. Their defence was superb, but when we scored they lost authority.*

Gerard Houllier

During the season Wenger had gradually converted fiery Freddie Ljungberg into a right winger who could score with his left foot. He grabbed the first goal in a 4–1 win against Everton, and, after Arsenal had won 2–1 at Derby, Ljungberg again scored the first against Leeds, who were beaten 2–1 on the Saturday before their Champions League semi-final second leg in Valencia, where Leeds lost 3–0. After the Leeds game Sylvain Wiltord was seen leaving Highbury with four suitcases, heading for Paris, where he spent Saturday night, Sunday and Monday. A club statement later said he had permission to attend a charity event and reporters who noticed his absence from training on Tuesday were told that Wiltord was 'injured'.

Among the many previews of the FA Cup final the most perceptive remark came from Arsenal's Head Youth Coach Don Howe who said, 'Steven Gerrard is going to be a tremendous player. I liken him to a young Stefan Effenberg at Bayern Munich. He is big, strong and gets around the whole pitch. He also has a terrific shot and we must not allow him the space if he moves towards goal.'

Jean-Marc Butterlin of *L'Equipe*, the French sports newspaper, reckoned that Wenger's strength lies in his close relationship with his players. 'He has a true love for them, as if they were his children,' said Butterlin. 'He expects a lot of them but he loves watching them develop into what he wants. For him, it is very, very important that each player keeps developing. His players are as important as his team. Thierry Henry and Nicolas Anelka are prime examples of players he's pampered while he watched them grow up. He says he likes players for the childlike side of their personality, for the purity of play while they are cocooned in his team.'

Staging the FA Cup final in Cardiff made the match a unique event for both sets of fans. Londoners and Liverpudlians mingled happily in the sunshine and the new Millennium Stadium had a more invigorating atmosphere than Wembley, plus better sightlines and adequate knee-room. Wenger picked all five of his French players, so Grimandi, a journeyman, was preferred in central midfield to Lauren, who had been player of the tournament in the African Nations in 2000 and an Olympic champion with Cameroon in Sydney in the autumn. Lauren had also scored Arsenal's first Premiership goal of the season – against Liverpool. Wiltord started rather than Kanu, who had scored only four goals all season after seventeen the year before. A manager's selections are often self-justifying, of course. If you pay £12 million for Wiltord you want to play him to justify your outlay, and if you are keen to unload him, you put him in the shop window and hope he scores. Bergkamp had missed the last nine games with an

Achilles tendon injury, so he was on the bench alongside Kanu, Parlour, Lauren and Manninger.

As expected, Liverpool defended deep, and nothing much happened for seventeen minutes. Then Vieira made a tackle on Heskey, poking the ball to Ljungberg, whose pass allowed Henry to race behind Hyypia, cruise round keeper Westerveld and shoot from a narrow angle. The ball was going into the net when centre-back Henchoz blocked it with his left arm, but assistant referee Kevin Pike kept his flag down. At the other end Michael Owen threatened but Adams stood his ground cleverly, and then, when Heskey flicked on Babbel's long throw, and Owen shot, Keown made a magnificent block.

At the start of the second half Seaman saved a Heskey header and then Pires gave Henry a one-on-one with Westerveld, but he bottled it. Where Ian Wright or Michael Owen would have seen only the goal, Henry saw the keeper, and his outstretched boot missed the ball by three inches. Henry collided with Westerveld, fell on his back, and flicked the loose ball to Ashley Cole, whose shot was cleared off the line by Hyypia.

Then Henry beat Henchoz and side-footed a silly shot which hit Hyypia and rebounded to Ljungberg, whose chip over the advancing Westerveld was headed off the line by Hyypia. Arsenal had so far produced four shots on target: one saved, one handballed and two cleared off the line.

After 72 minutes Liverpool, still very negative, ran out of luck. Carragher backpassed, Westerveld kicked wide to Babbel, who backpassed again, and this time the keeper scuffed his clearance to Grimandi, who volleyed to Pires and his slide-rule pass picked out Ljungberg's diagonal run. The sparky Swede took the ball sweetly round the keeper, clipped it into the net from seven yards, and Wenger leapt off the bench with both fists clenched. He had just seen a gem, one of his team's finest 'narrow' goals, a perfect combination between two wide players who baffled the Liverpool defence by linking with each other, missing out the strikers, to create a goal worthy of the occasion.

The game opened up immediately, and when Ljungberg's long pass released Henry, he swerved round Henchoz, who fell and diverted the ball with his trailing arm, so that the shot became awkward for Henry, and his side-foot stab was parried by the keeper. Incredibly, Henry miskicked the rebound and Hyypia cleared off the line for the third time.

Wiltord slipped three or four times, as if he was wearing the wrong studs, and he showed once again that he cannot play with Henry. By now the game was crying out for Bergkamp but Wenger brought on Parlour for Wiltord in 75 minutes. This was utter folly. It was really two changes rather than one, since Ljungberg switched into a striking role. Good substitutes, like Sheringham, are invariably technicians, not warriors, because warriors take a while to warm up, a point proved by Houllier's subs – McAllister, Berger and Fowler – whose skill allowed them to get into the game immediately.

As soon as Parlour came on, Arsenal's attacks stopped and their problems started. Keown had to make another superb tackle on Owen in the box. Unfortunately, the demoralised Henry had switched off mentally and was caught offside four times in the remaining eighteen minutes; Bergkamp might have revived him during that crucial period. Parlour played a role in Liverpool's equaliser when he got on the wrong side of Carragher and made a challenge he did not have to make. McAllister's free-kick ricocheted vertically off Keown's head, Babbel just beat Adams in the air, and Owen half-volleyed home, a fine strike by a great reflex player. So it was 1–1 after 83 minutes.

Extra time looked likely when Keown went forward for an Arsenal free-kick after 87 minutes, leaving Dixon and Adams at the back. Pires hit the free-kick feebly and as it bounced Kanu, who had replaced Ljungberg, did not compete with Heskey. The Liverpool striker brushed the Nigerian aside and pushed the ball to Berger, who launched a long 'Petit pass', a 70-yard defence-stretcher. The acceleration of Owen was electrifying, just like Overmars and Anelka in the 1998 final. He held off Dixon, sped wide of Adams and shot low across Seaman for a memorable winner. From Pires' free-kick to the goal at the other end took only eleven seconds. Seaman did not check his angles or advance to give Owen a smaller target.

Bergkamp came on for Dixon with 90 minutes on the clock, so a season which had started in controversy at Sunderland now ended in farce. Liverpool had never beaten Arsenal in any cup final and they should not have won in Cardiff, but at least the Millennium collapse gave the manager a perfect X-ray of his team. Football is a game of partnerships and Patrick Vieira had no partner. Thierry Henry had no partner either, so he carried too big a burden. The back five were magnificent and then, on a hot day, they fell part in the last ten minutes. Michael Owen's first goal had triggered a familiar ailment: Bayernitis. It was the concede-and-crumble scenario all over again. When Arsenal let a goal in they just went to pieces and started giving the ball away. As Gerard Houllier noted, 'As soon as Michael scored it was a different game. Their defence was superb, but when we scored they lost authority.'

Arsène Wenger had picked the wrong team in an FA Cup final, but he had looked like winning the game anyway. Attack had been his best means of defence for 83 minutes and attacking had worked so well that Seaman had only needed to make one save, which was one less than Henchoz. Parlour for Wiltord when Arsenal were 1–0 up was an inexplicable and disruptive substitution which he will probably regret for the rest of his days. Afterwards Wenger said, 'This is a little bit the image of our season. We always looked like we should win the big games but we can't finish it and we lose the concentration. We need some players because we've lost two big games, Valencia and now today, in the last fifteen minutes – and that is not a coincidence.'

Significantly, Wiltord was not in the squad for the last two Premiership games. On the Tuesday night at Newcastle Bergkamp played for an hour in the 0–0 draw which clinched the runners-up spot and an automatic Champions League place. If Bergkamp was fit enough to start in Newcastle, why did he not come on earlier in Cardiff? On the final Premiership Saturday Arsenal met Southampton in an emotional final match at The Dell, the home of the Saints for 103 years. Arsenal led 1–0 through Cole, and then led 2–1 thanks to Ljungberg, but eventually lost 3–2. Matt Le Tissier, a supreme technician, came on and scored the winner in the 89th minute. The only good news was that Wiltord had said he never wanted to play for Arsenal again.

At Wembley in 1998, after the FA Cup final win over Newcastle, I had asked Wenger, 'Are you specifically looking for a striker who can head the ball?' He smiled and said, 'That's a good question.' Three years later I was still waiting for an answer. The point had been emphasised on Wednesday 16 May when Liverpool played Alavés in a thrilling UEFA Cup final in Dortmund, winning 5–4 in extra time against nine men with a golden own-goal. Three of the Alavés goals were headers.

# 9. 2001/02: THE SEASON OF THE SQUAD

On 25 May 2001, Patrick Vieira told *L'Equipe* that he was in talks with Arsenal about leaving. He was still moaning about the departure of Petit and Overmars. Meanwhile, Wiltord and Lauren had admitted being lonely and homesick. The Frenchman loved nightclubbing and been fined for turning up late for training, but promised to change his ways, as bad boys always do. Wenger had allowed Wiltord to go on holiday early and he now said, 'I am very happy at Arsenal, but I know there have been mistakes. There is much more to come from me.'

Lauren had lived in Spain since the age of four and was on holiday in Mallorca with his wife. 'My first year in England has been positive, apart from the time I was out injured,' he said. 'It is always a joy for me to return to Mallorca; I have a lot of friends here and I miss them. I feel a bit nostalgic, but I am sure that next year I will feel more comfortable and not miss things quite as much.'

Feyenoord goalkeeper Jerzy Dudek had visited Shenley and agreed personal terms, but the Rotterdam club wanted £8.6 million and Arsenal had offered £6 million. As Poland's keeper he naturally wanted to protect that position if he joined Arsenal. 'I don't want to go to be a reserve. I have told them of my concerns. It would be too much to risk my international career.' Wenger said he wanted new players, but had to be careful and think about many things. 'It can be dangerous to bring in too many players at once and upset the spirit at the club. We need to strengthen and I will buy players, but two, maybe three, and in the right areas. I know that. We have to look at the options tactically, and with our formation, like Robert Pires and whether he could play in the middle. There are many ways of changing the team. It is more important that we build on what we have and strengthen from there and that means we will never sell Patrick. He will stay and be successful with us. We have come very close in the biggest games this season. It shows we need something extra, but it also means we are not far away and I think sometimes disappointments can inspire success.'

On Sunday 10 June, Wenger was in Yokohama as a television commentator to see Vieira score the winner as France beat Japan in the Confederations Cup Final. In the absence of Zidane, Pires had partnered Vieira in central midfield, and he talked about taking his Arsenal form into the tournament, which was exactly what Petit had done in 1998.

'All the French players who came to Arsenal under Wenger have exploded,' said Pires. 'Certainly, he has instilled confidence into my game. The success I've had with France in Japan was just a continuation of a really enjoyable year I had at Arsenal. Arsène has worked so hard on my confidence. The simple thing is he puts enormous trust in you. He has spoken to me a lot and made me aware of my place in the whole environment of the game. But then he knows me well, since I was at Metz.

'It's interesting how he works on you. At the beginning, he speaks to you a lot. Then he leaves you, lets you relax in your mind and become calm about what you're doing. Then, once you are on the pitch, it's up to you to demonstrate your worth back to him. The way he talks, it makes the pleasure of playing come back. He does it progressively until something sparks inside you. He says simple things and they make you want to work for him. He takes only six minutes to announce the team line-up and talk before each game. Then, the rest of it is up to us, to think while we're in the dressing room about what we are going to do.'

Wenger was reconsidering his personnel, seeking to define the missing pieces of the jigsaw. Clearly, Vieira needed a left-footed partner with a good passing range, Keown needed a younger partner with pace, and Henry needed someone who was quick enough to play with him, brave enough to get in where it hurts, bright enough to run behind defences at the right moment and skilful enough to play one-touch football at high speed.

Very few British strikers fitted that description, perhaps only Robbie Keane and Francis Jeffers, the Everton kid Wenger now signed for £10 million on the same day that Chelsea paid £11 million for West Ham's Frank Lampard. He said, 'I have signed Francis because he is a good player and has the qualities I need in my team. We play football based on mobility and technique here and he is a good runner off the ball. Maybe people will be surprised that I have signed an Englishman but I looked at his quality and not his passport. You need an English base and the right mixture at a club.'

Jeffers was twenty and had been injury-prone. He was a goal-poacher who knew where to run, and Wenger explained his virtues in considerable detail. 'Francis has the qualities we have missed in the team. He is obsessed with scoring goals and we haven't had a player like that. I want to develop him as a team player. As soon as I knew Francis was available I wanted him here. English players are used to the hardness of the Premiership. Francis knows what it means to go to Southampton or Newcastle and fight. He scored seven goals in the first nine games last season before he was injured and five of them were away.'

On Tuesday 19 June, he signed Giovanni van Bronckhorst, 26, from Rangers. The Dutchman said he had spoken to Wenger on Friday and it felt right: 'The ambition, the way he trains, the way the team plays, his vision really suited me.'

The Vieira situation, however, remained a major drama. The star flew back to London and told Wenger and Dein that he wanted to leave. Then he went on holiday to Miami with Sheryl, his girlfriend. Two weeks later he launched a stunning attack on Arsenal in *The Sun*, saying, 'I need to leave because I want to win more trophies and I just cannot see that happening at Arsenal. Certainly not over the next few years, anyway. Comparing Arsenal to the big clubs in Europe this season is going to be quite ridiculous.'

On the signings of Jeffers and van Bronckhorst, he said, 'Arsène Wenger has signed two 'hopeful' players who haven't proved themselves in the Premiership yet. One of them is a boy of twenty. You can't compete with the best clubs in Europe by making these kind of signings.'

Gilles Grimandi was adamant that these quotes had been made up because his friend never talked like that. Grimandi told his website, 'He will never get the same level of love, respect and admiration that he enjoys at Highbury anywhere else. He's like a God at Arsenal, I can honestly say I've never known anything like it.'

Recognising an agent's handiwork, David Dein issued a statement. 'Patrick Vieira is an Arsenal player and is not for sale at any price.' Wenger was deeply depressed by this turn of events, since he had developed Vieira into the complete footballer: warrior, ball-winner, standard-bearer, and, now, playmaker. The season's OPTA stats showed that Vieira was Arsenal's best passer of the ball with 1,500 passes, 300 more than anyone else, and 82 per cent of his passes were successful. He won more tackles than any of his team-mates, and scored five goals with four assists. He was one of the giants of the modern game, the finest player in the Premiership.

But was Patrick Vieira bigger than the club? Did he think he was bigger than Arsenal? If he did, could they keep him? Should they keep him? What were their options in this ugly situation? If Vieira was on £30,000 a week and Wenger thought he was half the team, should he double his wages, demand a big season from him, and sell him in June 2002? Clearly, if Frank Lampard was worth £11 million, Anelka was worth £23 million and if Figo was worth £37 million, then Vieira, who was 25 and in his prime, must now be worth £40 million.

Vieira had grown up in poverty in Dakar, Senegal, and when he was seven he emigrated with his brother Nicoro to join his mother Rose in Trappes, a Paris suburb mainly populated by immigrant families. He had captained Cannes at eighteen and come to Arsenal via AC Milan, for whom he played only twice. He now seemed to be at a crossroads in his life.

On Tuesday 3 July, a controversial transfer coup was announced: Sol Campbell had left Tottenham on a free transfer and signed a four-year contract with Arsenal. He was reported to be on a salary of £45,000 plus a huge signing-on fee paid in instalments over his five-year contract, making him the highest-paid footballer in British history.

One on one, Campbell, 26, was a magnificent gladiator, although he sometimes struggled to read crosses. His other main quality, after his athleticism, was his calm temperament. 'I tried to attract him here because he is the best,' said Wenger. 'After chatting to him I felt he is a very ambitious guy who wants to improve and play at the top level. That convinced me he is the right player for us.' He hoped that the arrival of Campbell would help him to persuade Vieira to stay, and he admitted that Campbell had asked him whether he was confident of keeping Vieira.

On 6 July he signed Ipswich goalkeeper Richard Wright, 23, for a reported £6 million fee. Freddie Ljungberg agreed a new five-year deal on 11 July, and he also signed young Japanese midfielder Junichi Inamoto on loan with an option to buy him for £4 million after one year.

Amazingly, Sir Alex Ferguson now accused Arsenal of double standards because they had signed Sol Campbell but refused to release Vieira. 'We know he has asked to leave,' said Ferguson. 'Are Arsenal going to condemn the boy for wanting to come to United?' It was, of course, nonsensical to compare Vieira and Campbell, since Vieira was in the middle of a long contract till 2004. Did Fergie really entertain hopes that Arsenal would sell Vieira to him? Or was it just a exercise to destabilise his rivals? The United boss soon bought Juan Sebastian Veron from Lazio for a British record transfer fee of £28 million.

There was intense speculation about whether Vieira would turn up for training on Monday 16 July, but he arrived at 9.42a.m. in his black Cherokee Jeep and left an hour after the other players, driving over the grass to a side exit to escape reporters.

Insiders soon whispered that when Vieira reported for training Dein and Wenger had sat him down and told him that Arsenal would hold him to his contract for the next three years. If he didn't like it, he could play for the reserves. But he was not going anywhere. This information explained Vieira's silence and his refusal to apologise for the media manipulation of his agent Marc Roger. But would Vieira sulk? Would he care as much as he did before? Would he play as well as he had done for the last five years?

On a happier note, Philippe Auclair did an interview in *France Football*, where Wenger talked in glowing terms about the talents of Robert Pires. 'Personally, I look at the player and what do I see? He asks for the ball, and then he gives it to a team-mate. Already that's not bad. Then, he passes it to a player who is in front of him. That is even better. Lastly, he gives it at the right moment. Not many players can do that. He can also accelerate, he's a team player, passes a lot. When he went to Marseille, I already wanted to sign him. For me he is a fantastic football player and, on top of all that, he loves what he does.'

On 5 August, Alex Manninger joined Fiorentina on loan, and Wenger then picked up Stathis Tavlaridis, twenty, a promising Greek defender who had trained with Arsenal for ten days. After warm-up games in Austria, the squad came back for a friendly at Norwich, where, surprisingly, Vieira wore the skipper's armband, even though Keown was playing. On Wednesday 8 August, Vieira was appointed club vice-captain, so he would lead the team when Tony Adams was absent.

Pires reckoned that the club would have faced an exodus if Vieira had been allowed to quit, saying, 'If you let a player of Patrick's stature leave, then your whole credibility is shot to pieces.' When France met Denmark in Nantes on 15 August, Pires scored the only goal of the game and dedicated it to Wenger. 'If I play so well with France it is because of Arsenal,' he said. 'I got my confidence back thanks to them, they trust me. I found there the quality of game I had lost. Every time I leave Arsenal to go and play with Les Bleus, Wenger tells me, "Play as you know and take initiatives." I've had the chance to play under excellent coaches in my career but there is something extra with Wenger, he deeply loves football and his players.'

With the new season about to kick-off, Wenger was saying he was happy to have more options. Most of his players were now between 20 and 26 years of age, so it was his youngest squad and last year's new boys were now bedded in. 'I'm very happy with the signings we have made, but just as encouraging is that we have kept the players who were here last year. The ones who arrived a year ago like Sylvain Wiltord, Robert Pires and Lauren should show the benefit of having had a season to get used to English football.'

## CAMPBELL RETURNS TO THE LANE

*We look very solid, especially away from home.*

Arsène Wenger

In the first game at Middlesbrough the team was Seaman, Lauren, Adams, Campbell, Cole, Parlour, Vieira, Pires, Ljungberg, Wiltord and Henry. They won 4–0 and Henry, who scored the first goal, said, 'I saw something today I never saw last season – we played as a team in attack and in defence. It's the most important thing in football.' Regrettably, Parlour earned a second yellow card for a mistimed tackle on Ehiogu.

On the following Tuesday night, they faced Leeds and referee Jeff Winter booked Bakke, Dacourt, Bowyer and Mills in the first seventeen minutes. When Mills was fouled by Pires outside the box, Winter allowed Ian Harte to take a free-kick quickly and Leeds went 1–0 up. Wiltord soon equalised with a diving header. When Alan Smith was injured, Batty came on and that gave Leeds three against three in the middle and pushed Bowyer onto Cole, who had been unmarked. That change shut the door and Kewell soon jinked round Lauren and passed to Viduka, who beat Adams and scored, giving Leeds their first league victory at Highbury for seven years, even though Bowyer and Mills had been sent off. Wenger said, 'It's a real blow for us to lose a game like this. If you're going to have a good season, you have to be strong at home. It's very frustrating.'

The conundrum facing every football coach is this: how do I make one part of my team stronger without making another part weaker? Interestingly, Wenger had re-configured his attack for these two games, using three players in midfield – Parlour, Vieira and Pires – with Ljungberg and Wiltord wide, plus Henry. The narrow midfielders had dominated against Leeds, but Arsenal had failed to score first. Henry and Wiltord rarely set up goals for each other and this system admitted their incompatability by playing them on opposite sides of the field.

After the Leeds defeat, Wenger gave van Bronckhorst his debut and started Bergkamp, not Henry, against Leicester. On a blazing hot day, Leicester struggled to keep the ball for more than a few seconds. Bergkamp played an advanced game at centre-forward, feeding Wiltord on the right, and Pires set up goals for Ljungberg, then Wiltord. When Henry came on, he made it 3–0. Then Vieira and Dennis Wise were sent off after going head-to-head in a one-sided game which had become calmer in the cruel heat. Kanu headed a fourth in stoppage time.

When Wenger came into the press conference, I asked him if it was the hottest day's football he had ever known at Highbury. He smiled and said, 'I felt we played in Yaounde or Angola. It was African heat. It looked like we were serious in the first half, tried to get a good pace in the game. And of course we dropped physically in the second half.'

Asked about Vieira's dismissal, he said, 'Patrick at that stage of the game was already physically a little bit tired. He had played his fourth game in nine days and maybe he was a little bit nervous. Because he has not, at the moment, really found his game.' The Sunday papers reported that it had been the hottest bank holiday in London since 1943.

The Champions' League deadline was approaching and Arsenal sold Silvinho, 27, to Celta Vigo, just in time for him to register to play in the UEFA Cup. In a remarkable twist, Liverpool signed Jerzy Dudek for £4.85 million and threw him in against Aston Villa the following day. Sander Westerveld had made a late error to lose a game at Bolton.

Arsenal were scheduled to play Real Mallorca, FC Schalke 04 and Panathinaikos in the Champions' League but France had arranged a friendly in far-flung Chile, a ridiculous journey. Wenger, angry before the trip, would be furious when he saw the impact on his team's next performance at Chelsea. Vieira and Parlour were suspended, but he rested Campbell, Ljungberg and Jeffers because he was thinking ahead to his 11 September date, saying, 'That gives me five fresh players for Mallorca.' At Stamford Bridge, Henry snapped up a rebound from a Pires shot, but Hasselbaink equalised with a penalty after Keown brought down Zola. Hasselbaink was then sent off after tangling with Keown.

On that Tuesday morning the Al-Qaida suicide hijackers crashed jets into the World Trade Centre and the Pentagon, a terrorist outrage which shocked the whole world and made UEFA wonder whether the eight games should go ahead that night. It was decided that Wednesday's games should be postponed, but Tuesday's should be played because thousands of fans had travelled.

Vieira led Arsenal for the first time in a competitive game and saw Ashley Cole make a crazy tackle on Albert Luque in the box and get sent off after only eleven minutes. Engonga cheekily floated the penalty down the middle, past Seaman, and that was the only goal of the game. Henry was clipped by Nadal in the box, but Danish referee Knud Fisker gave him a yellow card for diving.

Incredibly, none of Arsenal's five games so far had ended with 22 players and seven of the sixteen red cards so far shown in the Premiership had come in games involving Arsenal, so there was an avalanche of bad publicity. They went to newly-promoted Fulham and might have had six goals instead of one at half-time. Ljungberg scored the first goal and set up Henry for the second before Bergkamp made it 3–1 from Wiltord's pass. So Arsenal headed the table after five games and Wenger said, 'I think we can stay at the top. Why not? Other teams are dropping points. It could be a lot closer than last year. We look very solid, especially away from home. We look determined, mentally right.'

A frightening drama unfolded at Anfield during Liverpool's game against Leeds. Gerard Houllier spoke to the players in the dressing room, then complained to the club doctor of chest pains. He was taken to hospital immediately, had heart surgery that night, and a tragedy was narrowly averted.

Otherwise, Arsenal's autumn continued along familiar lines with a 1–0 defeat in Athens, where Henry berated the referee after the game, and a 2–1 win against Panathinakos at home. They qualified by beating Mallorca 3–1 at Highbury, which made Schalke in Gelsenkirchen a dead game. Vieira was rested, Parlour captained the team for the first time, and Luzhny was dismissed for an off-the-ball scuffle with Jörg Böhme as Schalke won 3–1.

They remained in the top two in the Premiership until their usual November slump began against Charlton with a 4–2 defeat in which Richard Wright was at fault for two goals. It was Wenger's biggest home defeat in the Premiership and he was very upset by the booing, but said nothing on the record. One could sympathise with his distress, since every team loses matches.

In the Worthington Cup, his second team beat Ferguson's third team 4–0 and after that it was White Hart Lane, which the tabloids hyped up with headlines like SOL TO FACE HATE MOB. On 17 November, sure enough, the Arsenal team bus was bombarded with bottles and beer cans. When Campbell had come on as a sub at Chelsea he had looked fat, and he was ponderous against Schalke. But now he was a well-conditioned athlete and Wenger said he was only a kilo above his optimum weight.

The fans held up abusive banners, released two thousand balloons with the word JUDAS printed on them, and jeered his every touch. But Sol Campbell announced himself as an Arsenal player with a thunderous tackle on Poyet, winning the ball. That tackle said: I am an Arsenal player now. He played superbly in a tight game and Pires eventually put Arsenal ahead with a 25-yard curler. In stoppage time, when Gus Poyet hit a volley from outside the box, Wright tried to catch the ball and fumbled it over the line.

Still, Campbell had earned the respect of his teammates on the traumatic day, and he now faced another challenge in Spain. Wenger warned that Deportivo were not the quickest side in the world, but could win matches just by passing the ball well. 'La Coruña are better than Barcelona at the moment,' he noted. 'They have tremendous intelligence.' He said that Richard Wright had a great game at Tottenham and then made a mistake in the last seconds. Wenger, more forgiving than Houllier when it came to goalkeeping blunders, added, 'Richard had a bad day against Charlton but 24 hours later he bounced back with a clean sheet against United in the Worthington Cup. That makes you think he has the calibre to play for Arsenal, because it takes a special strength of character to play here.'

Deportivo had just beaten Manchester United twice and they now had Diego Tristan, a powerful centre forward with guile. Wenger said, 'Sol was brilliant against Tottenham but, though this game will be mentally easier for him, it will be a lot more difficult technically. Against Spurs, it was all route one with lots of high balls and I know Sol and Martin Keown can always cope with that.

Against La Coruña, it will be a Brazilian type of game, with everything on the ground. They play on the break and Tristan always knows where to go. He is an intelligent player, brilliant at exploiting the spaces left by defenders. You cannot afford to let your concentration drop for one second.'

He admitted, 'Deportivo are one of the best teams, better than anything we faced in the first group. They are good enough to be European champions. We do seem to have a bit of a mental block when it comes to playing away in Europe and we have to get over that. My players have the character and determination to achieve something in Europe. This is the chance for them to show I'm right not to be worried by our recent record. We are not lacking quality, but there is a confidence problem at the back. We are being punished for every technical mistake we make. We just need to get through one game without losing concentration and we will be on the way.'

Early on, as Arsenal defended, Campbell made two good blocks but then blasted the loose ball against Tristan, only to see it ricochet to Makaay, whose shot bounced past Wright for 1–0. Soon after that, during a deceptively sleepy passage of play, Valeron launched a perfect diagonal pass to Tristan, who ambled inside Lauren and hit a shot which Wright should have saved at his near post. That mistake effectively ended the match after 25 minutes.

The game must have been among the longest of Wenger's career. Every tackle was too short, the passing was atrocious, and Henry, caught offside in the 5th, 24th, 32nd and 89th minutes, was cautioned when he petulantly lashed at the ball, kicking it away after conceding a throw.

Deportivo were organised, with good habits. They used the whole width of the pitch and were not scared to pass the ball backwards and sideways, while Arsenal played narrowly and impatiently, always trying to go forward. Mauro Silva anchored everything and Emerson, another tenacious Brazilian, was strong enough to dominate van Bronckhorst, and to mix it with Vieira. Wenger admitted it was wrong to start Richard Wright, even though the doctors had said his jarred knee was OK. Stuart Taylor had replaced him at half time.

The next game was against Manchester United at Highbury on Sunday 25 November, the seventeenth clash between the managers whose rivalry had defined English football for half a decade. Remarkably, United had only won two of their last nine games, while Arsenal had only won two of their last eight. Ferguson had lost authority because he was retiring at the end of the season, and Wenger seemed to have lost authority because he had not signed his contract yet.

'Alex has done marvellously well, but his club has such potential they will continue to be tough, no matter who comes in after him,' said Wenger. 'It will not be a relief when he retires. They have the money to buy a good manager, the money to buy good players. It will go on. United have twice our budget, but I don't envy that because, frankly, I enjoy our rivalry. I want to go as far as I can with my team.'

Santa Claus turned up a month early in the shape of a goalkeeper with a shaved head. United had scored with their first attack when Silvestre picked out Scholes, who beat keeper Stuart Taylor on his Premiership debut, but that was their only shot on target. The equaliser came when Gary Neville passed to Pires, who played the ball across to Ljungberg, whose jabbed shot flew sharply over Fabien Barthez and into the net. Barthez had made good saves to keep the score at 1–1 but after 80 minutes he booted Beckham's back-pass straight to Henry, who made it 2–1. Then Barthez raced out to challenge Henry for Vieira's lofted through pass and fumbled the ball, another gift for Henry.

At Ipswich, defender Titus Bramble made an early error, passing to Henry, who set up Ljungberg for 1–0. When the Swede was brought down by Mark Venus, Henry converted the penalty for 2–0.

Then it was the big night at Highbury against Juventus, who started impressively. Stuart Taylor made important saves, especially one from Del Piero, and Cole was outstanding in a hectic first fifteen minutes, while Kanu and Henry were clueless. When Vieira powered through for a shot after 21 minutes, Gianlugi Buffon spilled it and Ljungberg popped up to net the rebound.

Then Arsenal won a free-kick 22 yards out and Henry took one step and hit the ball over the wall and down into the top corner. Buffon took half a step towards the shot and stopped, knowing he could not reach a strike that was stunning in its velocity and accuracy. It was also utterly unexpected. If Henry could do that, why had he waited three years?

Juve then got a goal back when Taylor saved Trezeguet's shot and Campbell's clearance off the line hit the keeper for an unlucky own-goal. After that it was a very intense, absorbing contest, balanced on a knife-edge at 2–1. The rugged Montero had been reading Kanu like an open book, so Kanu was replaced by Bergkamp, who soon turned Montero inside out before flicking Ljungberg through for 3–1. Having created two goals for Freddie against last year's Italians, Lazio, Bergkamp now took eleven touches to conjure the *coup de grace* against Juventus. Would Wiltord have read that situation? Would he have made that run to score from Bergkamp's sublime pass? Not in a thousand years.

Overall, this thrilling 3–1 victory was what Arsenal had promised against Bayern Munich but did not deliver. It was the same brand of speed-football that sliced Bayern to ribbons for fifty minutes, but this time they sustained it and gave the manager his first win against the big boys. A year on from the Munich meltdown, Arsenal had finished the job. They were learning.

## WENGER SIGNS TILL 2005

*We can win everything.*

Arsène Wenger

Having now won four games in a row for the first time all season, the manager decided to sign his contract, so the media were summoned to the training ground on Friday 7 December.

David Dein, Danny Fiszman, Wenger and Peter Hill-Wood sat together at a long table backed by small posters that said LET ARSENAL SUPPORT ISLINGTON. The stadium decision was due at a council meeting on the following Monday night and Wenger's signature at this moment, after so much speculation and delay, suggested that approval of the club's plans would be granted at last.

'Good afternoon, ladies and gentlemen, and welcome,' said Peter Hill-Wood, who always relishes a role as the bringer of glad tidings. 'Arsène has agreed to sign a new contract with us which will keep him at the club till at least 2005. It's marvellous news. He's done an absolutely fantastic job since his arrival in 1996 and our future could not be in better hands.'

Wenger said that he hoped we would suffer him for a few more years. 'I've decided to stay because I believe I have a group of players that I respect and admire and have a lot of potential to bring this club to where I want them to be. That means at the top level in Europe and in the world. The directors have shared that kind of ambition with me. And that's why I decided to stay, giving me the freedom to work and to achieve our target. The club has a huge potential supporters-wise, and the fans have always been loyal to me since I'm here.'

He was asked whether this would encourage players to extend their contracts. 'Well, we have a strong bunch of players. All the young players have longer contracts and the experienced players have a big part to play as well in the future of the club. Overall, I think 99 per cent of the players will stay. When I'm committed, I'm committed. I don't accept get-out clauses for the players. You're in a project or out of it, and not in between. So if it goes well, you stay. I'm part of the future of the club and I will fight very hard to achieve our target. I'm not in or out. I'm in, and definitely.

'No matter where you work in the world, if you get up in the morning and you're not happy to go to your job, it's not worth doing it. The relationship I have with the directors of this club is predominant. You have a deep feeling when you make such a decision. I'm 52 years old, I know that I will not take five more contracts. In fairness, I had good possibilities, and when you face such a decision you have deep feelings in yourself that tell you the truth. Are you happy here, or not?'

Hill-Wood said that other clubs had asked to speak to Wenger, but he refused to admit that one of them had been Manchester United. Then the daily papers chatted to Dein, while, simultaneously, in the next room, the Sunday papers had an audience with Fiszman and Hill-Wood.

Dein emphasised that the manager was intimately involved in everything the club was doing. 'This development here at the training ground is Arsène's brainchild. He was concerned with every minor detail down to the teacups. And he's involved, obviously, in making sure that the new stadium's gonna be successful. We need a new stadium to compete with the biggest clubs in Europe because financially, without a new stadium, we cannot afford to pay the sort of salaries that we currently do.

'Personally, I always thought he was going to stay. To me, he's a miracle-worker. He revolutionised the club. We owe a lot to him. He has brought world class players to the club. He's developed players to world class stature. Together with Liam Brady, he's developed our youth policy to make sure we've got youngsters coming through, as you saw on Tuesday night. Our back five, when you consider, we had Stuart Taylor and Ashley Cole who came through our youth team. Without being unkind to Juventus, what did they pay for their back five? It's not just about money. It's that he believes in seeing that youth does develop through the ranks as well as combining with other talent, which he's been so successful in doing.'

He said he had known Arsène for fourteen years and had been privileged to see him operate at close quarters in France. 'I'd seen him work at Monaco, seen how he dealt with players, with the press, the public in general. His demeanour, his intelligence. He's a hybrid. He's highly intelligent, he speaks five or six languages. Cool, calm and collected. A great tactician. Knows a lot about medicine. It's very rare that you find that – he knows what an injury is all about. He knows when to bring players on and when to bring them off in a game. This is all part of a manager's ability. He has got an encyclopaedic knowledge of players. I don't think there's anybody I've ever met who could challenge him for his knowledge on players around the world. The ambition of the club is that one day when he gets to the point when he can't take it every day in a tracksuit, he'd be the ideal person to be technical director.'

Wenger said that the players each have ambitions and it is up to a coach to provide a framework in which they can express themselves. 'We can win everything, in my opinion, because we have a big squad and huge potential. I think we have shown that by beating Manchester United and Juventus in recent weeks. If we can beat teams like that quite comfortably, it tells you a lot about the potential of the players. You ask anybody at Juventus what they want to achieve and they will say they want to win the League and the European Cup. Ask anybody at Man United and they will say exactly the same. So, when we do what we have done to them, why should we not say that, too?

'My ambition is for Arsenal to become the best in Europe, starting this season. That means we've got to remove Man United and many other teams who have the same ambition. But I believe we can do it because we have young players, we have potential and we have stability. We have also gathered experience in the Champions' League over the past three years. That will help us a lot.'

He had no qualms about four more years in a very stressful job, saying, 'It's a choice between a passionate life and a really quiet life and for me that's no choice. I came into this job so I could stay in football and I thought it would lead me to extreme emotions and tell me a lot about myself. I was not wrong. Maybe I will die two or three years earlier. Maybe ten. But I could also have died with a boring life. It's the life I wanted.'

Philippe Auclair had introduced me to *France Football* editor Gerard Ernault and Arnaud Ramsay, another French reporter, and we chatted for a while and then went downstairs and asked the receptionist to call a taxi to St Albans station. Philippe explained that Gerard had come over to present the French Player of the Year trophy to Patrick Vieira today, before this press conference had been arranged.

As we were standing in the foyer, Vieira came down the stairs wearing a long navy blue mac, tight black trousers and snazzy silverblue trainers. He was carrying a large bag in one hand and a red mobile phone in the other and he asked Philippe if he needed a lift.

'There's four of us,' said Philippe.

'Oh, that's alright, come with me,' said Patrick.

So we asked the receptionist to cancel the cab and walked out to the car park where I stood by the passenger door of the black

Chrysler Jeep while the others piled in the back. Then Patrick appeared by my elbow and said, 'It's a left-hand drive.' I could not see the steering wheel through the dark windows.

We rolled out of Shenley and out of Hertfordshire and down past Totteridge and through Mill Hill and into Hendon and most of the chat was in French. Patrick, an easy-going, agreeable character, was just as relaxed as any other superstar on his way home from work. When Gerard asked where the players live Patrick said that Gilles was in Hampstead, Robert was near Baker Street, and, '*Thierry habite a cinq minutes de chez moi.*'

His radio was tuned to Choice FM, so I asked him if he ever listened to Jazz FM. He said he likes to listen to the station at night on long drives, but Choice during the day.

'Do you go to any concerts?'

'Sometimes, yes. The last one I went to was R. Kelly. It was good.'

'He produced Aaliyah's first album, didn't he?'

'Yes, he was married to her,' said Patrick.

I mentioned Tuesday night's success, saying that it must be a proud feeling to be captain of Arsenal when you beat Juventus 3–1.

'I didn't think we'd do that. It's a good feeling – but we lost to Charlton.'

'Arsène said that was complacency,' I said.

'Did he?' said Patrick, a little surprised.

We cruised down Finchley Road and turned left up Frognal and he dropped us at the bottom of Holly Hill, opposite Hampstead tube station and we said thanks and cheerio. Philippe has a close relationship with Arsène, so he was delighted by today's news and wanted to celebrate with a pint.

As we strolled down Hampstead High Street towards a pub he knows, George Graham came out of a shop two yards in front of us. He was wearing a black leather jacket and looked fit, fashionable, sporty, a bit macho, a working playboy. The poor boy from Glasgow became a footballer, then a Londoner, then a manager, then a millionaire and now he lives here with Sting, Boy George, Danny Fiszman and all the other Hampstead millionaires. George is a Sky Sports pundit now and has remained friendly with

Fiszman, so he knows what is going on at Arsenal. I had sparred with him at press conferences for eight years, developed a rapport, and enjoyed our one-on-one interviews.

He grinned, shook my hand, and said, 'Hi, how are you doing?'

George said he was impressed by how well Arsenal were playing these days and I introduced him to the French guys and told him that Patrick has just dropped us off.

'Will Vieira be here next season?' said George.

'I didn't ask him that,' I replied.

'Why not? It's your job!' he said, laughing.

Old habits die hard and George still likes to keep everybody on their toes. It was good to see him looking so well and it brought back many happy memories.


## ARSENAL 1 NEWCASTLE 3

*Some people round here don't know how to lose.*

Bobby Robson

Arsenal needed to beat Aston Villa at Highbury to stay second but they went behind when Dion Dublin flicked on and Upson reacted late to a run by Merson, who lobbed the advancing Taylor. Steve Stone's low shot made it 2–0, so Wenger gambled with two changes at half-time: Keown for Upson, Wiltord for Ljungberg. Immediately, Wiltord made it 2–1. Then Vieira robbed Samuel in the right back position, saw Henry just onside, and hit a superlative cross, left-footed, to his pal, who killed the ball perfectly, dummied Enckelman on to his knee, and slotted the ball past him for 2–2.

After that the pressure built until a pass from Pires released Henry, who slipped the ball neatly past Enckelman for a 92nd minute winner. Arsenal had so far won twelve games and Henry had scored in all of those victories. At the end of the season he said that this goal, while not his most beautiful, was his favourite.

On the following Monday night, Islington Council gave the go-ahead for the new stadium. Wenger took kids and squad players to Blackburn for the Worthington Cup quarter-final and they were thrashed 4–0. When asked about Inamoto he said, 'Well, I took him off at half-time and he wasn't injured.'

At home to Newcastle, they scored first when Henry hooked the ball across for Cole to turn back for Pires. Then Kanu missed two sitters, which would prove expensive. Referee Graham Poll gave Parlour an early yellow card after his arm caught Dabizas, and then sent him off for a slightly late tackle on Shearer, who asked the ref to be lenient. At half-time Henry walked off alongside Poll, shaking his head.

After an hour, Arsenal were guilty of dopey defending when substitute Lua Lua took a quick corner to the near post. Stuart Taylor was still organising at the far side and Henry was strolling back, the nearest player to Andy O'Brien, who headed in from two yards. It was a very soft goal. Then Cole feigned injury to get Bellamy sent off. When Bellamy's arm caught Cole on the neck he went down as if he had been punched and Poll gave Bellamy a straight red card.

Five minutes from time, Lauren Robert was through on Taylor and Campbell made, from behind, a magnificent recovery tackle, toe-ending the ball out for a corner. It might have been the best tackle of the season, but Poll awarded a penalty. A good referee looks at where the ball goes. Such incidents are like an l.b.w. in cricket – you can't give a decision if you're not a hundred per cent sure. Shearer scored from the spot and Robert made it 3–1 at the death to give the Newcastle their first win in London for 30 matches.

Graham Poll had certainly ruined the contest but when the final whistle went, the game was over. Henry, furious, approached Poll accusingly, shouting, 'Why did you kill the game?' Keown tried to restrain Henry but he was pushed away, as was Gary Lewin. Such a tantrum was silly, self-defeating and, ultimately, pathetic. As Bobby Robson said, 'Some people round here don't know how to lose.' Quite. Bellamy's red card was later rescinded on appeal.

At that moment in December it looked as if Arsenal's appalling disciplinary record, 39 red cards since Wenger arrived, would derail their title challenge. Henry looked set for a long suspension. Vieira, booked seven times in all competitions and sent off against Chelsea, was suspended for Sunday's game at Liverpool, and

Lauren would miss the Middlesbrough game after accumulating five yellow cards. Parlour would sit out the New Year's Day game at Leicester and the FA Cup third round tie at Watford.

The press slaughtered Wenger, saying that he never saw fouls by his own players, never condemned them publicly, did not punish them privately or even, it seemed, speak to them about discipline. But it was all ancient news, really. Wenger was prepared to live with the red cards and the bad publicity. His attitude was: we play the game very fast, we go for ball, and sometimes we miss the ball, so we get cards which are deserved, and other cards that are undeserved – that's my kind of football and I will never apologise for it because we are not a dirty team.

Many acres of newsprint had been devoted to this controversy, but Wenger had once summed it up in nine words when he said, 'I'm never going to tell them not to tackle.'

The next game was at Anfield, where van Bronckhorst was muscled over in the box by Henchoz. He got up without claiming a penalty but referee Paul Durkin gave him a second yellow card for diving. That injustice really ignited the team and, with Parlour playing out of his skin, they roared into a 2–0 lead.

The first goal was a Henry penalty after Ljungberg ran on to Kanu's pass and Dudek could not avoid colliding with him. Early in the second half Gerrard made a sloppy pass to Pires, who left him for dead and teed up a low cross for ever-ready Freddie to stab home from four yards. Litmanen netted a late header. It was Arsenal's first Premiership victory at Anfield for nine years.

At Chelsea, they fell behind when a Melchiot throw, chested by Hasselbaink, rebounded off Vieira for Lampard to fire low into the bottom corner. Campbell headed in a corner for 1–1 and eventually van Bronckhorst took a free-kick, Melchiot headed out, and Wiltord smashed in the winner.

The Middlesbrough match at Highbury was tense and messy, with both keepers unemployed except for Mark Crossley once saving a Pires shot, knocking it onto the post. Then Campbell miskicked a back-pass and Noel Whelan scored and Arsenal were 1–0 down at half-time. Pires hauled them back into it with a looping thirty-yarder, helped by Henry's obstruction on Paul Ince, which the referee missed. Bergkamp, on as a sub, won the game with a curling cross over the defence for Cole to head in.

In the FA Cup Third Round, they outclassed Watford and then drew Liverpool in the Fourth Round at Highbury. They had three league games before that and the first, oddly enough, was at home to Liverpool. Arsenal were one player short down the left side because Upson, while playing well at left back, lacked the attacking brio of the injured Cole, but at the other end Campbell and Keown were so tight that Michael Owen had no goal attempts. Anelka, on loan from Paris St. Germain, had one shot blocked. Bergkamp replaced Kanu, became the third man on the left, and they scored immediately. Campbell hit a long ball into the corner, Bergkamp held off Carragher cleverly, played a cute ball to Pires, and his pass allowed Ljungberg to stab in from six yards. Then Riise zoomed down the flank and scored from Gerrard's long diagonal pass as keeper Stuart Taylor froze. Taylor had one decision to make in the match and he got it wrong, so the game finished 1–1. The team was looking good, but could they win a trophy without a goalkeeper?

It was now mid-January and the fans were still wondering about Vieira. Arsenal needed him, France needed him, and Real Madrid thought they needed him, but Vieira's mediocre performances seemed to indicate that he did not want to be at Arsenal. His mind was not on the job. He tackled less often, gave the ball away more, and got sillier bookings than ever before. Then Wenger gave the players two days off and Vieira was spotted at Barajas airport in Madrid. The world's greatest club had apparently offered him £3.5 million a year for five years. Who could turn down that kind of money?

Some fans were dismayed; others angry. When Vieira was suspended at Anfield, Parlour had inspired the team and they won 2–1 with ten men. But when Parlour was suspended at Highbury, Vieira was not concentrating. There was plenty of time to score again after Riise equalised: 21 minutes. But how could Vieira concentrate on winning that game if he knew he would be on a plane to Madrid in the morning?

Sunday's visit to Leeds fizzled out into a 1–1 draw. Wilcox beat Luzhny to create Fowler's early header past Wright, who was back in goal, and then Pires started and finished the move for the equaliser. But Wilcox fell against Ljungberg, twisting the Swede's ankle and putting him out for the next eight weeks. Those two 1–1 draws put pressure on the game at Leicester, where van Bronckhorst lifted the anxiety by heading his first goal in a 3–1 win.

## ARSENAL 0 DEPORTIVO LA CORUÑA 2

*What he does is close to genius.*

Wenger on Bergkamp's goal at Newcastle

Arsenal v Liverpool was an FA Cup Fourth Round tie that had monsoon rain, gusting wind, a pulsating atmosphere, van Bronckhorst's best game so far, some dogged defending, a miss or two by Owen, and a sulky cameo by Anelka, who was withdrawn at half time.

We saw a collective sense of purpose, and a style of play, which had now evolved to the point where the team could prosper without Lauren and Ljungberg, and despite losing the injured Pires after twenty minutes, and despite the sending off of Keown and Bergkamp.

They only scored one goal, but they only needed one. When Wright kicked long, Henry controlled the ball beautifully on his body, played a one-two with van Bronckhorst, and crossed left-footed for Bergkamp to glance a header beyond Dudek from seven yards. It was champagne football: sharp early passes, lightning sprints, a sudden thrust into the box, an unstoppable goal.

In the second half there were three red cards. Keown impeded Owen on a breakaway and referee Mike Riley sent him off. Bergkamp, furious after a handball had not been given against Hyypia, made a malicious-looking tackle which just missed Carragher's ankle, so he walked as well. Then Carragher stupidly threw a coin back into the crowd.

A 3–2 win at Blackburn was a thriller in which Robert Pires started the move for the first goal, when Wiltord's cross reached Bergkamp at the far post, gave Henry a 60-yard pass for the second, and slipped Bergkamp in for the winner after Blackburn had levelled at 2–2. Playing like this, Pires made anything seem possible. Luzhny had been sent off for tripping Tugay.

At home to Southampton, Vieira went off injured, and then Cole got a knee injury which put him out for the next eleven games. Wiltord scored just before half-time but Richard Wright was a bag of nerves, blasting pass-backs here, there and everywhere. Southampton took over and Joe Tessem headed an equaliser. But Edu had looked the part, at last.

On 6 February, Manchester United PLC informed the Stock Exchange that they were in talks with Sir Alex about him staying on as manager. They had failed to tempt Eriksson, Hitzfeld and Capello.

Arsenal went to Everton on 10 February, a week before manager Walter Smith was sacked. Stepanovs was booked early on, as was Campbell, but after that Campbell held the defence together. He has a knack of playing athletically, and robustly, but not riskily, so he never gets a second yellow card. Everton were the better side in the first half but after an hour Vieira played a lovely chipped pass, Wiltord shinned it, the ball looped across the goal – and went in.

When the team was motoring, and enjoying this unbeaten run, new players coming in were jumping onto a moving vehicle and were carried along by the momentum. As February continued, Vieira was superb in a 4–1 win against Fulham and he blotted out Michael Ballack in a phenomenal 4–1 demolition of Bayer Leverskusen. At Newcastle he played with all his old flair, power and authority in a 2–0 victory. Why had he improved so much in those three games? Had he decided to stay?

Pires later described how Vieira kept the French boys together, on and off the field. 'Patrick is so important to the team. He gives us rhythm, his positional play is excellent and he always makes a good pass. He's intelligent and he's the soul of the team. When he's not playing well, the team are not playing well. Patrick, Thierry, Sylvain and me are close. I've known Patrick for eight years now. For us, he's also very important outside football. He knows London very well, and where to go out. But as far as his future is concerned it's his decision, not ours. Of course, it would be great if he stays.

But you know he's been here six years already, and so, whatever he decides, we will respect it.'

2 March saw a league game at Newcastle and Henry's delayed misconduct charge was to be heard by the FA on the following Wednesday. 'I cannot believe that Henry has not been in front of the FA yet,' said Bobby Robson. 'After all, it's coming up to three months since we played that game. Perhaps this shows what power Arsenal have in the game today.' The visitors made the break-through with an outrageous goal after eleven minutes. Vieira won the ball from Lauren Robert and played it up to Bergkamp, who passed wide and square to Pires and then cruised upfield, collected a crossfield pass from Pires, and flicked the ball, left-footed, past Dabizas, ducked in behind him, and side-footed past Shay Given into the corner from ten yards.

'Unbelievable,' said Wenger. 'You don't see that kind of thing too many times, but you're blessed when you come to a stadium and witness something like that. It wasn't only a magnificent goal, but an extremely important one. That's why I enjoyed it so much. What he does is close to genius. I'm always wary of using those kind of words, but I think in his case they're justified. He's a player who gets close to perfection.'

ITV pundit Ally McCoist made a complete fool of himself by doubting that dazzling Dennis had wholly intended this demon-stration of footballing magic, which was later voted Goal of the Season. McCoist was obliged to apologise in a later programme. Bergkamp, incidentally, had made the second goal that day, flighting a free-kick for Sol Campbell to score with a header.

After that 2–0 win, Wenger said he believed his team were good enough to claim a treble of Champions' League, Premiership and FA Cup, just as Manchester United had done in 1999. 'I just want to take the club as far as I can and like at every big club it is a construction,' he said. 'There is a scaffolding you build up and up and up. The club now has recognition in Europe but we want more. We want to become the biggest club in the world. I believe the club is in progression, it is on the move. If you look at the potential of Arsenal with the new stadium, you cannot say you want to be the second best in the world.

'I understand other clubs have the same target but I don't know why we should be behind anyone in our ambitions. The secret to becoming the biggest club in the world is having good players and making good decisions. Nothing more. And that is our goal. As long as our attitude and commitment is right, I expect us to win every game. But it is important to be vigilant because all our hopes can disappear very quickly if we get careless.'

With ten league games left, Arsenal were three points better off than at the same stage in 1998. In the next game, against Derby on 5 March, Bergkamp put Pires through for the winner, his eleventh goal of the season. Television captured their exquisite skill: Wiltord's diagonal pass went over a defender's head and Bergkamp, the king of two-touch, took one touch on the turn, then flicked into the stride of Pires, who guided the ball precisely four feet in front of himself and swept his shot past Andy Oakes, a young keeper who was having a good game.

It was their seventeenth match without defeat since losing to Newcastle at Highbury in December and Wenger said, 'The championship is now in our hands and as long as we win our games we don't have to worry about anyone else.' When the FA banned Henry for three games Wenger decided not to appeal as it would play on Henry's mind.

Meanwhile, Bergkamp had tipped Pires for the PFA Player of the Year Award, saying, 'He has been absolutely awesome all season and I've nothing but respect for the man. He has so much intelligence and skill it's terrifying. One of his main strengths is his ability to keep possession of the ball. I think he's possibly the best player I've ever seen at Arsenal in terms of holding on to the ball come what may. I'm a big fan of Robert and enjoy playing with him.'

For the FA Cup Sixth Round tie at Newcastle, the teamsheet contained four shocks. Pires, Bergkamp and Seaman were on the bench, while Ljungberg, who had missed twelve games, started after not playing for the reserves. They scored an early goal when Wiltord crossed low to the near post for Edu but then Lauren Robert accelerated on to Shearer's flick-on and fired past Wright, so it went to a replay.

In the Champions' League, Deportivo La Coruna and Arsenal both had seven points from four games and Wenger was again raising the stakes with upbeat comments. He said, 'If we beat La Coruna, we will qualify for the last eight – and I am convinced we will. The players are more confident now than at any other time since I took charge at Highbury six years ago.' To say this after being outplayed at the Riazor in November seemed reckless, but football is a game of sequences and Arsenal were really enjoying their 18-match unbeaten run.

The night promised a fascinating clash of styles, since Arsenal are spectacular sprinters who win games by overwhelming opponents, and Deportivo are canny passers who win by outsmarting them. Unfortunately, Arsenal had been playing an FA Cup tie while Depor were resting eight players at the weekend, and they looked tired. The match began promisingly but the crowd became quiet and apprehensive after twenty minutes as they saw their team run out of ideas. When Wiltord turned carelessly, Mauro Silva read the turn and backheeled smartly to Fran, who fed Romero's overlap run to the touchline. Romero cut the ball back to Valeron, Campbell went to ground for the block, and Valeron stroked home his shot with a matador's panache, an elegant, deadly thrust.

When Fran crossed, Tristan headed back, Valeron shot again from eight yards, and Seaman made a superb save. By then, after only 35 minutes, the game looked over. Then Vieira lost the ball to Victor upfield and did not chase back immediately as a captain should. Depor played six passes round and through the Arsenal defence as Grimandi missed a tackle, Vieira, back now, missed a tackle, Campbell missed a tackle, Luzhny missed a tackle, Lauren missed a tackle and then Naybet's shot was deflected in off Stepanovs. Deportivo destroyed Arsenal in that move, toying with them as no team has toyed with them.

After half-time, Arsenal cranked up the tempo for a while but it was a storm in a teacup. Hope flickered when Ljungberg came on and immediately raced behind the defence to touch Bergkamp's pass beyond Molina, who brought him down. But Henry's penalty was feeble and Molina saved it.

Deportivo won fair and square with sophisticated teamwork, sometimes reading Arsenal's passes before they had even decided to make the pass. They may not have the best players in Europe, but they might have the best shape, the sweetest rhythm, and the most fully-realised style of play. With two left-footed players, Fran and Romero, they had a good balance, and Mauro Silva was immense in a team that was well-equipped to defend a 2–0 lead. At the end, the Arsenal fans gave them a standing ovation.

This defeat, Wenger's first in seventeen European matches at Highbury, left qualification out of Arsenal's hands and facing a game in Turin against Juventus, who were bottom of the group and could not qualify. So Arsenal could win and still go out, but they could also lose and go through if Deportivo beat Leverkusen in La Coruna to win the group. Matchday 12 threatened to be a weird evening.

On Sunday afternoon, Edu scored at Aston Villa, Seaman made a sensational penalty save from Gareth Barry, Pires cleverly lobbed Schmeichel for a second goal, but a Dublin header made it 2–1 and gave Arsenal a tense last twenty minutes. Lee Dixon came on as a sub on his 38th birthday.

Juventus were one point behind joint-leaders Inter and Roma, so their minds were on the title race and they fielded a reserve side. When Wenger heard the Deportivo team, containing only Mauro Silva, Cesar and Naybet from the eleven who started at Highbury, he feared the worst. Ten minutes into the game, his assistant had a phone call from their man in La Coruna, saying that Depor were not up for it. Arsenal lost their game when Zalayeta scored with a header from a corner. The bottom line, on Matchday 12, was that Juve's reserves were motivated but Deportivo's reserves were not, losing 3–1 to allow Leverkusen to win the group. So Arsenal's European campaign was over for another year.


## LJUNGBERG SCORES SEVEN IN SEVEN

*This could be the first of many for me.*

Sol Campbell


Wenger had said boldly on Sky Sports that he was one hundred per cent certain that Arsenal would win the title. Had any manager ever said that since the league started in 1888? That he was one hundred per cent certain his team would be champions? It had always been one of the rules of football, as fundamental as having eleven players on each side and four corner flags, that a manager always said, 'We'll take each game as it comes.'

One of Dennis Bergkamp's lifetime dreams was to play in an FA Cup Final, so he was on fire in the replay against Newcastle on 23 March. Magisterial, razor-sharp, always thinking one move ahead, always purposeful, never flashy, never guilty of showboating, Bergkamp made a goal for Pires in 62 seconds, chipped against the bar in five minutes, scored from a Pires pass in ten minutes, chipped against the post in 22 minutes, and created the third goal in 49 minutes.

At 2–0, Newcastle fought back with admirable spirit, but just after half-time Luzhny made a run, got fouled, and Bergkamp sent the free-kick dipping down into the area for Sol Campbell to head in from seven yards. Newcastle kept playing, rarely fouled, had some decent shots and headers, and Kieron Dyer did well on his long-awaited comeback. But they were outclasssed, as Bobby Robson admitted. 'Arsenal were far better than us,' he said. 'They had a genius in Bergkamp. We didn't have a genius.'

Unfortunately, Pires, jumping to avoid a lunge by Dabizas, had landed awkwardly and damaged the medial ligament of his right knee. He had been the best player in the Premiership, but he would now miss the World Cup. Pires had scored thirteen goals and had assists in fifteen other goals. Only David Beckham, twice, and Nol Solano had ever accumulated fifteen Premiership assists in a season, and they played more games.

Arsenal celebrated Easter with two 3–0 victories and the ferocity of those performances seemed to contain an element of, 'Let's win it for Robert.' On the Saturday, they had some luck against Sunderland, but on Monday they played devastating football at Charlton. Henry raced on to Campbell's clearance to fire past Dean Kiely, sprinted to the corner flag, and kicked it out of the ground, a violent celebration we had never seen before. Then Henry turned Richard Rufus inside out to release Bergkamp, who glided round Kiely and crossed to give Ljungberg his first goal since his return.

Another sparkling move allowed Henry to make it 3–0 after 25 minutes. Manchester United went to Spain and outplayed Deportivo for a 2–0 victory which kept Ferguson on course for a European Cup Final in his home town of Glasgow on 15 May.

Talking about Bergkamp's form, and his finest goals, Wenger said, 'With Dennis in the team you expect him to create chance after chance for everybody. And with Robert Pires unavailable we rely more and more on that. Dennis is really confident at the moment and as creative as ever, but what is different this season is that he looks more physically fresh. Maybe that's because he has played less games this season, so he now looks very sharp. Personally, I like the goals he scores with his head – like the ones against Real Mallorca and Dynamo Kiev. When you see how good he is technically at heading the ball it's a shame that he does not score more like that. Also, I don't get to see my team score many headed goals, so when they happen I always enjoy them!'

The home game against Tottenham was level at 1–1 after 86 minutes. Ljungberg had scored from Bergkamp's pass and Sheringham equalised from a dubious penalty when Poyet ran into Seaman. Then Dean Richards wrestled Henry to the ground. Referee Mark Halsey gave another penalty. The immaculate Lauren waited for Kasey Keller to move and then rolled the ball gently down the middle.

The FA Cup semi-final was at Old Trafford, where Middlesbrough's substitute centreback, Gianluca Festa, scored an own-goal to send Arsenal to Cardiff again, while Chelsea beat Fulham at Villa Park with a goal by John Terry.

Against Ipswich, after an hour of tension, frustration and doubt, Ljungberg grabbed both goals from crosses, not passes. Bergkamp was energetic and productive, but Henry seemed to have lost his bottle. Would he score again this season? On that showing it looked unlikely. Was he carrying an injury we did not know about?

Arsenal were jittery against West Ham at Highbury and Kanoute was unlucky not to score when Ashley Cole kicked his shot away after it had crossed the line. Eventually, a majestic pass from Bergkamp released Ljungberg and he beat David James comfortably. Then Ljungberg crossed from the left for Kanu to make it 2–0.

By now, Ferguson could see that an unprecedented fourth consecutive Premiership trophy was likely to elude him, but he claimed that Arsenal might pay for an apparent 'over-confidence'. On 29 April, Arsenal went to Bolton, who were now safe from relegation. It was a massive match, bigger than the FA Cup Final, since they could blow the title if they lost, but Bergkamp laid on two passes in seven minutes to give Ljungberg and Wiltord the goals. They now had a lead of five points over Manchester United with two games remaining.

On a sunny Saturday, 4 May, Arsenal returned to the magnificent Millennium Stadium as favourites to win the FA Cup Final. Wenger dropped Edu, started Parlour, and preferred Seaman to Wright, who had played in the previous rounds. It was a harsh decision but the correct one.

Claudio Ranieri had figured out that Wiltord and Henry can rarely time their runs off the ball, so Chelsea defended with a very high line. Where Liverpool had defended the box the year before, and allowed Arsenal the space to create sweet passing moves, the blues defended the halfway line as much as possible, squeezing Bergkamp out of the spaces he uses to create his killer passes. Lampard did remarkably well against Vieira, whose passing was shabby.

In that tight first half, Bergkamp released Ljungberg twice with passes down the middle but the flag went up because Henry had strayed offside on both occasions. Wiltord crossed for Lauren, whose header deflected over the bar off Le Saux's head. Vieira then picked out Bergkamp's run with a diagonal pass from the halfway line but his header floated just wide. Hasselbaink was carrying a calf injury and when he and Gudjohnsen managed a one-two just before half time, Gudjohnsen was wrongly flagged offside. Then Gudjohnsen hit a dipping shot which forced Seaman to make the best save of the game.

Chelsea dominated after half-time and the first goal came from a counter-attack: Cole to Vieira to Parlour to Adams to Wiltord, who evaded Desailly and jabbed the ball to Parlour, who fired a 22-yard shot into the far corner of the net. It was a glorious moment for Romford Ray after a mixed campaign with three red cards and only one previous goal – against Gillingham. Then Edu found Ljungberg just inside Arsenal's half. Three red shirts faced six blues but the little man suddenly spurted forward with immense drive and optimism, beyond the blue defence, like a scrum-half going for the line. Amazingly, he held off substitute John Terry, stumbled, recovered and curled his shot round Cudicini for 2–0.

Fiery Freddie had conjured up a real do-it-yourself goal, his seventh in his last seven games. Charity workers in Cardiff had been soliciting donations in return for dye-jobs, so thousands of fans had red hair in tribute to the man of the moment and now, to the tune of the Andy Williams hit 'Can't Take My Eyes Off You', they were singing, 'We love you Freddie, because you've got red hair, we love you Freddie, because you're everywhere.'

At the final whistle, Tony Adams hugged Sol Campbell, who later said, 'I must admit it was really nice with Tony at the end. He's got a few winner's medals under his belt and hopefully I can join him – this could be the first of many for me. It's a start. I'm going to enjoy this. I've won the Worthington Cup with Spurs, but this is great. It's been a fantastic season, the way everyone in the squad has chipped in. It's nice that everyone has played a part in some unbelievable performances.'

UEFA chief Lennart Johansson, a lifelong Arsenal fan, handed out the medals one by one, with Tony Adams last in line. Adams and Vieira held up the trophy together. Would either of them be playing for Arsenal next season? The retirement of Adams looked likely and Vieira's flaccid performance suggested he might be at Real Madrid. Maybe he was just tired. A year ago against Liverpool he had been the best player on the pitch and lost. Now, against Chelsea, Vieira had been average and won. A funny old game, football. Arsenal were now one point away from the first League and FA Cup double ever to be won Cup-first.

## CHAMPIONS AT OLD TRAFFORD

*He's given people patience. And a lot of love.*

Tony Adams

In the Champions' League semi-final, Manchester United had lost to Bayer Leverkusen on away goals, so Ferguson's fairytale was over. When the press said Veron was a luxury player who had disrupted their shape, Ferguson erupted at Carrington, the training ground, swearing at reporters. Defending Veron, his parting words were, 'He's a f****** great player.' He added 'Youse are all f****** idiots.' Skipper Roy Keane also spoke out, questioning the commitment of some United players.

When reporters next saw Wenger, he mischievously asked, 'What are all these asterisks in the newspaper?' He said that he never thought that Arsenal might not win the title. 'It does not cross my mind. I don't know if Alex Ferguson is rattled or if he will congratulate us if we do it, but the table doesn't lie. It's always right. We have coped with the pressure and we will show it again in what is a big pressure game. You do not take your foot off the pedal when you are so close.'

He highlighted the turning point: the 2–1 win at Liverpool with ten men. He said that victory was the day the players really believed they could win the Premiership. 'This season is the season of the squad, a mental strength that has kept us together. What relaxes me is knowing the effort the team is putting in. I have never had to ask myself this question this season. I can go home knowing this team will give their last drop of blood for me.'

After the Cardiff consummation, Wenger said the players felt relief after such a long wait for another trophy. They had dinner together, but it was a low-key affair because everyone knew that the job was not yet done. He said, 'We expect United to be at their best, don't worry about that. They won't want to lose the title on their own ground, but we don't want to lose it, either. Winning the title at Old Trafford will have no special significance.'

Gooners who read that comment must have giggled. Winning the title at Old Trafford will have no special significance? Who did Arsène think he was kidding? It would be wonderful to win the title in Sir Alex F*******'s own back yard, but it would also be fantastic to win it with a win, rather than a draw. The league is about points, of course, but psychological ascendancy over your main rivals is very important.

Wenger made three changes: Keown for Adams, who had a knee injury, Edu for Henry, and Kanu for Bergkamp. Henry had 'a small knee injury'. Outside the stadium the United fans were not really buzzing, since they did not give Everton a prayer at Highbury on the final day. Wenger looked relaxed on the bench, because it was a win-win-win situation. He already had silverware in the bank and if he did not win tonight a draw would be enough for the title, and even if he lost Arsenal would still be champions on Saturday.

It was extraordinary how the match reflected the temperaments of the rival managers: United were spiky and energetic, while Arsenal were also combative, but in a more cerebral manner, more detached and in control of their game. The Red Devils started aggressively to show Keane they still had fire in their bellies, and they had a few near-misses before the real mayhem began. Referee Paul Durkin issued three yellow cards in six minutes after Scholes clattered into Edu, Phil Neville scythed down Wiltord, and Keane came in late as Vieira controlled a high-bouncing ball. Keane's boot just missed Vieira's thigh, but his arm smacked Vieira's face. That was the end of Keane and the end of the contest, really.

Edu was busy, competitive and positionally solid, the revelation of the night. When Silvestre moved up the left he lost possession to Parlour, who passed short to Wiltord, who found the diagonal run of Ljungberg, who beat Blanc and hit a low shot. Barthez saved and the ball rebounded to Wiltord on his weaker left foot . . . and he scored the goal that won the Double.

When the final whistle came, the beaming Wenger was hugged by physio Gary Lewin, Edu lifted Ljungberg off his feet, Wiltord and Lauren danced a jig of delight, and Wenger walked over to embrace Vieira. He had seen his men produce a truly heroic team performance, a classic of containment and counter-attack, with the defensive and offensive elements executed confidently. It was exactly the kind of away performance they needed in the Champions' League.

Winning the title again was even more satisfying than it had been in 1998, said Wenger, who regarded this Double as his greatest achievement in England. 'I feel very happy because this team got what they deserved and we did it in style. I personally believe that what this team has achieved is tremendous and will remain in history. We have 84 points, we have played 19 games away in the League without losing one and we have scored in every game. The character of this team is extraordinary. This is not only a team of good players. It is a team of togetherness. We wanted there to be a shift of power. Winning it in my first full season almost felt natural, but I have lost a few times since then and realised how hard it is.'

The papers gave high praise to the new champions the next day, when the best headline was on a Tim Rich piece in *The Independent*: WENGER'S INVINCIBLES CLAIM GRAND PRIZE IN BARE-KNUCKLE TITLE FIGHT.

There was a festival atmosphere at Highbury as Lee Dixon led out the side against Everton in his last game before retirement. After imbecilic defending by Alan Stubbs and Stepanovs, among others, they won 4–3. Henry, playing with his right knee strapped, scored twice and crossed for sub Francis Jeffers to head Arsenal into a 4–2 lead. Bergkamp had netted the first and generously set up the second for Henry, whose 24 league goals won him the Golden Boot.

Then came the presentations. The 22 players who had played ten games or more collected their medals as did Pat Rice, Gary Lewin and first team coach Bora Primorac. Then, at last, came Robert Pires and, as he held up the trophy, the other players bowed down to him in a we-are-not-worthy salute. The pantomime was amusing but also a sincere statement of thanks, for without the consistent creativity of Pires they would not have been collecting these medals as champions. He had been voted Footballer of the Year by the English journalists.

Liverpool had finished second, with Dudek and Riise proving to be phenomenal signings. Manchester United, now demoralised, were third after a 0–0 draw with Charlton, their first scoreless game in the Premiership for three years. Arsenal had 87 points, Liverpool 84 and United 77.

Tony Adams gave an interview to Sky, saying that the manager had won the League this time, not the players. He explained how much he enjoyed the day-to-day life at the training ground and praised Wenger's cool leadership and his shrewd deployment of the squad.

'It takes a man at the helm. Maybe '98 was the players winning it, but I do believe it's the manager that's won this one. Throughout the season he's been extremely confident, unflappable. I dunno how best to describe him. But he's been self-assured, he's been dignified, he's been calm, he's been trusting, he's been faithful. He's given people patience. And a lot of love. I think the man deserves all the credit he can get.'

Wenger managed his players with tolerance, accepting their mistakes without being punitive or judgemental. He was also patient because he knew that you succeed after you fail, not before, so he kept faith with the new players and gave them time to settle in. He said, 'I am convinced that the biggest problem in modern football is impatience with new players. There are many big examples of this impatience, like when Patrick was at Milan and Thierry at Juventus. All coaches are under a lot of pressure that if a player does not perform in the first six months everybody starts to question our buying policy. Arsenal fans were always very patient with our players and it has worked out. Take Pires this year and Pires last year.'

While 2000–01 had been the season when rotation did not quite work, 2001–02 was the season where enforced rotation, due to a succession of injuries, worked remarkably well. Bergkamp had needed a year to adjust to not starting every match. Arguably, Wenger's first choice team was Seaman, Lauren, Campbell, Adams, Cole, Ljungberg, Parlour, Vieira, Pires, Bergkamp and Henry, but that eleven never played once in the sixty games. He had ten in the first two games, missing Bergkamp, and ten in the FA Cup Final, when he was missing Pires. So it was, truly, the season of the squad, and it looked as if, from now on, all seasons would be like this. The concept of the 'first team' had become obsolete.

Back in May 2001, Wenger had talked about needing 'a depth of stability in defence', but five players had turned out at left back, including Juan, the young Brazilian who played against Gillingham, and there had been a bewildering succession of centre-back partnerships. Three goalkeepers collected medals, which was unprecedented.

Despite all that disruption, the improvement in their defensive record during February, March, April and May was staggering: they had not been behind in a Premiership game since Fowler scored at Elland Road on 20 January. Team spirit had played a big part, confidence had grown while the vehicle was motoring, but the consistency, the twelve clean sheets, still seemed somewhat hard to explain. Perhaps the return of Adams and Dixon, who were training with the team again, had made everything more solid. Lauren admitted that Dixon had given him tips about positioning, and he was now covering runs instead of ball-watching. The clean sheets really started when Seaman came back to the side in February, and Campbell's recovery pace meant that mistakes could usually be rectified.

The professor, a master of man-management and mind-management, had guided his team to a 29-game unbeaten run in domestic football. It was revealed that Wenger held a team meeting on 23 December where he asked the players to stop getting red cards. Bergkamp was sent off after that, against Liverpool, and Luzhny went at Blackburn, but maybe there was no mystery about their improved disciplinary record. Success generally improves a team's behaviour. Players get red cards when they are struggling and frustrated and losing, not when they are cruising and winning. Patrick Vieira had played more than anyone else, but produced only half a dozen great games in all competitions. He was pacing himself, like most of the French World Cup winners, planning to peak in Japan in June. Often he was sloppy in the first half, much better in the second, perhaps after Wenger had a word.

Freddie Ljungberg had been playing exceptionally well when he was injured in January. He came back in March and was red hot in April and May. He scored the vital first goal so often. Of his seventeen goals, eleven were first goals. Two of the other six goals were in matches where he had scored the first goal. He was the first player to score in consecutive FA Cup Finals for forty years.

Remarkably, Wenger had sorted out their away form in the Premiership. Their record had improved from five wins, seven draws and seven defeats to fourteen wins and five draws, so his next task was obvious: to improve Arsenal's away form in Europe.

How would he do that? By signing players who would slightly change Arsenal's style, allowing more flexibility and greater possession? Did he now accept that the high-tempo attacking which worked so well at Highbury, and which destroyed Juventus and Bayer Leverkusen, does not work away from home in the Champions' League?

They needed to keep the ball for longer, consolidate at the back, and score some goals from crosses. Their definitive away performance was in Lyon, when they kept possession well and Henry headed home a cross by Ashley Cole and they won 1–0. That match always looked like a template to follow for the future, but they never played well enough to repeat that victory, although they were close in Leverkusen.

On 13 May, Wenger was quoted in *L'Equipe* saying, 'I can't imagine finishing my life without winning the European Cup.' Two days later he flew to Glasgow to see the European Cup Final in which Real Madrid met Leverkusen. The German underdogs, without Ze Roberto and skipper Nowoty, outplayed Madrid, but they were beaten by a stunning volley from Zidane.

Wenger's contract was due to end in 2005, by which time he would have been managing Arsenal for nine years, but Ashburton Grove looked unlikely to open before 2005–6. In the meantime, he was still enjoying his daily work at Shenley and he loved the competition, the matches. As he said, 'It's the life I wanted.'

When George Graham was sacked in 1995, the directors had resolved that no future manager would ever have that much power again, but Wenger now oversaw a vastly expanded operation with many coaches, physios, masseurs and other full time staff. In 1996 Ashley Cole had been a 14-year-old boy looked after by a part-time schoolteacher who earned £45 a week, but now he was a 21-year-old playing for England in the World Cup.

Film director Orson Welles, a maverick genius, once called RKO Studios 'the biggest electric train set a boy ever had,' but Arsène Wenger would probably say that managing Arsenal was the biggest train set a French boy ever had. A man motivated by an ideal of how the game could be, he was now close to creating his perfect football machine: a stylish, athletic, attacking team which could keep clean sheets.

Since London is the biggest city in Europe, it was logical for Arsenal to try to become the biggest club in the world. A new stadium alone cannot do that, of course, but it could provide the money to make winning the European Cup more likely.

Or maybe Arsenal could reach the final next year. Could Arsène Wenger win the European Cup at Old Trafford in May 2003?

# 10. 2002/03: THE SEASON OF 15 DRAWS

Ronaldinho's free-kick is one of those unforgettable moments in English football history.

World Cup 2002 Quarter-finals, Shizuoka, Japan: the score is 1–1 and Brazil get a free-kick on the right side, 35 yards from England's goal. Roberto Carlos and Rivaldo let the youngster take it and he scores by floating the ball over David Seaman and into the far corner. The goal is no fluke. It is an outrageous free-kick by a Brazilian genius. His body shape proves it was deliberate, and he looks only at the goal, not at the players hoping for a header 12 yards out from the far post. Ronaldinho did not miskick that ball by 12 yards.

Such a moment had been coming for a long time. When a baseball player gets too old the Americans say he has 'lost a step' and Seaman, 38, had lost a step years before. Between 1989 and 1996 he had been well protected by the best defence in England, and when Vieira, Petit and Parlour were in midfield, he had even less to do. Seaman was the hero of Euro 96 and as the years rolled on he could still make great saves, but he did not command his penalty area after his ribs were broken by Ole Gunnar Solskjaer on 16 November 1996. He did not come out so much or so confidently, so his defenders were gradually pushed back into the goalmouth when defending crosses and free-kicks.

However, his decline had been a taboo subject. To criticise David Seaman MBE was unpatriotic and he had remained as Arsenal's No.1, while Richard Wright, who had never recovered from his trauma in La Coruña, was sold to Everton for £3.5 million. Alex Manninger went to Espanyol for £1 million and Wenger signed a Swedish keeper, Rami Shaaban, 27, from Djurgaarden IF for £600,000, plus the Lille center-back Pascal Cygan for £2.1 million, and Kolo Toure from the Ivory Coast for £500,000. He phoned PSV Eindhoven about Mark van Bommel, but PSV would not budge from their price of £15 million, so he bought Gilberto Silva from Atletico Mineiro for £4.5 million.

Retirements had created a leadership vacuum and left Dennis Bergkamp wondering, 'Who will do the shouting, organising and motivating without Tony Adams and Lee Dixon? That was always a major, major strength of both those players.'

In the Community Shield, Arsenal met Liverpool, and Gilberto scored the only goal, charging onto Bergkamp's pass to blast a left-foot shot through the legs of Jerzy Dudek. The following weekend the Premiership kicked off with 132 foreign players and just 88 Englishmen, and Arsenal's Rolls-Royce teamwork made it a short match against promoted Birmingham, as they raced to a 2–0 lead in 23 minutes. They went to Upton Park seeking their 15th straight league win, but Joe Cole and Frederic Kanoute gave West Ham a two-goal lead after 65 minutes. Then Henry scored a wonder goal, Kanoute missed a penalty, and Wiltord made it 2–2. If the Hammers had held on, their season might have been completely different.

Against West Brom, Arsenal cruised to a 3–0 lead in 24 minutes. It was far too easy and they came out for the second half with a different head on and Scott Dobie scored. After that goal, amazingly, Arsenal got the jitters. If Adams and Dixon had been playing, they would not have been so shaky when leading 3–1 at home. But they went on to win 5–2.

The Chelsea-Arsenal match was the tamest for ten years and Arsenal were dominating until Zola's 40-yard free-kick bounced three yards from goal and went into the net. Patrick Vieira was harshly sent off by referee Andy D'Urso after a tackle which Zola skipped over and another where Gronkjaer hurt himself by kicking Vieira's boot. A Kolo Toure header earned a draw.

After that, Arsenal won the next nine games by playing the most stylish, entertaining football they had played in their entire history. Fluent, powerful and confident, as champions should be, they could now spurt, score, slow it down, spurt again, score another, and stroll to the final whistle. Skipper Vieira was back to his regal best – concentrating well, striding forward and passing beautifully – the hub of a football machine that now had more gears. With Sol

Campbell developing into a better player than he had ever been at Spurs, Gilberto adding extra power, Henry demonstrating sublime skills at breathtaking pace, and Bergkamp pulling out all the stops for what might be his swansong season, Arsenal were playing keep-ball better than they had done at any time in the last six years.

So hopes were high for the Champions League campaign, which would begin at home to Borussia Dortmund on 17 September, followed by away games against PSV Eindhoven and Auxerre. But, after they had beaten Charlton 3–0 and Dortmund 2–0 and Bolton 2–1, Wenger made a comment for which he would be castigated. He said, 'It looks easy from the outside when we dominate some games – but it is a consequence of a big effort and a lot of hard work by the players. If we have the right attitude, we can go through the season unbeaten. I'm not tempting fate by saying what I believe.'

Arsenal kicked off in Eindhoven and lost the ball, but Ljungberg won it back, released Henry on the left, and he crossed for Gilberto to grab the fastest goal in Champions League history in 20.07 seconds. Ljungberg made it 2–0, Henry doubled the tally to 4–0, and Vieira said, 'We know we can beat anybody. We feel really strong.'

Toure made the first goal and scored the second in a spectacular 4–1 win at Leeds, and, in Auxerre, new boy Gilberto grabbed another priceless goal. 'They're capable of scoring within five seconds of getting the ball back,' said coach Guy Roux. 'Their forwards have devilish skill like I haven't seen in a long time.'

In *France Football*, Vieira said he would far rather win the Champions League with Arsenal than with Real Madrid and he noted that Arsenal played with more freedom than France, so Thierry Henry can score at any time. 'He can make the difference at any given moment, and to stretch the point, you could say that we all play for him, in a way.' A revealing line: 'We all play for him, in a way.'

Vieira was exceptional in a 3–1 win over Sunderland, whose player-coach Niall Quinn said, 'They're playing football like they're the kings of Europe, not just the kings of the Premiership.' And it was that victory which overtook Manchester United's previous benchmark of 29 Premiership games unbeaten.

## ROONEY SHATTERS THE EUPHORIA

*Arsenal are the strongest team in Europe at the moment*

Roma coach Fabio Capello

After that came an international break which worried Wenger. England drew 2–2 with Macedonia, and Seaman took more flak when Artim Sakiri scored directly from a corner. France thrashed Slovenia 5–0, flew to Malta and went 3–0 up in an hour, but Jacques Santini left Henry, Vieira and Wiltord on for 90 minutes.

The Arsenal team had not played together for 14 days, so they lacked their normal fluency at Everton, who were a rejuvenated side. Ljungberg got the first goal, Radzinski equalised, and a tight battle developed. But then Everton's chunky substitute Wayne Rooney controlled a high ball from Gravesen and smashed a dipping 25-yard shot in off the underside of the bar. Rooney became the Premiership's youngest-ever goalscorer five days short of his 17th birthday.

In that moment a bubble was burst, a state of euphoria destroyed. Footballers who had forgotten what it was like to lose came back to earth with a painful bump, as the magic carpet was yanked from under them. Arsenal's aura of invincibility was suddenly shattered.

Cleverly, Wenger hailed Rooney as the greatest prospect in English football, declaring, 'He is the biggest talent I've seen since I arrived in England. There has certainly not been an under-20 player as good as him since I became a manager here. We were beaten by a special goal from a very special talent.'

On his 53rd birthday, Wenger welcomed Auxerre to Highbury, who started at a high tempo and went 2–0 up in 27 minutes and then sat deep and blotted out Henry, whose one good run set up a goal for Kanu. After that, Arsenal were denied further chances, being forced to hit long balls. It was like Senegal beating France. At Blackburn, Edu volleyed an own-goal and then equalised from a free-kick, but Tugay slid a ball between Campbell and Lauren for Ostenstad, whose square pass gave Yorke the winner. Arsenal had 27 shots and Brad Friedel made 14 saves, some of them world class. The champions had now lost three games in a row.

In Dortmund, the home team hit the post twice in 14 minutes before Arsenal got out of first gear. Henry scored with a free-kick, but had a poor game, giving up too easily, which annoyed the fans. Seaman had no chance with a Gilberto own-goal, but bottled a 50-50 with Jan Koller, who touched the ball, jumped over him and fell. The replays showed no contact and Wenger said, 'Like on many occasions, the referee made a difference. All credit to him, he scored a good second goal for them. I was happy for him. He deserves a good mention.' Four consecutive defeats was Arsenal's worst run since 1983 and Wenger had responded with sarcasm.

Liverpool stormed seven points clear by beating West Ham at Anfield, but Arsenal scraped home at Fulham, courtesy of a surreal own-goal by Steve Marlet. A relieved Wenger said, 'I would have preferred to win this match with a different goal, but I'll take that one. If you lose four, it has to be a concern because confidence is a fragile thing. We're not used to losing runs.'

In the Worthington Cup Arsenal's Second XI went 2–0 up against Sunderland at Highbury and then conceded three headers to lose 3–2. At home to Newcastle, Wiltord scored, and that 1–0 win cut the gap at the top of the Premiership, with Liverpool losing at Middlesbrough. Rami Shaaban made his debut against PSV Eindhoven in the Champions League, Seaman having strained a groin muscle, but Arsenal had already qualified and it was a 0–0 draw. Toure was sent off, but Cygan played solidly, as did Shaaban. For the second group stage they were drawn against Valencia, Roma and Ajax.

When Spurs came to Highbury on 16 November, Henry, deep in his own half, controlled Vieira's header on his body, exploded away from Etherington, swerved past Steve Carr and Ledley King, and aimed a left-foot shot just inside the post – an electrifying solo goal. The 3–0 win put the champions back on top.

Gilberto had flown to South Korea to play for Brazil, so Edu started at Southampton, where Bergkamp scored the first goal. James Beattie replied from a free-kick awarded for a fair challenge by Cygan on Delgado. When Campbell brought Delgado down, referee Paul Durkin gave him a red card and Beattie's penalty put the Saints ahead. Then Toure headed into his own net off Delgado for 3–1. There were more chances at both ends before Pires, replacing Bergkamp, made it 3–2.

Rome loomed as a huge test for Shaaban. He had kept clean sheets against PSV and Spurs but he now saw Cassano's miscued shot dribble in off the post after only four minutes. Amazingly, Henry equalised within two minutes and after that both sides kept it tight until the last fifteen, when Henry scored two more goals. Roma coach Fabio Capello accepted defeat graciously, saying 'Arsenal are the strongest team in Europe at the moment. They punish you at the first mistake and are always united. They run for each other the whole time. They never stop.' Back home, Henry starred in a 3–1 win against Aston Villa at Highbury, but Cygan and Campbell looked dodgy against Vassell and Dublin.

As December started, Manchester United were motoring after wins against Newcastle, Basle and Liverpool and their next game was Arsenal at Old Trafford. In a Sky interview, Tony Adams urged his team to stop treating the Premiership as their No.2 priority. Adams tipped United, suggesting that Arsenal's defending in domestic games was not as professional as it was in Europe. It was a good call: United were fiery and won 2–0. Arsenal were still top but their sequence of scoring in 55 Premiership games had ended.

Adams criticised the midfield balance, saying, 'I can now say publicly what I used to say to Arsène Wenger privately on occasion, that the most crucial area of any game is getting the numbers and balance right in midfield. Freddie Ljungberg and Robert Pires are wonderful players going forward, but I don't think you can play them both away from home. I believe Arsenal are missing Ray Parlour.'

The second group stage of the Champions League continued at Highbury against Valencia, whose left winger, Vicente, reckoned that Henry often 'lacks character at key moments'. He added, 'I've seen him play lots of times and he tries to be so elegant that he might as well go on to the pitch wearing his dinner jacket. He's too laid back. If you keep him tightly marked he hardly makes a contribution.' On the night both teams seemed to respect each other too much and a keenly anticipated clash fizzled out in a 0–0 draw.

Only Cole, Parlour, Campbell and Keown were really up for the following derby at White Hart Lane, a 1–1 draw in which Seaman embarrassed himself by trying to dribble round Robbie Keane. It looked as if Adams was right: the foreigners were concentrating on the Champions League. So the key question became: How long can a team keep fluctuating from bad to good without losing the ability to be good when it wants to be good?

In the run-up to Christmas, a 2–0 home win over Middlesbrough put Arsenal two points above Chelsea, but at West Brom they struggled to create openings, and Dichio headed home a Koumas corner. Then Jeffers clipped in a neat equaliser. Vieira, superb throughout, blocked Adam Chambers' clearance and the ball rebounded for Henry to score the winner. Unfortunately, during training on Christmas Eve, Rami Shaaban broke his leg.

Liverpool at Highbury was a tale of two penalties. Gerrard's long pass found Baros looking for Campbell's outstretched foot to trip over. He went down and Danny Murphy converted. Baros could not have scored from such a narrow angle and sometimes a defender has to say: 'OK, you've beaten me, now beat my keeper!' Jeffers came on for Wiltord and spun onto Bergkamp's jabbed pass into the box, Riise put an arm across him, Jeffers dived, and Henry smashed the penalty down the middle.

December had been a disappointing month with only two wins in six games, but January began well as Chelsea arrived to find Vieira in super-gladiator mode. Arsenal led 3–0 after 83 minutes before a loss of concentration let Chelsea pull back to 3–2. The players looked tired after four games in 11 days, especially Gilberto, who was now running on World Cup legs, but they had maintained their five-point advantage at the top. Never before had Arsenal earned so many points by New Year's Day. Centre-back Matthew Upson, disillusioned by his lack of first-team action, wanted a move, so he was sold to Birmingham for an initial £1 million during the January transfer window.

They now had easy games against Oxford, Birmingham, West Ham and Farnborough, and four wins took them to Anfield for a thriller which again showed how Arsenal failed to kill off opponents. Henry scored early and almost created another goal five minutes before the interval, then Heskey set up Riise for a scorching shot into the far corner. Seaman had no chance and neither did Dudek when Bergkamp's shot deflected off the heel of Henchoz for 2–1. When Baros came on, Wenger took Bergkamp off and brought on Luzhny as a third centre-back. By removing Bergkamp, Wenger was saying to Liverpool, 'You have the ball for the next six minutes'. Baros and Luzhny chased a ball which looked over the line before either touched it, a dubious corner was cleared, but Diao crossed and Heskey headed in for 2–2.

The Fulham game was poised at 1–1 for an hour until substitute Jeffers changed the game, creating the winner for Pires. Despite the team's dodgy moments, Bergkamp said he felt part of something really special. 'I don't want to get too philosophical, but I honestly think that this Arsenal side have rewritten the rules of football.'

At Newcastle a fast and furious battle developed. Henry made it 1–0, but early in the second half, Cole gave the ball to Laurent Robert, who beat Vieira and Lauren to rifle in the equaliser. There was more than half an hour left and only a late save by Seaman denied Newcastle victory. Another draw meant that after 27 games Arsenal had 57 points and Manchester United had 54.

The FA Cup took Arsenal to Old Trafford. Henry and Bergkamp were rested, and also Gilberto, who was recovering from Brazil's friendly in China. Scholes kicked Vieira twice to start a fracas, and van Nistelrooy kicked Keown and slammed his arm into Lauren's forehead. Vieira, furious at these assaults, was booked for dissent.

Then Beckham flighted a 40-yard pass for Giggs, who went round Seaman and Campbell, but fired over an open goal. That was the turning point. When Edu took a free-kick, the wall jumped. The ball hit Beckham's shoulder, wrong-footing Barthez for 1–0, and then a swift move set up Wiltord, who swerved past Wes Brown and thumped in the second. Remarkably, Seaman did not have one shot to save.

Media frenzy erupted when the front page of Monday's *Sun* carried a photograph showing Beckham arriving for training with a cut over his left eyebrow. The injury occurred in the dressing room when an angry Ferguson kicked a loose boot, which hit Beckham's face.

Ajax coach Ronald Koeman knew how penetrating Arsenal had been against PSV, but he could also see that they were predictable. His side, with seven players of 21 or under, started shakily at Highbury and conceded an early goal to Wiltord. Then De Jong made it 1–1 and Ajax settled down and contained Arsenal by defending deep, attacking wide and improving as the game went on, with the little South African, Pienaar, typifying their effervescent spirit. It is at such moments that Wenger seems to be a very conservative selector, too rigid in his thinking. He has a master plan, a way of playing, and a first eleven which is set in stone, Edu had done enough in Manchester to keep his place.

When Arsenal won 5–1 at Maine Road, Manchester City manager Kevin Keegan said, 'Arsenal, in my opinion, will win the Champions League. They're on a different planet.' Amsterdam was next and Wenger admitted that 'other teams adapt to your style of play'. But, positive as ever, he added, 'We've taken a big step forward in Europe over the last three years and now believe we can win anywhere against anyone.'

This time there was less fire and trickery about Ajax, who played in a more functional, programmed style, which worked until Vieira made a magnificent tackle, got up, found Henry, who found Pires, who put Bergkamp in on the right. But he scuffed his shot beyond the far post. The Ajax kids prevented similar counter-thrusts by skirmishing energetically just inside Arsenal's half, the zone from which their killer passes are so often launched, and defending the box in depth against a side which does not score from crosses. Meanwhile, Roma had become the first team to win a Champions League game in Valencia.

March kicked off with a 2–0 home win against Charlton which put Arsenal eight points clear, so the season now depended on the next four games – Chelsea, Roma, Blackburn and Valencia. Two games at home, then two away. The treble was still possible, but Ashley Cole, their only left-back, was out for a month after a hernia operation.

The Chelsea cup tie was a superb contest for an hour. John Terry scored with an early header, Cudicini saved Henry's penalty, Jeffers levelled, and Henry bamboozled the advancing Cudicini with a spin to put Arsenal 2–1 up at half-time. The game turned on the double substitution of Pires and Wiltord for Jeffers and Ljungberg in 64 minutes. After that, Arsenal lost shape and fluency, and when Toure came on for Henry there was no goal threat. Chelsea, already chasing the game, were further galvanised. Zenden's corner was flicked into the danger area by Melchiot, where Campbell kicked the ball against Lampard and the rebound dribbled over the line to set up a replay.

The Roma game was yet another draw. Vieira played out of his skin, but nobody else did, and Arsenal could not defeat ten men after Totti was sent off for jumping into Keown arm-first and slapping him on the ear. Montella missed a late header and it finished 1–1.

In another *Observer* piece, Tony Adams said that Wenger goes on long walks round the training ground, mulling over the selection most suited to the next match, and asks physio Gary Lewin which players are feeling stiff or tired. 'Then he will look at the statistics he has from the games. He will see which players are in the best shape. For example, he may look at the chart of, say, Robert Pires. He may have run 14 kilometres during the last game and compare it to another midfielder – Ray Parlour, for instance. If he is deciding between the two for a spot in the team, he will look at those figures. If Robert has run more than Ray, then he will deduce he is in better shape and he will get the nod. He is what I call a physiological manager. He goes a lot on physical shape.'

At Blackburn, Arsenal were without Vieira, Campbell and Cole, so it was a cruel blow when Keown pulled a hamstring. He went off when the score was 0–0, and the defence collapsed, with van Bronckhorst exposed by Keith Gillespie. Duff and Tugay scored.

Wenger's fiftieth Champions League match in charge of Arsenal would be a moment of truth. They would qualify for the quarter-finals, if they won or drew in Valencia, but they had just drawn with Chelsea, drawn with Roma, and lost at Blackburn, so form was not on their side and neither was history: Arsenal had never won in Spain.

Surprisingly, Pires was given the Bergkamp role, with Ljungberg on the left and Wiltord on the right, and they faced canny veterans who were especially good at containing quick-passing thrusts through the middle, which was more than could be said for the defenders at the other end. When Cygan followed Juan Sanchez into midfield, Aimar released Carew to rifle a shot inside Taylor's near post. Then Pires slipped Henry through to side-foot his trademark shot round Canizares. Nobody scores a one-on-one from 19 yards so sweetly. But Wiltord idiotically lost the ball to Vicente, who crossed for Carew to head the winner. Ajax drew 1–1 in Rome, so Valencia won the group with nine points, followed by Ajax on eight, Arsenal on seven and Roma on five.

A European campaign, which had started so marvellously in Eindhoven, had ended with yet another crushing disappointment, but Patrick Vieira now showed his colossal competitive spirit by putting the team on his back and carrying them to two wins in three days against Everton and Chelsea. With Vieira playing like this, a double Double was still possible and the title race promised to be the most exciting finish in the eleven-year history of the Premiership.

## COLLAPSING INTO CARDIFF

*I hope that, for the next 20 years, we will have seasons as disappointing as this one.*

Arsène Wenger

Arsenal's regained momentum was now interrupted for England's crucial Euro 2004 qualifier against Turkey, with Wayne Rooney making a fine debut in a 2–0 victory.

Unfortunately, when the team re-assembled at Villa Park it looked a feeble imitation of the outfit that had hammered Chelsea 3–1. Ljungberg gave them the lead, but deputy left-back Toure miskicked an Alback shot into his own net and the last half hour was pitiful. Arsenal's eight-point lead had vanished in 29 days and they now led United only on goal difference.

The following weekend United won 6–2 at Newcastle while the FA Cup semi-finals brought predictable wins for Southampton against Watford, and Arsenal against Sheffield United. Ljungberg scored again, Vieira went off with a serious knee injury, and Seaman clawed a Peschisolido header off the line at the death.

At Highbury, Vieira led the team out against Manchester United with his knee bandaged. Van Nistelrooy raced away from Campbell to score, and Vieira had to limp off. Arsenal then got lucky, as Cole's shot was deflected in off Henry's calf, and when Henry, clearly offside, took a Gilberto pass and netted with no flag raised. But Giggs replied immediately with a header and it finished 2–2. Late on, Sol Campbell threw an arm that caught Solskjaer and referee Mark Halsey gave him his second red card of the season. Campbell was now banned for the last three games, plus the FA Cup Final.

To keep the contest going until the last day, Arsenal now needed to win at Middlesbrough and Bolton. Skipper Ray Parlour was the catalyst at the Riverside, making more tackles in the first 20 minutes than Gilberto had made since Christmas, and setting the tone. Cygan also played well in a 2–0 win. But United beat Blackburn 3–1 and they now topped the table on 74 points with three games to play. Arsenal had 71 points with four to play, so if both teams kept winning, they would finish level on 83 points and the title would be decided on goal difference, goals scored, or, possibly, a play-off.

At the Reebok, Bolton, who were fighting relegation, dominated a goalless first half. Henry created a tap-in for Wiltord, Pires side-footed a second, but then Okocha crunched Ljungberg's ankle. It looked as if Bergkamp would replace the crippled Swede, but Luzhny came on. Then, suddenly, Cygan pulled a calf muscle, and a Gardner tackle put Lauren out of the game with a twisted ankle.

Incredibly, three players had gone off injured in the 15 minutes since Pires had put them 2–0 up. Luzhny scuffed a clearance and Frandsen's shot rebounded to Djorkaeff, who made it 2–1 and then produced a dipping free-kick which went in off Keown's head. Champions should defend better than that. It was another lead lost, another draw, another bitterly disappointing day. Wenger made a comment he had never made before, admitting that his players 'wanted to do the minimum to win'.

The team that could not hold a lead never got in front when Leeds came to Highbury on 4 May. Wilcox hit a very long pass and Kewell deftly handled the ball towards his left foot and hit a sensational cross-shot past Seaman. Keown did not appeal, none of the officials saw the handball, and, astonishingly, the Sky commentators and studio pundits missed it as well.

Henry headed the equaliser after Parlour's 30-yarder was tipped onto the post by Robinson, and Harte hit a free-kick which went off Cole's head to make it 2–1 to Leeds. Still, Arsenal were playing well and Henry found Pires, who set up Bergkamp for 2–2, and they looked like winning when Henry stepped inside Mills to hit a swerving shot against the far post. There was still time and it looked as if Henry might score, but substitute Jermaine Pennant ignored a pass to Bergkamp, preferring to turn the other way into three Leeds players. Matteo took the ball off him and released Viduka, who was coming back in an offside position. The flag stayed down and Viduka scored the goal that gave Sir Alex Ferguson another title.

In the final analysis, Arsenal lacked experienced defensive cover and lost 14 points in away games when they were leading. The team could lift you up to the skies but could not nail down a result. They were the most attractive attacking team in England, but you don't get points for artistic impression. Professional football is about results and their results were not quite good enough. They drew 15 of their 59 games in all competitions. Manchester United were champions because they won 13 of their last 16 league games and drew three.

Back in the Sixties, the legendary Matt Busby had told Best, Law and Charlton to just go out and play. Busby's philosophy was 'We are the stars, let them mark us'. Forty years later, Ferguson's rivalry with Wenger tended to obscure what their teams had in common: Arsenal always come to play, and Manchester United always come to play. Maybe Arsène Wenger was really just Sir Matt Busby with a BSc.

Ten days before the FA Cup Final, Southampton suffered a 6–1 humiliation at Highbury, so boss Gordon Strachan chose damage limitation tactics, dropping right-winger Fernandes, pushing Telfer forward and introducing Baird, a young right-back, to tighten up that flank.

It was a one-sided final in which Henry missed early chances and Pires scored his 16th goal of the season. Vieira and Campbell, two spinal players, were badly missed, so Arsenal were too inhibited to kill the game off. Brett Ormerod eventually hit a terrific volley which skipper Seaman palmed away and after that scare it was keep-ball and time-wasting. That led to drama in stoppage time when Matt Oakley swung over a perfect corner and James Beattie powered in a header, which Cole blocked on the line. Bergkamp was the classiest player on the pitch and Gilberto had his best game for three months.

Thierry Henry, who had racked up 24 Premiership goals and an unprecedented 20 assists, won PFA Player of the Year and FWA Footballer of the Year, plus Goal of the Season for his slalom against Spurs, but he had still not scored in a final.

Seven years on from his ambassadorial arrival on that sunny autumn Sunday, Arsène Wenger had stayed true to his mission statement. Arsenal were playing stylish, power football, scoring dozens of thrilling goals, breaking many records, and had collected five trophies. No manager in Arsenal's history had kept them in the top two for six years in a row and one of his comments after Cardiff reminded us that the Arsène Wenger we love most is the droll Professor who says things like, 'I hope that, for the next 20 years, we will have seasons as disappointing as this one'.

In the Champions League semi-final Real Madrid were beaten by Juventus, who met AC Milan in the final and lost a penalty shoot-out after a 0–0 draw.

Madrid were again linked with Arsène Wenger, who was alleged to be frustrated by the delay in building Ashburton Grove, and to have had a meeting with them in Paris. But while Wenger would probably love to manage Raul, Ronaldo, Figo and Zidane, would he enjoy managing Jorge Valdano, the sporting director, and Florentino Perez, the president who bought their superstars? One recalled the words of Tibource Darrou, the fitness coach Wenger uses in Antibes, in a new book, *The French Revolution*. He said, 'The day Arsène stops managing Arsenal, he stops managing for good.

What he lives here is a dream. He did not need to invest one penny, but he manages the money of the club, he is the boss. What else could he dream of?'

# 11. 2003/04: THE SEASON OF 38 GAMES UNBEATEN

In the summer of 2003, Wenger signed Jens Lehmann, a goalkeeper from Borussia Dortmund for £1.5 million. He was 33 and was first seen in two friendlies in Scotland.

Against Celtic, the German claimed high balls with authority and looked a big improvement on Seaman, who had been offered a coaching job, but preferred to join Manchester City. Kolo Toure played centre-back at Parkhead, which was a radical selection and a fascinating experiment for all concerned, including the new goalkeeper.

In the first half, Francis Jeffers was abysmal, and Celtic scored when Liam Miller was allowed to hook in an overhead shot from seven yards. Toure had gone AWOL and the other three defenders were too deep. Since the team now had a 'keeper willing to punch crosses, they should have been defending further out. Immediately, Wenger put Cygan on for Toure. In the second half, Arsenal settled down and Kanu equalised.

Could Kolo Toure become a Premiership centre-back? Until now he had been a utility player, a rough diamond with skill, strength, bravery, pace and energy to burn. His distribution and positional play would need to improve.

When Arsenal played Rangers at Ibrox, an Edu shot deflected into the top corner and the game became a stroll. Lauren scored a penalty, Campbell made it 3–0 with a header, and the team was already showing glimpses of the power football that wins Premiership titles. Lehmann shouted, pointed, organised at set-pieces, and kept a clean sheet.

In the Community Shield against Manchester United, we saw why Jeffers would never be an Arsenal player. It was 1–1 after 73 minutes and he was fouled by Phil Neville: they tangled, Neville held Jeffers's leg, fell – and Jeffers kicked him while he was on the ground. Jeffers was sent off and, as soon as possible, loaned back to Everton for the season. United had won the penalty shoot-out.

The first three games against Everton, Middlesbrough and Aston Villa were won by 2–1 and 4–0 and 2–0. Sol Campbell had been sent off at Goodison after 25 minutes for tripping Gravesen, but they still took a 2–0 lead. At Manchester City, Seaman bottled a 50-50 with Pires to give Ljungberg the winner. Against Portsmouth at Highbury their form dipped, as it often does before European games, but a crafty dive by Pires earned a phoney penalty and a draw.

Sol Campbell's father was seriously ill, but he played against Inter Milan in the Champions League and Arsenal conceded early goals to Julio Cruz and Andy van der Meyde. Wiltord was abysmal, running offside, falling over the ball, unable to pass. When the Spanish referee gave Ljungberg a penalty, Henry's shot was easily saved by Toldo, and at half-time Ljungberg bawled out Pires as they walked off for playing a cross-field pass that was intercepted, leading to a third goal by Obafemi Martins. It is very rare to see Arsenal players accusing each other of mistakes.

Bergkamp and Kanu eventually replaced Pires and Gilberto. When Henry played a ball through for Bergkamp it was a 50-50 with Materazzi, so Bergkamp jammed his foot on the ball, turned his backside into Materazzi, knocked him over, and had a shot which was deflected off Cannavaro's toe, Toldo saving. Arsenal had needed that aggression at 7.45 pm, not at 9.00 pm when they were 3–0 down and the game was over.

Next game, the manager had to shake it up. Pires had played badly against Portsmouth and Inter, so he was dropped for Sunday's visit to Old Trafford, along with Wiltord. Wenger decided to play for a draw, so he rested Campbell, whose father had died, brought in Keown, put Ljungberg on the left, started Parlour and Bergkamp, and made sure it was a tight, scrappy game.

Nothing much happened until Vieira got two yellow cards in the 78th and 80th minutes. The first was harsh, for a tackle on Fortune. Then Ruud van Nistelrooy jumped into Vieira with no intention of playing the ball. Vieira fell, then flicked his foot and pulled it back. Van Nistelrooy knew that Vieira's foot could not have reached him, but he jumped back and turned to referee Steve Bennett as if to say 'Did you see that?' He tried to get Vieira sent off, Bennett obliged, and that infuriated the whole Arsenal team.

When Forlan and Keown dived together for a cross, and both missed the ball, Bennett gave a penalty in the last minute, but van Nistelrooy slammed it against the bar. The game finished 0–0, the players taunted van Nistelrooy for his sly gamesmanship, and a brief scuffle developed. As usual, Wenger played down the controversy, saying, 'We have played ten games of 90 minutes and for five seconds we didn't behave. We did not behave as we want to behave. It was no more than that.' Arsenal were eventually fined £175,000 and five players were suspended and fined: Lauren (four matches, £40,000), Keown (three matches, £20,000), Vieira (one match, £10,000), Parlour (one match, £10,000) and Cole (£10,000). The discipline was much improved after this game, with only one further red card all season.

On a wet Friday at Highbury, Newcastle were the visitors. Henry scored first, Dyer set up Robert for 1–1, Ljungberg hit the post, Gilberto made it 2–1, then Dyer supplied Bernard for the best goal of the game. It could have finished 2–2, but Jenas handled and Henry clipped the penalty sweetly down the middle as Given dived left.

In the Champions League, Matchday 2 is always a massive night for all the clubs who lost on Matchday 1, as Lokomotiv Moscow and Arsenal had done. The defence played well in a goalless game in Moscow. At Anfield, Jeremie Aliadière, 20, was preferred to Wiltord. Liverpool's first half was the best football they had ever played against a Wenger team and Harry Kewell scored a fine goal. Edu miscued a header which dribbled in for 1–1, and later set up Pires, who curled the winner round Dudek from twenty yards.

Ken Bates had sold Chelsea to the Russian oligarch Roman Abramovich, who bought eleven new players for £110 million in one summer. Despite his redundant personnel, Claudio Ranieri's team had started the season very well and they came to Highbury as league leaders.

Edu's free-kick deflected past Cudicini to put Arsenal ahead, but then Crespo went off the pitch, sneaked back on, and hit a stunning shot for 1–1. Cudicini made a rare blunder when he allowed a Pires cross to go through his legs and hit Henry on the knee and bobble into the net. Arsenal had played calmly, confidently, and, for once, Plan B worked. Parlour and Wiltord had lacked the craft to deliver a final ball, but the arrival of Bergkamp and Kanu transformed the game, with Bergkamp making three passes that nobody else on the field would have seen. However, Henry showed the extent of their new pragmatism by walking the ball to the corner flag to run down the clock. In seven years, Wenger's teams had never done that before, except in the FA Cup Final against Southampton.

Inter sacked Hector Cuper two months into his third season and they lost 3–0 to Lokomotiv Moscow. In the Ukraine, Arsenal were beaten 2–1 by Dynamo Kiev, but it was their best Champions League performance in a defeat. A slip by Edu and a blunder by Lehmann, miskicking outside his box, cost them two goals. Back home, a point at Charlton kept them on top, the kids were magnificent in the Carling Cup game against Rotherham, winning a penalty shoot-out, and at Elland Road in the FA Cup Third Round, Arsenal were 4–0 up before Alan Smith got his consolation goal.

## INTER MILAN 1 ARSENAL 5

*If we go out of the Champions League, I'll beat myself up and feel really upset. Unfortunately, I do that every season.*

Arsène Wenger

In the Champions League their position was now serious, almost terminal, since they needed to win their next three games, which looked improbable. At Highbury, Dynamo Kiev pressed fiercely at times, while shunting back into their box at other times, making it a very difficult test, but an interesting one. Pires was everywhere, sprinting, shuffling, thinking, performing at the outer limit of his abilities, using everything he had ever learned, while Ljungberg had three near-misses. In the second half, substitute Wiltord crossed into the box and the ball glanced off the top of Federov's head towards the far post, where Ashley Cole dived to head the goal which kept their European season alive. A big goal – 5 November, Cole, 88 minutes.

On the Saturday, Spurs arrived to face a team who were too tired to play their beautiful game. Lauren kicked the ball against a Spurs player and it rebounded for Anderton to score, but Pires equalised when Henry's shot rebounded off Keller. Even when Arsenal were losing 1–0, they were better than Spurs, and they won with a shot by Ljungberg which hit Steve Carr's boot and looped over Kasey Keller.

Birmingham–Arsenal was Wenger's 400th game and he surprised us by starting teenager Gael Clichy in left midfield, playing Pires and Edu centrally, recalling Cygan, and switching Toure to right back. His new captain was Bergkamp, who turned the clock back five years with a magisterial display, and Henry provided three marvellous assists in a 3–0 win.

The San Siro, without the injured Vieira, now looked like a mighty challenge for a team who had won only two of their last thirteen Champions League games.

'I won't be fulfilled if we don't win the Champions League,' admitted Wenger. 'But I know I'll never be fulfilled no matter what I achieve as a coach. I'll always have problems accepting that I can lose in any competition. One of my strong points is my hunger. When I look back on my career, I always think about what we've lost rather than what we've won. So, if we go out of the Champions League, I'll beat myself up and feel really upset. Unfortunately, I do that every season.'

He said that Arsenal were respected, that they sold out stadiums everywhere they played, and that the games they had lost were always very, very close.

On that particular night, the game was not close because Arsenal produced a colossal team performance and thrashed Inter 5–1, the club's biggest win in Italy. Afterwards, Lehmann made an emotional speech, telling his teammates that he had never known such a strong team spirit. Wenger later said, 'It was a special moment when Jens got up and spoke in the dressing room. He realises there is a special spirit here.'

Against Fulham, they failed to score for the first time in 47 Premiership games because most of their 24 shots were feeble. The team had done well without Vieira, who missed twelve games between 4 October and 14 December, but he made his comeback in the Carling Cup against Wolves alongside Spaniard Cesc Fabregas, sixteen, and six other youngsters, and they won 5–1. Vieira said, 'Cesc is a fantastic prospect who reads the game very quickly and knows what to do when he receives the ball. He has a brilliant future.'

You could now see the AW hallmark, the 'house style', because the youngsters played just like the first team, making early passes in a way that looks relaxed, but also very fast. No other team plays quite like Arsenal because no other coach places as much emphasis on the skilful teamwork needed to attack with explosive pace and score so many one-on-one goals in such a pure way. A week after the 5–1 humbling of Inter in Milan, we saw Wolves being sliced apart by the rapier football of Wenger's talented hopefuls.

Gilberto had some average games, and the fans grumbled, but he always made the defence look more solid. A strategic player, he only catches the eye when he bursts forward. The rest of his work is invisible to those who do not know how to see it. Gilberto cuts off angles, shadows runners, jockeys dribblers, and makes interceptions. He is a team player, a shape player, a continuity player. Clearly, Edu puts his foot in, and makes more forward passes. But in some games it may be risky to use a midfielder who moves around as much as Edu in a team that already has a midfielder who roams around like Pires.

At Leicester, Gilberto silenced his critics with a power sprint into the box to head home Bergkamp's cross in 60 minutes, but Cole was sent off for a two-footed tackle on Ben Thatcher and sub Craig Hignett made it 1–1.

Against Lokomotiv, Arsenal started at a very high tempo, scored an early goal, and played quite patiently after that. Pires produced his most complete performance since his injury and the way he took the first goal was phenomenal, jabbing the ball up ahead of himself, spurting into the box by taking two strides that were longer than usual, and firing precisely inside the near post. That goal settled the team, calmed the crowd, stopped everybody being nervous. Henry also supplied the pass for Ljungberg to make it 2–0.

The Swede, talking about the games that should have been won the year before, admitted, 'The boss told us we had led 1–0 in eleven matches we didn't win last season and that was very irritating. Sometimes, when we had the lead last year, we stopped playing football and started having fun. We had fun instead of killing the game. The boss told us to change that this season.'

On the following Sunday, Blackburn made a game of it and then Toure broke to give Bergkamp a goal against the run of play. That 1–0 win restored Arsenal to the top of the table on a day when Chelsea lost 2–1 at home to Bolton. Wenger used a mixture of young players and his first-team bench in the Carling Cup at West Brom, where a 2–0 win kept his amazing record of never having lost to opponents from a lower division in 23 games over seven years.

## WENGER SIGNS JOSE ANTONIO REYES

*Reyes was a Galactico in the making because, let's face it, he's got absolutely everything as a footballer.*

Ivan Helguera

Wenger knew that the Champions League contained better teams than Lokomotiv Moscow, and he needed another goalscorer, so during the transfer window he made a bid for Robin van Persie, a big winger who had one year left on his contract. When Feyenoord wanted £3.75 million, he turned his attention to another young star that his scouts had watched over 40 times: José Antonio Reyes of Sevilla.

Reyes had scored 21 goals in 84 Primera Liga appearances and was the most fouled player in La Liga. In his last three seasons there had been 283 fouls on him.

Real Madrid captain Iván Helguera said, 'Reyes was a Galactico in the making because, let's face it, he's got absolutely everything as a footballer. His dribbling and speed on the ball makes life hell for defenders.'

Wenger said, 'We have a game based on movement, technique and pace, and he has all of that. He is a good investment as he's twenty and is already an international. He can play everywhere, up front, on the left flank or even on the right, like any good offensive player. He can be adaptable and replace everybody, so we'll use him wherever we feel that we need him.

'He needs time, but he's a special player and I genuinely believe the younger you move, the more chance you have to adapt. It makes you a stronger person. The language barrier is not a problem. When players are on the same wavelength, the ball is the best communicator. José will bring audacity and maintain our dynamic way of playing.'

He added, 'We want to be the best and if that is the aim you have to take gambles. But these have to be as calculated and well-thought out as possible. A big investment on a very young player is certainly less risky than with older players. If you make a major investment on someone who is over 27, your return today is zero.'

The acquisition of Reyes was a big deal, but cleverly structured. Arsenal paid around £10 million, with £6.5 million due immediately and the rest over the next four years. They will owe another £7.5million if Reyes makes 125 appearances and a further £1.6 million if they win the Champions' League between 2004 and 2008.

Apart from the appearance of Reyes as a sub, Arsenal versus Manchester City was just another game, another wet Sunday, another 4-5-1 line-up, another session of attack v defence, another 2–1 home win in a 23-match unbeaten run in the Premiership, another Henry wonder-goal. But Reyes looked so good for twenty minutes that the date of his Premiership debut was worth noting: 1 February, 2004.

Having pulled out all the stops to beat Wolves on Saturday, when Henry scored twice in a 3–0, Arsenal looked tired in the first half against Southampton. Pires scored the only goal from Henry's pass. Reyes had come on against Wolves and he started at St Mary's, where he stayed in the middle, took a lot of kicks, and did not complain, although Vieira complained to the referee on his behalf.

The first Premiership game of 2004 was at Everton, where they drew 1–1. And then Wenger made six changes for the FA Cup Fourth Round tie against Leeds, who played five in midfield.

Lehmann allowed Viduka to block his clearance and score, but Arsenal fought back and won 4–1.

They now met Middlesbrough four times in January, outclassing them in the Premiership before winning 2–0 at Aston Villa, then beating Boro 4–1 in the FA Cup Fourth Round. The Carling Cup semi-final was over two legs, which they lost 1–0 and 2–1 with weakened teams.

In the FA Cup Fifth Round tie against Chelsea at Highbury, Bergkamp and Reyes were the two strikers. Arsenal were lucky when referee Paul Durkin disallowed a Gronkjaer header from Lampard's cross, as replays proved that the 'goal' was onside. Then Lehmann miskicked the ball out of his hands to Parker, who volleyed to Mutu, whose shot flashed between Toure's legs and into the net. In the first half, José Reyes had made good runs and chased every defender, but nothing he did came off. However, Reyes proved that if you graft, you can work your way into a game that is passing you by.

Soon after Edu came on for the injured Parlour, Reyes scored with two left-foot shots, the first from 25 yards, the second from ten yards. Edu was fast and tidy, tackling sharply and raising the tempo, Vieira was awesome, and Bergkamp played as if another FA Cup Final would mean everything to him.

Henry was restored for the Premiership game at Stamford Bridge, a 2–1 win which removed any doubts that Arsenal would be champions, even before Manchester United drew 1–1 with Leeds. After 26 games, Arsenal were seven points ahead of United and nine ahead of Chelsea.

Their Champions League opponents in the new round of sixteen were Celta Vigo, where they made history with the club's first win in Spain, by 3–2 against a side who were sixteenth in the Primera Liga. Back home, they beat Charlton 2–1 and went nine points ahead of United with eleven games left, and everyone talked and wrote talked about whether they could stay unbeaten in 38 Premiership games.

Their FA Cup Sixth Round tie was at Portsmouth, where there was tremendous interplay between Ljungberg, Reyes and Henry in a 5–1 victory. Although Reyes did not score, he was marvellously mature and hardly wasted a ball. Very few players who are as exciting as Reyes are also economical. He knows where to run, where to pass, when to hold the ball for another split-second, when to accelerate, when to stop and play it square, when to dribble from the centre circle to the edge of the box, how to pinch the ball on the halfway line and give a simple pass. After only six weeks in England, Reyes could do all the things that Wiltord had been unable to do since arriving in August 2000.

The draw for the Champions League quarter-finals paired Chelsea and Arsenal, while Real Madrid would play Monaco, Porto met Lyon, and AC Milan faced Deportivo La Coruna.

Arsenal now faced a challenging schedule of nine games in 30 days, and at Blackburn they were lucky to get a foul when Craig Short connected gently with Henry, who scored from the free-kick. Pires made it 2–0 late on. After a delayed kick-off at Bolton due to gales, Pires and Berkgamp scored world-class goals, but a Campo goal made it interesting.

In the Champions League at Stamford Bridge, Chelsea were the better side and scored first. After 53 minutes, Lampard hit a probing ball that Lehmann had to come for and Gudjohnsen got lucky as he charged down the 'keeper's clearance to score from a tight angle. Then Arsenal raised their game and Cole's cross found the head of Pires, who nodded perfectly inside the post. Going into the second leg, the tie was nicely balanced.

On 28 March, Manchester United came to Highbury, where a 1–1 draw kept Arsenal 12 points above them. Henry did nothing for 50 minutes, then scored with a thunderous shot from 30 yards. Unfortunately, Wenger's use of three subs in the last 23 minutes disrupted the team. Gilberto for Reyes was unfathomable, Cygan for Ljungberg made no sense, and as soon as he took off Pires, and put on Bergkamp, Saha tapped in the equaliser. Although we knew by now that Arsène Wenger is good at everything except substitutions, it was disappointing to see such an attacking coach now waving the white flag from the bench.

Still, Arsenal were unbeaten after 30 league games, a record start to a Premiership season, and if they won their next two games, this disappointment would be forgotten.

In the FA Cup semi-final against United at Villa Park, Bergkamp must have been amazed to start alongside Aliadière, who had not played for three months. Why didn't Reyes play? Because, we assumed, Wenger did not want to risk injury to him. After half an hour a low cross from Giggs was buried by Scholes and the contest was over. Arsenal's game is pass-and-move, but there was no movement. Edu looked up again and again to see . . . no run! No movement at all!

In the second half, Arsenal created little until Reyes and Henry came on for Aliadiere and Pires. Reyes was suddenly a huge threat to United, producing three moments of pure genius, so Scholes kicked him on the knee. The tackle was so late that it missed the bus back to Manchester, but Scholes got off with a yellow card. Having said that, United wanted it more, a lot more. Basically, if you are not 100 per cent up for it, and not fielding your best team, you will never beat Manchester United in an FA Cup semi-final.

So a very big, very dramatic match arrived on Tuesday 6 April. It was, as pundits love to say, a moment of truth: a Champions League victory in the second leg against Chelsea, by any score, would justify the failure at Villa Park. On the night, 35,000 tense, jittery Gooners saw an opening period that was fast, compressed, hectic, with many passing errors by both sides. Henry missed two early chances, rushing shots from promising positions.

Claudio Ranieri knew how Arsenal launch their killer breaks from the middle third, so Chelsea denied them space everywhere, conceding only a yard or two on the flanks, which led to the kind of goal Arsenal rarely score. Lauren crossed, Henry headed back, and Reyes fired a shot through the legs of 'keeper Ambrosio, just before half-time. A huge explosion of happiness rocked Highbury.

The Tinkerman took off the gritty Parker and sent out the pacy Gronkjaer to push Cole back, a shrewd change. When Lehmann parried a Makelele shot to Lampard, he made it 1–1, and after that it was all Chelsea. Cole had to clear a Gudjohnsen shot off the line, Arsenal fell back far too deep, and eventually Edu and Lauren failed to track the run of Wayne Bridge, who fired across Lehmann into the far corner.

The big-handled bauble, the Holy Grail, the cup that every star footballer wants to hold, was still out of reach. The dream had been possible, had been vivid, but then it just flickered, faded, and slipped away, yet again.

The anonymity of Henry was the main talking point. Once again he had been a paper tiger in a big game. Was he fit that night? He pulled a muscle, went off, came back on, and was substituted. If he was not fit, why did he start? Makelele said, 'When Thierry Henry is only fifty per cent, you can see it immediately.'

When Arsenal came out against Liverpool, we could see the hangover: they were slow, sloppy, lethargic, unrecognisable. Hyypia scored an early goal and after that Liverpool just wanted to defend their lead. As Arsenal started to find their game, Henry's shot went inside the post for 1–1, but just when it looked as if they would go in level, Gerrard hit a through-pass to Owen, who scored. Campbell and Lehmann had switched off. After two big defeats, a half-time score of 1–2 was the most perilous moment of the entire season.

As Wenger has said, success in football is fragile, so you can lose six months' work in four days. But not this time. Immediately after the interval, Arsenal came back with a vengeance. Henry gave Ljungberg a pass which he volleyed to Pires, who buried his shot inside the near post, Henry slalomed round Hamann and Carragher and sidefooted past Dudek for 3–2, Bergkamp put Henry through for 4–2. After that handsome victory, Ranieri said it was Arsenal's title, a comment which gave Chelsea permission to draw 0–0 at home to Middlesbrough and lose 3–2 at Villa.

After a frustrating 0–0 on a bumpy, sticky pitch in Newcastle, Thierry Henry scored four goals in a 5–0 thrashing of Leeds, so Arsenal could now win the title at White Hart Lane with four matches to spare. In a lunchtime kick-off, Newcastle beat Chelsea 2-1, so even a draw at the Lane would give them the title.

After three minutes, Vieira scored, and half an hour later he supplied a perfect assist for Pires to make it 2–0. Then Henry started showboating, thinking the game was over, and Jamie Redknapp pulled a goal back. A Pires shot hit the bar, and the volatile Lehmann put his glove on Robbie Keane's head, pushing him down as a corner came over. The ball glanced off the bar, but the German shoved Keane, who pushed him back. Referee Mark

Halsey booked both men and gave a penalty, which Keane slotted. Arsenal won the Premiership, but a 2–2 draw took some of the gloss off the glorious day.

Wenger then signed winger Robin van Persie from Feyonoord for £2.3 million. He was twenty and now wanted to play as a half-striker, like Bergkamp.

Could the new champions keep concentrating and avoid defeat in their four remaining games? Inevitably, their efforts dipped in a tedious 0–0 against Birmingham. At Portsmouth, Lehmann was their best player in an exciting game in which Yakubu made it 1–0, but eventually, when Henry's cross into the box was headed out, Reyes smashed the ball into the net. At Fulham, Reyes dispossessed sloppy 'keeper Edwin van der Sar to score the only goal.

The final game was at home against Leicester on 15 May and Paul Dickov stunned Highbury with an early header for 0–1, but Arsenal came back thanks to two fabulous passes by Bergkamp. The first went to Ashley Cole, who won a penalty from which Henry equalised, and the second allowed Vieira to waltz round 'keeper Ian Walker and roll in the winner.

So Arsenal were unbeaten all season in 38 Premiership games and achieved something which had eluded the legendary Tottenham, Liverpool and Manchester United teams. History had been made and Thierry Henry made even more history by becoming the first player to retain the Football Writers' Association Footballer of the Year award. He had already won the PFA trophy.

More than 250,000 fans turned out to cheer the victory parade from Highbury to Islington Town Hall, where Wenger thanked the fans for their support and told them that Ruud van Nistelrooy's penalty miss at Manchester United in September and the comeback against Liverpool were the decisive days of a record-breaking season. 'It is the biggest moment since I arrived here,' he said. 'My dream has always been to play a whole season unbeaten. It's something unique, because no other manager can say that in the top League. I'm very happy, I'm proud of my players.'

So that was that. Arsenal were champions again and everyone was delighted, none more so than David Dein, who said, 'Arsène is unique – the best signing we have ever made. At the time it was not an easy decision to appoint him – one newspaper headline screamed: "Arsène Who?" Now I sincerely hope that, after what he has achieved, Arsène will stay at the club for the rest of his life. He has undoubtedly transformed and revolutionised the club. This club now sets new standards in the English game. What we have achieved this season is extraordinary. It has resounded around Europe. I know that from the number of e-mails and faxes I have received from clubs far and wide.'

In an interview in *Champions* magazine, Wenger had talked about working with players. He said, 'What I look for in a young player is game intelligence, speed, technique, but even if they have just attitude and technique, you can build on that.What makes you saddest of all is to see talent but no desire to achieve something.'

He sees himself as a teacher, a facilitator, someone who provides a vehicle which can fulfill the aspirations of individuals. 'Players need to express themselves. It's very easy for communication between a manager and a player, or between players for that matter, to be superficial. Players want to learn and if they feel deep down that you are only interested in them as a number in a team or to fit into a tactical system, they won't be as happy and they may not play as well. And when they feel they have no more to learn from you, that you can't develop them, that's when a player is likely to leave.'

Eight years on from his arrival in London, it appears that the Professor has created the best dressing room in the world, but we shall never know that for sure. We only know that it has music and eight nationalities and a very tall Frenchman from Senegal and a very calm boss who does yoga every morning and only shouts at his players once a season.

Footballers certainly appreciate his man-management skills. 'Arsène is someone who gives everything to his players,' said Vieira. 'We are now at the stage where we trust him as a coach and also as a human being. We can talk to him about football, about personal life – everything. I know in public he rarely says we've done wrong, but that's because he's protecting us.'

A visionary with a lot of stamina, a polymath who uses knowledge from outside football, Wenger is also a dynamo who has generated big cash flows. He has created an infrastructure with his deluxe training complex, which is like a campus for millionaire athletes and wannabes, a facility which always impresses new players. José Reyes, arriving in January and seeing snow being melted by undersoil heating, said, 'They've even got a fire under the grass!'

Back in 2003 Arsène Wenger and Gérard Houllier were each given an honorary OBE, and Wenger said, 'There was scepticism when I arrived in England, but this shows that I have now been accepted by the country. It is recognition that I have tried to do my work properly. I have learned to be mentally strong because it is not always easy. I learned to improve because people are always demanding more and football means so much here. I have learned to master my job because there is so much involved in it, and I believe I have become a more complete manager than I was when I arrived here.'

In the summer of 2004, after Liverpool had finished 30 points behind Arsenal, Houllier was sacked. Arsenal's Frenchman had raised the bar so high that he made his rivals look mediocre.

Chelsea appointed the cocky, clever Jose Mourinho, 41, who had just won the UEFA Cup and the Champions League for Porto in successive seasons. Owner Roman Abramovich was 35 and a young man in a hurry, so he employed another young man in a hurry. Spurs brought in Frank Arnesen as their new technical director, replacing David Pleat, and then hired Jacques Santini, the manager of the French national team. Santini had guided Lyon to the French league title in 2002.

A workaholic, Arsène Wenger wants to take a world-class team into Ashburton Grove in two years' time. His success has made the new stadium necessary, and possible. He will be 55 in October, and we know that, in the fullness of time, he will leave Arsenal, but when he does he will leave more than a legacy. He will leave a future.

# INDEX